The D-Day Landing on Gold Beach

Bloomsbury Studies in Military History

Series Editor: Jeremy Black

Bloomsbury Studies in Military History offers up-to-date, scholarly accounts of war and military history. Unrestricted by period or geography, the series aims to provide free-standing works that are attuned to conceptual and historiographical developments in the field while being based on original scholarship.

Published:

The 56th Infantry Brigade and D-Day, Andrew Holborn

The RAF's French Foreign Legion, G.H. Bennett

Empire and Military Revolution in Eastern Europe, Brian Davies

Reinventing Warfare 1914-1918, Anthony Saunders

Fratricide in Battle, Charles Kirke

The Army in British India, Kaushik Roy

The 1711 Expedition to Quebec, Adam Lyons

Britain, Germany and the Battle of the Atlantic, Dennis Haslop

Military Transition in Early Modern Asia, 1400-1750, Kaushik Roy

The Role of the Royal Navy in South America, Jon Wise

Scotland and the British Army 1700-1750, Victoria Henshaw

War and State-Building in Modern Afghanistan, edited by Scott Gates and Kaushik Roy

Conflict and Soldiers' Literature in Early Modern Europe, Paul Scannell

Youth, Heroism and Naval Propaganda, Douglas Ronald

William Howe and the American War of Independence, David Smith

Postwar Japan as a Sea Power, Alessio Patalano

Forthcoming:

Reassessing the British Way in Warfare, K. A. J. McLay

Australasian Propaganda and the Vietnam War, Caroline Page

Australian Soldiers in the Boer and Vietnam Wars, Effie Karageorgos

English Landed Society and the Great War, Edward Bujak

The D-Day Landing on Gold Beach

6 June 1944

Andrew Holborn

Bloomsbury Academic
An imprint of Bloomsbury Publishing Plc

B L O O M S B U R Y
LONDON • OXFORD • NEW YORK • NEW DELHI • SYDNEY

Bloomsbury Academic

An imprint of Bloomsbury Publishing Plc

50 Bedford Square	1385 Broadway
London	New York
WC1B 3DP	NY 10018
UK	USA

www.bloomsbury.com

BLOOMSBURY and the Diana logo are trademarks of Bloomsbury Publishing Plc

First published 2015
Paperback edition first published 2017

British Library Cataloguing-in-Publication Data

A catalogue record for this book is available from the British Library.

ISBN: HB: 978-1-4411-8328-6
PB: 978-1-3500-2782-4
ePDF: 978-1-4411-3817-0
ePub: 978-1-4411-7340-9

Library of Congress Cataloging-in-Publication Data

Holborn, Andrew.
The D-Day landing on Gold Beach: 6 June 1944 / Andrew Holborn.
pages cm
ISBN 978-1-4411-8328-6 (hbk.)
1. World War, 1939-1945--Campaigns--France--Normandy. I. Title.
D756.5.N6H6243 2015
940.54'21421--dc23
2015006523

Series: Bloomsbury Studies in Military History

Typeset by Deanta Global Publishing Services, Chennai, India

May the great God, whom I worship, grant to my country and for the benefit of Europe in general, a great and glorious victory: and may no misconduct, in any one, tarnish it: and may humanity after victory be the predominant feature in the British fleet.

Nelson's Prayer before Trafalgar, 21 October 1805.

Good night then: sleep to gather strength for the morning. For the morning will come. Brightly will it shine on the brave and true, kindly upon all who suffer for the cause, glorious upon the tombs of heroes. Thus will shine the dawn. Vive la France!

Winston Churchill: broadcast to the French people, 21 October 1940.

Once more the supreme test has to be faced. This time the challenge is not to fight to survive but to fight to win the final victory for the good cause. Once again what is demanded from us all is something more than courage, more than endurance, we need a revival of spirit – a new, unconquerable resolve. After nearly more than five years of toil and suffering we must renew that crusading impulse on which we entered the war and met its darkest hour ....
At this historic moment surely not one of us is too busy, too young, or too old to play a part in a nationwide, a worldwide vigil of prayer as the great Crusade sets forth.

King George VI: broadcast to the nation, 6 June 1944.

Contents

List of Illustrations

Acknowledgements

A large number of people and organizations have helped me complete this study of the D-Day Landings on Gold Beach. First and foremost, I must thank all the veterans who have allowed to me interview them and have often followed up with phone calls, e-mails and even copies of personal diaries. Both their deeds of seventy years ago and their continued interest in this project have been an inspiration.

Andrew Whitmarsh, the development officer at the D-Day Museum and Overlord Embroidery in Portsmouth, was very welcoming, and allowed me access to their extensive archive. As usual, the regimental museums I had contact with were very helpful; these are always worth a visit. As well as having many artefacts on show, they often have an extensive archive. The Normandy Fellowship website allowed me to use a number of pieces from their collection, as did Geoff Slee of the Combined Operations website. As will be seen in the endnotes to chapters, several relatives of men who landed on Gold Beach allowed me to use sources and memoirs now in their hands.

The veteran members and the officers who run 49th (West Riding) Infantry Division Association (Polar Bears) also provide constant inspiration and interest. I am proud to be an associate member. One of those members taught me at school, and obviously helped nurture a lifelong interest in sport and history.

I would also like to thank the Icon Design Partnership, Brighton, for drawing up the maps which accompany this book from my very rough sketches.

Family have also played a significant part, as I have been able to visit Normandy virtually every year since 2004, sometimes more than once; and as well as putting up with the writing, they have often been more or less willing companions in exploring the area by foot, bicycle and car.

Lest we forget.

Andrew Holborn
Devon, December 2014

List of Abbreviations and Glossary

AA	Anti-aircraft
ACV	Armoured command vehicle
AFPU	Army Film and Photographic Unit
AVRE	Armoured Vehicle Royal Engineers
BARV	Beach armoured recovery vehicle
Bde	Brigade – 3 battalions of infantry
BEF	British Expeditionary Force
Bn	Battalion
Bren gun	Very well-engineered British LMG made by Enfield from a Czech design, hence BR (Bruno) + EN (Enfield)
Brig.	Brigadier – officer in charge of a brigade
Capt.	Captain – officer in charge of a company, usually promoted to major
CIGS	Chief of the Imperial General Staff (UK)
Cmdo	Commando – either an individual specially trained soldier or a unit of around 450 men. In the Second World War, there were Commando units from the army, RN and RM
Coy	Company – 120 infantrymen commanded by a captain/major
Cpl	Corporal – NCO in charge of a section
Crocodile	Flame-thrower Churchill tank
CTC	Combined Training Centre
CWGC	Commonwealth War Graves Commission
DD	Duplex drive tank. Tank capable of 'swimming' ashore
DG	Dragoon Guards
Div.	Division – 3 brigades plus supporting arms

DLI	Durham Light Infantry
DUKW	Amphibious cargo vehicle based on US GMC 'Deuce and a half' 2.5 ton truck
FOB	Forward observation bombardment (naval)
FOO	Forward observation officer (usually RA)
FS Knife	Fairburn-Sykes fighting knife, issued to commando troops
FSMO	Full service marching order
Gen.	General – officer in charge of a division
GOC	General Officer Commanding
HAA	Heavy anti-aircraft (3.7 inch AA, British/88 mm Flak, German)
HARDS	Slipway constructed for loading landing craft
HMS	His Majesty's Ship
IO	Intelligence officer
ITC	Infantry Training Centre
LAA	Light anti-aircraft (40 mm Bofors/20 mm Oerlikon)
LAD	Light aid detachment – Brigade vehicle repair workshop
LCA	Landing craft assault
LCA (HR)	Landing craft assault (hedgerow) – adapted LCAs each firing twenty-four 30 lb spigot mortar bombs to clear beach obstacles
LCF	Landing craft flak
LCG	Landing craft gun
LCI	Landing craft infantry – (L) large
LCOCU	Landing craft obstacle clearance unit
LCT	Landing craft tank
LCT (R)	Landing craft tank converted to fire up to 1,000 rockets
LMG	Light machine gun
LSI	Landing ship infantry
LST	Landing ship tank
Lt	Lieutenant (or second Lt) in charge of a platoon
Lt Col.	Lieutenant colonel – officer in charge of a battalion

MG42	German machine gun used in LMG (bipod) or MMG (tripod) role with a high rate of fire, over 1,200 rounds per minute. Often called a 'Spandau' by veterans
ML	Motor launch
MMG	Medium machine gun (Vickers UK)
MO	Medical officer
MP40	German 9 mm sub-machine gun. Well engineered and often coveted by British officers and NCOs as a replacement for their issued and more cheaply engineered Sten gun. Often erroneously termed a 'Schmeisser' by veterans
MT	Motor transport
NCO	Non-commissioned officer
OCTU	Officer Cadet Training Unit
ORs	Other ranks
PIAT	Projector infantry anti-tank. Designed on the spigot mortar principle, it fired a hollow charge warhead. Also useful when attacking buildings
POW(s)	Prisoner(s) of war
RA	Royal Artillery
RAC	Royal Armoured Corps
RAF	Royal Air Force
RAMC	Royal Army Medical Corps
RCN	Royal Canadian Navy
RCS	Royal Corps of Signals
RE	Royal Engineers
Regt	Regiment – German equivalent of a British brigade
REME	Royal Electrical and Mechanical Engineers
RHU	Reinforcement holding unit
RM	Royal Marines
RN	Royal Navy
RNVR	Royal Navy Volunteer Reserve
SBG	Small box girder – assault bridge carried by AVRE

Sgt	Sergeant – second-in-command of platoon
SHAEF	Supreme Headquarters Allied Expeditionary Force
SMG	Sub-machine gun – Browning (Commando issue), Sten gun – British; MP40 – German
SRY	(Nottinghamshire) Sherwood Rangers Yeomanry
Sten gun	Cheaply made, but effective, British SMG. Designed by Shepherd and Turpin (ST), manufactured by Enfield (EN)
Stutzpunkt	German resistance post – company size
SWB	South Wales Borderers
TCV	Troop carrying vehicle
U-boat	*Unterseeboot* – German submarine
USN	United States Navy
WN	*Wiederstandnester* – German resistance post, platoon size
WO	War Office or Warrant Officer

Introduction

This study of the D-Day landing on Gold Beach was an idea formed while completing a previous study of an infantry brigade that landed here on D-Day as an attached unit to 50th Division.[1] There were already studies covering this event in the form of battlefield guides, such as *Gold Beach. Inland from King – June 1944* and *Gold Beach – Jig. Jig Sector and West – June 1944*,[2] and a further work produced in the *Battlezone* Series – *Gold Beach*.[3] However, while the above works give details about these operations on D-Day, along with some of the background planning and training for the assault, this work seeks to look more deeply into the long journey made by the British military, from defeat in Europe during 1940, through the planning, organization and development which finally led to a late decision in February 1944 to add a landing on Gold Beach to the D-Day plans for an invasion of France. There is also an examination of the German Army in Normandy showing that, although, compared with the Russian front, Normandy was a safer place to be, any German soldier guarding the coast had to keep on his toes. Intermittent raiding by British forces, in particular on the coastline, had to be constantly guarded against. Similarly, the pre-D-Day air bombing brought casualties and confusion to both German forces and French civilians. The fraught but successful landing and exploitation south, east and west on 6 June 1944 and developments later from the beachhead complete this study.

Great things were expected of the landings on Gold Beach. They were made on a two-brigade front and were planned to move swiftly far inland and provide an incursion deep into occupied Normandy within forty-eight hours. In fact, this deep penetration was only achieved by August 1944. A formidable mass of men and materiel from the 50th (Northumbrian) Division and its supporting units was thrown ashore on D-Day, with powerful units such as 7th Armoured Division expected to follow within hours, and 49th (West Riding) Infantry Division within days. Had success been as swift and devastating to German arms as expected, the problems experienced in attempts to capture the city of Caen on D-Day by units from Sword and Juno beaches, and the controversy surrounding its capture much later in July 1944, probably would not have become an issue for historians to argue over ever since.

An important point which will become clear during the narrative is that the landings on the British and Canadian beaches were not as straightforward as sometimes portrayed. Those on Gold Beach were fraught with danger and difficulty, as were the landings on Juno and Sword. It will also become apparent that prior training in the months leading up to D-Day was not always useful to the troops involved. Most of the units involved in this landing received insufficient training and were often based in areas unsuitable for the type of training required. No unit, for example, trained with an eye to the close countryside of the bocage. Initially

50th (Northumbrian) Infantry Division was not expecting to be used as the assault division, but only as a follow-up unit to the invasion. This division had only recently returned from long service abroad, beginning in 1940 in France and then throughout the Middle East campaign and into Sicily by 1943. It required many replacements on its return to the United Kingdom and felt that it deserved a rest. Many of the veteran men of 50th Division suffered from malaria, which manifested itself during the pre-D-Day period and afterwards in Normandy. Originally, 49th (West Riding) Infantry Division had been in training as an assault landing division, but Montgomery was insistent that one of his 'trusted' units should lead the assault, so roles were reversed between 50th and 49th Infantry Divisions. Similarly, 56th (Independent) Infantry Brigade, 47 (RM) Commando and many of the armoured and other units attached to 50th Division for D-Day had received hasty training, and many had not seen any active service in the war.

Montgomery illustrates his view by noting that the majority of his units available for Overlord lacked combat experience and that, although they had been training 'energetically' in England, 'their notions and doctrine had become theoretical'. He therefore set about the task of inculcating a sound battle technique by exchanging officers from Eighth Army formations like 51st (Highland) Infantry Division, 50th (Northumbrian) Infantry Division and 7th (Armoured) Division with units of little experience. 'I endeavoured to spread our available experience as much as possible.' He also made changes among the senior army commanders of battle formations, 'again with the object of making good as far as possible the inevitable lack of battle experience I found so prevalent'.[4] To command the British Army in Normandy, he brought home General Dempsey from Italy, who served well for the rest of the war in Europe and is an often unsung leader. It is interesting to compare this stance by Montgomery with how most of the units lacking in experience fared in Normandy; in fact, the new units did as well as anyone. As an example, by the end of August 1944, the 49th (West Riding) Infantry Division, which sported a polar bear emblem as its divisional sign, had been named the 'Butcher' Polar Bears by its German counterpart after a series of vicious battles where its men were opposed by SS troops.

From the outside, 50th (Northumbrian) Division was a tough, experienced division of fighting men from the north of England, men from the cities of Newcastle and Durham or the rugged countryside of the north-west. But the logic was flawed. By the end of 1943, many men felt that they had done enough and that there were plenty of trained men back in the United Kingdom who had not fought yet. There had been a mutiny (often called the Salerno Mutiny) by men from the division in Italy, which doubtless led to some of the feeling of ill will continuing into 1944. Five hundred men from 50th Division and 51st Highland Division found they were to be returned to combat units other than their own. Some of these men had recovered from wounds or illness. A number of them refused orders, and in the end, 192 were charged with mutiny under the Army Act, the largest number of men ever to be so charged in the British Army.[5] Montgomery was not involved in this event, but he blamed the senior officers and described the resulting confusion as 'appalling'.[6] Also, towards the end of 1943 in Sicily and Italy, and later in England in 1944, when Montgomery talked to the troops en masse at battalion level, he knew he was not always well received.

Further, by the end of 1943, one of '50 Div's' experienced infantry brigades was new to the division and could hardly be described as being 'Northumbrian'. A brigade made up of county battalions from the south of England, comprising 1st Hampshire, 2nd Devonshire and 1st Dorsetshire, called 231st Infantry Brigade (also known until 1944 as the 'Malta' Brigade), had guarded Malta through its worst hours and then fought in Italy. A further consideration is that, by the end of 1943, replacements for dead and injured soldiers were not necessarily from the original recruiting areas at all. By 1944, a British battalion of infantry (around 850 men) contained men from throughout the United Kingdom and Ireland, and the original idea of loyalty to the county regiment was at least diminished. Although many officers still retained regimental county loyalties, from New Year 1944, many replacement officers came from a variety of backgrounds; several hundred officers at least were retrained as infantry officers from the Royal Armoured Corps as surplus to requirements. Englishmen, for example, were sometimes surprised to find themselves in Highland regiments who wore kilts when not in battledress. One Irishman claiming to be ex-Irish Republican Army served with 2nd Glosters. Perhaps the most interesting example concerns the number of soldiers of German, Austrian or Italian nationalities who served in the British Army. The brigade major of 56th Infantry Brigade was called Beuttler and had won a Military Cross (MC); in 2nd Glosters, the liaison officer to the brigade was named Burkhart, and Lt Nordbruck won an MC for disabling a German tank. 2SWB had two officer twins from the Austrian nobility called Thurn-Vallessina, who were known almost inevitably and affectionately as 'left and right Thurn'. Toni Mansi served with 2nd Essex and was badly wounded at Tilly-sur-Seulles. He was visited in hospital in the north of England by his mother, who spoke virtually only Italian. Perusal of Commonwealth War Grave cemetery lists will, from time to time, throw up a name with 'Alias' attached. The real family name is usually provided. Many of these men were fighting with British forces, and their aliases protected a family in an occupied country, but a number of them were German, Austrian or Italian and fought with an alias to protect their family at home in case of capture or death.

Initially, for the assault follow-up phase, 56th (Independent) Infantry Brigade was attached to 50th Division 'under command'. This brigade comprised three battalions of infantry, hastily put together, who had not been in combat as units since 1940. They were 2nd South Wales Borderers (SWB), 2nd Essex and 2nd Glosters. This addition of nearly 3,000 infantrymen further diluted the northern 'feel' of 50th Division. Finally, some of the attached armour for the assault was also inexperienced in combat. To be fair, the men attached to all these units acquitted themselves well in the ensuing conflict, but prior to June 1944, they were unknown quantities until they had been in action for some time. Certainly, something that 50th Division was able to provide was a very highly competent and organized central command structure, as would be expected from a unit as experienced as this. Later in Normandy, when units were moved from one division to another, the 2nd South Wales Borderers intelligence officer lamented the lack of the 'highly professional' intelligence and command system that they had had access to when under the command of 50th Division.[7]

Gold Beach itself lies between the Normandy coastal villages of La Riviere in the east and Le Hamel in the west. This stretch of coast is found between the great ports of

Le Havre and Cherbourg. On landing, exploitation was expected west as far as Port-en-Bessin and south at least to Bayeux. The minimum aim for the end of D-Day was the joining of hands with US forces coming ashore on Omaha Beach to the western flank and, on the eastern flank, joining with Canadian troops from Juno Beach landings, and exploitation south to cut and take a line along the east–west Caen to Bayeux main road and railway line. Further, hoping against hope, this was merely a jumping-off point for a drive through Bayeux, south through Tilly-sur-Seulles and far inland to take Villers-Bocage by the end of D+1; Montgomery even seemed willing to sacrifice an armoured brigade to achieve this objective. He wanted to concentrate the armoured units soon after landing and an armoured brigade group to push forward on the afternoon of D-Day; 'speed and boldness' were required. 'To be successful, such tactics must be adopted on D-Day; to wait till D plus 1 would be to lose the opportunity, and also lose the initiative.' Montgomery went on to say that he 'would even risk the total loss of the armoured brigade groups – which in any event is not really possible'.[8]

But these optimistic plans for exploitation from Gold Beach were already dashed by the evening of D-Day. The poor weather, confusion and casualties of the landing meant that the timetable of advance from the beaches went seriously awry. By the time it was back on track within a few days, powerful German divisions such as Panzer Lehr and 12 SS Panzer had arrived on the scene. Exploitation south of Gold Beach through Bayeux towards Villers-Bocage was blocked at Tilly-sur-Seulles by Panzer Lehr. Only six days after D-Day, from 12 June, an attempt by elements of 7th Armoured Division to reach Villers-Bocage by a right hook rather than a left proved disastrous, as the first four of only the few infamous 'Tiger Tanks' (Mark VI Panzers) operating in Normandy caused great destruction to units of 7th Armoured Division tanks and transport in the confines of the streets of Villers-Bocage. This attempted penetration ended in confusion and withdrawal as further German reinforcements arrived on the scene.

While the final chapters will describe the Gold Beach landing, an analysis of the changes in circumstance, thought and direction of the war from 1940 to 1944, changes that affected the final landing operation, will be made. Undoubtedly, the United States joining the war in 1941 made an enormous change to the possibilities of an Allied return to Europe, and without the United States, a successful invasion of the French coast and exploitation through the battle of Normandy and after could not have been achieved by the British alone. However, I hope to point out in this work that without British efforts, this invasion could not have taken place. Over many years, the efforts and abilities of the British Army in Normandy have been played down by a number of authors. Even in the seventieth anniversary year, US involvement is often shown much more to the fore than the British effort, and one author even suggests that 'the memory of the D-Day landings has been gradually Americanized at the expense of the British' and points out that films such as *Saving Private Ryan* (1998) 'simply reduced the D-Day landings to a purely American affair'.[9]

What is often overlooked is that Britain, with the great help of its empire and commonwealth, had more than pulled its weight since 1940. Britain endured bombing and at the same time prosecuted war in the Western Desert, then in Sicily and Italy, kept large areas of its empire around the world garrisoned, carried out an extensive and expensive campaign in men and materiel in the air and at sea, and, from 1941, became embroiled in war in the Far East. Reverses in the Desert Campaign, Crete, Hong Kong, Singapore and Dieppe, and bombing and rationing at home, battered morale. It is a wonder that the British were able to play such an important role in the Second World War for so long. By 1944, Britain was having great difficulty in finding enough men and materiel for the armed services, industry and farming – despite the conscription of women into the armed forces, farms and factories, and US help with materiel.

At the end of a successful prosecution of the war in Europe, Britain was facing the prospect of further high casualty figures when helping with the invasion of Japan, the East Indies and Malaya, continued fighting in Burma, and a war that was planned and expected to last at least throughout 1946. Churchill was forever demanding his chiefs of staff to slim down the supply and administration 'tail' of the armed forces to provide more and more men to the various fronts – 'One set of men are sent back again and again'[10] – yet in an industrial war with armed services requiring a large administrative and supply 'tail', this was a very difficult feat to achieve, and, unlike the First World War, many men in military service never saw front-line action. Churchill knew that the infantry and other front-line troops were returned to the battle as soon as they had recovered from wounds, and experienced troops such as 50th Division were used time and time again. This seemed not only unfair, but also a practice that degraded the fighting arms. Later in 1944, older men, who had served, for example, in anti-aircraft batteries in the United Kingdom, were remustered as infantry after only a short period of retraining. Similarly, men from the RAF, Royal Navy and Royal Marines serving on ships found themselves as infantry in north-west Europe. The lack of appropriately aged and trained men resulting from casualties created huge problems for the British Army throughout 1944–5.

The critical area of the British Army that became increasingly short of trained personnel, then, was its fighting arms: artillery, armour and especially infantry. It was precisely these units that would be in the forefront of any invasion of Europe, and very high casualties were predicted for the assault phase; perhaps so much time was spent in planning this phase that the next important phase, of immediate exploitation, was not looked at so carefully. As we know from events, it was in Normandy that the British Army bogged down, faced as it was with operating in difficult and easily defensible countryside while pulling onto itself the preponderance of the better German armoured forces. But Montgomery had received warnings and should have been aware of the difficulty of fighting in Normandy. Chief of the Imperial General Staff (CIGS) Brooke had direct experience in this area from 1940, and Montgomery claims that Williams, his head of intelligence staff, as well as underlining that Rommel would try to stop the invasion on the beaches, pointed to 'stiff resistance in the bocage country as we pushed inland'.[11]

Not on D-Day, as planned, but seven weeks later on 19 July, the city of Caen fell, and only then could the ground south and east of the city be exploited. Villers-Bocage was only captured on 14 August, nearly ten weeks later than hoped for. To the east of Gold Beach, Canadian troops on Juno Beach had won through on D-Day despite some fierce resistance, especially in the streets of the fishing town of Courseulles, and then similarly were held up as an increasing number of German units arrived. From Sword Beach, a successful exploitation was made to the British Airborne bridgehead, but then stalled against increasing resistance. US troops had suffered two major losses of men in the landing on Omaha Beach and the airborne landings in the Cotentin Peninsula.[12] Only the landings on Utah Beach had gone comparatively smoothly, but again found increasing German resistance as troops moved inland and linked with the airborne troops to advance in three directions: north to capture Cherbourg, west to cut across the neck of the Cotentin Peninsula and south to join with the troops from Omaha and exploit into the hinterland.

In all cases, the expected speed of advance was slowed by weeks against intractable German defence, and not until the end of August was the German Army fully in flight from Normandy, with many of its units smashed within the famous Falaise Pocket. Nor was the German Army the only enemy that the Allies faced. The summer of 1944 proved to have among the worst weather for decades. Contemporary photographs and war diaries, both official and personal, chart the often wet and windy conditions. This not only hampered the build-up through the ports and beaches but also caused problems for troops operating in the often poor conditions. From 19 to 21 June 1944, a 'great storm', the worst in forty years, wrecked the US *Mulberry A* at Omaha Beach and damaged *Mulberry B* at Arromanches.

In all of this historical background, what cannot be doubted is the bravery of the men directly involved in landing from the sea or air. None will admit that they were particularly brave, but to travel across rough seas, feel seasick and land ashore in the teeth of enemy fire, or travel by air to drop in the darkness, and hold all that together and carry the fight to the enemy operating in countryside often well known to them, can be nothing but brave. The majority of these soldiers, sailors, airmen and marines were ordinary people conscripted and trained for their task. Many had never faced battle before. This study has been informed by interviews with men who were directly involved in the events. A number of these interviews have been carried out by the author; others were supplied through various regimental museums and the offices of the Portsmouth D-Day Museum and the D-Day Fellowship, to whom grateful thanks are extended. Although some historians are not keen on oral history, this author believes that it provides a crucial element and social dimension to any historical study where this evidence can be used. The accounts of veterans add immediacy to any historical study and sometimes throw a different light on accepted accounts of events. In some cases, letters and personal diaries were made available.

As well as the important veteran testimony, much primary evidence has been examined, some of which is rarely used in accounts, and again sources include the regimental museums, the D-Day Museum and, of course, the National Archive Centre at Kew. Unit war diaries vary in their quality, and were usually written by a battalion or regiment intelligence officer, often aged nineteen or twenty. Those that are well written and might also include map references giving positions and times, patrol reports, appendices, maps and even aerial photographs can prove to be very useful indeed to the researcher. In others, a whole week of intense fighting is succinctly described in only a few lines of prose. The war diaries used are listed in the endnotes for each chapter, and a comprehensive list of primary and secondary sources appears in the bibliography.

Secondary written sources can also be very valuable, and despite over seventy years separating the present from D-Day, they still maintain a controversial aspect.

Since 1944, historians have taken different and sometimes seemingly completely opposite stances about different areas of the campaign. From a British point of view, these opinions and controversies range around the fighting prowess of the British and Canadian soldier and the leadership displayed at all levels. Some of the older texts were written soon after the events, often by people directly involved. Surprisingly, it took until 1962 for the British official history of the campaign to be published. *Victory in the West. The Battle of Normandy* by L. F. Ellis has often been criticized for a bland covering of events and partiality towards General Montgomery. Despite this, it also sometimes knocks the British achievement on D-Day: 'At times there was little evidence of the urgency which would have to characterise operations if they were to succeed fully'[13] and, when discussing the progress of 56th (Independent) Infantry Brigade after landing, writes: 'It had taken four to five hours to advance about three miles, though virtually unopposed, and Bayeux was untaken.'[14] In the first instance, Ellis takes some time following the statement to describe problems accounting for the apparent lack of urgency; in the second case, the very good reasons for the time taken by 56th Brigade are not mentioned. The chapters covering Gold Beach and 50th Division in *Victory in the West* were informed by an important primary work for this study, published in 1950 and written by Lt Col. Warhurst, who took part in the invasion: *D-Day: 30 Corps and Gold Beach*. These official narratives are put together by the careful scrutiny of battalion, regiment, brigade and other unit war diaries and the interrogation of key people within a few years of the events. Similarly from the naval side, and published in 1947 by the Historical Section of the Admiralty, *Battle Summary No. 39. Volume 1. Landings in Normandy* is a very useful guide to naval operations. For Gold Beach in particular, the *Report by the Naval Commander Force G.*, authored by the naval commander Douglas-Pennant, was submitted to the Admiralty only several weeks after D-Day on 15 July 1944, and was obviously an important primary source for this study. The very comprehensive nature of the reports by Warhurst and Douglas-Pennant, written close in time to the events, are of great use and interest to researchers.

Montgomery as ground force commander wrote two books after the war. *Normandy to the Baltic* was published in 1946, to be followed by *The Memoirs of Field Marshal the Viscount Montgomery of Alamein* in 1958. Montgomery's memoirs are to an extent controversial, and later editions carried a near apology to General Auchinleck. However, they do include copies of contemporary notes and letters and are sometimes written with humour and candour. Montgomery fell out with many of his subordinates and superiors, including Eisenhower, and part of the story of the events in Normandy is bound up in the character, personalities and rivalries of the generals involved. Montgomery has often received a bad press, and there can be little doubt that he was often undiplomatic within an allied team and very difficult to get on with. Often he is accused of rewriting the script afterwards to suit himself. But an important question to ask is: Was anyone better suited to the task? A comprehensive three-volume biography of Montgomery has been written by Nigel Hamilton, who had promised Montgomery that he would only publish after the field marshal's death. The three volumes are *Monty, the Making of a General 1887–1942* (1981), *Monty, Master of the Battlefield 1942–1944* (1983) and *Monty, The Field Marshal 1944–1977* (1986). General Morgan was tasked with the pre-planning of Overlord, and in 1950, he published his memoirs of this time as *Overture to Overlord*. This again gives a useful contemporary account and shows the difficulties faced by Morgan in his task. Later he joined Eisenhower's staff, and he and Montgomery seemed to be at odds with each other, with Montgomery being rude about the pre-planning, but not giving credit to someone who was only allowed to plan within severe constraints.

From the German side, an important document is the result of the post-war interrogation of Generalleutnant Wilhelm Richter, and is titled *The Battle of the 716th Infantry Division in Normandy. 6th June – 23rd June 1944.* Various Fuhrer directives, telegrams and naval documents have also been used. These documents, which can be obtained from the US archives, were the results of post-war interrogation or document translation by the US military. There are also British regimental accounts published from the late 1940s to the late 1950s, indicated in the text, which also add to our knowledge of events. Many of these were very well written. Of course, whether a Montgomery autobiography, battalion war diary or interrogation script, all such contemporary, or near-contemporary, accounts need to be read and understood for bias within the context of the events, inter-service and international rivalries, and the personality of the writer.

From the 1970s, historians have had open access to the war diaries of units involved in the Second World War through the British National Archive. One of the most important works to come from this period is *Decision in Normandy* by Carlo D'Este. In the 1994 edition, D'Este encapsulates the Normandy controversy by writing: 'Montgomery's so called master plan became one of the most debated and least understood stratagems of his military career. It generated nearly endless debate and to this day arouses fierce reaction in his critics and admirers.'

Later historians picked up themes introduced by D'Este and extended them. The highly regarded author Max Hastings, in *Overlord. D-Day and the Battle for Normandy 1944* (1984), holds the viewpoint that US and British Canadian troops were not quite up to it compared with the excellence of the German Army; Stephen Ambrose in *D-Day* (1994) clearly undervalues the British/Canadian contribution; while in *Clash of Arms* (2001), Russell Hart uses authors such as D'Este, Hastings and others to discuss the British Army's lacklustre performance in the campaign. On the other hand, Robin Neillands in *The Battle of Normandy 1944* (2002) refutes the claim that British troops were too slow or that they lacked drive in the attack, while John Buckley in *Monty's Men. The British Army and the Liberation of Europe* (2013) makes a very strong case in arguing overall for the efficiency of the British Army and its commanders in 1944. Buckley has also made another very useful contribution to understanding the campaign in *British Armour in the Normandy Campaign* (2004). All of the above are deserving of being widely read by students of D-Day and the Normandy campaign. In this book on Gold Beach, it is hoped that the overall effectiveness of the British/Canadian Army will be clearly shown with final thoughts in the conclusion. Part of the 'story' of the Gold Beach landings that this author wishes to amend is any idea that the landings went ahead easily and straightforwardly, as shown in some accounts of D-Day on this beach. They did not, and a significant number of men lost their lives and many more were badly injured in order to secure the beachhead and advance inland.

The Gold Beach area today is a tranquil place, which has returned to its nineteenth- and early-twentieth-century status of small seaside resorts backed by an international reputation for seafood gastronomy. In summer, the beaches are visited by many, but they never attain the size of crowds at Brighton or Blackpool. Since the 1980s, Gold Beach below the high tide mark has been altered by the establishment of extensive oyster beds. The main German coastal positions remain and can be easily seen. Few can be explored, and those that can are potentially dangerous. Coastal erosion also means that the shoreline has receded many metres and some fortifications can only be seen at low tide. There is no doubt that the main coastal attraction is the small town of Arromanches, which comes alive with visitors from Easter onwards and is beginning to establish an increase in holiday visitations throughout the year. In front of this quiet fishing village was built one of the two famous *Mulberry* harbours to provide shelter to shipping supplying the build-up after the invasion for several weeks. It is the survival of *Mulberry B* that has ensured for Arromanches a place in world history and one centre of British D-Day commemoration.[15] It has many small friendly bars and hotels and a campsite. Parking in its narrow streets and car parks is often difficult, and in peak periods such as D-Day, a car park is opened in a large field above the town. Situated here on the seafront is one of the well-known *Musées* covering the Battle of Normandy; in particular, this one charts the building of the *Mulberry B*, of which extensive remains can still be seen. Even today, seventy years after the landings, British veterans gather in the square every 6 June in front of the *Musée* for a moving ceremony and service in the evening, to be justly applauded by a large crowd.

Inland are important areas of agriculture, and further south of Bayeux, this often turns to animal farming, particularly cows, for dairy produce. Many areas of the famous bocage have been irrevocably changed by the destruction of the earth banks to increase the size of fields since 1944 as farming practices became modernized. Normandy itself remains an important cultural and gastronomic area, with its dairy produce in particular exported around the world. Bayeux displays remarkable architecture from a number of periods, and its escape from destruction in 1944 was nothing short of miraculous. Despite plans for 56th (Independent) Infantry Brigade to capture it on D-Day, including an artillery bombardment with air support if necessary, it thankfully escaped fairly undamaged during 6–7 June 1944. As well as its cathedral, Bayeux is the resting place of the famous embroidery known as the Bayeux Tapestry depicting the Norman invasion of England.

The tranquil and often laid-back nature of the Normandy of today was not always so. The name Normandy was derived from the word 'Northmen', and part of the area was settled by the Vikings in the ninth century. From a British perspective, it was most famously the base for William Duke of Normandy (the Conqueror). His successful invasion of England is believed to have been launched from St Valery-sur-Somme in 1066. The HQ of Rommel at the Chateau De La Roche-Guyon was built in the twelfth century. Guy De La Roche fell at the Battle of Agincourt. Since 1984, Normandy has been divided into two regions: Basse-Normandie and Haute-Normandie (Lower and Upper Normandy). The former consists of the Departments Orne, Calvados and Manche, while the latter consists of the Departments Seine-Maritime and Eure. Lower Normandy was to be the focus of the Allied invasion; it includes the city of Caen and supports towns such as Bayeux, Lisieux, Saint-Lo and the port of Cherbourg. Rouen is the regional capital of Upper Normandy, with Le Havre being its large and famous port at the mouth of the River Seine. The existing political division into Lower and Upper Normandy still causes some controversy today, with calls frequently made to politically reunite the two areas.

During the Franco-Prussian War of 1870–1, tough battles were fought along the banks of the River Seine, and Rouen, Dieppe, Fecamp and Boulbec were occupied by the Prussian Army for a time. After the Franco-Prussian War, the area recovered its prosperity. By the early twentieth century, economically and gastronomically, Normandy was known for its fish and other seafood and dairy farming, with Camembert cheese perhaps its best-known product. Cider and an apple brandy known as Calvados were widely produced. The Norman coastal belt not only became fashionable to visit by the French middle classes, but also received many visitors from Britain and the rest of Europe. Fishing villages such as Courseulles, Ver-sur-Mer, Asnelles and Arromanches became small-scale resorts with a number of large new villas and hotels.

Normandy was also a favourite with many artists. Perhaps the best known of the impressionists to paint in the region was Claude Monet (1840–1926). His painting depicting Le Havre port, *Impression, Soleil Levant* (1872), helped to coin the term 'Impressionism'. Oddly, this popularity with some British families meant that, despite attempts at deception by changing the orientation and names on invasion-planning maps, many officers quickly worked out the invasion areas within the pre-invasion camps in the New Forest. With an allusion to the Bayeux Tapestry, it was an in-joke to remind each other 'not to forget their knitting!'[16] The excellent aerial photographs available also revealed the destination to some. Casting a magnifying glass over one photograph, a signals sergeant pointed out to his signals officer the name and numbers on a road sign showing the distance from Vaux-sur-Aure to Bayeux.[17] At least by this time the camps in the New Forest had been 'sealed'.

There was a small mining and quarrying industry across late-nineteenth- and early-twentieth-century Normandy. Coal and iron ore were mined, and a number of types of stone were quarried in the region. Much of this stone found its way into the construction of the strongly built farms, hamlets and villages that dotted the countryside, and many proved to be more than troublesome centres of German resistance to the advancing Allies in 1944. Coal was a disappointment when mines flooded, but an important iron ore industry developed between Caen and Falaise. The need to transport over 3,000 tonnes of ore per day, increasing visitor passenger potential and the potential of moving other products to railheads and ports caused an extensive series of light railways alongside roads or canals to be developed, both inland and along the coastal strip, from the end of the nineteenth century and into the twentieth century.

The original design of track was done by Paul Decauville (1846–1922), and the Decauville system of light railway became famous on the Western Front during the First World War. A number of swing bridges had to be constructed, one of which was the predecessor of the bridge at Benouville, famously known as Pegasus Bridge, the first structure to be captured in the early hours of D-Day by Major Howard and his glider-borne troops.

However, by the early 1930s, these small railways were declining due to the improvement in roads and main-line railways in Normandy. One of the last, the line from Caen to Luc-sur-Mer, ended its service on 6 June 1944 due to the D-Day landings on either side of Luc-sur-Mer, Juno Beach (Canadian) and Sword Beach (British). The first train of the day was abandoned at Luc-sur-Mer.[18] One of the small remaining railway shelters on Gold Beach was mistaken by Stanley Hollis for a pillbox as his landing craft assault was approaching the beach, and he fired on it with a Bren gun from the craft during the Green Howards' run-in to the beach on D-Day. Famously he burnt his hand on the hot barrel, a moment of thoughtlessness on this day of days causing even a very experienced company sergeant major in the British Army to become careless. Before the day was out, he would become the only man to win a Victoria Cross (VC) on D-Day. On landing, one of his men reported that the building was 'only a bloody bus shelter Sarn't Major'.[19] The shelter still exists with an explanation board attached.

1

Preparing the Way and Planning
Overlord 1940–3

By June 1940, much of Western Europe was under German occupation, allied to Germany or neutral. Britain was totally isolated, relying on her empire and later the United States for sustenance and support. Hitler and his generals were surprised that the British, led by their new Prime Minister Winston Churchill, continued to fight, and raiding of the now enemy coast by British forces began within days of the French surrender. As time went on, these raids became bolder and with more purpose than just to 'Butcher and Bolt'.[1] However, it was soon evident that little effort or research had gone into amphibious operations. The development of amphibious operations was another casualty of lack of money and drive after the First World War, not only because of the economic depression but also due to a lack of appetite for war. Political moves aimed towards appeasement and disarmament, plus the memory of the military disaster that attached itself to the Gallipoli landings in 1915, militated against such developments.

By 1930, there were only three experimental landing craft in Britain. However, by 1938, with the realization that the probability of war was increasing, the Inter Services Training and Development Centre (ISTDC) was established with a view to 'study and advance the technique of combined operations'.[2] In time, the work of the ISTDC designed and produced the Landing Craft Assault (LCA), a small ten-tonne landing craft carrying approximately a platoon of men and able to land them in shallow water. Second, a Landing Craft Mechanised (LCM) was also designed and built, which was a twenty-tonne craft for the landing of stores or vehicles in shallow water. An adapted LCA became the Landing Craft Support (LCS), which was able to emit a smokescreen. The LCA and LCM, alongside the Landing Craft Tank (LCT), were later to become the key landing craft for delivering invasion forces to beaches and the inshore workhorses of any invasion. An LCT of 300 tonnes, capable of delivering not only tanks but a range or mix of vehicles, stores and men, was still undergoing sea trials in October 1940.[3] A further craft, capable of carrying 200 men at a time across the English Channel, was not designed until 1942, when 1,000 were ordered from the United States. This vessel was named the Landing Craft Infantry (Large) (LCI (L)).[4]

Whether by luck or by design, ISTDC was established at Portsmouth, where 9th Infantry Brigade was also tasked for special operations. In the summer of 1938, on 6 July, an unusual exercise was arranged by the commander of 9th Infantry Brigade at Portsmouth. Using Slapton Sands in Devon as a landing area, the three battalions of infantry carried by two troopships were landed by naval cutters, whalers and ships' lifeboats, showing that even by 1938 landing operations had hardly moved forward since the days of Nelson – or Gallipoli. A battleship, two cruisers and five destroyers gave bombardment support to the landing, and airpower was provided by a squadron of Swordfish biplanes from HMS *Courageous*. Artillery, light tanks and transport were put ashore by flat-bottomed barges with ramps. The landing was a success and had been very well planned on 30,000 sheets of foolscap paper.[5] Despite showing up a degree of unpreparedness for amphibious warfare in terms of modern landing craft, it had been an exemplary exercise, showing what could be achieved jointly by the three services. The commander and brains behind this exercise was one Brigadier Bernard Montgomery.

During the Norwegian and French campaigns, some of the valuable landing craft were lost. British soldiers were usually transported by converted small liners. In extremis, in Norway and at Dunkirk, a destroyer could crowd a battalion of 800 men aboard. The continuing work of the ISTDC and the reviewing of amphibious operations led to some deep thought and progress in what became known as 'Combined Operations'. Lessons drawn from the 1940 Narvik operation in Norway included, first, the need to follow a Combined Operations policy and, second, that clear instructions were required by all commanders taking part in such operations. Third, the proper planning and collaboration of all services and units involved in any combined operation was essential. Attention was given to the correct order of loading and unloading shipping, and there was a need to ensure the use of proper maps and intelligence. Narvik also convincingly showed that the use of airpower to support a landing force was crucial.[6]

Although displaying a very confident stance over raiding enemy coasts from 1940, Churchill always had at the back of his mind the harsh criticism he had faced over several military operations he had been involved with as a politician. Each of them had involved landings. In the eyes of some of the press and public, he remained responsible for the failure of expeditions to defend Antwerp in October 1914, the Gallipoli campaign between April 1915 and January 1916, and the post-war operations to aid the anti-Bolshevik Russian Army. A famous Low cartoon of January 1920 had Churchill in plus fours and holding a double-barrelled shotgun standing over six dead cats, four of which were labelled 'Sidney Street', 'Antwerp Blunder', 'Gallipoli Mistake' and 'Russian Bungle'. The caption read 'Winston hunts lions and brings back cats.'[7] In July 1943, he seemed preoccupied with the success or failure of the Allied landings in Sicily. His daughter-in-law Pamela felt sure that he related these fears to Gallipoli and the Dardanelles.[8] Thoughts of failure in landing operations and the high casualties they might entail haunted Churchill until the end of the war.

After the evacuation of British forces from France in 1940, these feelings were not helped by the failure to take the strategically valuable enemy base of Dakar in late September 1940. Operation Menace was an attempt to take French West Africa from Vichy French rule. A strong force was led by an aircraft carrier, two battleships, five cruisers and ten destroyers, escorting several transports carrying 8,000 troops, including Royal Marines and Free French. The aim was to negotiate with the Vichy forces and persuade them to capitulate to forces led by General de Gaulle, the Free French leader. However, Governor Boisson refused to negotiate, and a three-day battle ensued. An attempted landing failed due to the coastal fortifications and the desire of Frenchmen not to kill each other. The task force thus withdrew, having lost six aircraft and with several ships damaged. This was a humiliating result, which partly caused de Gaulle to lose his standing with the British. It was an early example of the problems associated with not having specialist training and landing craft when attacking a fortified port.[9]

One result was the realization that something had to change to ensure proper training for amphibious forces; therefore, a Combined Training Centre (CTC) was set up at Inverary on the shores of Loch Fyne from October 1940. When it reached its full establishment, it could accommodate up to 15,000 troops in more than half a dozen nearby camps, including the naval centre for operations, HMS *Quebec*, named after the operations around the storming of Quebec by General Wolfe in 1759. Its task was to provide and maintain the craft for training operations and accommodate the training personnel. The other camps catered for infantry, tank and engineer units. Between 1940 and 1944 around a quarter of a million men passed through it. Very many of the infantry battalions that were to land on D-Day completed an amphibious landing course there between late 1943 and D-Day.[10]

There was already a War Office department for Combined Operations, established in June 1940, led by Admiral Sir Roger Keyes. Keyes was notable for a very long period of service, starting with anti-slavery patrols out of Zanzibar in 1890. His pedigree for such a post was apparently unassailable, having been involved in planning the Dardanelles campaign, the anti-submarine Dover Patrol, and planning and leading the famous raids to cripple the German submarine bases at Zeebrugge and Ostend in 1918. He had been a Conservative MP and played an important part in liaising with the Belgian king early in the Second World War.

Having been born in 1872, perhaps the only problem was his age, though he was still reckoned to be fit and aggressive for the task. 'Commandos were raised and trained in their own ferocious style of warfare; landing craft were built, and crews entirely drawn from the Royal Naval Volunteer Reserve were trained; ships were earmarked for amphibious warfare; special equipment was designed.'[11] In fact, Keyes was aggressive enough to call the chiefs of staff cowards to their faces. His task was not an easy one when building new units and demanding more and more equipment and the best men at a time when the country was in dire straits. He often found his job very frustrating, and increasingly fell out with other departments. Churchill removed Keyes: 'I reached the decision with much regret on personal grounds that the appointment of a new and young figure at the head of the overseas organisation would be in the public interest.'[12]

The new head of Combined Operations from October 1941 was Louis Mountbatten. A favourite with Churchill, he received quick promotion from captain to commodore and then to vice-admiral in 1942. Mountbatten would have preferred a sea command, but Churchill recognized the powers of diplomacy and will that Mountbatten would need to succeed in the role. Churchill tasked him with turning 'the south coast of England from a bastion of defence into a springboard of attack'.[13] Also, by the end of 1941 the attack by the Japanese on Pearl Harbor was to catapult the United States directly into the war and change the situation completely. One of Mountbatten's early suggestions was to instigate a Combined Signals School at HMS *Quebec* for signallers from all three services. Early raids on the Norwegian islands of Vaasgo, Maaloy and the Lofoten Islands were planned and executed under his command from 26 to 28 December 1941. The aim was to destroy fish oil factories, a power station, wireless stations and fortifications. The raids, against only light resistance, were a great success and provided a propaganda coup as well as destroying over 15,000 tonnes of shipping. Also, an Enigma code machine and a set of German naval codes were captured. Over 120 prisoners were taken, and nearly 300 Norwegians returned to Britain to serve in the Free Norwegian forces. British forces lost 20 men killed and 59 wounded, while the Germans had over 150 killed. These raids kept important resources from the Germans and showed that the British were able to strike in remote areas. Importantly for the future invasion of France, it forced Hitler to keep large numbers of troops stationed in Norway.

Within two months a second successful operation, code-named Operation Biting, was planned to capture important parts of the German Wurzburg radar, photograph the installation and return parts to Britain. The Germans had reorganized their defences against air attack, and, like the Chain Home System established in Britain before 1940, radar became the eyes of this defence. However, the German radar system was adapted for gun-laying rather than pure reporting of enemy activity. It was important to capture and understand new parts of this system. By coincidence, a Spitfire of the Photo Reconnaissance Unit (PRU) had photographed what looked like a Wurzburg radar dish on the clifftop north of Le Havre near the village of Bruneval. A lone villa nearby was the obvious HQ of the Wurzburg operatives.

Over the night of 27/28 February 1942, a unit of 120 parachute troops with an RAF expert on radar landed near the village of Bruneval and attacked the lone house and Wurzburg radar installation. There was some fighting at night in the snow, during which the nearby villa was taken and held, and a group that had landed in the wrong place had fought through to the main party via Bruneval. They were successful in their task, taking some photographs by flash bulb, and sawing off and carrying away important pieces of the machine. The group were taken off by sea in a small number of landing craft and transferred to motor gun boats for the journey back to Portsmouth. Two parachutists had been killed and six were missing, later captured.[14] They had captured two Germans, one was an operator of the Wurzburg. After detailed examination, including evaluation of the manufacturer's tags, it was found that about a hundred of these radars were produced each month and that the radar contained no anti-jamming device. This was to be important, because it was found that the simple expedient of dropping aluminium strips, called 'window', would disrupt German radar. Also, the raid caused the Germans to wire in and mine the areas surrounding their radar sites. Lack of animal grazing allowed the grass to grow much higher around these sites, which now became more easily identified in reconnaissance photographs. Before D-Day, this made it easier to target the radar installations. The important point is that this was a model of small-scale raiding and combined operations, and showed that all three services could plan and work successfully together.

On 11 February 1942, the German battleships *Scharnhorst* and *Gneisenau*, with the heavy cruiser *Prinz Eugen*, had sailed from Brest through the English Channel to the German port of Wilhelmshaven. This event, known popularly in Britain as the 'Channel Dash' and by the Germans as Operation Cerberus, shocked Churchill, as British forces had seemed powerless to stop the German ships. With the Channel guns down for maintenance, only Swordfish aircraft got anywhere near the ships, and all were lost. It appeared that large German naval units could operate successfully in the English Channel. What if the greatest remaining German battleship, *Tirpitz*, was released from Norway?

One month later, on 28 March, 'our biggest and most dramatic raid took place'.[15] The main aim of Operation Chariot was to put out of action the huge dry dock in the port of St Nazaire in France, so that the *Tirpitz* could not use St Nazaire, where it could more easily be a threat to Atlantic shipping. If *Tirpitz* was damaged, the dry dock at St Nazaire would be the only one on the French coast capable of repairing it. A number of subsidiary targets included gun positions, bridges, pumping and power stations, and any U-boats or shipping in port.

Seventy bombers were to provide a diversion for Chariot, but on the night, only ten aircraft bombed any targets, due to the poor conditions. The RAF had been told only to bomb clearly visible targets, one bomb at a time, to avoid casualties among the French townspeople. In fact, this tactic alarmed some German officers, who believed an airborne landing might be taking place. The assault was led by a commando force of 173 men from two commando units and 92 men from another six commando units to gain experience. The navy provided another 357 men. One aspect of this raid was unusual: the old destroyer HMS *Campbeltown* had explosives hidden in her bows, and was to ram the main lock gates with the explosives timed to go off later, destroying the gates and rendering the dry dock useless. HMS *Campbeltown* was to carry some of the attacking force, while the remainder were carried in eighteen motor launches of varying types.

The flotilla left Falmouth at 1400 hours on 26 March. The 400-mile journey across to the Brittany coast was hazardous: a U-boat was encountered and unsuccessfully attacked, and the Admiralty signalled that German surface forces were in the area. The approach to the target was five miles up the River Loire, under German observation and covered by batteries ashore. The landing and demolition force was especially highly trained for the raid; some practice had been carried out on similar facilities in Southampton docks. The targets were divided between three main groups, with each group sub-divided down to a total of sixteen smaller units of between thirty and five commandos, depending on task.[16] The raid was successful, but costly in terms of lives and loss of the motor launches. In total, 169 men were killed, and 215 became prisoners of war. Five men managed to evade capture and made their escape to freedom via the Spanish border. Remarkably for a small action, five Victoria Crosses were awarded and over 100 other medals and awards were made.[17]

The results had wider implications than the denial of the dry dock. Hitler was mortified that the British had displayed the guile to approach up a defended river, and the vulnerable nature of the French coast was openly displayed. British raids were becoming larger in scale and ambition. Hitler made Von Rundstedt lead an enquiry and, not satisfied with his report, had the whole matter investigated by General Jodl. The upshot was a bitter row between the German Army and Navy. However, the high casualties also pointed to problems with the British investment in materiel. During planning, both the role of the RAF and the number and type of naval craft had been greatly reduced and changed. The Admiralty was not prepared to risk using a larger force, or craft such as landing craft, in the venture. Instead, the motor launches, which were very vulnerable to enemy fire and only lightly armed and armoured, were used, and there was no covering bombardment force. Bomber Command did not want to commit large numbers of aircraft, there were always fears during the planning about civilian French casualties, Churchill finally placed further restrictions on the bombing force just prior to the raid, and the weather on the night was not favourable to the bombers. The German report into the action acknowledged, first, that heavier and more continuous bombing by the RAF would probably have allowed the British Navy to approach unimpeded and, second, that had the British used more men and larger ships, the raid would have been an even greater success.[18]

This raid placed Mountbatten more firmly in the role at Combined Operations and future planning for invasion: 'Dickie's [Mountbatten] show at St. Nazaire, though small in scale, was very bracing. ... I made him Vice-Admiral, Lieutenant-General and Air-Marshal some weeks ago.'[19] The RAF and army rank may have been honorary, but he now had an equal seat at the Chiefs of Staff Committee, and, as Churchill noted to Roosevelt, 'He will be in the centre of what you mention about the joint attack on Europe.'[20]

The next major British action on the coast of France remains controversial because of the very high casualties sustained by the British force, mainly made up of Canadian soldiers and commandos. This was the 'raid' on 19 August 1942 on Dieppe. Afterwards, the Germans were able to claim a victory because of the many casualties and loss of equipment that the attacking force sustained; however, it has also been claimed that many valuable lessons were learnt that stood the eventual planning for D-Day in good stead and hence saved many lives in 1944. The raid in force on Dieppe had been planned as Operation Rutter earlier in 1942. Canadian troops were chosen for a number of reasons. Recognized as tough soldiers, many were getting bored waiting in England. They had been one of the major defensive forces available throughout 1940, and were highly trained. Canadian politicians had given the go-ahead for their use in any viable operation, and by the end of 1941, the 1st Canadian Army had been formed with 125,000 men.[21] As the planning for Rutter went ahead, the Canadians went through a rigorous commando-like training period. Tank support to the landing was to be provided using a number of the new Churchill tanks, the Royal Navy was to provide extensive fire support for the landing and the troops ashore, and the RAF was to provide bombing prior to the landing and fighter cover to bring the Luftwaffe into the air in order to win an air battle over the Continent, while still protecting the shipping below. Also, it was originally planned to land parachute troops on either side of the port to destroy the German coastal batteries that flanked the town. However, when all was ready, Rutter was cancelled on 8 July due to continuing bad weather and the fact that two important ships of the landing force had been hit by bombs the day before. The attack on the gathered shipping in the Solent by four German fighter-bombers, probably Focke-Wulf 190s, also fuelled speculation that the Germans had somehow got intelligence about the raid.[22] The Canadian troops dispersed back to their camps.

From early 1942, there was pressure on Britain from its two main allies. First, the Russians asked for a 'second front' to relieve pressure on them; there were genuine fears at this time about how Russia was faring. Second, pressure for some sort of major British action, perhaps commitment, against the Continent came from the United States. There had already been a round of planning for a landing on the Continent, called 'Roundup', if Germany looked as though it might suffer an internal collapse, or, if the Russians looked likely to collapse, another plan was formed, known as 'Sledgehammer'. The actual areas of invasion looked at during these sometimes vague planning meetings included the Pas-de-Calais, Le Havre, the Channel Islands and the Cherbourg Peninsula. One of the greatest problems to be faced remained shipping and landing craft for an invasion. In the end, it was only because the United States took on a significant programme of landing-craft building that by June 1944 just about enough landing craft were available for use in the European theatre of operations. A second important consideration was that the Allies had to have control of the air over the Continent for an invasion to succeed.

Later in 1942, an invasion plan called Wetbob was also being investigated: putting ashore two British armoured and four infantry divisions, supported by seven commando units and four parachute battalions, while the United States provided a further armoured division, two infantry divisions and another parachute battalion. Such an invasion would have fulfilled the requirements of Sledgehammer. This is significant for the eventual planning for D-Day. The area chosen for such an assault was either side of the base of the Cotentin Peninsula, so that the troops landing on each coast would meet and form a broad front that could not be sealed off by German attacks on the narrow peninsula, and a drive could be made north on the port of Cherbourg. Also, rather than an attack on a point or port, the initial landings were to be over open beaches. The commandos were again specifically tasked to take out flanking batteries. Planned for October 1942, this plan was quietly shelved, as Britain and the United States eventually agreed upon Operation Torch, the invasion of North Africa.[23]

However, a raid in force on the French Channel coast could now test some of the ideas and theories. So Rutter was resurrected, and renamed Operation Jubilee on 20 July 1942. The aim was to test German defences and gain experience of handling a large landing force: a mini, limited invasion. Other aims were to examine a nearby German radar station and test the new LCTs in action. There were potential problems with this resurrection of Rutter. Not least was security, due to the previous standing down of the invasion force of several thousand men. Montgomery, who, as general of South Eastern Command, was responsible for providing the troops, claims that he seriously disapproved: 'When I heard of this I was very upset; I considered it no longer possible to maintain secrecy.'[24] Further, Montgomery wrote to General Paget, the commander-in-chief of Home Forces, recommending that the raid be cancelled and, if so desired, another target be chosen and planned for. Within ten days, Montgomery was removed completely from the scene when he was ordered to take command of

8th Army in North Africa. Unlike Wetbob/Sledgehammer plans, Jubilee would directly attack a heavily defended port rather than open beaches.

Commandos landing on either side of Dieppe were substituted for parachutists to destroy the flanking coastal batteries, so that poor weather would have less of an effect on the forces involved. The preceding air bombardment was eliminated due to fears of alerting the enemy and making the streets of Dieppe impassable to the raiding force through rubble. The naval bombarding contingent was restricted to only six smaller destroyers and a gunboat.

On 19 August 1942, the raid was mounted. The attacking force consisted of over 6,000 troops, including 50 US rangers. Some 5,000 troops were Canadian. It was a disaster: 907 Canadians were killed and nearly 2,000 taken prisoner. In the air, 119 aircraft and 93 airmen were lost. Out of the thousand British troops involved, 52 were killed, as was one US ranger. The Royal Navy lost 75 killed and over 250 prisoners of war. The Germans were on the highest state of alert: the orders for the German 302 Infantry Division on watch in the area read: 'The night 18/19th can be regarded as suitable for enemy raiding operations. Commanders of coastal defences are to maintain troops at the Threatened Danger Alert.'[25] The landing areas were all overlooked, and behind the main beach at Dieppe lay a typical beach wall and an esplanade. The beach itself was wide and devoid of cover. Few men made it across the esplanade; most were pinned down on the beach. Most of the tanks could not make it over the sea wall and were brought to a halt on the beach. There can be no doubting the bravery of all the troops concerned, Canadian, British or American. It was impossible to make headway against the storm of fire coming from German positions. By 1100 hours, the order was given to withdraw.

Mountbatten claimed: 'It is only in the most immediate sense that Dieppe can be called a catastrophe. The losses of course were very disturbing.'[26] He then goes on to enumerate the benefits that came from the raid. Churchill confirms Montgomery's stance, but then goes on to say that he thinks it important that a large-scale operation should take place that summer. Oddly, he then says that, because of the speed of organization required between Rutter and Jubilee, 'no records were kept'.[27] While regretting the casualties, Churchill also goes on to say that the raid was a 'mine of experience'.[28]

This is not the place to examine the arguments for who was right or wrong. Mountbatten has been especially held up as accountable, although both Brooke and Churchill seemed eager for the raid to go ahead and, bearing in mind some of the raiding and experiences of Combined Operations, some of the planning seems naïve at best.[29] The destruction and loss of such a large, able fighting unit in an experiment like this surely could not be justified at this time, even if it was claimed that the lessons learnt saved so many lives on D-Day and ensured a successful landing on a vast scale.

An interesting side issue was the decision to use the Churchill tanks. Thirty of these were landed, and all thirty were captured, yet this was a virtually new tank and a gift to the Germans. Armed at the time with a two-pound gun in the turret and a three-inch howitzer in the body, this new tank was still having many teething troubles. Quite a number of tanks were disabled on the beach, some through broken tracks caused by the pebble beach – a weakness that should already have been apparent, as some training had been carried out in Britain on similar beaches. The sixteen tanks that got off the beach[30] could not penetrate into the town, due to the number and size of concrete anti-tank obstacles the Germans had erected on the sea front and blocking roads off the esplanade into the town. This, equally, should not have surprised anyone, as the British had been constructing similar anti-invasion obstacles since 1939. The engineers on foot who should have accompanied the tanks and destroy any obstacles were mainly pinned down or dead on the beach. The German appreciation of these tanks after inspection was not very gratifying. Despite this very inauspicious start, the Churchill tank in various guises was to return to France on D-Day and perform excellent service on the British beaches, having been adapted to specialist roles.

Important lessons were understood and learnt from Jubilee in analysis carried out afterwards and published in a report of October 1942. It was finally realized that a direct attack on a fortified point such as a port was too costly, that attacks needed to be developed around the flanks of any such target and that specialist close inshore support ships needed to be developed: 'The lesson of greatest importance is the need for overwhelming fire support, including close support, during the initial stages of the attack. … Without such support any assault on the enemy occupied coast of Europe is more and more likely to fail as the enemy's defences are extended and improved.'[31] It was realized that planning and training of selected troops had to be exemplary and that troops must train adequately with their naval counterparts, so that everyone understood each other's role. When fired upon, troops should not go to ground, but needed to move in order not to be pinned down. In future, much more live ammunition was to be expended during exercises and training to get men used to the sound of gunfire very close to them. Communications between the land forces and any commander at sea had to be greatly improved, especially where the use of floating reserve troops was concerned. Also, any plan needed to have flexibility built in and a variety of options available to any commander once ashore. New techniques of landing and support were to be developed and precise timings adhered to. One of these techniques was prompted by the relative failure of the tank support through their inability to cross the sea wall or operate inland. In future, it was decided that tanks could contribute to close and overwhelming fire support on the way into a beach and, once landed, must be able to be quickly deployed to suppress enemy fire and available to be called up at a moment's notice to lend fire support as the landing progressed inland. Another positive effect in the end was the continued improvement to the Churchill tank design and its adaption for a number of crucial roles by June 1944 alongside the Sherman flail tank.

At the same time as the events described above were taking place, there had been major meetings of politicians and military to try to plan the strategic journey ahead. Roosevelt had always supported Churchill and the British in carrying on their war against Germany as much as he could, while the United States remained neutral until very late in 1941. From 1940, supplies of weapons and ammunition had made their way to Britain and Commonwealth countries from the United States, critically helping to rearm the army after Dunkirk and the Home Guard. From early in his time as prime minister, Churchill had corresponded with Roosevelt on a personal level. Churchill believed that 'In this way our perfect understanding was gained.'[32] In all, Churchill reckoned that he sent Roosevelt 950 messages, receiving 800 in reply. 'What we had was lent or leased to us because our continued resistance was deemed to be of vital interest to the great Republic.'[33] On 30 December 1940, Roosevelt, in one of his famous 'fireside chats' to the American people, declared that the United States must be the great arsenal of democracy, and that if Britain went down, the United States would be living at the point of a loaded gun.

Between August 1940 and January 1941, there had been high-level military consultations between the British and Americans resulting in staff agreement, known as American–British Staff Conversations or ABC-1. These had concluded with the idea that in any future global war it was the Germans who would need to be beaten first in Europe and the Atlantic. It was after this that British planners started to look at Operation Roundup in case of German collapse, though little concrete achievement was possible at this stage. It assumed that the Germans had given up hope of victory and were withdrawing to their border. The plan was to disrupt this withdrawal by landing at several points between Deauville and Dieppe, initially dominating an area of land between the River Seine and Calais, and pushing north later to Antwerp and eventually the German border. It has been pointed out that this scatter of landings with small forces indicated the weak British position at the time.[34]

From 22 December 1941 to 14 January 1942, the Arcadia Conference was held in Washington, DC. It officially reaffirmed the strategy of Germany first. The important point for this study is that, during these conferences for Roundup and Arcadia, the principle was that the United States and Britain would work together to defeat Germany first, and that this must mean an invasion of Europe launched from Britain. Thus, the early seeds of Operation Overlord were sown. Further meetings were held in London during April 1942, at which the initial plans for the build-up of US troops in Britain, called Operation Bolero, were agreed, with the idea that there would be an invasion of the Continent perhaps later in 1942, or definitely in 1943. At this conference, Mountbatten stated that the plans for an attack on the Continent, which fell short through lack of resources, would 'all be changed when the great flow of American forces began, and we should be able to plan that real return to the Continent, without which we could not hope to bring the war to a successful conclusion.'[35]

For the British in particular, it was not just a question of materiel or production; there were real issues of manpower if British industry and agriculture were to supply all that was needed. There was a shortage of labour in Britain: by the summer of 1941, 49 per cent of the working population were employed on government work, and the army was kept at a size of two million.[36] Not only were men conscripted for military service and work, but women too. Britain was the only nation to apply this measure. By 1943, a crisis point had been reached, and in early 1943, by applying what was called the manpower budget, it was realized that more people were needed in industry than could be found, there were no extra groups to undergo conscription, and there was a labour gap of one million.[37] Yet during 1943, Britain had armies fighting in North Africa, then Sicily and Italy; it kept further forces in the Middle East and was fighting the Japanese in Burma. In all theatres of war, the Royal Air Force, Royal Navy and Mercantile Marine played vital roles. Men would be needed in large numbers for the forthcoming invasion of Europe, and beyond lay the spectre of an eventual invasion of Japan.

Despite the entry of the USSR and the United States into the war by the end of 1941, early 1942 was not a good time for British fortunes. In the Far East, Hong Kong had fallen to the Japanese on Christmas Day 1941, and Malaya and Singapore had surrendered with an army of 100,000 men on 15 February 1942, thus also weakening the British military and political position in the Far East and India. In August came the news of the disastrous Dieppe raid. In the desert war, the British could never seem to hold onto any gains for long, and Rommel built himself a near-mystical reputation with Allied troops. In June 1942, he struck again, capturing Tobruk and driving British forces back to within seventy miles of Alexandria, where he was finally halted at El Alamein. Not until a two-week battle during October–November 1942 was he driven from the Alamein position by British forces led by the new 8th Army commander, Lt General Bernard Montgomery, who had replaced General Auchinleck in August. On 19 August, the day of Dieppe, Churchill had visited his new desert general in Montgomery's map wagon: 'There he gave us a masterly exposition of the situation, showing that in a few days he had firmly gripped the whole problem.'[38] Churchill expected immediate action, but was disappointed. Montgomery's way was to leave nothing to chance, but to wait until he had satisfied himself as to the logistical build-up and satisfactory planning had taken place. Among other things, delivery of the new Sherman tanks from the United States would put this arm on more than equal terms with the Afrika Corps and the Italian Army. Also, massive use of artillery was to be made. Churchill may not have been happy with the wait until Montgomery was fully prepared, but he noted a complete change of atmosphere and spirits after Montgomery took charge. Churchill was later to write of the successful end of the Battle of El Alamein: 'Before Alamein we never had a victory. After Alamein we never had a defeat.'[39] Montgomery, who had already shown himself as an able commander during the retreat in France 1940, an excellent trainer of troops in South East Command and a clever self-propagandist, thus took a further step on his journey to becoming the British public's most popular general since Wellington.

While these events had been taking place, discussions continued between the British and the Americans about the problem of a landing in Europe. There were a number of challenges to be considered. First, although it had been established that Germany would be dealt with first, there were problems with a lack of landing craft. Prosecuting the war in the Far East, the United States needed many craft, and few could be spared from the hard-fought Pacific campaign. This helped British interests because of the vulnerability of Australia and New Zealand, and in any case this would eventually have to be the route for the invasion of Japan. Still in the Far East, India was threatened, and control of the Indian Ocean had been lost. Britain was very short of shipping, and many ships were still being lost in the Atlantic and the Arctic. The British, led by Churchill and Brooke, also emphasized the danger of not successfully prosecuting and completing the desert campaign. The lack of materiel during the first half of 1942 and the success of the Afrika Corps and the Italian Army in the desert maintained the fear of loss of the Suez Canal and the Middle Eastern oilfields.

If any attempt was made to land in Europe in 1942 to bolster the USSR, the initial burden would fall on the British. Previous planning for Sledgehammer had shown that the only area within reasonable air cover from British fighter planes was the Pas-de-Calais, and an examination of the beaches here showed that they were not suitable for landing craft, and the exits from the beaches often led up easily defendable gullies through tall cliffs. Also, any landing in force here, provoking a strong German counter-attack and withdrawal, would mean that it might be very difficult to recover retreating troops from the coast, as the Bruneval raid nearly showed. These varied problems and worries throughout 1942 gave the British a distinct lack of enthusiasm for invasion of the Continent at that moment, and the feeling that the war in North Africa had to be settled first. In fact, during the April 1942 conference, Brooke reversed the idea that any landing in Europe was to bolster the Russians in adversity; rather, Sledgehammer should only be attempted if the Russians had won a considerable victory and Germany was on the back foot. The most useful part of planning for Sledgehammer was helping to decide the future area of invasion.

With this in mind, a plan for an invasion of French North Africa, named Gymnast, had already been raised at the Arcadia Conference. It relied to a great extent on the co-operation of the French Colonial forces present in this area under the rule of Vichy France. As the year progressed, the British side seemed much keener to pursue this operation than an attack on the Continent, which seemed unlikely to be successful, and agreement over definite proposals for Gymnast, renamed Torch, was reached in July 1942, about the same time that Rutter was being resurrected. At the first meeting to discuss plans for Torch, Churchill raised the idea that, if the invasion was successful and all North Africa cleared of the enemy, it might be possible to attack Sicily and Italy.[40] Brooke still found the Americans in favour of Europe and not North Africa. He was convinced that any landing in Europe would not survive the winter, and would just lead to the loss of six divisions.[41] Arguments continued for two days until Roosevelt wired to say he favoured the North African plan. By 24 July, Brooke reported that, despite his apprehensions, the Americans had 'produced a paper containing almost everything we had asked them to agree to at the start'.[42] Among other things, a pet idea of Churchill's, an invasion of Norway, had been sidelined, although a Canadian division was issued with Arctic clothing and made to look as if it were off to Norway, doubtless feeding Hitler's fear of the vulnerability of his northern conquest. An American general, Eisenhower, was chosen to lead the invasion; he had made a good impression on Churchill at an earlier meeting in Washington.

The final plans for Torch were issued in late September, and the series of landings, originally planned for October or earlier, were pushed back to 8 November 1942. Among other problems and hold-ups were issues with the number and state of landing craft and the training of the troops. Landings were effected at Algiers, Oran and Casablanca. The Western Task Force sailed directly from the United States, the other two from the United Kingdom. It was thought that Vichy French forces in the area might have sympathy with the United States, but were unlikely to be sympathetic to British troops because of the bombardment of the French fleet at Mers-el-Kebir in June 1940 by the Royal Navy. Therefore, British forces used some US equipment and uniforms, and aircraft had their British identification roundels changed to the US star. Overall, the landings were successful, but there was fairly fierce resistance from French forces in some places, which ended when the French Admiral Darlan ordered his troops to cease fire. The Allies found the unwelcoming attitude of the French surprising; however, a political solution was found quickly enough, and the Allies could concentrate on gripping Axis forces in North Africa in a pincer movement, the whole point of the operation. One result of the landings was that the Germans occupied Vichy France and made for the Toulon naval base, where the French sailors scuttled their ships so that they did not fall into German hands. The battles across Tunisia did not always go to plan, and the US troops had ample opportunity to learn their trade. By 13 May, when the last of the Axis forces surrendered, the Allies were able to count 320,000 prisoners of war or dead and all their materiel. After the campaign, Eisenhower reported on how well the two nations had become integrated and worked very well together at the level of command. Many valuable lessons were learnt both by the army, navy and air commanders and by the ordinary men on the ground: 'In the event, the American, British, and French forces that had been engaged had become battle-hardened, had tested their ability to fight together as comrades-in-arms, and had won in the end a confidence that was inspired by overwhelming victory.'[43] As the first joint UK/US landing, Torch had proved a very important operation. On 15 November, with the battle at El Alamein and Torch successful, Churchill ordered the ringing of the church bells in Britain.

Even before victory in North Africa was assured, the Allies had met at Casablanca in January 1943 to thrash out future strategy. The British view for the future was finalized by 29 December 1942,[44] and Churchill outlined it in four parts: first, to knock Italy out of the war, bring Turkey into the war and give the Axis no time to recover; second, to increase the bombing of Germany; third, to maintain aid to Russia and finally build up Bolero to a great scale to re-enter the Continent around August or September 1943.[45] The main ideas had already been endorsed by Roosevelt in November 1942,[46] but at this time the US War Department was set against it. As well as Roosevelt and Churchill, a large party of high-ranking military officers from the United Kingdom and the United States met at Casablanca. There was discussion on the British side as to whether Sardinia or Sicily would be the next target after North Africa was secure. In the end, the better aerodromes and less opposition in Sardinia were eschewed in favour of Sicily. The US team wanted to hold North Africa and enter France next. It took the ten-day conference to settle matters in terms of invading Sicily, with the longer-term aim of putting Italy out of the war. The agreement of Roosevelt and the great shortage of shipping required to invade Europe were the main points in bringing round the US staff to the British view. For the British, one very good outcome of knocking Italy out of the war would be establishing control over the Mediterranean Sea and allowing the reopening of the Suez Canal to shipping, providing security and a shorter journey each way for the countries of the British Commonwealth and Empire in the Far East and Antipodes. Churchill also had a scheme to involve Turkey in the war and attack Germany via Romania and through the 'soft underbelly' of Europe. This would also allow supplies to be sent to Russia via the Mediterranean and Black Seas. To some who saw little future in becoming embroiled in the Balkans, or possible post-war British political aspirations, this was a throwback to ideas of 1914–18 and imperial dabbling.

The landings on Sicily, code-named Husky, took place on 10 July. Rather like Torch, the invasion spots were dispersed in the original plan, something against which

Montgomery argued vociferously. After being informed that he would command the British force, he wrote to his commander, General Alexander, on 17 March 1943: 'I am NOT happy about the present plan for HUSKY. In my opinion it breaks every common sense rule of practical battle fighting, and the present plan would have no hope of success.'[47]

After some argument, the plans were revised along the lines desired by Montgomery, Eisenhower as usual playing the diplomat, something he was already becoming used to. The invasion was preceded by an airdrop by US paratroopers and a glider-borne British air landing brigade. Strong winds scattered the parachutists and gliders, some landing in the sea. However, the fighting spirit and will of the scattered troops caused many problems for the defenders. Equally, the weather caused problems for the sea landing force, but, interestingly, caused the defenders to believe that landing operations could not be carried out in these conditions – a mirror to D-Day in Normandy. Seven assault divisions were ashore and the port of Syracuse captured by the end of the first day, a success which caused Churchill to telegraph Eisenhower: 'It is a tremendous feat to leap on shore with nearly 200,000 men.'[48] In terms of naval involvement, the planning included an Eastern Task Force under the US Rear-Admiral Hewitt and a Western Task Force led by the British Admiral Ramsay. Ramsay had been deputy naval commander during Torch, and had planned the landings from the naval point of view. Including the landing craft, over 2,500 ships were involved. With his earlier experience of organizing the Dunkirk evacuation, and having been involved in the Ostend and Zeebrugge raids during the First World War, for which he had received a Mention in Dispatches, he had a clearly established curriculum vitae of amphibious operations. The battles for Sicily were harder than expected, and the German and Italian air forces had some success in attacking Allied shipping, raising fears of similar problems in an invasion of France.

Italy surrendered secretly in the hope that the Allies would be able to follow up and land in Italy without the Germans taking over the country. This was a forlorn hope, and the Germans increased the number of their divisions in Italy from two to seven during August. The German Army fairly successfully evacuated forces from Sicily by 17 August 1943, and British forces followed, crossing the Straits of Messina and landing in Calabria, the toe of Italy, on 3 September. This was successful, but Montgomery had predicted that it would be a waste of time and would simply strand the British Eighth Army 300 miles south of US forces, due to land later at Salerno and quickly get north to Naples. He was correct; landing against light opposition, the British had to march north relatively slowly against Axis blocking actions. The enemy had also already believed that a main landing would come at Salerno or even further north, and had disposed their main forces accordingly. The US landing on 9 September was met with severe opposition; both advances were severely held back, and the success of the landings was threatened for over a week. The German Army was already disarming Italian forces, and sometimes military action, especially near Rome, took place between the ex-partners. The Allies came through, but the German Army began a slow withdrawal north, fighting hard throughout and falling back on prepared defensive lines. Perhaps the most famous of these included the area of Monte Cassino, which took over four months to capture. Not until 4 June 1944 did US forces enter the open city of Rome. Montgomery was criticized for insisting on full artillery cover and preparations for the British part in the landings, but claimed that he had not received adequate intelligence or even a realistic objective during the planning phase. His reputation with the Americans for methodical and overwhelming, but very slow, build-up of forces was beginning to grow. The Montgomery view was: 'You would think we would learn by our mistakes, but apparently not. Some of the things I was asked to do, and the way the whole party was stage managed, is past all belief.'[49]

Three major invasions had now given the Allies much important experience. The commanders of the two nations representing their army, navy and air components had to meet, plan and execute the three operations. The problems of control of operations, lack of landing craft and other shipping, and best use of airpower had all been practised for real. Not all had gone right by any means, and a resolute enemy had provided some nasty surprises. Together with the raiding carried out on the coast of France and the disaster of Dieppe, very valuable lessons had been learnt. American amphibious operations in the Pacific were also adding to operational knowledge and strategy, but they, too, required large numbers of landing craft. While very large armies were actively involved in the North African and Italian land operations, other armies were being gathered and trained in the United Kingdom, and planning for an invasion of France in 1944 was going ahead. The Casablanca Conference had agreed the moves in Sicily and Italy, but had also set in train the detailed planning required to carry out an invasion of France as soon as practicable. So, in March 1943, General Frederick Morgan was told that the responsibility for this planning would fall on him. Curiously, he reports being told of his appointment by Mountbatten while in a lift full of people at Combined Operations HQ in London! This seems to give somewhat of an insight into Mountbatten's nature and the times they were living in. Morgan's new title described his post admirably: chief of staff to the supreme allied commander (designate) or COSSAC, a title made up by Morgan himself.[50]

Initially, Morgan had been chosen to lead First Corps under Eisenhower's command in autumn 1942. However, by March 1943, his force had been dissipated as reinforcements to the North African armies. It was at this point that Morgan was nominated as COSSAC. Having met Eisenhower fairly briefly twice, and also being known as a good organizer, Morgan was an obvious man for the task, especially at that time the commander for the invasion of Europe was expected to be British, and military thinking of the time expected the chief of staff to be of the same nationality as the commander. In true British style, everything had to be done quickly, and Morgan recounts how he had effectively stolen his driver and car from First Corps HQ; including two batmen and an aide-de-camp, this made up the entire initial staff. Morgan 'established squatters rights' in an unoccupied office he had found in Norfolk House, and for equipment used a couple of chairs and desks found in the room together with some sheets of paper and a pencil found on the floor.[51] After a lunch at Chequers in early April 1943, he received the prime minister's blessing. Morgan seems to have ably set about constructing a viable invasion plan.

As his staff grew, he made sure that American officers had equal status as well as involving the naval and air side of things. All was not smooth sailing, and Morgan recounts how he had to reconcile not only different nationalities, but also different arms of service. He understood that fighting in Europe would be very different and require different techniques from those so far successfully applied in late 1942 and early 1943 in the Mediterranean theatre of war. This fact was sometimes difficult to get across to men from this theatre, who felt they had tried and trusted techniques and did not see why they could not be exported to other theatres. In fact, Morgan realized that he had to plan for three things: first, diversionary operations through the summer of 1943 to keep the Germans occupied in the west of Europe so that they could not easily risk reinforcing the Italian or Russian front; second, a quick entry into Europe if the Third Reich disintegrated; and finally – and most expectedly – to prepare for an all-out assault on north-west Europe as early as possible in 1944 under the code name Overlord. Outline plans for this latter task were to be in the hands of the chiefs of staff by 1 August 1943, with a projected invasion date of 1 May 1944.

Diversionary operations in 1943 were carried out under the umbrella name of Cockade, using three ruses. The Germans did not buy into any of them, as their intelligence indicated that, with all their commitments elsewhere, the Allies could not land in Europe as early as 1943. The first and most visible of these was Operation Starkey over 8/9 September 1943. The Germans were to be led to believe that an invasion, or at least a large raid, was being carried out in the Calais/Boulogne area of the Pas-de-Calais. By the use of a visible 'invasion force' of ships and landing craft, German reactions were to be monitored, and the expectation was that the Luftwaffe would be enticed to take to the skies, and by a large air battle the Allies would score a great victory. A difficulty Morgan faced was the ever-decreasing number of landing craft. He describes the need for landing craft in Sicily/Italy as 'insatiable'.[52] He was also refused the use of a bombarding battleship, as being too valuable to lose, and the numbers of bombing aircraft expected to be used were greatly reduced, so that the air war being carried out against Germany would not be diminished. Despite this, on the day of the feint attack, nearly 300 heavy bombers hit six German airfields in the hinterland of the Pas-de-Calais and industrial targets in the suburbs of Paris. Also, over 200 medium bombers hit coastal targets in the area on the day.

During August, troops (Exercise Harlequin) and shipping gathered in southern Kent around Hythe and Folkestone, and there was a perceptible increase in German air reconnaissance and some bombing. Dummy and real landing craft had been gathered in the Thames estuary and the Solent. From a Kent resident's point of view, the exercise was very visible. Colonel Foster, of the Home Guard and Air Raid Precautions (ARP), kept a diary throughout the war. On 17 August, 'Eastern Command took over the coast area today. All morning the sky was full of [Allied] bombers. I counted 36 Fortresses in one force and 32 Liberators in another.'[53] By 23 August, Colonel Foster noted that the Hythe area was being heavily used as an armoured vehicle and lorry park, and later in the month the town was full of men from the Royal Tank Regiment and No. 5 Commando; smokescreens were laid in the English Channel; heavy bomber raids across the coast continued; and flotillas of destroyers patrolled up and down, releasing smokescreens when fired upon by the German heavy artillery in the Pas-de-Calais. On 8 September Foster reports heavy bombing of Boulogne – visible from the English coast – and on 9 September fifty barges loaded tanks and men from Hythe beach and took to sea, returning later to disembark them. All the while, heavy bombing raids on the French coast, including Calais and Boulogne, continued. But by 13 September, all the extra military had left the area and it had returned to normal.[54] An officer of 2nd Glosters, Basil 'Jim' Stephens, took part in the exercise and remembers it as 'an interesting exercise, a pretend invasion force approaching within five miles of the coast of France to gauge German reaction. There was none!' Stephens remembers the bar on his ship remaining open all night.[55]

The immediate results of Starkey were disappointing. No great German air armada emerged to be shot from the skies; Morgan was told that a German artillery officer was heard over the radio 'to ask if anyone knew what all this fuss was about?'[56] One positive outcome was that, by using convoys from Kent and Portsmouth to make a sham attack towards Calais, the idea was reinforced in the German mind about the probable area of invasion being the Pas-de-Calais. Also, Starkey was used to see how effective British double agents could be in planting bogus information into German minds. When the BBC broadcast that it was only an exercise that had been taking place in the English Channel and not a raid, as had been fed to the Germans by double agents, the same agents and their handlers came up with the story to the German intelligence service that actually the raid had been called off due to Italy surrendering to the Allies, and the same opportunity was to be afforded to the Germans.[57] What Starkey also did was provide practice in large-scale and combined movement and administration for all involved. This is a crucial part of all such undertakings, and successful administration was vital to the preparation and execution of Overlord. Large army formations were moved and had to be housed and organized near their embarkation points, and later embarked in assault craft. The naval and merchant navy had to be organized, as did the air forces. 'The practice in moving a great army rapidly through concentration and assembly areas in England to embarkation points, and putting on board ship, was in reality, the rehearsal for the vast operations of June 1944.'[58]

The two further ruses, Operations Tindall and Wadham, were of much lesser stature than Starkey. Wadham pretended that an American invasion of Brittany direct from the United States would take place a fortnight after Starkey. Six infantry divisions, two armoured divisions and an airborne division were notionally to be involved. Tindall was a little more plausible, as it involved an air landing at Stavanger in Norway as well as landings by sea by units stationed in Scotland. Unlike Starkey, neither of these plans involved any real action. All three formed part of a greater deception plan, later known as Bodyguard after Churchill's later conversation with Stalin at the Teheran Conference in November 1943: 'In wartime truth is so precious that she should always be attended by a bodyguard of lies.'[59]

Three scenarios were also planned under the code name Rankin in case of some sort of German collapse in the west. Rankin A was a plan to return to Western Europe in the event of weakening German morale and strength, Rankin B covered the eventuality that the Germans would voluntarily leave France and Belgium and Rankin C planned for the case of unconditional surrender by the Germans. Each relied on some crack in German resolve due to pressure exerted via the Italian campaign, the war in Russia, internal German conflict, or any combination of the three. Morgan describes how there was little enthusiasm for the Rankin scenarios, and that a plan was only submitted on 13 August 1943, and in outline only, as the main events could not be exactly foreseen. As Morgan points out,[60] success in North Africa, Sicily and Russia and the invasion of Italy all took place during this planning period, and, in any event, any of these occurrences during 1943 or 1944 looked unlikely. Churchill also had little faith in a German collapse during 1943. Writing to General Ismay on 18 April for the Chiefs of Staff Committee, Churchill wrote: 'A German collapse being extremely unlikely and not to be counted upon this year, and neither American reinforcements nor landing craft ...'[61] This was the preamble to the orders to be given to Morgan, and, interestingly, Churchill made it clear that, as far as he was concerned, Morgan only required a small planning staff. One useful aspect of Rankin was that eventually, at the end of the war in 1945, the plans were used for the liberation of Norway and the Channel Islands.

Morgan had to work within certain restrictive parameters alongside the date of 1 May 1944. He was given an expected total of twenty-nine divisions for the assault and build-up; five infantry divisions could be loaded into the available shipping and landing craft, with two more divisions able to follow up immediately. He was told that two airborne divisions could be used, and possibly one French division would be available. Very soon afterwards, though, this number was recalculated, and he was told that both landing craft and aircraft capable of carrying paratroops or towing gliders for the assault would only be available in even smaller numbers. So his final plan for the assault reckoned that only three infantry divisions could be landed by sea, with a follow-up of two tank brigades and a US regimental combat team, and fewer than two airborne divisions as support to protect the flanks of the sea landing. This was a much smaller assault plan than he believed to be required in the first place, but it was what the operational planning staff had to work with. The balance would be the follow-up forces of eighteen divisions to expand the bridgehead, reckoned to be ashore within fourteen days, by which time fourteen airfields would have been established ashore, operating up to thirty squadrons of fighter aircraft. However, this would be after what Morgan describes as 'an awkward pause for a day or two after the assault until the next important reinforcement could be landed'.[62]

Morgan and his staff had to contend with other worries aside from the lack of landing craft and aircraft. Problems had to be faced over the use of bombing aircraft for Overlord. Air Chief Marshal Harris and Major General Carl Spaatz, heads of the British and US strategic bomber forces, respectively, believed that Germany could be brought to its knees by bombing alone, and, as Starkey had shown, were reluctant to lend any bombing aircraft to what they saw as sideshows. It seems from the testimony of Morgan that initially there were two main schools of thought for a landing area: either Pas-de-Calais or Normandy. The answer to this was thrashed out at a 'course' for all officers concerned with planning at Largs in Scotland. Normandy was chosen, as it was seen that the Pas-de-Calais was too difficult to assault for various reasons: poor landing beaches, few adequate beach exits, tides and currents, and the much more significant number of fortifications, many hardened and equipped with heavy artillery. The Normandy beaches between Cherbourg and Le Havre, especially about Bayeux, offered many landing places with good exits, and there was a possibility of capturing these two important ports, especially Cherbourg, by flanking moves. Also, this stretch of the coast offered a number of smaller ports, and the bay was relatively sheltered by the Cotentin Peninsula. To some extent, previous background work already carried out in these areas for other schemes was helpful due to the amount of information available. The area offered good potential for the construction of aerodromes and for the use of airborne troops. 'We thought in terms of a lodgement area bounded to the east by the Seine, to the south by the Loire, which seemed to be well suited for development by both ground and air forces.'[63] In later planning, it was realized that these two river boundaries could also be used to isolate the lodgement area by the destruction of road and rail bridges.

So, by the latter part of 1943, Morgan had produced a workable plan for the invasion of Europe. As we will see, this was radically altered, but the amount of groundwork and organization carried out under Morgan was very important. Without that work already in place on the eve of 1944, it is doubtful whether Overlord could have taken place that year. A great deal had been accomplished in a short space of time. Another benefit was the apparent excellent relations and ability to work together that had been built up over time between a planning team that was not only inter-service but bi-national. During this time, it had also not been apparent who was to lead the invasion. Initially, it was expected to be a senior British general, perhaps Brooke; then more likely Marshall, the US Army chief of staff. In the event, Churchill would not spare Brooke, and neither would Roosevelt spare Marshall. The men were too important to their respective leaders at home. Later, in December 1943, Eisenhower was chosen as commander of the Supreme Headquarters Allied Expeditionary Force (SHAEF), with Montgomery as commander of 21st Army Group, in charge of ground forces for the invasion and development of the bridgehead.

A Quiet Backwater of War?[1]

With the onset of the Second World War in 1939, the people of Normandy were probably as perplexed as anyone with the lack of action on the border with Germany. Through the autumn and winter of 1939–40 and into the spring continued a period called the Phoney War by the British, *Drole de Guerre* by the French and Sitzkrieg by the Germans. But on 10 May 1940, the Germans struck swiftly, carrying out a method of war that would be called Blitzkrieg or 'lightning war'. German forces advanced through Luxembourg, Holland and Belgium. Despite some valiant fighting, the Allies could not hold out against the German onslaught. By 21 May, German forces had reached the English Channel around the mouth of the River Somme. By 23 May, General Gort had decided to evacuate the British Expeditionary Force (BEF) through the Channel ports, with the majority of his army falling back on Dunkirk. Boulogne was taken on 25 May, though the Royal Navy managed to evacuate over 4,000 British soldiers from there. Calais fell early on 27 May, with the loss of two battalions of infantry and a battalion of armour. Churchill dispatched the following message to Calais for Brigadier Nicholson at 2100 on 26 May: 'Every hour you continue to exist is of the greatest help to the BEF. … Have the greatest possible admiration for your splendid stand. Evacuation will not (repeat not) take place.'[2] This loss of a whole brigade ordered by Churchill was to show British support for the French. Meanwhile, strenuous efforts were made to evacuate British troops from Dunkirk, and between 27 May and 4 June, 224,686 British troops and 141,445 Allied (mainly French) troops were evacuated.[3]

Despite the earlier aberration of stopping outside Dunkirk to let the Luftwaffe deal with the encircled British and French troops, the German Army continued to advance and cut off and capture the large numbers of British troops south of the River Somme. Dieppe, a large British Army medical centre, had already been evacuated by the end of May. In the Canadian Commonwealth War Graves Cemetery at Dieppe lies an unusual victim of 1940. Brigadier Mary Janet Climpson, aged fifty-six, of the Salvation Army had been working with her husband and others of the Salvation Army, providing help to British troops, writing letters home, visiting hospitals and conducting religious services. When it became obvious that they would have to leave France, the Climpsons journeyed to Dieppe in a military convoy. On the way, the column was attacked by German planes on 20 May, and Mary Climpson was a casualty. Her body was quickly interred on the outskirts of Dieppe.[4]

On 9 June, Rouen fell to the Germans without a fight. The bridges across the River Seine had been destroyed, and the German follow-up to the French and British withdrawal south of the River Seine slowed, partly because two-thirds of 51st Highland Division was now trapped north of the Seine and had to be dealt with.[5] Eventually, the 51st Division retreated to the small port and fishing village of Saint Valery-en-Caux. But on 12 June, two of its brigades were forced to surrender. Around a third of all buildings in the town had been destroyed or badly damaged. Rescue of over 2,000 men by the Royal Navy had been severely hampered by thick fog and German occupation of the clifftops either side of the narrow estuary. The third brigade of 51st Division had already been detached and eventually escaped via Le Havre. Leading the advance on Saint Valery-en-Caux, and within a week on Cherbourg, was a German general named Rommel.

Bill Robinson of 2nd Glosters was wounded and evacuated via Le Havre. Initially, after leave, before Christmas 1939 he had been sent to join 2nd Glosters in France. During May 1940, he was away from the battalion with his lorry. Outside Rouen, an attack by JU87 Stuka dive-bombers attacked his convoy of vehicles and he was wounded. 'Shrapnel hit me and I was given morphine. They put a big red X on my forehead to show that. I was put on a hospital train and got away from the docks and ended up in hospital at Stanmore in Middlesex.'[6] He was actually lucky: 2nd Glosters suffered high casualties defending the road to Dunkirk at Cassel, many of the remainder were captured and the battalion had to be completely rebuilt in Britain. In 1944, Robinson was to land on Gold Beach on D-Day with 2nd Glosters.

The port of Le Havre was bombed by the Luftwaffe on 11 June, and with the oil refineries in flames, it was decided to evacuate civilians across the River Seine. One of several ships sunk by the Luftwaffe was the *Niobe*, with 810 crew and civilians killed. From Le Havre, the Royal Navy evacuated over 2,000 troops to England, but also transported nearly 9,000 to Cherbourg to continue the fight. The navy only lost the troopship *Bruges*, which was bombed and then beached to prevent it from sinking.

Not only British troops were still cut off from the main army. The 1st Canadian Division and the 52nd (Lowland) Infantry Division had been taken to France to defend the west and became known as 2nd BEF. Having been evacuated from Dunkirk, General Sir Alan Brooke (later CIGS) was sent to command them. Having arrived in England from Dunkirk on 30 May, Brooke had an interview at the War Office with Dill, the current CIGS, on 2 June. When told he was to 'return to France to form a new BEF', Brooke remarks that 'this was certainly one of my blackest moments'.[7] Arriving in France on 13 June, Brooke realized that there was little hope of a successful campaign, and on the evening of 14 June, held a difficult conversation with Dill, then Churchill, on a poor telephone line, eventually persuading Churchill that it was necessary to evacuate. A rearguard action was carried through the Cotentin peninsula, and between 15 and 18 June, most of 1st Armoured Brigade and 52nd Infantry Division were evacuated. At around the same time, 1st Canadian Division was taken off from St Malo, and altogether it is estimated that around 52,000 men got away. Further evacuation took place from the Brittany ports of Brest, St Nazaire and La Rochelle, and later from around Bordeaux. There were evacuations on a smaller scale from the French Mediterranean up to the middle of August 1940.

One disaster which occurred during these evacuations was the sinking of the *Lancastria*. Moored off St Nazaire, she was sunk by bombs on the afternoon of

17 June with the loss of over 3,000, possibly as many as 6,000, lives.[8] Burning oil and Luftwaffe strafing killed some in the water. News of her sinking was suppressed by Churchill, and a full enquiry has never taken place. Charles Willis, with the Royal Army Service Corps, witnessed this event. Going to France, his unit was responsible for carefully laying out dumps towards the forward areas. Unfortunately, the German attack meant that they had barely completed their task before having to retreat, destroying the dumps they had laid down. The time needed to do this meant that they could not reach Dunkirk, and they were eventually evacuated out of St Nazaire. Here, Charles witnessed the sinking of the *Lancastria*, being 600 yards away at the time. He noted that, to him at least, one bomb appeared to go down the funnel of the ship.[9] Charles later served in Sicily and Italy, and by early 1945 was a platoon commander in Holland.

This period gave Brooke an insight into the difficulties of operations in the Normandy *bocage*. *Bocage* describes very small fields surrounded by high banks, usually topped with a dense tree cover and interspersed with orchards. Deep narrow lanes divide the fields, usually overhung with trees, and a spread of farms and hamlets strongly built of the local stone produces terrain ideal for defence. This type of country existed extensively south of Bayeux, and spread south and west into the Cotentin peninsula. In 1940, Brooke could have little dreamt that in four years' time he would be involved in planning and organizing an invasion of this area.

Despite some very gallant fighting by units of the French Army, the British withdrawal signified that even Churchill had lost hope that the German Army could be held on the European mainland as in the First World War. With the surrender of France on 22 June, France was divided into two: an occupied northern and western part down as far as the border with Spain, and a southern semi-independent part under the leadership of Marshal Petain centred on the town of Vichy, with Vichy France forced to participate in a collaborationist policy with Hitler. When the Allies invaded North Africa in November 1942, this 'free' area was occupied by German and Italian forces. In Normandy, towns like St Valery-en-Caux and Le Havre had suffered much destruction and many casualties, but the countryside suffered little damage. Across France, many would never see sons or husbands again, and many more had to wait until the end of the war for loved ones to be released from Germany. The cost to the French Army of those few weeks in 1940 was 90,000 killed and nearly two million taken prisoner.

As far as the British were concerned, this short campaign had cost the British Army 68,710 men, either killed, died of wounds or disease, missing, wounded or prisoners of war. The Royal Air Force had lost 1,526 killed, wounded or made prisoners of war. The casualties of the Royal Navy were heavy in men and ships. Left behind in France were 2,472 pieces of artillery, 63,879 vehicles (including tanks), 20,584 motorcycles, 76,697 tonnes of ammunition, 415,940 tonnes of supplies and stores, and 164,929 tonnes of petrol.[10] This high price was to have a great impact on British planning for months and years to come. The loss of materiel alone caused anxiety regarding the defence of Britain in case of a German invasion of the British Isles. As early as the second week of May 1940, and before Dunkirk, the British government had foreseen the possibility of coastal raids, inland parachute drops or German invasion. On the evening of 14 May 1940, a broadcast by Anthony Eden, secretary of state for war, invited males between the ages of sixteen and sixty-five to join the Local Defence Volunteers (later the Home Guard). While Britain feared invasion, its ally had surrendered, and across the Channel, the people of France began four long years of occupation.

Cherbourg, like Le Havre, was an important port, able to handle large ships and heavy goods. The potential use to the German Navy was obvious. The following gives an idea of what German occupation could mean for an important Norman port city:

> German soldiers patrolled the streets to control movement, all businesses remained closed, driving was not permitted, and many were forced to house German soldiers in their homes. These guests often took French cars, money, and supplies. The occupiers did not permit Cherbourg's citizens to gather or leave the city, and the nightly curfew began at 22.00 hours. There was no gas or electricity in the city for several weeks, and overnight 6,000 people lost their jobs. ... More than one month passed before they allowed fishing to resume, but restricted it to specific zones with an armed German soldier on each boat. Rationing also affected the fishing industry, limiting fuel and replacement parts. In addition, all the restrictions made it difficult to maintain the fishing industry and the local fish market.[11]

The invading power made France cover the cost of the occupation. The Germans set the value of the Reichsmark at a very favourable rate against the franc, at eight francs higher than the preoccupation value. Food and raw materials were seized. The French suffered very real deprivation during the occupation. Food shortages, and even malnutrition, in the larger towns and cities were normal. Gas was rationed and power cuts frequent at times. As time went on, even a rich farming area such as Normandy suffered rationing, and prices on the black market soared. In the countryside things could be better, but only by hiding foodstuffs and running the risk of arrest and imprisonment or deportation to work camps in Germany. Clandestine listening to the BBC was equally risky. Of course, all firearms had to be handed in, affecting the farming community through a loss of hunting rifles. Only German stations, Radio Paris and National Radio could be listened to, and all of these were heavily censored. The tricolour French flag was replaced by the swastika in the occupied zone; there were many parades, and German military bands were often to be seen playing martial music.

From 1942, Jews throughout France were rounded up and transported to concentration camps, where more than 70,000 were killed. A further 3,000–4,000 died before leaving France, at concentration camps set up within France or in massacres on French soil. A further 30,000 members of various political parties were also executed, and deaths of members of the resistance organizations are estimated at above 60,000.

In *Directive No. 18*, November 1940, Hitler stated that the aim of my policy towards France is to co-operate with that country in the most effective manner possible for the future conduct of the war against England'. France was required to be a non-belligerent power, allowing German war measures on French territory, including France's African colonies, and to guard against any attempts by the British or de Gaulle to gain power in the French African colonies. By the following month, in *Directive No. 19*, plans were to be drawn up in case of need for the rapid occupation of unoccupied France and bringing the French fleet and remaining air force under German control. Any opposition was to be 'ruthlessly suppressed'. Interestingly, the Italians were not to be informed about German plans.[12]

Normandy suffered its share of deaths through resistance. Early in the German occupation, the first outward sign of resistance was the publishing of underground news sheets. German soldiers were generally happy to be stationed in this historic and agriculturally wealthy area. Second-line units equipped with low-quality transport and arms, and, later, units resting from the Russian Front, occupied the area.

In Britain, Churchill was showing his aggressive nature even before the final evacuation of the British Army from Normandy and Brittany. In a letter to General Ismay dated 4 June 1940, Churchill proposed that 'to keep the largest number of German forces all along the coasts they have conquered …we should set to work to organise raiding forces on these coasts where the populations are friendly'.[13] He proposed forces between 1,000 and 10,000 strong. He continued in the same week to emphasize this message. Only two days later, he was writing about the 'butcher and bolt' policy.[14] He expanded this to suggest that a port like Calais or Boulogne could be taken and held for a significant length of time, with retreat to our shores only when the enemy had made preparations to retake such a place. In typical bloodthirsty fashion, he described such a force as 'leaving a trail of German corpses behind them' and stated that a landing in force could proceed inland as far as Paris.

Broadly speaking, the area of Normandy and Brittany was to receive several raids from 1940 onwards. Unfortunately, the first raids met with little success. On 24–25 June, Operation Collar – a raid in the Pas-de-Calais by 115 commandos from 11 Independent Company – landed in four different locations. After spending eighty minutes on shore, they got back to their boats unscathed, except for one man wounded on Stella Plage in an exchange of fire. The group landing at Le Touquet silently killed two sentries, but were forced to swim out to their boats when a stronger German patrol approached.

On 2 July 1940, Churchill wrote: 'If it be true that a few hundred German troops have been landed on Jersey or Guernsey by troop carriers, plans should be studied to land secretly by night on the islands and kill or capture the invaders. This is exactly one of the exploits for which the Commandos would be suited.'[15] The proposed operation – Operation Ambassador – was carried out by elements of 3 Commando, only just in formation, and again by elements of 11 Independent Company.

On 8 July, Lieutenant Nicolle was landed on Guernsey by submarine and was picked up three days later. He discovered that fewer than 500 enemies were on the island, the majority at St Peter Port, although several machine-gun positions lined the coast. Leaving from Dartmouth, two destroyers led a group of six RAF Air-Sea Rescue launches, to be used to land the troops on the night of 14/15 July. The force of 140 men was split between H Troop of No. 3 Commando and No. 11 Independent Company. While 3 Commando were to kill and capture German soldiers, No. 11 Independent Company were to wreck the island's airfield. Although the commandos successfully landed, they did not engage any German forces. They found a barracks and machine-gun post empty. When the time came to withdraw, it was realized that the party would have to swim out to sea. At this point, three commandos confessed that they could not swim and had to be left behind. A fourth appears to have been lost when a dinghy overturned. No. 11 Independent Company lost two of their launches on the journey over due to engine trouble. As they approached the coast with their remaining craft, one hit a rock and the other landed on the Island of Sark through poor navigation. The four soldiers left behind were all captured. Overall, this was not an auspicious start to commando operations, and Churchill was furious, calling it a 'silly fiasco'.[16]

Problems included lack of time or up-to-date intelligence to help with developing a plan. The RAF launches used on the early raids were only quick stand-ins, as the originally supplied craft were found to be inadequate. The launches themselves had only basic navigation equipment. They were not shallow draught vessels, and could not go close in, requiring deep wading by the troops, with the risk of wet equipment and weapons failure. Their relative failure was more to do with lack of experience and adequate equipment than any lack of will on the part of the men involved. These were the forerunners, developing and trying out techniques which, as the war years progressed, would be improved and honed to a very high standard of success.

Important and successful raids were later carried out in Norway, but the coast of France was to continue to see quite a number of raids of varying size up to D-Day. The Bruneval and Dieppe raids carried out in Normandy and the St Nazaire raid in Brittany were all carried out in 1942, and those at St Nazaire and Dieppe showed by their size and intent that the British had the confidence to land on the coast of France in large numbers. Small-scale raids continued, two of which, in September 1941 and September 1942, led to the loss of commando lives on the beaches that were later to become famous on D-Day.

Operation Deepcut, which took place over the night of 24/25 September 1941, consisted of sixty-five men split into two parties from 5 Troop: No. 1 Commando landing at St Vaast-la-Hougue on the north-eastern side of the Cherbourg peninsula, north of what was to become Utah Beach, and the other party at Courseulles, on what was to become Juno Beach. The two parties were transported across the Channel in HMS *Prince Leopold*, an ex-railway ferry converted to a small troopship, then each party was transferred to smaller craft towed inshore by motor gun boats. The party at St Vaast killed two Germans, and took a wounded prisoner back to their boats after a brief firefight with a German bicycle patrol. The wounded man died on board. The Courseulles group landed at the wrong place, further east, at Luc-sur-Mer. As they tried to force a way through the apron of barbed wire on the sea wall, they were heavily fired upon, and two were killed. The rest immediately retreated, and returned to HMS *Prince Leopold*. The two casualties, Privates Edwards and Evans, were buried with full military honours by the German garrison of Luc-sur-Mer in the churchyard, next to the body of a Spitfire pilot (Squadron Leader Pitcairn-Hill DSO, DFC) washed up on the beach at Luc-sur-Mer the year before.[17]

The second raid which took casualties in the D-Day landing area was Operation Aquatint. When this raid took place over the night of 12/13 September 1942, the Germans in coastal areas were on high alert after the Dieppe raid of August and other coastal raids, near Barfleur on 14/15 August and against the Casquets lighthouse off Alderney over 2/3 September. The Aquatint party believed they were off St Honorine, but in fact were off St Laurent-sur-Mer (later Dog Sector, Omaha Beach area). The party of eleven landed, but became involved in a lengthy firefight. Their motor torpedo boat, waiting out at sea, was also engaged and hit. On land, three of the raiding party were killed and four captured. Four of the commandos had managed to escape. Later, three of these were captured by a German unit on a training exercise. One was sent to a prisoner-of-war camp, from which he later escaped. One of the other two died or was killed, and the fate of the final member is not known. They may both have been executed. The final free person – Captain Hayes – was passed through a Resistance escape line, but was betrayed and captured in Spain and handed back to the German border guards. He was executed in July 1943. The whole escape network appears to have been compromised. Of the eleven-man commando team, one member was French, another Polish, a third Dutch and a fourth a Sudeten German. A new Commando – No. 10 (Inter-Allied) Commando – was being raised from European men in the army, who had been screened with a view to coastal raiding and usefulness in providing translators, interpreters and interrogators. The three men killed on landing are buried in the local cemetery at St-Laurent-sur-Mer cemetery, not far from the very famous United States Cemetery wherein are buried or commemorated nearly 11,000 US men who died on D-Day or the later Normandy campaign.

By October 1942, 'Commando' raids were having such an effect that Hitler ordered that no commandos should be spared, even if they appeared to be surrendering. In or out of uniform, armed or not, they were to be 'killed to the last man in battle or flight'.[18] Some captured commandos could be kept briefly for interrogation, but afterwards they were to be immediately shot. Hitler justified this order by explaining that the British and Americans were landing men by sea and air who acted in a way similar to the partisans in the east.

> Especially brutal and underhanded are the methods of the so-called commandos, which, as has been established, even include former criminals who have been released in enemy countries. Captured orders show that they are instructed not only to tie prisoners, but even simply to kill defenceless prisoners when they find that these interfere in any way with their missions. Finally orders were found demanding that prisoners be killed as a matter of principle.[19]

The United States entered the war in December 1941, and, despite the attack by the Japanese on Pearl Harbor, agreed to a policy of 'Germany first'. From 1942, many of the raids along the French coast were undertaken with a view to gaining specific intelligence about the possibility and suitability of beaches for an invasion. A series of raids in late December 1943 and early 1944, codenamed Hardtack, were carried out specifically for this reason, and No. 10 (IA) Commando took part in at least eight of these, mainly on the Normandy coast and the Channel Islands. In May 1944, No.10 Commando also took part in eight raids, code-named Tarbrush. By now, perhaps, we should definitely be using the term 'reconnaissance'. On one of these raids, 17/18 May, Tarbrush 10, the two commandos involved – Captain Wooldridge and Lieutenant Lane (an alias) – were captured, and were famously interviewed by Rommel on 20 May. 'Fifteenth Army should have turned them over to the SS Security Service. Speidel, however, had given them instructions to send them to La Roche-Guyon, and, with Rommel's consent, had them moved to a prisoner-of-war camp, which probably saved their lives.'[20] Their actual task was to photograph one of the beach obstacles known as

'Element C'. Also, interestingly, the Tarbrush series of raids took place further north of Normandy, in the Pas-de-Calais, perhaps as part of the subterfuge concentrating on this area. Some of the previous Hardtack operations were cancelled, as they were to have taken place on actual Overlord beaches.[21]

By the middle of the autumn of 1940, it was obvious to Hitler that no landing on the shores of Britain could be contemplated until 1941. The first German occupation forces settled down in Normandy. Later, when the war with Russia and the North African campaigns were in full swing, many soldiers appreciated that they were able to carry out their military service in a quiet area with the advantages and privileges of a conquering army. On the coast, the army had to keep awake to the possibility of the small, deadly raids by the commandos; even inland, parachutists might be dropped. At sea, movement was difficult, faced with the Royal Navy, and small coastal battles were not unknown. As time moved on, an increasing threat of attacks on coastal shipping by the RAF and, later, the US Air Force became another worry. When the war situation looked promising from a German point of view, Hitler could talk about how he would deal with Britain after the defeat of Russia, and how the British would be defeated in North Africa, and then Gibraltar and Malta eliminated. Finally, an invasion of Britain could take place.[22]

But the German High Command always considered the broad experience and skill of the Royal Navy and the ingenuity of the British Army, and realized that it was not beyond the wit of the British and their American allies to force a landing on a less well-defended area of the coastline. With increasing raids by the Allies, the few fortifications that had taken place on the Channel coast were only adequate around important harbours and the mouths of estuaries, with the one important exception of the heavy batteries erected around Cap Gris Nez commanding the Straits of Dover. These guns could actually reach British shores; 148 civilians were killed and 255 seriously wounded by these guns bombarding the Kent coast.[23]

With this thought in mind, Hitler issued *Directive No.40*[24] on 23 March 1942 under the title 'Command Organization along the Coast'. Its first principle stated that 'in the near future the European coasts will be exposed very seriously to the danger of enemy landings'. It was recognized that even limited landings would seriously disrupt German coastal traffic and tie down naval, army and air forces. It was believed that an important airbase might be captured and utilized, and important materiel captured and turned to the Allies' use. This directive also makes it clear that the Germans were aware that the Allies had 'numerous armoured landing craft suitable for carrying tanks and heavy weapons', and that any attack might well include 'parachute troops and airborne landings on a large scale'. Also, attacks could take place on an open coast. As well as stressing that a high state of alert was constantly necessary, the notion that one man should have overall control of the defence was emphasized. In France, Belgium and the Netherlands, this was to be the commanding general, armed forces, west. It was made clear that it was preferable not to allow the enemy to land, and that if the enemy made it ashore, they must be destroyed and thrown into the sea by immediate counter-attacks. Already, a fear about the perceived vulnerability of the Channel Islands seems to have been borne in mind: 'The enemy must be kept from establishing himself on any islands which, if he had possession of them, would represent a danger to the mainland and to coastal shipping.' Improvement of fortifications and setting up strongpoint defences even in less likely landing areas with all-round defence were included in the directive. It was pointed out that a fortification might have to hold out for a long time, and should never have to surrender due to lack of supplies, ammunition or water. Although many fortifications had already been improved or added to the French coast since German occupation, it was *Fuhrer Directive No. 40* that set in train the building of the so-called 'Atlantic Wall' as an impenetrable barrier against landings by the Allies.

In an addendum[25] to *Directive No. 40*, added on the eve of the St Nazaire raid by the commander-in-chief navy, Admiral Raeder, it was made clear that the directive was issued because of 'the constant enemy threat to the coasts of the occupied countries'. It showed that the many pin-prick raids had highlighted the vulnerability of coastal sectors. The Royal Navy and RAF seemed to have the capability of accurately delivering commando raiders at will. Now, with the might of the United States added, suddenly the coastal springboard for an optimistic attack on the enemy (Britain) was seen as the opposite, a vulnerable area inviting attack. Also, this addendum explained that the German naval forces were only under the command of the army commander as far as any fight for the coast was concerned. Large-calibre land-based guns in naval service, such as those defending ports and mining activities, were to remain under the control of the navy for the defence of convoys and support of naval forces. Raeder also made it clear that naval forces remained under his command, and hinted that undue pressure from the army commander should be referred to him, as 'the naval commanders and stations involved are also engaged in the tasks remaining under my command in the coastal sectors'. A circular telegram from the Fuehrer Headquarters of 5 December 1942 attempted to make sense of this by specifying that the navy had sole control of the batteries controlling the coast, and only those batteries set up temporarily and unsuitable for firing out to sea would be placed at the disposal of the army. The army had complete charge of land operations. For batteries that could fire at land and sea targets, sea targets had priority, but if there was disagreement, the Armed Forces High Command would settle the matter.[26]

The German military organization at the top left a lot to be desired, and stored up problems for future commanders. In supreme command of the German armed forces, with oversight of the army (Heer), navy (Kriegsmarine) and air force (Luftwaffe), was the Oberkommando der Wehrmacht (OKW), led throughout the war by Keitel. Each of the services had its own command: Oberkommando der Heeres (OKH), Oberkommando der Marine (OKM) and Oberkommando der Luftwaffe (OKL). During the war, OKW gained more power over operations, but was increasingly dominated by Hitler and his personal staff. From the spring of 1942, mixed messages, muddled thinking and petty jealousies between the different arms of service were storing up problems for the future.

What followed on 28 March 1942 shocked Hitler and the German High Command. Operation Chariot succeeded in destroying the dry-dock gates at St Nazaire and other important dock facilities, and rendered the large dry dock unserviceable to the German fleet.

After Chariot, Raeder issued an intelligence summary on 11 April discussing the lessons to be learnt from the St Nazaire raid. 'The British are determined and able to attack our extensive coastline more frequently and on a larger scale than heretofore.'[27] In this document, it is made clear that the threat of invasion of England by German forces has ceased, and that, with the bulk of the German Army and Air Force concentrating on Russia, the German Air Force and coastal defences have been weakened considerably in the west. The lack of patrol and minelaying craft is bemoaned, and the increasing likelihood of further Anglo-American operations on the coast of Europe underscored. A list of probable targets is explored, from the Lofoten Islands to the Spanish border on the Atlantic coast. In the north, landings by Anglo-American forces could link with the Russians, while in the south, the accepted wisdom still remained that any raid in force or invasion would have at its heart the taking of important ports or submarine bases. A clear need to increase the number batteries along the Atlantic and Channel coasts by September was indicated. The pressure exerted from Britain on German defences, and fears of an Allied landing in force, were already quite high four months before the raid on Dieppe.

The person entrusted with the direction of army operations in France and Belgium was Field Marshal Gerd Von Rundstedt. He is usually portrayed as one of the remaining aristocratic officers in the German Army, and his task was difficult. He had already retired once before the war. Then, he was reinstated and commanded Army Group South, successfully invading southern Poland. He led the invasion of France, commanding Army Group A. He was promoted to field marshal, moved to command Army Group South for the invasion of Russia, and was in command during the capture of Kiev in September 1941, destroying about a third of the Russian Army in the process. However, he was dismissed for ordering a tactical retreat in November 1941. During the campaign in Russia, he had suffered a heart attack, and was now aged sixty-five. Already a heavy smoker, he also took to fine wines; a reaction, perhaps, to having to follow orders he thought unreasonable. However, Hitler immediately had doubts about sacking one of his best generals – almost a talisman – and reinstated him in the post of (acting) commander-in-chief west (Oberbefehlshaber West (OB West)) from 8 March 1942, and in a permanent post from 1 May, at the age of sixty-six. In regard to Rundstedt, Hitler is reported to have said to Keitel later in 1944, after another episode of Rundstedt being relieved and reinstated: 'You know the respect Rundstedt enjoys, not only in the army but in the other services too, in the navy and air force is absolutely unique. He can get away with anything, and I have nobody who enjoys quite the same respect as he.'[28]

The Dieppe raid in August 1942 landed over 6,000 mainly Canadian troops. Despite the fact that the raid was repulsed with large casualties to the British forces, and the German High Command treated Dieppe as a propaganda coup for themselves, it was clear that the British were building their potential for a landing and beachhead on the continent. It was obvious to both sides that the Allies would be very foolish to again attempt a direct assault on a defended Channel port. With small commando raids on the coast and occasional raids in force such as St Nazaire and Dieppe, the German command was in a difficult position. Running campaigns in Russia and the Mediterranean made it difficult to supply all the men who were needed to build and defend the 'Atlantic Wall'. Increased bombing of Germany and industries in the occupied countries made it difficult to supply materials such as steel and concrete to make such a 'Wall' a reality.

From the very beginning of the German occupation of Normandy, coastal field fortifications had been constructed. Often no more than earth and timber constructions, these consisted of open artillery pits, machine-gun positions and trenches. These were constructed in the first instance by the troops manning them. In terms of overhead protection, they were limited. Protection for such positions against infantry and armoured attack was provided by barbed wire and minefields. Second, trained engineers from the divisional strength were responsible for the organizing and recording of minefields. In what remained an active food and industrial area, these minefields had to be clearly marked, for civilian and soldier alike. Any flame-throwing equipment was also the remit of divisional engineers, and the advice of engineering officers was sought in the design and layout of field defences. Trained army construction battalions also erected pillbox-type constructions, in which the concrete did not exceed a metre in thickness. The greater tasks of building and arming thicker concrete constructions capable of withstanding prolonged bombardment were carried out by fortress engineer and construction battalions overseen by the Organisation Todt (OT). As well as heavy gun emplacements in France, the OT was responsible for the building of U-boat shelters and, by 1944, the launch bases for V1 flying bombs and V2 rockets.

Before the war, Dr Fritz Todt had been the inspector general of the German highway system, and was then tasked by Hitler with overseeing the construction of Germany's defensive West Wall in 1938. Following this, and the successful completion of the Autobahn system, the OT became responsible for increasing military construction, in which, as the war progressed, larger numbers of labourers were foreign volunteers or forced labour, while the overseers and planners were German and wore a khaki uniform. Todt held the honorary rank of Luftwaffe general. By 1944, in France the OT had mustered 112,000 German and 152,000 French workers.[29] It was not unusual for foreign workers to be beaten and treated as slave workers by the OT; the German OT overseers were not popular with the military, often being seen as criminals using their position to escape armed service. Todt was killed in a plane crash in February 1942, and his place was taken by Albert Speer.

Despite this apparent activity of building an 'Atlantic Wall', the man responsible for defending it was far from happy. The increasing offensive power of the RAF and the Royal Navy, and the build-up of American troops in the United Kingdom, worried von Rundstedt because of the slow speed of defence building and draining of manpower from the west to other fronts. Between April and December 1943, he lost five armoured, two motorized and twenty infantry divisions, to be replaced by units from the German Reserve, which were not comparable in strength or experience. Their usefulness in carrying out offensive action was limited, and they were armed with a great variety of captured weapons, especially heavy infantry weapons and artillery. This made ammunition supply difficult, and in the case of invasion, resupply might become impossible. Rundstedt spent several months in 1943 writing a report on the state of coastal and inland defences and military personnel, and presented this in October 1943. It was impossible to build fixed fortifications along the entire coastline, and the speed of building was well behind schedule anyway. Rundstedt laid out his thoughts on a defensive campaign, which, as well as units on the coast, would require a strong reserve of armoured and motorized formations which could be manoeuvred to where they were needed.

The Germans were not at all sure of where a landing would take place; their best bet was the shortest sea crossing between England and the Pas-de-Calais. But they were also concerned about the possibility of landings from Norway to the Mediterranean coast of France. This uncertainty was not helped from 1943 by the wide web of deception woven in the United Kingdom, called Operation Fortitude, to keep the Germans guessing as to the landing areas. Indeed, the Germans believed that there would be more than one landing. By 1944, British and American 'ghost' armies existed in the south-east of England and in Scotland, kept alive by a stream of spoof radio traffic. Indeed, the 'army' in south-east England was run by US General Patton, whom the Germans saw as a very dangerous adversary. The success of this approach meant, for example, that OKW kept nearly 300,000 soldiers in Norway and important units like 2nd SS Panzer Division Das Reich (seventy-eight Panzer IV, seventy-nine Panzer V and thirteen self-propelled guns)[30] in the south of France near Toulouse, and 28,000 soldiers remained until the end of the war in the Channel Islands.[31]

In response to the paper by Rundstedt, Hitler issued *Fuhrer Directive No. 51* on 3 November 1943.[32] It stated that, although energy and military resources had been concentrated on the Eastern Front, it was time to face a more pressing threat – an Anglo-American invasion of the west in the following spring or even earlier. *Directive 51* also made the point that increased efforts would be made to fortify the west, especially in those areas from where the V1 and V2 rocket bombs would be launched. This was the Pas-de-Calais region, the expected area of Allied invasion. The possibility of diversionary attacks was not discounted. Denmark was seen as one strong possibility for diversionary attack, and was to be heavily reinforced. The point was made again that any Allied bridgehead must be immediately destroyed rather than the war of manoeuvre Rundstedt envisaged.

In detail, *Directive 51* expected all Panzer and armoured infantry divisions to be equipped with ninety-three Panzer IV or assault guns with heavy (88 mm) anti-tank weapons by the end of December. By the end of 1943, the 20th Luftwaffe Field Division should be re-equipped with assault guns as an effective mobile reserve. The 12th SS Hitler Jugend Panzer Division, 21st Panzer Division and other infantry reserve divisions, all stationed at the time in Jutland, should be brought to full strength as soon as possible. All other reserve tank units were to receive extra Panzer IV, assault guns and heavy anti-tank guns. Each static coastal division was to have 1,000 extra machine guns distributed within it. The transferring of units from the west was to end. All available aircraft were to be released from home defence, and extra airfields established in the west. The navy were ordered to finish all coastal installations speedily, with investigation into adding further coastal batteries and minefields. Also, the navy was to be combed out to provide extra men for land fighting or security duties. Enough U-boats should be moved to protect the northern shores, even at the expense of operations in the Atlantic. Similarly, the SS was expected to provide further land-fighting units and personnel for patrolling and security tasks. The final note of *Directive 51* should have persuaded everyone to work at the maximum:

> All persons of authority will guard against wasting time and energy in useless quibbling about jurisdictional matters and will direct all efforts toward strengthening our defensive and offensive power.[33]

A clear indication of the change of pace Hitler required in the west was the appointment in December 1943 of Rommel as inspector of coastal defence, reporting directly to Hitler on the implementation and progress of *Directive 51*. His two tasks were (a) to study the preparedness of the coasts occupied by Germany and submit further proposals for improving the defences and (b) to arrange operational studies for offensive operations against an enemy landing force.[34] This caused difficulties between the staffs of Rommel, von Rundstedt, the Luftwaffe and Kriegsmarine, but this talisman of the German Army was placed centre stage. The differences in class, age and experience between Rundstedt and Rommel would mean that there would always be a gulf between them. Blumentritt, chief of staff at OB West, stated in post-war interrogation that 'the chain of command was complicated and muddled'.[35] Some of the command problems were solved on 15 January 1944 when Rommel was made commander of Army Group B, consisting of Fifteenth (north) and Seventh (south) Armies, which protected the coast north of the River Loire – the area in which a landing was most expected. The boundary between the two armies was along the River Dives, east of Caen.

After the German and Italian defeat in North Africa, it had been difficult to place Rommel in a useful command. There had been times when the stress of command had told on him, manifesting itself in physical illness, and he had to be rested several times. But Rommel was close to Hitler, and had shown in France in 1940, and earlier in the desert war, that he was a general of vision, even if sometimes he was accused of recklessness, often by leading from the front and occasionally becoming cut off from command. Leading from or near the front was not unusual for a general in the German Army, but Rommel had a reputation for taking risks and being too long away from his HQ. However, his high reputation with the British had seen the sacking of a number of able British generals in the desert war before the appearance of General Montgomery, and even caused General Auchinleck to issue an order to his Desert Command that Rommel was not a magician, bogeyman or superman, and that it was undesirable for troops to credit him with supernatural powers. When talking of the enemy, the terms 'Axis Powers', 'the Germans' and 'the enemy' were to be used instead of 'Rommel'. Churchill equally showed the power held by Rommel over the desert campaign when he exclaimed in 1942: 'Rommel, Rommel, Rommel! What else matters but beating him!'[36] This new task seemed ideal for a man of his talents and energy, and he jumped into it with vigour. Vice Admiral Ruge reports the many visits Rommel made in the first few weeks of his appointment to all the threatened areas, from Denmark to the South of France.[37] Ruge was appointed as naval adviser to Rommel, and was an expert in the field of naval mines and mine warfare.

Rommel came to his post with some clear thoughts. He was one of only a very few German generals in the west who had already had to operate under the threat of

Allied air superiority and crushing Allied artillery concentrations. Also, the British expertise in the use of minefields in the desert had impressed him. 'We again and again found ourselves in the position of having to overcome an enemy who had established himself with large numbers of anti-tank guns, and even in some places tanks, deep in the mined zone. This fighting was of extreme severity.'[38] He was convinced that the Allies had to be defeated on the coastal crust and that, as well as heavily fortifying this area, tanks should be placed in small, heavily defended units near to the coast. Generals Rundstedt, Geyr von Schweppenburg – the Panzer group west commander – and Heinz Guderian – inspector general of armoured troops – believed that the correct tactics were to mass the armour well away from the coastal area around Paris and manoeuvre them into a classic counter-attack as the Allies penetrated inland. These two opposing views caused great vacillation in OKW, and eventually an unsatisfactory compromise was reached, which included referring to Hitler the decision to release Panzer units to the coast. Normandy was thought to be a possible Allied target for a landing, but main German strategy was still wedded to a landing in the Pas-de-Calais and the misconception that the Allies would have to capture a major port. When discussing his thoughts with General Bayerlein on 17 May 1944 on Schweppenburg's, Guderian's and OKW's lack of appreciation of the effect of Allied air power over the battlefield, Bayerlein reports Rommel as saying: 'Our friends from the east cannot imagine what they are in for here.'[39]

After an initial inspection of the Danish coast, Rommel set up his HQ in a chateau at Fontainebleau which had once belonged to Madame Pompadour. Later, from 9 March 1944, he moved with his staff of over 100 to the Norman chateau at La Roche-Guyon on the north bank of the River Seine, about 50 kilometres from Paris.[40] From his inspections, he grasped that the much-vaunted Atlantic Wall was nothing like that portrayed in German cinemas. He had already written in August 1943 that infantry companies should be reorganized to include more anti-tank weapons and quadruple anti-aircraft guns.[41] Now he realized that the infantry at the coast was too weak, and the establishment of self-propelled guns and all forms of anti-tank weapon was sorely lacking. 'With the coastline held as thinly as it is at present, the enemy will probably succeed in creating bridgeheads at several points and in achieving a major penetration of our coastal defences.'[42] He knew that the Allies would also call on strong airborne forces, used in conjunction with forces landed from the sea, to take and hold large areas of land behind the coast, causing the failure of any relief force by cutting road and railway communications. Added to this was the power of the Allied air force to dominate the battlezone and beyond. On this belief rested his judgement that operational reserves and tank forces had to be kept close to the coast in order to throw the Allies back into the sea before they had time to consolidate. With what he had to hand, he organized a great number of defensive measures, relying mainly on offshore obstructions, minefields and anti-glider poles.

Under Rommel's guidance, enough spare explosive was found in France to manufacture millions of anti-personnel mines. By 20 May 1944, over four million mines had been laid on the Channel coast,[43] the majority in the period after March. Stakes and other ram-log obstructions were placed below high water, often with a mine or artillery shell lashed to the top. Concrete and steel tetrahedra were constructed and laid in the same areas. Another obstacle was the so-called Element C or Belgian gates, which were large gate-like obstructions with a height of 2.5 metres and a width of 3 metres. Made of steel and with a weight of 1,400 kg, they were a formidable obstacle. British raiding missions bought some parts back for evaluation after cutting pieces from them in pre-D-Day reconnaissance missions. Originally, they had been placed as protection by the French and Belgian armies in the Maginot Line and Belgian forts, and could be rolled into position to block gateways or roads. In 1940, the Belgians even constructed the KW defence line from them, forming a wall of steel from Koninkshooikt to Wavre. By May 1944, the Germans had removed over 23,000 of them from their original sites and placed them along the low-tide line or blocking ditches behind coastal dikes.[44] The idea was to create a deep defensive line in the sea, from the high-water line outwards, of four belts of underwater obstacles. Only two were completed in Normandy by D-Day: one at the high-tide level in 2 metres of water, and the other at half tide of a 4-metre tide. It had been found that many of the timber obstructions could be quickly placed by the use of a power hose to excavate a hole rather than using manual labour. A constant problem was whether or not mines and shells would remain effective after immersion in sea water and the continual repair works to obstacles required after storms.

Rommel strove hard to insist that all coastal positions were hardened in concrete, camouflaged, well wired and surrounded by mines, so that they became near-impregnable islands of defence armed with machine guns, mortars and at least light anti-tank weapons of 37–50 mm in calibre. Behind the coast, artillery and other positions were constructed of open earth and timber 'field positions' to give defence in depth. Where possible, areas were flooded as a further obstruction, and to force Allied troops into killing corridors covered by artillery, mortar fire and machine guns. To disrupt inland glider and parachute landings, stakes were placed in obvious areas. These 3-metre-high stakes became known as 'Rommel's asparagus', but the addition of shells and wiring them together to form barriers across fields could not be completed in time. Arming of obstacles with a million captured shells was only sanctioned several days prior to D-Day.[45]

There were increasing problems with progress towards achieving defence targets as D-Day neared. The Allies made an increasing number of attacks throughout the region north of the River Loire, destroying radar stations, defence works, bridges and canal locks, putting railway junctions out of use, destroying railway engines and rolling stock, and attacking airfields and industrial plants. The battlefield area was being isolated from the rest of German-occupied Europe, and Rommel's fears came true. On 20 May, it was reported that only 50 per cent of the landing stakes were in place. Placement of 900,000 stakes in the area had been required. In the inland area, only 15 per cent of defence work was reported as completed, while 15th Army HQ reported a lack of cement, wire, iron and wood. Seven days later, Northern military district reported that 67 per cent of the fortification schedule was ready for use, but only 3 per cent had been reinforced with concrete. Forty-eight gun positions were still in the course of construction, and land obstacles were now 25 per cent completed. It was reported by 15th Army HQ that 70 per cent of its plan was complete, but that cement, wooden frames, building materials and tools were lacking. On the same date,

7th Army reported that only 14.4 per cent of its summer construction programme was complete, and noted a similar lack of equipment and tools. Also, of 1,600 railway trucks of cement expected, only 159 had arrived. One week after that, and only three days before D-Day, the reports were similar, with 7th Army adding that the poor transport situation was significantly holding up work. It appeared that 15th Army employed around 30,000 soldiers and 36,000 civilians, while 7th Army had around 37,000 soldiers and 63,000 civilians engaged on the building projects.[46] By June, units were far from completing construction of the planned defences.

There remained the problem of the quality of troops and equipment. Blumentritt in post-war interrogations described how the German infantry in the west had no organic transport, while along the Atlantic Wall there was not enough motorized transport, and what transport there was included a mix of often captured vehicles from different countries and a reliance on French drivers. Occasionally in Normandy, a British unit would recover from the Germans transport *it* had lost in 1940 at Dunkirk! The coastal defence infantry divisions were in last place in order of efficiency, occupying a rigid defence system on a broad front. Most had only two infantry regiments, weak artillery and very limited mobility. Their weapons were no match for a modern army, and they lacked the tactical ability to carry out mobile warfare. In terms of weaponry, there was not enough field artillery ammunition for light and medium pieces, and the large number of foreign weapons in use made for a very complicated supply of different weapon parts and types of ammunition. Blumentritt also identified the number of different types of tanks and vehicles as causing similar problems with repair and spares. Similarly, the coastal guns, from six different nations and with varying calibres, required a variety of ammunition, which was limited.[47] Schweppenburg, commanding Panzer Gruppe West, backed up Blumentritt with his post-war interrogation report, stating that 'the operational staff of Von Rundstedt knew that the infantry divisions were short of artillery, anti-tank weapons and supply units. Infantry units were seen as having poor fighting qualities.'[48]

The invasion area of Gold Beach was no exception to these problems. The unit tasked with protecting this area since late spring 1942 was 716th Infantry Division. German infantry divisions were normally made up of three regiments, each of two battalions of infantry and one fusilier battalion. Hence, a German regiment was approximately equivalent to a British infantry brigade. A German infantry division also had as part of its organic make-up an anti-tank battalion, an engineer battalion and an artillery regiment of three battalions.[49] Each infantry regiment was made up as follows: I Battalion (Companies 1–4), II Battalion (Companies 5–8) and III Battalion (Companies 9–12). Company 13 was the Howitzer Company, and Company 14 the Mortar Company.

By D-Day, 716th Division also included three Ost Battalions made up of volunteer Soviet prisoners of war led by German officers and NCOs. These men had 'volunteered' for service in the German Army, doubtless to escape the often awful conditions Russian prisoners were kept in. Raised in May 1941 and sent to defend the Caen area from May 1942, it was classed as a static formation garrison, and as such had little transport of its own. In any event, it was the horse that was utilized by the German Army in Normandy, a situation which persisted up to the day of invasion. By 1 June

1944, OB West reported that the division numbered 7,771 men.[50] The commander of 716th Division was Generalleutnant Wilhelm Richter, and he believed that his area of coastal defence, from the mouth of the River Orne to north of Bayeux (originally much further west, to the mouth of the River Vire), was very favourable for Allied attack. He claimed in post-war interviews that his immediate superior, General Marcks, was of the same opinion, and this was why the sector guarded by his division was cut in November 1943 by two-thirds. He further stated that the 'defensive fortifications in the coastal sector of the Division (often known also as Calvados) were in no way sufficient to repel the attack of a modern army'.[51] He further talked about the two lost years, 1942–4, when little was done, and that once the process was speeded up from January 1944 the increasing destruction of the French railway system caused many difficulties in providing construction material. Richter noted that many of his fortifications were not completed or organized, and that defence in depth was lacking in the interior behind Gold Beach as well as other areas. The laying of mines, both at the coast and around fortifications and inland communities, appears to have been nearly completed, and strongpoints were wired in, but not as much as hoped for, due to a shortage of wire.

Since the arrival of Rommel, things had been speeded up, but were far from complete by June 1944. His battery positions included dummy positions and alternative positions for his artillery, but Richter stated that 'since February 1944 the gun emplacements that were being fortified were bombed once or twice each week'. By June, Richter also claimed that his infantry was only 1 per cent deficient in men, but that self-propelled assault guns and tanks were not provided for 716th Division, and it was about one-third deficient in horse transport for the batteries and more greatly deficient in harnesses and horse equipment. Each of its regiments probably had similar light weapons, including forty-eight machine guns, six 50 mm mortars and nine 80 mm mortars. Ost 441, one of 716th Division's eastern battalions, only had twenty-eight machine guns and five mortars.[52] It has been said that few German divisions were as weak as 716th Division.[53] In his own critique and report of Richter's evaluation, Generalleutnant Max Pemsel[54] mainly agreed with Richter, but underlined that German naval experts considered a landing on the coast of Calvados 'improbable' due to the reefs that lay off the coast, but that the navy had not taken account of the gaps in the reefs around what became the actual landing beaches.

One big change affecting the western side of Gold Beach and Omaha Beach occurred in March 1944, when, to reduce the width of 716th Infantry Division's front, a new infantry division was inserted along this coastal sector: 352nd Infantry Division took over duties from the coastal village of Le Hamel/Asnelles westwards, including Port-en-Bessin, both places being within 50th Division's expected exploitation of the beachhead on D-Day. Commanded by Generalleutnant Kraiss and comprising the 914th, 915th and 916th Infantry Regiments, this division was raised as a fully mobile field division with many younger recruits, ten Sturmgeschutz III assault guns, and fourteen Marder self-propelled anti-tank guns in its Panzerjager-Abteilung. Its artillery regiment had forty-eight howitzers: twenty-four 10.5 cm and twenty-four 15 cm. None of the batteries were motorized, and they only had a single load of ammunition. But the self-propelled and assault guns gave the capacity to move troops on the vehicles.

By 1 June, OB West was reporting that this division had a complement of 12,734 men.[55] However, although on the face of it this sounds a very powerful unit at this stage in the war, the assistant chief of staff of 352nd Infantry Division, Oberstleutnant Ziegelmann, did report problems with the slow arrival of equipment causing the training programme to be curtailed, which he attributed to labour shortages in Germany and the bombing raids leading to a lack of materiel. He also stated that the young soldiers from the class of 1925/26 had been severely affected by food shortages in Germany and were not physically fit to start with, but with milk purchased from local farmers their physical abilities improved. Fifty per cent of the officers were experienced in combat, but by 1 March 1944 nearly a third of their complement of NCO posts still remained unfilled due to candidates not possessing the requisite experience.[56] From March 1944, when it was committed to the Bayeux coastal sector, its soldiers worked nine hours a day improving the area defences, plus three hours of training. One assumes that the soldiers of 716th Infantry Division were similarly employed. One major difference between the two divisions was in age: while the 352nd Division troops had an average age of eighteen to nineteen, the 700 series of divisions had an average age of over thirty.[57] Ziegelmann also remarked that, when taking over the sector, the 726th Regiment (from 716th Infantry Division) was backward in training due to providing reinforcements to the Eastern Front, the lack of ammunition for training and the poor condition of their transport. Despite these protestations, it must be remembered that it was the 352nd Division, and units under its control, that caused the near-disaster to the US landing on Omaha Beach and caused considerable problems and casualties to some units of 50th (Northumbrian) Infantry Division landing on the right flank of Gold Beach.

Although it only covered the western part of the Gold Beach landing area, it is worth looking at the power of 352nd Division overall. Each of its infantry and fusilier battalions had sixty light machine guns, three heavy machine guns and twelve 80 mm mortars. The 914th Regiment and 915th Regiment gun companies had two 15 cm howitzers and six 7.5 cm howitzers. The 916th Regiment was only equipped with two 15 cm and two 7.5 cm infantry howitzers. Each regiment had an anti-tank company with three 7.5 cm Pak 40s. There was an anti-aircraft company, with nine motorized 3.7 cm Flak, which could also be turned on ground targets. Its pioneer battalion had three companies, including thirty-seven machine guns, twenty flame-throwers and six mortars. The field replacement battalion had five companies, with a total of sixty-two machine guns, six 80 mm mortars, a 50 mm anti-tank gun, a 7.5 cm anti-tank gun, one 10.5 cm howitzer, one infantry howitzer and two flame-throwers. On D-Day, parts of 916th Regiment were located along Omaha Beach, with one battalion from the 716th Infantry Division attached; 915th Regiment was in reserve south-east of Bayeux, while 914th Regiment was deployed around Isigny.

Generally speaking, by June 1944 the defences along the Atlantic Wall were not completed, but the energy of Field Marshal Rommel in his task had ensured that many improvements had been made in a relatively short time. Defences consisted of strongpoints known as Stutzpunkt, of which the only one identified on Gold Beach was situated on the cliffs east of Arromanches. Otherwise, the series of mutually supporting positions were known as resistance nests or *Wiederstandnester*. On all beaches, these were backed by artillery positions, many still in open pits, but a smaller number well protected in concrete casemates.

The *Wiederstandnester* were the most numerous of the defensive positions, manned by thirty to fifty men, and are often described as platoon positions. Generally speaking, they were armed with mortars, machine guns and often a light anti-tank gun. Soldiers had concrete shelters to live in when on duty. These were usually constructed 'dug in' to provide a low silhouette to the enemy, and some were covered over with earth for further protection. The heavy infantry weapons – anti-tank guns, machine guns and mortars – were housed in concrete pillboxes or sometimes open (unroofed) concrete-walled positions. Sandbags were used to provide further protection in and around both concrete and open positions. Weapon positions were connected by trenches, sometimes underground. Positions were well camouflaged with nets and difficult to make out. Bushes and trees were cleared, and, if necessary, buildings demolished to give open fields of fire. The whole was well surrounded by barbed wire and mined with both anti-personnel and anti-tank mines. The soldiers manning the position entered and left by clear paths known to them. In short, all these positions were very difficult to assault by infantry alone. Prior bombardment and the close support of tanks were going to be essential to reduce these minor fortresses.

One very common concrete position seen along the Atlantic Wall was the *Ringstande*, more commonly called a 'Tobruk' by the Allies, and named after the port city of Tobruk in Libya, where these fortifications were first encountered. Essentially a concrete-hardened slit trench with a protected entrance at the rear or side, the top circular opening allowed a mortar to be fired from below ground level or a machine gun to be mounted on a circular rail. Some had obsolete French and German tank turrets added. Some larger concrete bunkers had *Ringstande* incorporated in their construction. Where there were high sea walls protecting coastal buildings from erosion, the walls were often heightened by the Germans. At La Riviere and Le Hamel, this evidence can be detected today. At La Riviere today, the wall does not seem very high, due to later deposit of material, but in 1944 it stood much higher. Not only were the tops of these walls wired, but baulks of timber were installed, coming out horizontally for 2 or 3 metres, wired around and providing a roof of strands of barbed wire. This effectively meant that attacking troops below the walls would have great difficulty in laying scaling ladders up against the walls. Even smashed down by prior bombardment, the remains would add to the debris in areas that needed to be quickly scaled or crossed by men under fire. The area on the land side of a sea wall was covered by machine guns firing on fixed lines, and, of course, mined.

Most of the anti-tank guns mounted in the coastal strip were obsolete infantry or tank weapons able to fire 37–50 mm shells, but larger and more effective anti-tank weapons in the range of 75–88 mm were housed in very well-constructed concrete bunkers firing in enfilade across a beach. Despite very comprehensive Allied aerial photographs and intelligence gained from resistance groups, by D-Day it was not appreciated that these particular positions were protected on their seaward side from sea bombardment by a protective wall.

Stutzpunkt positions were similarly constructed but larger. They were manned by around a hundred men, and were often called company positions.

The Gold Beach landing area is approximately 6 kilometres wide. It consists of a very wide sandy beach at low tide leading to a low bank, behind which is marshy ground known as Le Marais. Le Marais is 200 metres wide at La Riviere and 750 metres wide at Le Hamel. At high tide, the sea comes near to the bank on normal tides. In the middle of the beach, two small streams join and exit to the sea: La Gronde Ruisseau (the word 'Gronde' is transcribed as 'Grande' on some maps, leading to some confusion on D-Day as to its size) and Le Hable de Heurtaut (spelt Heurtot on 1944 maps). Behind Le Marais on the La Riviere side of the beach the land rises fairly steeply to 50 metres, running across the back of Le Marais for 4 kilometres, after which it turns inland and south-west above the small village of Meuvaines. This feature dominates the eastern side of the valley running inland and is called the Meuvaines Ridge. Behind the far western side of Asnelles/Le Hamel, the ground rises to 55 metres, and, where it reaches the coast, forms a cliff for over a kilometre until it reaches Arromanches to the west. This feature forms another ridgeline running from the sea to the south-west parallel to the Meuvaines Ridge. Between the two lies a fairly flat valley some 2.5 kilometres wide, dominated by both ridges.

By June 1944, its defences may not have been complete, but they were considerable. Moving from east to west along the coast, starting at La Riviere, the first *Wiederstandnester* (WN) that 50th Division would have to overcome on the coastal crust was WN33a, with a main armament of two 75–50 mm guns. WN33, at the west end of La Riviere, had an 88 mm gun firing in enfilade across the beach to the west and two 50 mm guns. A few hundred metres inland was WN34, near the Mont Fleury lighthouse, which sported a 75 mm and a 50 mm gun. Over 1.5 kilometres west along the coast, near the Hable de Heurtot, WN35 had a series of bunkers and a 50 mm gun. One kilometre inland of this, at the top of the rise and covering a track inland from WN35, WN35a was probably armed with a light gun in a small series of bunkers. Two kilometres west at the Cabane de Douanes (Customs House), WN36 was a series of bunkers including a 50 mm and 37 mm gun. A kilometre away was probably the strongest position along this portion of coast. WN37 had a series of bunkers, pillboxes and Tobruks, based around a fortified sanatorium at the eastern end of Le Hamel. Here was a 75 mm gun housed in a casemate enfilading the beach to the east, and also a 50 mm gun. At the other end of Le Hamel was WN38, with a 50 mm gun in a small casemate protected from sea bombardment. Between the ends of Le Hamel, a number of the houses had been fortified by sandbags and concrete, an anti-tank wall ran through the western end of the village, and an anti-tank ditch, mines and barbed wire protected its landward side. The whole of Le Hamel's seaward approach was fronted by a high sea wall. Between them, the anti-tank guns at WN33 and WN37 could produce crossfire covering the majority of the beach.

From the western end of Le Hamel (and the western limit of the planned effective landing area of 50th Division), the ground rises to cliffs before descending again to the coastal village of Arromanches, situated in a hollow in the hills. On the cliff above St Come-de-Fresne, WN39 had an 88 mm gun in a casemate and a 75 mm gun. On the slope of the hill above Le Carrefour, overlooking to the east the Meuvaines valley, was WN40, with other positions south of it. Back at the coast and on the clifftop guarding a Wurzburg radar array, WN42 had a number of bunkers, 20 mm anti-aircraft guns and

Photo 1 The gun emplacement at Le Hamel. WN37 was the emplacement that, along with the fortified sanatorium, caused all the problems at Le Hamel. The protecting arm is hardly damaged and despite the pounding it took throughout the day damage can only really be seen on the landward side. Behind it stood the Sanatorium now gone and replaced by modern buildings. Surprisingly many buildings in other parts of Le Hamel survived. Left of the photographer in the car park there is a Tobruk and behind the position in the sea wall is another Tobruk, curiously with an upturned anchor concreted in. The author believes the anchor and concrete plug was added after 6 June as a tying up point within the Mulberry Harbour.

Photo 2 The 88 mm gun emplacement at WN33, La Riviere. The flanking side wall protecting it from gunfire from the sea is obvious. The sea wall was higher in 1944. Behind this emplacement is another open 50 mm emplacement.

a 75 mm gun. On the descent into Arromanches, WN43 had a casemated 105 mm gun dominating the town and firing west, and on the opposite coastal cliff, above Tracy-sur-Mer, WN44 housed a 47 mm gun. In all, over 2,000 men defended this stretch of Gold Beach coast in several heavily fortified positions. Inland, on the hills south of Arromanches, and astride the road from Arromanches to St Come-de-Fresne and Meuvaines at Le Puits de Herode, was WN41, armed with at least one heavy gun. Further inland, 2 kilometres south-west of WN41, was a field position for four 105 mm guns, and a further two 105 mm guns were situated 2 kilometres south-west of Ryes. Four more were at Vaux-sur-Aure, and another two 105 mm were stationed just north of Bazenville. All of these were in open field positions.

Two casemated batteries were situated in the area. The first, at Mont Fleury, between Ver-sur-Mer and La Riviere, consisted of four 122 mm guns. In fact, only one was in a completed casemate by D-Day, but the position was fronted by an anti-tank ditch and several bunkers, trenches and pillboxes, and was the scene of Stanley Hollis's first acts of D-Day bravery.

The second casemated battery of four 100 mm guns was located in fields south of Ver-sur-Mer and called the Marefontaine battery (WN32) after the nearby farm; again, it was not complete. One further battery needs to be mentioned. The Longues battery (WN48) was situated on the coast between Arromanches and Port-en-Bessin and was armed with four 150 mm guns in separate casemates. Also, in an open emplacement, it had a 122 mm gun for night illumination, searchlights and 20 mm anti-aircraft guns. A two-storey concrete fire-control bunker using modern fire-control methods was built near the edge of the cliffs forwards of the battery. The whole position was well defended and ready by May 1944.

Photo 3 The Mont Fleury battery. This particular photograph shows the still incomplete casemate and the method of building with concrete block walls and an infill. A second incomplete casemate lies behind. All buildings in the photograph are post-1944.

Photo 4 The German view towards Gold Beach from Mont Fleury. The view looking north and west from the Mont Fleury position. In 1944 to the front was the anti-tank ditch. Its dominating position over the beach is clear. The current remains of Mulberry B can be seen. The houses at the coast were not there in 1944 and they mark the area near Les Roquettes this side of them and WN36 sea side of them. This was the 1st Dorset D-Day target but actually where 1st Hampshire landed. Either side of the car on the road the track leads downhill north to WN35 and uphill south to WN35a.

Only the main defences have been mentioned. It must be remembered that in the area there were also a number of field positions for machine-gun and mortar teams, as well as artillery pieces. The Meuvaines Ridge, in particular, was a dominating feature over the ground to its west, where many 50th Division units would funnel through. The high ground opposite, where the Puits de Herode (WN41) was situated, similarly dominated the surrounding countryside. The coastline between La Riviere and Le Hamel took the shape of a flattened arrowhead with its point at Le Hable de Heurtot. The 77 mm gun at Le Hamel and the 88 mm gun at La Riviere meant that the whole of Gold Beach could be kept under an enfilading crossfire for as long as these two positions survived.[58] Also, it is interesting to compare reconnaissance photographs. Those taken of Gold Beach in the late spring of 1944 show few preparations, but just over two months later the enormous changes taking place are obvious. Many obstacles had been placed in the landing-beach area; over 2,500 were eventually cleared after D-Day, 1,413 obstacles in 3,200 yards from Jig Beach landing area and 1,042 obstacles from King Beach over 2,500 yards.[59] These developments greatly worried the British planners and it was obvious that any landing would be seriously opposed.

Revised Plans, Neptune, Force
G and K, and Airpower

One of the important issues decided by the US and British Chiefs of Staff Committee in 1943 was how the leadership of Overlord was to be arranged. This was to consist of an overall commander and deputy commander, plus a commander of ground, air and naval forces. Initially, General Marshall from the United States was a strong favourite as overall commander; General Brooke, too, had his name in the frame as possible ground forces commander. However, both Roosevelt and Churchill felt that these were their right-hand military advisers and could not be spared. Indeed, Roosevelt is reported to have told Marshall: 'I feel I could not sleep at night with you out of the country.'[1]

Churchill claims that Roosevelt only told him of his decision to retain Marshall at the Cairo conference in early December 1943. Churchill reports this as taking place privately in Roosevelt's car while on a visit to the Pyramids. At the same time, Roosevelt suggested Eisenhower as supreme commander for Overlord, and Churchill agreed that 'we had the warmest regard for General Eisenhower, and would trust our fortunes to his direction with hearty goodwill'.[2] Normal procedure would then have been to appoint an American ground forces commander; however, as early as September 1943, the Americans themselves had reported that only British generals such as Alexander or Montgomery had the desired battle experience or reputation to be ground forces commander of 21st Army Group, the organization tasked with the invasion.[3]

A number of people, including Eisenhower, wanted Alexander as army commander, and Churchill could not make up his mind. By this time, Churchill had become unwell again and was in bed with pneumonia at Tunis. Here, with General Brooke, he discussed the candidates for the Overlord post. Observations were exchanged between Deputy Prime Minister Atlee and the War Cabinet in London. Brooke favoured Montgomery, but that choice might not be favoured by either Eisenhower or Churchill.[4] In the end, their decision was to pick Montgomery. On 18 December, Churchill sent a telegram to Roosevelt telling him that the War Cabinet had decided on Montgomery. The choice of Montgomery would give both the United States and Britain confidence, and Montgomery was a public hero in the United Kingdom.[5] Air Chief Marshal Tedder was proposed and accepted as deputy supreme commander. On the same day, Churchill told Brooke of his promotion to field marshal, effective from 1 January 1944, for all the excellent work he had done as chief of the imperial general staff. With Admiral Ramsay confirmed as overall naval commander, British officers held many of the leading roles in the preparation and execution of Overlord.

At this time, it was also decided to bypass German resistance in Italy and to capture Rome by a landing at Anzio early in 1944. This further complicated the landing-craft problem, as it meant that they could not be released back to the United Kingdom for some time. The landing at Anzio on 22 January 1944 (Operation Shingle) became a problem for the Allies. Unexpected and very determined German resistance was encountered. The Allies became entrapped for a time in the beachhead area. This infuriated Churchill, who clamoured: 'I had hoped we were hurling a wildcat into the shore, but all we got was a stranded whale.' The continued need to supply the landing by sea exacerbated the lack of LCTs for Overlord. Yet another complication was a plan to land in southern France, utilizing the resources of the Mediterranean Allied forces as a diversion to Overlord. This plan, agreed in outline in early December 1943, was called Anvil, and later Dragoon. It was finally rescheduled for after the Normandy landings, and eventually took place on 15 August 1944. Montgomery always thought this was one of the greatest strategic mistakes of the war.[6] It was after the series of meetings at Cairo and Teheran in December 1943 that the problems of, among other things, landing craft and best tides pushed Overlord back to early June.

On 23 December, Brooke sent a personal signal to Montgomery to let him know that he had been accepted as army commander for Overlord, and this was officially confirmed the following day on the BBC.[7] Eisenhower was displeased, but the ever-ebullient Montgomery was convinced that an Eisenhower and Alexander team would be a disaster, reporting in his diary that it was impossible to get decisions out of Alexander and that Alexander's HQ was inefficient. Montgomery believed that, whereas he always had a clear plan and then only held discussions about its implementation, Alexander came to conferences without any clear plan and only formulated one after discussion.[8] Brooke, incidentally, more or less agreed with him in a diary entry made on 14 December 1943, while visiting Montgomery at his HQ on the Sangro River in Italy.[9]

Montgomery travelled to Eisenhower's HQ at Algiers on 27 December, and they seem to have discussed the plans for Overlord as known to them. For the initial landing and battle in Normandy, US land forces were to come under the command of Montgomery. There is a discrepancy of views here about the plan as laid out under Morgan. Because of the paucity of landing craft and the timescale involved (then early May 1944), Morgan had reduced the five-division assault to only three. Both Eisenhower and Montgomery grasped that this was much too weak a punch. Eisenhower had remarked on this as early as the end of October 1943, one of his subordinates reporting that Eisenhower said 'not enough wallop in the initial attack'.[10] Further, in his foreword to Morgan's book *Overture to Overlord*, Eisenhower states that he communicated his concerns to his chief of staff and Montgomery.[11] One could assume that this was at the meeting between them in Algiers on 27 December. On the other hand, Montgomery claims this as his idea. After the meeting with Eisenhower, Montgomery had returned to Italy and taken an emotional farewell of his Eighth Army staff. He then travelled on to meet Churchill, who was still recuperating in Marrakesh. Churchill reports that he gave Montgomery the newest version of the Overlord plan to read, and after reading it, Montgomery said 'this will not do. I must have more in the initial punch'.[12] Churchill was, however, delighted with the exuberance of Montgomery in his new role. Also, in his own *Memoirs*, Montgomery tells the prime minister at Marrakesh that he has not seen the plan.

His most important points to Churchill were that there were not enough troops in the assault and that the landing was planned on too narrow a front for exploitation. Montgomery uses the word 'impracticable'.[13] It is an interesting insight into the nature of Montgomery, considering how relations between Montgomery and Eisenhower were to develop, both during the rest of the war and afterwards. Here, it seems, Montgomery allowed the self-promoting part of his nature (with the prime minister in this case) to get the better of him.[14] It is worth noting that later Churchill was to write: 'Eisenhower and Montgomery disagreed with one important feature of the plan. They wanted an assault in greater strength and on a wider front.'[15]

After this meeting, Montgomery flew home to the United Kingdom. Within a few days, after further examination of Morgan's plan, he was more than ever convinced of the need for change, and convened his first meeting as land forces commander. After a brief presentation of the COSSAC plan, which included the reason for choosing Normandy and the lack of landing craft and transport aircraft, Montgomery called for a break of twenty minutes. When he took the floor, he told the planners to go away and re-examine the possible landing areas and extend the area of search, looking again between Brittany and Dieppe. He gave them twenty-four hours. This was Montgomery stamping his authority on the project. The next day, after Admiral Ramsay explained naval difficulties, Montgomery moderated his views. By day three, the demands were for a landing as far west as Utah beach on the east side of the Cotentin, with a view to taking Cherbourg quickly and opening it as a port; also, to take Caen on day one, although the planners believed this was not possible. Apparently, Montgomery was not convinced by the idea of a floating pontoon harbour (Mulberry), but was convinced that it was essential to take a port early. Finally, he insisted on a five-division front in order to swiftly take a large area for follow-up troops to exploit the invasion quickly, or they could get someone else to command. The basic changes were taken on board.

Montgomery had shown his quick, decisive nature and got things moving. One witness recorded that his action 'was like a breath of fresh air' and another 'the incredible decisiveness that followed his arrival'.[16] Montgomery writes that in early 1944, 21st Army Group HQ was a 'well dug in static headquarters which had never been overseas and had never had any operational experience'.[17] He set about changing this by bringing in a number of staff officers whom he had purposely brought back from Italy. They knew how Montgomery worked, and he trusted them. This caused much resentment, and Montgomery states that in the London clubs it was common at the time to hear the remark 'the Gentlemen are out and the Players are just going in to bat'.[18] It was not the first or last time that Montgomery was seen as a maverick, operating outside the accepted rules of the upper military class. Another problem Montgomery foresaw with the British Army in the United Kingdom was that, although they had been well trained, they lacked battle experience, and officers and men did not know 'the tricks of the trade' that soldiers experienced in battle had learnt the hard way and saved many lives. Also, before D-Day, he claims to have used another unpopular but useful way of spreading experience by simply exchanging some experienced officers from units that had served in Africa, Sicily and Italy with inexperienced officers who had never left the country. Montgomery realized that the planning and preparation that went into operations were very important, but it could all come to nought if the junior officer, NCO and ordinary soldier were not up to their tasks.

By early 1944, the army in the United Kingdom had a number of things going for it. First, in Britain there was a large body of highly trained men who had not seen action. Some had stood on the British coast prepared for invasion, some had retreated at Dunkirk, but since 1942 they had become part of a highly trained, organized and proud army, having recovered from the shock of France and 1940. Second, with them was a leavening of experienced units that had been brought back to rest after fighting in the Mediterranean. Third, there was equipment and arms aplenty; although not all up to the standard of German arms, they were certainly available in greater number. Already, there were over three quarters of a million US Army personnel within the United Kingdom. They might not always be welcome, with 'overpaid, oversexed and over here' becoming a more common moan, but without overwhelming US support a European invasion simply could not have succeeded, and the numerous monuments raised in the United Kingdom to their passing and their exploits since 1944 pay just tribute to the true feelings of the British people. The Royal and US Air Forces would dominate the skies over Europe; the navies would continue to dominate the seas. The great battles on the Eastern Front would continue to starve the German Army of men and materiel. Torch, Husky and Italy had shown that a winning team of combined nations could operate together, and hence display both confidence and competence. Montgomery, as leader of the ground forces, was a man who cared for his men and 'kept them in the picture', had so far shown an incisive and decisive brain, showed authority and was mainly trusted by his subordinates.

Eisenhower was relieved of his Mediterranean duties, and arrived back in the United Kingdom on 14 January to take up his post as supreme commander. Brooke had been visiting the king at Sandringham, and first met Eisenhower after lunch on 17 January, when he reports that Eisenhower was in very good form and discussed the curtailing of landing craft for Anvil. Brooke believed that a paper on this, presented by Eisenhower on 24 January, was Montgomery's idea. In fact, he thought that Eisenhower held no strategic outlook and, from an operational point of view, should not be in post. However, Brooke does say that Eisenhower made up for all this by the way he worked on Allied co-operation.[19] In contrast, Brooke had to admonish Montgomery several times for upsetting various people, including the king! The British may have had some very good and experienced generals, but could any of them have carried out Eisenhower's task so successfully? On the same day as Eisenhower arrived in the United Kingdom, Montgomery began a six-day tour of all the US divisions in Britain. He addressed groups of 3,000–5,000 men from the bonnet of a jeep using a loudhailer. The accent and some of the British language may have made some men laugh, but overall it was a great success, and the US troops were amazed that their commander would take the time to travel and speak to them personally. Montgomery made a second similar tour of British troops in February. Along with his visits to workplaces and factories, Montgomery was appearing as headline news and feted as a national hero.

On 21 January, at a meeting attended by the commanders-in-chief (Eisenhower, Montgomery, Air Marshal Leigh-Mallory[20] and Admiral Ramsay), a new plan was decided. The addition of two landing divisions was definitely agreed, as was the extension of the landing area from 25 to nearly 50 miles, with British forces landing north-east of Bayeux (Gold) and US forces landing at the base of the Cotentin (Utah). Airborne forces were to pin each flank. The lack of belief in the Mulberry prefabricated harbours was underlined, and one important task of the US forces was to take the port of Cherbourg. Yet, no real alternative had been examined in case the Germans destroyed the dock facilities and mined the harbour. Leigh-Mallory explained the need now for a further eight fighter squadrons and 200 extra troop-carrying transports. He wanted transports, crews and glider pilots available for training two months before D-Day. Ramsay required two more naval assault forces to lift and support the extra divisions, with a considerable increase in strength, especially in bombarding ships and minesweepers. The landing-craft problem was now even more accentuated. Two hundred and twenty-four cargo ships and half of British coastal shipping would have to be found from the Merchant Navy and at great inconvenience to the civilian population.[21] A British naval perspective states that the requirement for two extra assault areas and divisions was 'like a tidal wave sweeping into a shallow estuary and causing violent and often unforeseen effects in sheltered creeks many miles from the source of the original disturbance'.[22] Part of the upshot of the 21 January meeting was the paper on Anvil, mentioned in the previous paragraph, in a bid to retrieve more landing craft. Not the least of the naval problems was the continued threat posed by major units of the German fleet, including *Tirpitz*, destroyers, minesweepers and S-boats (motor torpedo boats known to the Allies as E-boats), and, of course, the German U-boat submarines.

Considering the size and complexity of the operation, one must underline the competence and drive needed by the various staffs and units in order to prepare and succeed for D-Day barely four months after this conference. It also needs to be said that, although by 1944 considerable experience had been gained by the Allies working together in the European theatre in large operations, combining landings by sea and air, an attack from the United Kingdom across the English Channel was a very different proposition, simply because of the influence of tides and unpredictable weather, and the need to provide overwhelming air superiority. These were all factors that had counted to a lesser degree in the Mediterranean theatre of war. It must also be said that so far plans had only been discussed in brief outline, compared with the complexity of detail that had to be thought-through, planned, organized, trained for and enacted in each of the five sea landing areas and three airborne landing areas. This was in addition to the intelligence gathering, bombing and feint attacks that were included to confuse the enemy. The final orders for preparations were issued on 1 February, only sixteen weeks before D-Day.

Nor must it be thought that all this preparation was carried out in peace and calm. On the night of the 21 January meeting, the Germans started what was to be called the 'Baby Blitz' across Britain, lasting into May 1944. London was the target throughout

January and February, with some very significant raids. Also hit were Hull, Bristol, Portsmouth, Weymouth, Plymouth, Torquay and Falmouth, as well as smaller towns. The early raids were simply retaliation for Allied bombing; later raids were intended to disrupt the harbours and build-up of landing craft. The largest raid, of over 400 aircraft, occurred on the very first night. Later raids usually consisted of fewer than 200 aircraft. It would be wrong to overstate the physical effects of these raids; many failed to drop much on their targets; but for soldier or civilian, American or British, German bombers droning over Britain had some effect, and boosted the German propaganda machine. In all, during these four months of raids, the Luftwaffe lost around 330 aircraft,[23] mainly bombers, and ultimately the offensive was a failure. 'A major consequence was that the eve of the invasion found the German bomber force in the west on the verge of bankruptcy.'[24]

Operation Neptune, the naval task required of Admiral Ramsay, was immense. His outline orders were 'to secure a lodgement on the continent from which further offensive operations can be developed. This lodgement area must contain sufficient port facilities to maintain a force of 26 to 30 divisions.' It would be required to land between three and five divisions a month thereafter.[25] Each of the two task force areas was assigned a senior naval officer to command it. In the British, or eastern, task force area was Rear Admiral Vian, while the US, or western, task force area was commanded by Rear Admiral Kirk. The three assault areas in the east between the small ports of Ouistreham and Port-en-Bessin were named Sword (3rd British Infantry Division), Juno (3rd Canadian Infantry Division) and Gold (50th British Infantry Division). The two assault areas in the west were named Omaha (US 29th and 1st Infantry Divisions) between Port-en-Bessin and the River Vire, and finally Utah (US 4th Infantry Division) from the River Vire north on the east coast of the Cotentin peninsula. Each of the main assault divisions had various additional units under command, such as US rangers, commandos and specially trained beach units. Two US airborne divisions, 82nd and 101st, were to be landed the night before the assault in the Cotentin peninsula to support the sea landings, hold open causeways crossing flooded areas inland, and restrict the movement of the German Army. On the eastern flank, the British 6th Airborne was to land north-east of Caen and hold the crossings over the River Orne and the Caen Canal. Ramsay characterized Neptune as 'the safe and timely arrival of the assault forces at their beaches, the cover of their landings, and subsequently the support and maintenance and the rapid build-up of our forces ashore.'[26]

Up until 1944, all the training facilities had been geared for a three-division landing. The expansion to five assault areas, adding Gold and Utah, gave Ramsay another problem to add to the lack of landing craft. 'Training facilities and assault firing areas had originally been designed to cater for a three divisional assault, and it was not easy to expand these.'[27] It was noted that the new naval assault forces had to cram six months' training into three, similarly to the army units concerned. Certainly, a great deal of expertise could be shared. Force 'J' (for Juno Beach) had started training as far back as October 1942, spurred to overcome the problems found on the Dieppe raid. It took part in the invasion of Sicily, and then returned to Britain, and worked from September 1943 with 3rd Canadian Division around and beyond the Isle of Wight area training over the winter. This included several assault and ferry exercises. Force 'S' (for Sword Beach) had been formed in October 1943 and was busy training in Scotland.

Opposition from the German Navy could not be ignored. It was true that the main elements of the German fleet had been dealt with. The *Scharnhorst* had been sunk during the Battle of the North Cape on 26 December 1943, and Germany's only remaining battleship, the powerful *Tirpitz*, was bottled up in a Norwegian fjord. In fact, the vulnerability of *Tirpitz* in even this remote place was emphasized on 3 April 1944, when Royal Navy Fleet Air Arm aircraft attacked the *Tirpitz*. While Wildcat and Hellcat fighter planes strafed the decks and shore anti-aircraft batteries, two waves of Barracuda dive-bombers, thirty-nine aircraft in all, hit the *Tirpitz* several times, causing severe flooding, killing 122 of its crew and injuring over 300 more. Its anti-aircraft armament and signals equipment had also been severely damaged. When attacked, it had been about to take part in sea trials after being repaired following a previous attack by X Craft midget submarines in late September 1943. Kriegsmarine surface forces near the projected invasion area were reduced to five destroyers (slightly smaller than the British light 6" gun cruisers), nine to eleven torpedo boats (about small destroyer size), fifty to sixty E-boats (S-boats or, properly, *Schnellboote*, fast torpedo craft), a similar number of R-boats (*Raumboote* or small minesweepers and coastal escorts), twenty-five to thirty M class minesweepers and up to sixty miscellaneous small craft. A further six destroyers and ten torpedo boats could be sent from the Baltic area. It was reckoned that there were about 130 U-boats in the Biscay area, with twenty-five smaller U-boats able to be sent from the Baltic.[28]

In the Atlantic, the war against the U-boats had been all but won. This, the longest of all campaigns in the Second World War, was vital to the continued effective resistance of Britain during the early years of the war and the continued transport of food, men and arms from the United States. In all, during the Second World War, the U-boats accounted for fifteen million tonnes of Allied shipping, over 2,700 merchant vessels.[29] But between September 1943 and May 1944, the U-boat arm lost 146 submarines.[30] Convoys crossing the Atlantic were closely protected by escort vessels, and a system of support groups, including escort carriers, roamed the convoy routes. Improvements in anti-submarine tactics, including new weapons and radar, and the increasing effectiveness of British and US aircraft operating from land, meant that, although still a danger, the U-boat arm had lost its potent effectiveness of earlier years. Also, if the Germans believed that their S-boats might be a potent weapon against the Allied invasion, they had not counted on the British extending their radar cover by sending radar-controlling frigates with attached units of motor torpedo boats to blockade S-boat ports and deal with any found at sea. It was reported that this might 'prove to have been an important tactical surprise and may well have had a most disturbing effect upon the enemy's plans for counter measures at sea'.[31]

The official British naval history of Neptune states that 'no single topic was discussed more during planning than that of H-Hour'.[32] H-Hour was the moment the first assault troops actually landed. All timings, therefore, were either plus or minus H-Hour. Because of various complications, H-Hour varied from 0630 to 0745 across the five assault beaches. It was required that the landing should take place on a rising tide, to allow landing craft ease of disengagement, and also that a second tide, to allow follow-up troops to land, should occur well before darkness. A final consideration was that a long enough period of light before the assault should be available to ensure effective observed bombardment of targets on the beach and inland. A month or so before D-Day, this issue became further complicated when reconnaissance showed that the Germans were laying obstacles underwater. The number of craft of all sizes required rose to over 7,000. The efficiency of the British and US joint naval staff involved is highlighted by the fact that a naval outline of the operation was issued on 15 February 1944, with a near-final plan by 28 February. On 10 April, the final plan was issued. It was huge, comprising 7,000 sheets of foolscap paper, including plans and appendices. Later, the Admiralty issued an instruction that captains only needed to study the part of the plan that applied to them, and not digest the whole issue. However, it has been pointed out that greater portions needed to be read for officers to understand the context and wider roles.[33] Warships of all types numbered 1,206; various types of landing craft numbered 4,127; ancillary craft, including tugs, rescue, cable-laying and salvage vessels, numbered 423; and 1,260 merchant vessels were required.[34]

The various landing operations already carried out by the Allies in Europe and the Pacific had shown the advantages of naval fire support to suppress enemy beach defences and deal with any unexpected resistance. On Gold Beach, this was provided by Force K. Force K was a mix of cruisers, destroyers and armed landing craft. The Force K flagship was HMS *Argonaut*, with ten 5.25 inch guns. Three other cruisers and a gunboat provided heavier gunfire support: HMS *Ajax* with eight 6 inch, *Orion* with eight 6 inch, *Emerald* with seven 6 inch and HMNS (Netherlands) *Flores* with three 5.9 inch guns. Escort and bombardment duties were also provided by the larger fleet destroyers HMS *Grenville, Jervis, Ulster, Ulysses, Undaunted, Undine, Urania, Urchin* and *Ursa*, carrying 4.7 inch guns, with the smaller Hunt class destroyers HMS *Cattistock, Cottesmore, Pytchley* and ORP (Polish) *Krakowiak* carrying 4 inch guns. In the initial bombardment, HMS *Belfast*, giving support on neighbouring Juno Beach, was to fire on an important Gold Beach target, the Marefontaine battery, with her twelve 6 inch guns. This fearsome array of gunfire was augmented by armed landing craft capable of giving very close-in fire support: six Landing Craft Gun (Large) (LCG (L)), which were converted tank landing craft. Their tank hold was covered in and strengthened, and they carried two 4.7 inch guns. The area below was living accommodation and storage for the ammunition. They also carried two 20 mm Oerlikon guns and a crew of approximately thirty-five. Close-in suppressing light gun and automatic fire was provided by six Landing Craft Support (Large) (LCS (L)) armed with a 6 pounder anti-tank gun in a Daimler armoured car turret and seven Landing Craft Flak (LCF), firing 40 mm Bofors and 20 mm Oerlikon guns. A further eighteen Landing Craft Assault (Hedgerow) (LCA (HR)) fired twenty-four spigot mortars, the naval 'Hedgerow' anti-submarine weapon, onto the beach to clear obstacles and mines. They were towed to the beach behind LCTs carrying specialized engineers. Finally, a frightening and potentially lethal spectacle was provided by eight Landing Craft Tank (Rocket) (LCT (R)), which fired up to 1,000 5 inch barrage rockets at a time.[35] The 1,000 missiles were fired in just ninety seconds and had a range of around 2 miles. By the time final plans were in hand, it had also been decided that self-propelled guns of the Royal Artillery regiments would be allowed to fire from their LCTs on the run into shore.

As well as this firepower, any of the escorting frigates, sloops or minesweepers could be called upon by the naval commander to help add weaponry if required. Other landing beaches had battleships attached, and a number of battleships were kept in reserve for bombardment. Threats posed by the large guns at Le Havre across from Sword Beach and eventually, later in the campaign, those at Cherbourg would have to be countered. Equally, other groups gave protection from U-boat attack – six anti-submarine trawlers were attached to the Gold Beach covering force – and air attack. Four anti-submarine warfare support groups in south-west approaches to the Channel were at sea, mainly destroyers, frigates and corvettes. Six more naval groups, including three escort carriers, patrolled to the west of Land's End and the Scillies.

Sea mines posed a problem, as German and British minefields would have to have lanes cut through them on the way across, and mines could be laid during and after the landings by the Germans using small ships or aircraft. To deal with mines, the Gold Beach groups would be preceded by two minesweeping flotillas: eight fleet minesweepers of the 6th Minesweeper Flotilla, led by Comdr. JC Richards, and another eight fleet minesweepers of the 18th Flotilla, with Comdr. AV Walker in charge. Each flotilla had four Danlayers attached.

The Danlayers placed lit and flagged Dan buoys marking the safe passages. Closer inshore, ten British Yard minesweepers of 150th British Yard Minesweeper Flotilla ('Yard' was the class, designed to work in ports and harbour approaches) and ten motor minesweepers of the 7th Motor Launch Flotilla had the task of clearing the mines. The minesweepers were themselves preceded by shallow-draught motor launches pre-sweeping to protect the larger vessels. Two lanes were cut for each of the five landing beaches. The larger minesweepers turned back to sea when this was done, enlarged the lanes and took position on a line called the Trout Line to defend the anchorages from U-boat or E-boat attack. To further discourage German U-boats and surface vessels, minefields were to be laid along the Brittany coast, and a vigorous U-boat-hunting campaign was carried out to the north, preventing U-boats from arriving from the Baltic or Norway.

Commodore Douglas-Pennant was the naval officer responsible for the naval side of the landings on Gold Beach. 'Force G started at a considerable disadvantage to the other two (British) forces, as it was not formed until 1 March 1944.'[36] Yet all of Douglas-Pennant's fleet had to assemble in the Solent and Southampton by the end of May.

In fact, Douglas-Pennant himself only arrived back in Britain from India by air on 17 February 1944, and reported to Admiral Ramsay that evening at Norfolk House, where he received the news that he was to command Force G. Initially, he set up his HQ at 66 Ashley Gardens, London, together with the staffs of XXX Corps and 50th Division. This greatly facilitated early joint planning between the navy and the army. A week later, Force G was officially formed in the area between Portland and Poole in Dorset, centred on Weymouth, where the port and naval base was officially HMS *Grasshopper*. Douglas-Pennant joined this embryo force on 14 March, setting up his HQ in the Royal Hotel, now renamed HMS *Purbeck*. With him came the advanced HQ of 50th Division, so that very close links were maintained and strong bonds formed. Douglas-Pennant reports that his relations with the General Officer Commanding (GOC) XXX Corps, General Bucknall and Major-General Graham of 50th Division 'were always most happy and our respective staffs worked throughout as a team'.[37] His force transferred to the Southampton/Solent area on 28 April. In his report on the preparation and landings on Gold Beach, Douglas-Pennant shows that, as well as the very short time period for training, the units had to face other considerable problems. There was a lack of landing craft for practices, and Force G had to carry out four major exercises, Smash I–IV, at Studland Bay during April 1944. Each assault brigade was landed, and then the follow-up brigades, including all the extra units allocated. Finally, a full divisional dress rehearsal on Hayling Island, called Exercise Fabius, took place in May. When initially set up in the Portland/Weymouth area, Force G only had four LCT, three Landing Ship Infantry (LSI), two LCH, two LCF and a Landing Craft Personnel (Large) LCP (L) flotilla. Eventually, Force G expanded to well over 250 landing craft and ships alone, without counting escorting or bombardment forces.

On D-Day, all five forces, U, O, G, J and S, accompanied by the fleet minesweepers, were to sail to an assembly point south-east of the Isle of Wight and then sail down one of ten allotted channels, numbered from west to east, swept clear of mines, two channels per beach. Gold Beach convoys were allotted channels five and six.

The Gold Beach naval commander reports that at Portland, and later at Southampton, the local naval authorities were unable to adequately provide proper facilities, and this extra burden, therefore, fell on his staff. He did not receive a full complement of staff until later, as they were engaged in other areas, so they were unable to train together.

Beach gradients were an important piece of information required for beaching craft, and much of this arrived too late to be of help for training exercises. Radio aids were fitted to craft very late, and in two cases were only used for the first time on the day of the landings. Douglas-Pennant also comments that only four out of thirteen of his destroyer force were available for training with Force G, and four of them he only met on D-Day! He quotes HMS *Cottesmore* reporting that the exercises carried out at Studland were invaluable. As a further example, he reports on the condition of the six LCG (L) which supported the landings: 'The LCGs attached to Force G, namely LCG (L) 1, 2, 3, 13, 17 and 18 were some of the original 20 which were fitted out at very short notice for operation HUSKY. Due to lack of time they were only fitted with the barest essentials to enable them to operate.'[38] Finally, the headquarters ship for Force G was HM LSH *Bulolo*, LSH standing for Landing Ship, Headquarters. This ex-Australian liner only arrived in the United Kingdom on 17 April, and even then needed fitting out with extra communications equipment. Before D-Day, she was only available to take part in Exercise Fabius. Douglas-Pennant points out that *Bulolo* had already carried out LSH duties at Oran, Sicily and Anzio, and notes that the experience already gained by her 'ship's company of seamen, soldiers and airmen in these operations was of great value in ensuring that the Headquarters communications organisation worked efficiently and smoothly'.[39] However, in his report, he regrets that his staff and the officers of *Bulolo* were not able to collaborate in the four earlier Smash exercises.[40]

One of the very important groups of ships under his command were the eight LSI which carried the assault battalions and unloaded them into LCA for the run to shore. Each LSI carried around eighteen LCA. Seven of the LSI had the prefix *Empire*; these had been built for the Ministry of War Transport in the United States and had been converted into large troop-carrying assault ships sailing under the Red Ensign of the Merchant Navy. *Empire Arquebus*, *Empire Crossbow* and *Empire Spearhead* – all able to carry 1,310 troops and eighteen landing craft – plus HM LSI *Glenroy* (a larger vessel in RN service able to carry 1,098 troops with twenty-four landing craft) – would carry 231st Brigade in convoy G1, and *Empire Halberd*, *Empire Lance*, *Empire Mace* and *Empire Rapier* (capacity the same as the other *Empire* ships) would carry 69th Brigade in convoy G2. The commodore became anxious about the crews of some of these ships, as his narrative explains, and the story gives an insight into the problems which may be faced by a democratic nation even during the midst of the greatest of wars: 'During the training period it was agreed between the Board of Trade, the Admiralty and the men's Trade Unions that the ships lifeboats in the Empire Class LSI could be replaced by LCP (L).'[41] This had been done, but then, about ten days before D-Day, the crew of the SS *Empire Mace* at Southampton refused to sail for the Solent unless the lifeboats were replaced. The crew apparently stopped all work, despite the efforts of the local Ministry of Transport representative. Douglas-Pennant felt that he had no option but to give in, and to avoid further problems he had all the lifeboats replaced in the other Empire ships. He states that it was 'not until the Force sailed for the operation was I free from the anxiety that some similar complaint, this time not so easily remedied, might result in one of my LSI not sailing and lead to the dislocation of the whole assault'.[42]

Part of Douglas-Pennant's command was formed by the Canadian 264th LCI (L) flotilla. Each of these craft transported up to 200 soldiers. They were used to transport the follow-up infantry battalions of 56th (Independent) Infantry Brigade and 151st (DLI) Infantry Brigade to Normandy. The craft were originally US LCI (L), and twenty-four of them were made available and accepted by the Canadian Cabinet War Committee to be commissioned as HMC (His Majesty's Canadian) LCI. A memorandum issued on 21 December 1943[43] makes it clear that 'they are manned by the naval service [i.e. not Merchant Navy], they become a unit of the Canadian Navy, the loan was distinct from lend-lease procedure and in the event of loss there was no obligation to return the craft'. Maintenance, repairs and operational costs were to be met by the Canadian Naval Board. All the LCI (L) had been built in US shipyards, and made their way in independent convoy groups across the Atlantic to the United Kingdom. Their condition by early 1944 aptly describes the problems faced by landing-craft crews of all types. The LCIs given to the RCN (Royal Canadian Navy) were all Mark Is, the twenty-four from the United States and six from Britain to make up three flotillas. 'They had seen hard service in the Mediterranean landings from Sicily onwards. With the wear and tear of operations, lack of training to the crews, especially in Diesel engine maintenance, plus the loss of tools, the craft were described as being in a "shocking condition". Repair yards were already hard pressed with landing craft by the hundreds and tools were still in short supply.'[44] Important items like tachometers and temperature gauges were unobtainable. The maintenance parties, though, worked long and hard over the winter and spring, with tools being coaxed from the RN and even the army. It is noted, though, that these problems gravely reduced the time for training. One example was LCI (L) 299, which was not ready for service until 1 June. Other LCI (L) had to wait for a month before finding a dry dock clear for them; some were simply landed and work commenced while they were beached. The RN landing craft suffered the same fate. It was an indicator of the pace of various landings, the paucity of landing craft and the rush to get so much done with little resources and limited time. At the same time, flotillas were taking part in minor training exercises – manoeuvring, beaching, night navigation and firing exercises – at the rate of at least one per week, leading to further maintenance headaches. As well as the Canadian flotilla, Douglas-Pennant had under his command several elements of the US Navy. One US unit from 70th Division provided three LCI (L), joining with the Canadian flotilla to ship 56th (Independent) Infantry Brigade, and eighteen other LCI (L) from two more US units (61st and 62nd Divisions) to ship 151st Brigade. The LCI (L) carrying these two brigades were the most important part of convoy G3. Douglas-Pennant reports that he received 'at all times the most cheerful and willing co-operation' from the attached US and Canadian units.[45]

Thirty Landing Ship Tanks (LST) would join in four further D-Day Gold Beach convoys. They were often known with black humour as 'Large Slow Targets', and would arrive off Gold Beach between 1200 and 1500 on D-Day. Each could carry a significant amount of material. A typical load might include eight jeeps, twenty-one 3 ton lorries, six 15 cwt trucks, eighteen tanks and 177 troops.[46]

Of the British-built LCT, 160 LCT Mk 5 and Mk 6 were sent to the Royal Navy under lend-lease agreements. With a crew of around twelve, including two officers, the LCT could carry several tanks or self-propelled guns, or a mix of vehicles.

A good description of what it was like taking over a landing craft and meeting a new crew is provided by a 23-year-old New Zealander. After serving as a seaman, Eric Krull was sent for officer training at HMS *King Arthur* at Hove, and then, after some leave, had to go and help commission an LCT, which became a Gold Beach vessel.

> At Lowestoft we picked up ours. In the shipyard it was just a mess. Well the yards and that, they were making these landing craft in this particular yard and it was just a mass of bits of steel and grubbiness all round and we had to commission it as they say. So we had to clean it up and then the crew arrived. Accommodation for the officers situated below the bridge was in a cabin with a bunk each and a washbasin. As with many small ships the crew could be a motley bunch. When the crew arrived I thought 'gosh!' What have we got here? And they were all dressed up in all sorts of clothing. They must have been posted from various places like Portsmouth and other naval bases. English, Scots – and hard cases, aged about 20–21 at most. They were Ordinary seamen, one was I think an Able seaman, the coxswain he had previous experience and he was pretty good.[47]

The officers were paid around £4 a week, the crew much less. As they were in a small and uncomfortable craft, they all received extra pay known as 'hard lyers'.

Another interesting insight into operations and training is given by William Cooke. He had joined the Royal Navy at the age of seventeen and a half in August 1943 and completed his basic training at Skegness (Butlins Holiday Camp). He was then sent on a course in January 1944 as a telegraphist at HMS *Drake*, a training establishment at Crownhill, Plymouth. Training gave him skills in Morse and coding. His mother was a GPO telegraphist, so he already had a good knowledge of the task. There followed a period with Combined Operations at Portland, where he received further training in operating from land. Training was carried out in pairs, with a view to training men to operate from the beachhead operating transmitters for the Forward Observation

Bombardment (FOB) observers. However, he was drafted to join LCT 1087, an Mk IV LCT. The skipper was Dick Lloyd, with Sub. Lt McDonald. They were also the flotilla lead craft, with Lt Comdr Langley aboard. Their control ship was the frigate HMS *Nith*. LCT 807 was one of 865 Mk IV LCTs built in the United Kingdom. At 57 metres long and nearly 12 metres wide, it was capable of carrying nine M4 Sherman tanks or six Churchill tanks. LCT 807 was one of the many craft completed not long before D-Day. Work started on building it on 27 January 1944, and it was launched on 22 March and commissioned on 4 April. William Cooke's diary entries show that he joined LCT 1078 on 26 March at Weymouth. Shortly after this date, their flotilla of twelve craft sailed for Southampton.[48]

Another very important task that the navy continued to facilitate after the landings in Normandy was the maintenance of the armies. This required the provision of a ferry service from sea to shore and a cross-Channel service. During D-Day, all vehicles landed fully loaded with fuel, food and ammunition. Follow-up forces, Force L for the eastern (British) beaches and Force B for the western (US) beaches, landed reinforcement troops and material immediately following the landings. Force L was loaded at Tilbury and Felixstowe, and assembled at Southend, Sheerness and Harwich. Their convoys would have to run the gauntlet of fire from the large German coastal guns in the Pas-de-Calais. Rear Admiral WE Parry was appointed in early 1944, with his HQ in the east coast port of Harwich, as the commander of follow-up Force L to Gold Beach. This was made up of six convoys carrying 7th Armoured Division, 3rd Canadian Division, 51st Highland Division, 22nd Armoured Brigade, support units of I and XXX Corps, and 21st Army Group HQ. On arrival in the Gold Beach area, Force L came under the command of Cmdr. Douglas-Pennant. Force B loaded at Plymouth and Falmouth, and assembled at Plymouth, Falmouth, the Helford River and Fowey.

To ensure further delivery of materials and men and the evacuation of casualties, the two landing beaches of Gold and Omaha were to have a prefabricated harbour assembled, each approximately the size of Dover harbour. These two harbours were code-named Mulberry A (US) and Mulberry B (British). The British Mulberry was to be constructed offshore the small pre-war resort and fishing village of Arromanches. A second important plan concerned the delivery of fuel. This was dealt with in two ways: first, ship-to-shore pipelines were laid by D+18 days, so that tankers could unload off the beaches, and second, ten pipelines were laid from Sandown on the Isle of Wight to west of Cherbourg by D+75 days. These pipelines were called 'Pipe Line Under the Ocean' or PLUTO. During planning, it became clear that it would take some time for the Mulberries and PLUTO to be completed, so the naval officer in charge, Rear Admiral Tennant, came up with a further idea[49] that seventy obsolete ships could be used as breakwaters by sinking them in a line off each beach to provide some shelter inshore. These five breakwaters were called Gooseberries, numbered 1–5, with No. 3 off Gold Beach. They were to arrive on D+1 and D+2. The Gold Beach Gooseberry was laid according to plan, except that one ship was misaligned as it sank. The ships were scuttled by placing 10 lb charges in each hold. When blown, the ships took around half an hour to sink. Superstructures remained generally above water. Apart from anything else, they proved a great boon and shelter to the ferry service that the Navy and Royal Army Service Corps provided for the unloading of vessels offshore.

The two Mulberries at Gold and Omaha were constructed of concrete caissons called Phoenix, towed to Normandy and sunk to form protective harbours, each with two entrances. Metal piers, pontoons and articulated roadways were also floated across and assembled to provide unloading facilities inside the new harbours. This equipment was collectively known as 'Whale', and could float up and down with the tide. Heavy floating metal 'Bombardons' were placed outside the harbours as additional breakwaters. These two harbours, reckoned to amount to some two million tonnes of prefabricated steel and concrete, were floated across to Normandy from Britain after D-Day and constructed in situ. They required the use of 'every available tug which could be mustered in Britain and from the United States'.[50] Altogether, there were 213 Phoenix ferroconcrete caissons of varying size, from 2,000 to 6,000 tonnes, twenty-three floating pier-heads, 10 miles of Whale roadway and ninety-three Bombardons to be brought across. The Phoenix were assembled at Selsey and Dungeness, with a reserve in the Thames; the Bombardons were assembled at Portland; the Whale roadway in the Solent and at Selsey.[51]

It was planned that maintenance of the armies over the beachheads would only cease when the Seine ports were opened. Ready to follow on after D-Day were 205 pre-loaded Merchant Naval stores coasters, seventy-four vessels carrying motor transport and fifteen ships carrying personnel, all assembled between the Thames and the Bristol Channel.[52] 'An important point to notice is that no reliance was placed on any railways being available for at least the first three months of the operation and so the L of C [lines of communication] was planned to be entirely road operated.'[53] As the assault and follow-up troops moved forward from Gold Beach, the area behind the beach was to be organized into an enormous maintenance area for the storage and distribution of all the needs of XXX Corps. Various units were formed into 104 Beach Sub Group to facilitate this, including, in the first instance, such tasks as clearing the beach area of mines and obstructions and similarly making safe areas required as stores compounds. The initial build-up of supplies by D+3 was expected to include 'four days expenditure of ammunition for the forces expected to land by D+5, fifty miles worth of petrol, oil and lubricants (POL) per vehicle expected ashore on D+5 and two days supplies for the forces ashore by D+5'.[54] Working within the beach area were not only army troops, but RAF and naval units, some of whom were to be landed on D-Day.

The RAF and USAAF (United States Army Air Force) were also to play very important roles before, during and after D-Day. The air forces were tasked with a number of operations. From 1939, the only way of hitting back directly at Germany was by strategic bombing; then, after the 1940 Battle of Britain, fighter sweeps across north-west Europe took place in larger and larger numbers to hit ground targets and force the Luftwaffe into the air for combat. These sweeps were only limited by weather and the range of the Spitfires and Hurricanes involved. As time went on, and more bombing aircraft and a wider range of types of aircraft, such as the De Havilland Mosquito and Bristol Beaufighter, became available, the air could be used more frequently and effectively in the war against the U-boats and on shipping strikes. Once lease-lend, and then later when US air forces became established in the United Kingdom from 1942, the range of aircraft types increased again, including workhorses like the Douglas Havoc/Boston series of medium bombers, the twin tail boom Lightning and fighters like the Mustang and Thunderbolt. Airpower was also used for dropping parachute and air-landing (glider-borne) troops. Supplying resistance forces in Europe, and dropping or landing agents and materials, were carried out by specialist squadrons, and, to cause maximum disruption to help the Normandy landings, the French and Belgian Resistance were to be fully involved, along with specialist units from the Special Air Service. Much information was gathered by the largely unarmed photo-reconnaissance units, and was especially useful in building up (literally) a picture of the landing beaches and interpreting the results of air strikes. Finally, by 1944, the new German V weapons (*Vergeltungswaffen* or reprisal weapons) worried the Allies greatly. Only air attack could effectively counter the threats from the V1 flying bomb and the V2 rocket until the V-weapon sites themselves were overrun by ground forces.

The strategic bomber force leaders of the time, Harris (RAF) and Spaatz (US), both believed that the war could be won mainly by the use of strategic airpower and bombing. After the January 1943 Casablanca Conference, the British and US Bomber Commands in the United Kingdom were given a directive to destroy and dislocate the German military, industrial and economic system and also undermine the will of the German people to offer armed resistance. Submarine and aircraft manufacture, transportation and oil plants were to be the primary targets.[55] It was not until January 1944, when the US Air Force in the United Kingdom was massively reorganized, that the 8th Air Force really came into its own. One development that allowed 8th Air Force to roam more freely over Germany by day after November 1943 was the introduction of the highly improved P51 Mustang fighter plane, that could fly with the bombers all the way to Germany and back. Fitted with a Rolls-Royce Merlin rather than its original Allison engine, and equipped with drop fuel tanks, this aircraft could escort bombers to Berlin and back, and take on the Messerschmitt 109 and Focke-Wulf 190 on at least equal terms. The inequality of numbers soon told, and now it was the Germans suffering large losses of aircraft. The bomber offensive continued, with bombing raids on all targets, but a priority was to destroy Luftwaffe capability, on the ground and in the air, and the German aircraft industry. This joint US/UK (Combined Bomber Force) offensive, christened Operation Pointblank, was ordered from June 1943 and confirmed at the Quebec Conference in August 1943. However, there was going to be some argument about using the strategic bombers as priority targets changed moving closer to D-Day.

Until very late in the day, the 'Bomber Barons', Harris and Spaatz, were arguing that Germany could be fatally weakened and forced to surrender through bombing alone, whereas Roosevelt and Churchill, plus most other chiefs of staff, saw bombing as significantly weakening Germany before a final fatal blow was delivered through European invasion. A move was enforced to ensure that strategic bombing would help the invasion, isolating the battlefield by destroying railway centres and road and railway bridges. This, in essence, became known as the 'Transportation Plan'. Allied leaders, especially Churchill, were worried about casualties to French civilians. On 4 March 1944, experimental attacks were ordered on six railway marshalling yards. The first such raid, on Trappes, proved highly successful, with civilian casualties low.[56] On 25 March, a list of twenty-six such targets was issued, with Harris now worried that they might not all be hit by June. Eisenhower, as supreme commander, issued a directive on 17 April that 'all possible support must be afforded to the Allied armies by our air forces to assist them in establishing themselves in the lodgement area'.[57] By the eve of D-Day, bomber forces would confuse the enemy, dropping aluminium foil or 'window' to create two perceived invasion threats (operations Taxable and Glimmer), and over 1,000 British aircraft alone would bomb German coastal gun batteries.

That the raids by bomber aircraft on railway targets, plus opportunistic fighter-bomber attacks on individual railway trains, were highly successful in causing grave problems to the communications system is shown by post-operation reports. The number of workers employed in repairing railway damage rose from 1,300 on 11 March 1944 to over 12,000 by 3 June in the railway region 'Nord' alone.[58] Pre-D-Day, over 10,500 tonnes of bombs were dropped on railway targets in area West, and over 19,000 tonnes on area North, the two most important regions affecting communications with Normandy.[59] In January 1944, over 210,000 railway wagons were moving across the whole of the French railway system. By 2 June, this had been cut to only 65,000.[60] Attacks on bridges proceeded during May, and virtually all the bridges on the Rivers Seine and Loire were cut or seriously damaged by D-Day, seriously hampering German movement and reinforcement. Commencing on 21 May, the Allied Expeditionary Air Force (AEAF) began large-scale fighter sweeps aimed at targets of opportunity, such as road, rail and canal transport, as well as the Luftwaffe. On that day alone, we are told that over 1,200 Allied fighters ranged over north-west Europe.[61] On 15 May, a German Transport Ministry report noted that the air raids in Belgium and France had 'caused systematic breakdown of all main lines; the coastal defences have been cut off from the supply bases in the interior. Large scale movements of German troops are practically impossible', and by 3 June, another report concluded that the whole railway system of Belgium and northern France had been seriously crippled: 'Paris has been systematically cut off from long distance traffic. The most important bridges over the lower Seine have been destroyed one after another.' The German authorities were apparently considering giving up on repair work as 'useless'.[62]

To defend the west in 1944 from the inevitable Allied invasion, Goering believed that the Luftwaffe should concentrate all its forces to ward off the landings within the first few hours of attack, a position similar to that of Rommel. Sperrle, commanding Air Fleet 3, was tasked with establishing air superiority over any invasion area, with the capacity to attack the beachhead troops and ships day and night, thus supporting the ground forces. The Luftwaffe had around 100 airfields and landing grounds within a radius of 350 miles of Normandy. However, the majority of these were stationed north and north-east of Paris, and not closer to the coast, because of the fear of Allied air-landing operations against airfields and the dominance already virtually established by the Allies in the air by mid-1944 over western France.

By May 1944, the Luftwaffe units which were to face the invasion were already in a parlous state. Constant battle over France and raids further afield to the English coast to disrupt invasion preparations had cost dearly. The Luftwaffe was greatly reduced in numbers and suffered from a lack of trained and experienced pilots and aircrew. By the end of May 1944, Air Fleet 3 had only 510 serviceable aircraft: 125 fighters, 198 bombers, 27 ground attack aircraft, 51 night fighters, 72 reconnaissance planes and 37 heavy fighters. Between January and May 1944, German fighter-pilot losses had reached 25 per cent, and total Luftwaffe losses of aircraft through Allied action numbered over 6,000. Fuel shortages and casualties meant that pilot and aircrew training time had to be greatly reduced, leading inevitably to less experienced men reaching front-line squadrons. Between April and June 1944, production of synthetic oil, which supplied 90 per cent of the Luftwaffe's aviation fuel needs, had fallen from 178,000 tonnes to 53,000 tonnes.

The Allied bombing of airfields led to units being withdrawn further from the eventual scene of invasion, with the result that the Luftwaffe would have the extra disadvantage of reduced operation time over the battlefield. By D-Day, the Allied air forces would bring to bear more than forty times more aircraft than the Luftwaffe, and German planes would only relatively rarely be able to penetrate Allied air space effectively. From 6 June until the beginning of July, the Luftwaffe would lose an average of thirty-eight fighter planes per day – over 1,000 in less than a month.[63]

4

50th (Northumbrian) Infantry Division

For the landings on Gold Beach, Montgomery had chosen the main infantry assault force to be the 50th Infantry Division. Pre-war, it had been a first-line Territorial Army division, and had been organized as a motor division, meaning it could travel into battle motorized rather than marching. Its distinguishing, and soon to be famous, shoulder patch showed a 'TT' in red on a black background. The TT represented the pre-war recruiting area between the Rivers Tyne and Tees, and covered in part the ancient area known as Northumbria since Saxon times: hence, Northumbrian division. After the 1940 retreat from France, 50th Division was reorganized as an ordinary infantry division. As with most units, it had to leave its transport behind in France. Fighting in France, where it arrived in January 1940, around Arras, some of its units met the enemy led by a general they were to face in the future and grow to respect: Erwin Rommel. The division remained on duty in Britain until April 1941, when it left for North Africa. It was heavily involved in campaigns there, including the Battle of El Alamein, until it advanced to Tunisia, and was then involved in the Sicily landings and campaign.

The division was part of XXX Corps, and Montgomery had written to Brooke in September 1943 that XXX Corps could go home to Britain; he saw no possibility of employing them in Italy. He lauded them to Brooke as a 'superb team' that had taken part in 'every sort of fighting', and added that they could be studied as a model set-up in England. 'Such an experienced Corps would be worth untold gold when it comes to a cross-Channel venture.'[1] On 30 August 1943, Montgomery had visited each battalion of the Durham Light Infantry (DLI) Brigade, serving with 50th Division, in turn. He addressed one battalion in a dried-up river bed, telling them how well, long and hard they had fought under his command, and that they could enjoy a rest. He added that, if he ran into trouble in Italy, he might send for them, as he liked to have 50th Division wherever he went. Apparently, a great groan rose from the battalion. Montgomery then remarked that, of course, 'he might be going home'. Cries of 'Ha, bloody ha!' greeted this remark, and boos as well as cheers rang out.[2] Returning to England in November 1943, predictably 50th Division was earmarked as one of the assault divisions for Normandy, taking over a role that 49th (West Riding) Infantry Division had been training intensively for, while 49th Division – known as the Polar Bears after its time in Iceland and its distinctive shoulder patch – reverted to a follow-up infantry division, 'a result of General Montgomery's wish to have one assault division with battle experience, for which 50th Division was selected'.[3]

When 50th Division became the assault division for Gold Beach, it was already one of the most famous British divisions of the war. It had seen action in France during 1940, in Egypt, Cyprus, Iraq and Syria until February 1942, in North Africa until April 1943, and then Sicily. It had been returned from the Mediterranean to the United Kingdom in late 1943. The division had originally comprised two brigades of infantry, 150th Brigade and 151st Brigade, but by September 1943, it was composed of three infantry brigades, 69th Brigade, 151st Brigade and 231st Brigade. Of these, 151st Brigade had been with the division from the very beginning of the war, 69th Brigade from July 1940 and 231st Brigade from October 1943: 69th Brigade, under Brigadier Knox, was made up of the 5th Battalion of the East Yorkshire Regiment and the 6th and 7th Battalions of the Green Howards, also based in Yorkshire; 151st Brigade, under Brigadier Senior, was made up of the 6th, 8th and 9th Battalions of the DLI. These two brigades gave the division its distinctive northern Tyne/Tees flavour. The recently joined 231st Brigade, under Brigadier Sir A. Stanier, had a southern, even West Country flavour, comprised of the 1st Hampshire, 1st Dorset and 2nd Devon infantry battalions. They had had the harrowing experience of serving as 1st (Malta) Infantry Brigade in Malta from 1939, and were used to being called the 'Malta' Brigade, with their own distinctive shoulder flash of a white Maltese cross on a black background. The 'Malta' Brigade was redesignated 231st Infantry Brigade in April 1943.[4] From July 1943, it had been involved in the Sicily landings and fighting in Italy. Withdrawn back to Sicily in September 1943, the battalion had then joined 50th Division prior to returning to the United Kingdom.[5] The division arrived back in the United Kingdom, probably feeling it deserved a well-earned rest after being away and on active service for so long.

The 1st Dorset reached the River Clyde on the evening of 4 November 1943. 'It seemed almost unbelievable that this could be home and actually the United Kingdom.'[6] They disembarked on 6 November, and a Highland regiment band played them ashore. They then moved to Essex and were billeted in the Halstead area. Soon, virtually the whole battalion was sent on leave. Harold Lewis was an experienced soldier with 1st Dorsets, who had joined the Army in 1936 and seen service on the North-West Frontier of India, then moved to Malta in 1939 and eventually to Sicily. Coming home to the United Kingdom, he remembers the fear of a U-boat and the ships zigzagging in case of torpedo attack. The band piped them ashore at Greenock. Concern was shown by relatives when they went home on leave, as the men seemed so thin and had lost so much weight in Malta and Sicily. In fact, Harold recounts that they had better rations from the time that they embarked on board ship.[7] The 8th DLI arrived in the same convoy, and shared a similar experience. After leaving their troopship *Sibajak,* they moved to the railway station at Gourock, and while waiting for the troop train to take them south, were treated to tea and buns by the WVS (Women's Voluntary Service) and were played to by a band of the Cameronians. A holiday spirit gripped the battalion on their journey south, but this was dampened as the train passed through Newcastle, Durham, and their other home towns without stopping. Throughout their journey, when the train slowed through towns or at stations, they were cheered, and, for their part, men displayed captured enemy mementos from the carriage windows. Flags and welcoming messages were chalked on walls and hoardings. It appeared clear to all that a famous unit of the Mediterranean War had arrived home. Their destination was the small Suffolk town of Haverhill. Again, after several days of organization, parties of men were sent home on leave for between fourteen and twenty-eight days, depending on time served abroad.[8] The 5th East Yorkshire landed at Liverpool on 7 November, and travelled by train to Thetford in Norfolk. The whole unit then went on nearly a month's leave until 6 December.[9] Oliver Perks had been commissioned in May 1943. He had already seen considerable service, including wounding, in the desert. Now, as a member of 90th Field Artillery Regiment RA, a field artillery unit of 50th Division, he was returning home, coincidentally via his home town of Bristol:

> Then we had our trip back to the UK. We stayed off Algiers briefly and had a look at the town. And then on back home and round the north of Ireland. And then the convoy split up there, and our ship then came on down and I got up one morning and looked out and we were sailing up the Bristol Channel between Steepholme and Flatholme, and in due course came into Avonmouth. As it happened my mother had been on the quay the day before with the WVS [Women's Voluntary Service], dishing out kit to shipwrecked sailors. If she had seen me she probably would've had a fit because as far as she knew, I was still in Italy. On arrival, it was rather funny. There were a lot of military policemen on the quay and ours were some of the first troops to come back from the Middle East at all. Somebody started with our troops taking the mickey out of the police, shouting out, 'Yaaah, pale face!' The police were very embarrassed, but they couldn't do anything about it, but it made them look a bit silly.[10]

These accounts of the homecoming of 50th TT Division are typical. The Clyde, Liverpool and Avonmouth were the recipient of many convoys taking the long way home to avoid the threat of U-boats and E-boats in the English Channel: a reminder that, in a few short months, the largest invasion armada in history had to safely negotiate it. It appears that, once home, 50th Division and its supporting units went virtually immediately on home leave for up to four weeks. The reference in Oliver Perks' account of homecoming to mickey-taking of the military police and shouts of 'palefaces' was the risk one ran when coming across men from a desert unit, who were very suntanned and felt they had been out fighting a long time while others lingered at home. A similar piece of advice would be to 'get your knees brown!' or the inevitable 'get some time in!' No doubt this was a very welcome interlude for the officers and men after long and dangerous service abroad. When they returned to their units, they do not seem to have been urgently put back into training, nor, indeed, was 50th Division in a particularly good area to carry out the training for the task they were eventually given.

The 7th Armoured Division, which had been formed in Egypt after the 1938 Munich crisis, had also served throughout the desert war and in Italy. Again, from November 1943, this force returned home as one of the most experienced armoured divisions. Like 50th Infantry Division, it ended up stationed around Norfolk – an area not conducive to practising the type of armoured warfare it would be required to carry out in Normandy. Eisenhower and Montgomery were not to arrive in the United Kingdom for several more weeks; the invasion plan was still based on General Morgan's outline, and 50th Division were not part of that plan. In fact, for some, this was a time of waiting to see what the new boys thought up, while others were frustrated by the seeming inertia.

After the Christmas leave was over, the veteran units started to receive much-needed reinforcements. Many of these were young men who were called up, and induction into the army was not always a happy experience. Their memories of this time are worth recording. Still really fledgling soldiers, they were joining a very famous fighting division, and were often overawed by men whom they saw as being older (perhaps sometimes by only a year – but at eighteen or nineteen years of age small age differences are seen disproportionately), and much more experienced, even heroic.

What follows is anecdotal evidence from soldiers who joined 50th Division from its arrival back in England, both private soldiers and junior officers at the time. The oral evidence shows in many respects that the training received was not always consistent, and perhaps some of the required skills for the task ahead were not driven home, although the training was clearly sometimes quite tough. The accounts also give good examples of how soldiers were called up, trained and moved to their final parent units, and their personal and initial thoughts on army life and concrete evidence for the reinforcement problem: that especially the army was very short of infantry, and that men with aptitudes for other types of service or technical trades found themselves in the 'Poor Bloody Infantry' through desperate need. Most of these men were called up in 1943, and the accounts give a good insight into the times and problems that had to be faced in the main body of 50th Division. Some of the later accounts are by men serving with the commandos who landed on Gold Beach, both with 47 RM Commando and those with a specific task. Their anecdotes show that their training, although very thorough and sometimes difficult, did not go hand in hand with the general divisional training of 50th Division between February and May 1944.

Tom Hewitt of 2nd Devons[11] joined the army in March 1943, and, after basic training at Colchester, was sent to join 2nd Devons. He was not too keen on the way they were treated at times: 'no better than a farmers' dog'. He started working life in farming, but had then trained locally in Devon in the motor car trade as an apprentice mechanic. Engineering skills was not accepted on his papers; at the end of his ten-week basic training, his civilian job was listed as 'storeman', and hence 'I had to join the bloody infantry! But I did learn a lot in the Army despite this. I was pretty green on most things as a seventeen year old! We did lots of marching and training with rifles came later; lots of double marching to get us fitter.' Ordinary people in the street could be heard complaining about the way the soldiers were treated by the NCOs. Even during a war as desperate as the Second World War, some basic principles of democracy were adhered to, and civilians did not by any means kow-tow to the military. After basic training, they learnt fieldcraft and rifle drill. After ten days' leave, Hewitt was sent to Carrickfergus in Northern Ireland. Here they took part in even more intensive training, getting used to living in the outside environment among the Irish mountains. Eventually, he was sent to join 2nd Devons in the New Year. A number of exercises were specific for D-Day, including some mock landings on the south coast. He feels he was not long with 2nd Devons before D-Day. They went to the New Forest in May 1944. 'Guards all around the New Forest and we weren't allowed out. We lived in leaky Bell Tents and the place was a quagmire at times.' He remembers that some reinforcements came from other battalions of the Devonshire Regiment.

David Bushell[12] joined 1st Dorsets, and completed his basic training in a similar way to Tom Hewitt, but in Cheshire. He remembers this as 'changing clothes all day long, depending on whether they were doing rifle drill, Physical Education or field craft'. They seemed to have many inoculations 'for all the known diseases we were likely to catch'. After the six weeks, they were then put through a series of tests to decide their aptitude. Despite his engineering aptitude, he was sent to join the Dorset Regiment, and went to complete his next ten-week training period at Colchester. Here they moved up a gear, and went into specific infantry training: rifle shooting, route marching every day, grenade training and learning to use other weapons like the Bren gun. The route marches were of 10 or 20 miles, and also they had to complete 5 or 10 mile-long 'forced marches' that sometimes involved them running in full kit. After this, he underwent several weeks of more intensive toughening-up training in the Pennines in rainy weather. Their clothes seemed to be always wet, and they lived in primitive conditions, in a leaky barn with a trough of icy water to wash in outside. They were now training using live ammunition and explosives, and Bushell reports that there were a number of casualties, including two or three deaths.

In January 1944, he joined his designated battalion. The 1st Dorsets were in Essex.

> After several weeks we went and did some non-specific training along the coast around Southsea. Then we finished up in Scotland for ten days training and then returned to the New Forest near to Fawley. We were in nine feet high Bell Tents, ten soldiers to a tent, and had to keep all our kit in our own little area and tied the rifles up to the centre pole at night. It was a nightmare for anyone trying to get out for a pee at night!

Then some Americans arrived, and the Dorsets were very jealous of the nice square US tents with proper beds, four men to a tent, and the lovely smell of their cooked breakfast. They went out on LSIs and carried out at least two mock invasions of the Dorset Coast. These included landing from the LCA. Another time, they were expected to stay fully dressed in case of German E-boats. They were told that they went to within five miles of the French coast.

> We did two major exercises like this; the third one was the real thing. Some men were sick because of the greasy food we were fed on ship. In the sealed camps we did not do any training or marching, we were just killing time really. We were still very envious of the Americans as we were being fed by our own quartermasters.

Alan Norman[13] also became a new member of 231st Brigade as a junior officer. He had followed a route that quite a number of infantry junior officers had taken, via the Royal Armoured Corps (RAC). It seems that too many junior officers had been trained for the RAC, and when found surplus to requirements and that infantry officers required for the invasion were in very short supply, they were simply transferred after a short infantry conversion course.

> I was commissioned in the RAC in June 1943. I had been a trooper with the RAC, but went up to Sandhurst Officer Cadet Training Unit and was commissioned into 147 RAC which were originally a territorial battalion of the Hampshire.

As supernumerary we were sent on a short course and transferred to infantry. I went to 1st Hampshire in early January 1944 in A Company and joined them at Long Milton in Suffolk as a full Lieutenant. We were in a large hall and shared a room with two other officers.

On the day of arrival, he was still wearing his black RAC beret:

When we were stood up in the mess having a cup of tea I had the subalterns around me, and to be honest I was shooting a bit of a line about the tanks. Then someone said, 'you haven't met our Colonel?' And of course there was this young 26–28 year old with two badges on his shoulders and I had not realised one was a crown! So I felt quite small. He had commanded them in Italy and so on.

Norman carried on wearing his black beret until one day he got a note and a package from the adjutant. The note said: 'I would be very much obliged if in future you would wear the enclosed hat. NB You owe me £4. 10s for the hat.' Norman remembers the adjutant as a rather suave ex-stockbroker called Frank Walters. 'He was a very calm chap – laid back would be the words used today!' An interesting point made by Norman is that the soldiers were well aware of the forthcoming invasion of Europe. Because of the appetite for finishing the war, walls in streets and railway stations were often covered in graffiti saying: 'Second Front now' or 'Help Joe Stalin'. 'Some of the soldiers were a little bit on the bolshie side towards the invasion and having to take part.' He noted that the battalion was much depleted, although there were still quite a number of regulars left from before the war. His platoon was not brought up to full establishment numbers until perhaps as late as March 1944. 'When we got recruits, I was appalled at the level of their ability and experience. There were about ten reinforcements needed in each platoon.'

Landing craft practice consisted initially of having craft drawn or taped out on the ground. They practised demolishing barbed wire obstacles with Bangalore torpedoes. The Bangalore torpedo was a series of explosive tubes, which could be screwed together to form a longer tube of the required length. It had an igniter in the end, which you pulled to set off the delayed explosion after pushing the tube under the wire. Also, they used the 75 grenade, also known as the Hawkins grenade or mine, for demolition in a chain of grenades joined together with an instantaneous fuse, and at the far end a slow fuse allowing the firer to withdraw some distance. Each chain of five or six 75 grenades was about 4–5 feet long. Tossing the chain across Dannert wire demolished it. The 75 grenades could also be laid as an anti-tank device. During one exercise, Norman was warned to ensure that his men were properly briefed on one particular part, as Montgomery was present. The rumour was that on a previous exercise, Montgomery had asked a private to explain the exercise to him; this was badly done, and Montgomery had the captain who had briefed the exercise reduced to subaltern rank!

We went up to Inverary. I was surprised that there was still snow on the ground. We were also always hungry so we were always going up to get an extra meal at a tea-total hotel. On the larger ships the men stayed in hammocks and then climbed down to the smaller landing craft on netting, then land and go up a big hill, dig in on very poor hard soil. Then back to the landing craft and disembark on a landing stage. We came back down to Fawley by troop train to a tented camp maintained by American troops. We had several minor exercises. Time after time I would have to have a landing craft taped out and we would practise disembarking. Or fitness training carrying and throwing logs or a twenty mile route march. When we left our camp we went through the American camp and everything they had was beautiful compared to what we had. I remember we came back from one exercise and some of the men, not liking being held in the camp, tossed several Bakelite blast grenades at the American guards!

Norman remembers his first big exercise with 1st Hampshires at Studland Bay (Exercise Smash), and that 'we were landed beautifully, probably water only up to mid-calf. There were "enemy" dug in firing Bren Guns overhead to get us used to the noise and also on the exercise some of the LCT (R) were used firing rockets. When they landed, they also used "new" compo [composite] rations. The individual ones had a handful of boiled sweets, a meat cube and some compressed milk and sugar. They also contained some non-sweet and sweet biscuits. Tea was also in cubes. "When we made the tea it was appalling!" But some of the older veterans reckoned it was better, as at least they had a range of menus. They said that in Italy and Sicily, they only ever got Menu A and Menu B, as the other better compo menus never used to get past the base quartermasters! A final full divisional exercise – called Exercise Fabius – was held on Hayling Island in May'.

Exercise Fabius started like all the others. They were loaded onto lorries and taken into Southampton. Every so often, military police on motorcycles lined the route, and the vehicles were not allowed to stop. Then the lorries stopped in a residential area, and they got out and formed up in prearranged landing serials. In their landing serials, they marched out of the area and down through some public parks. They often had to stop and wait while other units were sorted out. Once Norman was impressed when a commando in another unit showed him his 'Bergan' rucksack, which was full of guncotton, one assumes for demolition. The commando told him it weighed 100 lb! Eventually they arrived at the working-class terraced house area near the docks, where the local people were shouting and cheering them. Norman was amazed at how generous these poor people were to the troops, giving them apples or cigarettes. On these exercises, the officers had arranged to sleep on stretchers on the decks. Norman was surprised to see, as they landed and came up to the top of the beach, lines of houses with people looking down from windows at them, and in one bathroom a man shaving. He got the impression that in this case, the people were not too keen on seeing them! They were taken off in the afternoon in an LCI (L) manned by Americans. By this time, the sea had turned really rough. 'We had to get in the sea up to mid-thigh to embark. Then they realised that they were grounded and had to be pulled up by another British ship. There was story going around about E-Boats in the Channel.'

I learnt two good lessons on these. On the first exercise I decided not to carry all my weapons and ammunition and put it on the follow up transport. Then when we were afloat I began to worry and consider 'what if this is the real thing and I have hardly any ammunition with me?' I never made that mistake again. The second one was that after a night out on the exercise my platoon sergeant reminded me that I had to bring in both sentries before we marched off – I nearly left one behind!

Later at the assembly area, they watched the new Churchill Crocodile flame-thrower tanks. Another tank, called 'The Snake', pushed an enormous Bangalore torpedo, which then exploded, destroying a wide area of barbed wire. They had to be part of the exercise and charge through after the explosion. They were also pretty impressed by the Petard Armoured Vehicle Royal Engineers (AVRE) tanks, which threw a large 'dustbin' bomb to destroy concrete positions. Like the Projector, Infantry, Anti-Tank (PIAT), this worked on the spigot mortar principle, except that the bomb was much larger.

Norman's reference to E-boats in the English Channel was almost certainly due to the disaster that had befallen US Troops taking part in Exercise Tiger. Aiming to practise a landing similar to the 'Exercise Smash' series, but at Slapton Sands in Devon, a follow-up convoy of US LSTs was attacked by E-boats in the early morning of 28 April, several LSTs were sunk or damaged, and nearly 1,000 US servicemen lost their lives. While the tragedy led to improvements in Allied radio co-operation, life-vest training and a larger number of small craft to pick up survivors of any craft sunk on D-Day, the event pointed out how vulnerable such shipping could be to attack, and the loss of the landing craft could be ill afforded.

Peter Goddin became a staff captain on the brigade staff of 151st Brigade. He had joined the Territorial Army in April 1939, and served as a private in the Royal Army Medical Corps in France from November 1939 until evacuation at Dunkirk. Sent for officer training, he was commissioned into the Queen's Own Royal West Kent Regiment in December 1940. After a variety of staff jobs in the United Kingdom, he received promotion to captain.

> Then out of the blue at the end of April 1944 I received a notification from the Military Secretary's department that T/Capt P. R. Goddin RWK was to report forthwith as Staff Captain to 151 Infantry Brigade. The Brigade was under canvas in a camp in Nightingale Woods outside Southampton and was due to land on Gold beach on D-Day. I found that my predecessor had succumbed to nervous exhaustion and had been hospitalised three days previously. In the six weeks prior to D-Day I wondered at times if I too would succumb.[14]

Charles Eagles became a member of 9th Battalion DLI in December 1943. He joined S Company, which was formed in February 1944 and attached to C Company. This group of about thirty-five members was on call to the battalion to deal with booby traps, deal with explosives and demolish objects like bridges. He had joined the army in February 1943, and did his initial six-week training with the Northumberland Fusiliers. Interested in boxing, and wishing later to become a professional boxer, he was at the time a 'keep fit fanatic'. From there, he was then sent to the Royal Army Service Corps for further training, but 'bored out of my mind I volunteered for Commandos and went up to Achnacarry and did six weeks Commando training there'. This was later in 1943. Unfortunately, he was injured towards the end of his training, and ended up in hospital for three weeks. He was given the opportunity to repeat the course when he became A1 fit again, but, deciding against this, he ended by being posted to the DLI in December 1943. With other friends, he volunteered to join the new S Company in 9DLI. Training here made him familiar with and used to handling explosives. As well as demolition work, occasionally explosives went into a nearby pond and brought up some fish! It appears from the description given by Charles that at this stage in 9DLI, the components of S Company – engineers, anti-tank, mortar etc. – were distributed among the rifle companies rather than working as a fifth full (mechanized with Bren carriers) company, as happened in other infantry battalions in 1944.

Eagles remembers that, by around the end of January 1944, he was aware that they were going to be involved in the forthcoming invasion. He felt that they were all very fit, and the work and training they did enabled them to get used to working together. They did lots of marching and double marching, assault courses, floating a gun across a river, practising blowing down trees and making booby traps. 'We went to the south and were under canvas, but some were in houses and barracks.'[15]

Bert Cooper was called up in April 1943, and completed his basic training at the DLI Depot near Brauncepeth Castle, where the DLI Regimental Headquarters were. The main camp, south of the village of Brauncepeth, consisted of over 100 huts. Then he was moved to the King's Own Yorkshire Light Infantry until November 1943, and then transferred to a holding unit in Romsey, from where he was sent to 5th East Yorkshire battalion as late as April 1944. He had missed quite a lot of training, but does remember a practice landing on the Isle of Wight. He was serving twenty-eight days' detention at the time because he and a friend had 'escaped' from the camp at Winchester. They had not seen their families for some time, and just wanted to see them before D-Day. By this time, they were well aware that 5th East Yorks was going to be one of the assault battalions. Eventually, after several detours, they got a lift as far as Grantham, and then another lift in an army lorry got Cooper home to Scunthorpe. He stayed for about a fortnight before giving himself up and being escorted back to Winchester by two Canadian MPs. He remembers that later, one man from Leeds managed to get completely away and was not seen again. This wish to see families 'one last time' is a recurring theme in the accounts of both veterans and the newer replacements. He was still serving part of his twenty-eight days' sentence on board ship bound for Normandy!

Dennis Bowen enlisted as a boy soldier of fifteen years old in 1941 into the East Yorkshire Regiment at Beverley. Like many boy soldiers, his service was as a band boy. Boy soldiers served until seventeen and a half years of age, when they started receiving regular pay. From eighteen years of age, service counted towards a regular soldier's pension. Bowen was then sent to join the 70th Battalion. Battalions of regiments numbered '70th' were battalions for 'young soldiers', and were often used for guarding important points like airfields, barracks or factories. After this, he went to the Richmond Infantry Training Centre. Beverley Barracks had been bombed, and Richmond was the Green Howard Regiment ITC. Promoted to 'local' (unpaid) NCOs and used as demonstrators for recruits, Bowen was here for several months.[16]

John Milton[17] was an officer with 6th Green Howards. He had left school and joined the army in 1942. He was well qualified from Blundell's School, and made use of this advantage when becoming an officer. After leaving school, he farmed near Ripon for two years, and, like many of the very young, and those too old for 'active' military service, he was also a member of the Home Guard. He volunteered for the Green Howards, and as a volunteer, was excused from his reserved farming occupation. He completed his initial training at Richmond, the Green Howards' HQ. Determined to be the best, he was promoted to corporal, and then helped train recruits, until he was sent to an officers' training unit on the Isle of Man. He joined the 6th Battalion early in 1944 at Thetford in Norfolk. He was in B Company. He remembers that they had to go to Scotland to Inverary in order to undertake landing craft training. This was quite tough, as, alongside the training, the weather was very cold, wet and miserable. Later, they did more training in the south of England. He cannot remember details of specific exercises, but knows that:

> I had to watch my step very carefully with the NCOs because they knew a lot more about war than I did. My Platoon Sergeant had won the Military Medal in North Africa; he only had one eye but had got himself upgraded and came back. Later he was one of many to be killed.
>
> We moved to Winchester and we had to stay in camp. That is where we got ready for D-Day. An amazing story is that I wrote home to my mother and father and the frank on the envelope said 'Winchester!' I have been amazed so many times that the Germans couldn't work out where we were to land! Other officers in fact joined after I did, including three young Norwegian chaps.

Charles Hill[18] was also a member of 6th Green Howards, D Company, the same company as Stanley Hollis, who won the VC on D-Day. Hill was called up for military service two weeks after he was eighteen, towards the end of May 1943. Going to barracks in Northampton, he was quickly sent to Skegness, to the Derbyshire Miners' Welfare Home, for ten weeks to put on some more weight, as on entry to the army he was only 9 st 2 lbs in weight. The military use of the Miners' Welfare Home was not unusual; the author has interviewed at least three veterans of the North West Europe Campaign from different regiments who were sent to be 'built up' at the same camp at different times during 1943/44.[19] Soldiers could be referred there for all sorts of physical problems. Charles was told that he would put on half a stone, which he did; however, he further reports that within a month of rejoining for training, he had put on another stone! This was a reflection of the slightly better food and the army exercise regime. But Skegness was not run as some sort of glorified rest home:

> Eventually I went down to 10st 7lb and kept that weight for most of my life. We were still exercising, running and firing, doing PE and so on. The instructors at Skegness were terrible! They gave us special exercises. For ten weeks we were not allowed shoes, only our Army boots for runs around Skegness and route marches. We had plimsolls for the gym. We had to go into the sea to swim; they would throw you in if you didn't want to go!

After Skegness, he was sent to the Infantry Training Centre at Lincoln, and after training there, he was sent to Thetford to join 6th Green Howards. It appears from this that the period of time in Skegness also covered his initial ten-week basic training period. In the forest at Thetford,

> We had to pick up the autumn leaves to keep the place tidy. Discipline! There were a lot of Americans around there. A lot of men played cards, I never won a hand! Card sharps or what! Then in the New Year we went to Inverary and we lost two

fellows up there through live ammunition accidents. Aircraft came strafing and so on. While we were training there the commanders of the LCAs told us we had to get into the water deeper than normal as they didn't want to damage the propellers. Then with live ammunition flying about we would have run up this hill to the top of the hill firing. I think the two who were killed were caused by ammunition (artillery) dropping short. Then we came back by train to Bournemouth which took 24 hours. On the way we suffered a train accident when an American lorry crashed off a hump back bridge and landed on the first carriage and coach. There were some killed and injured. In a very short time ladies living locally produced cups of tea and Americans turned up with a field kitchen. We though, were still stood up in the carriages playing cards!

The railway accident was at Henstridge on 13 March 1944. One person was killed and seven injured.[20] A number of casualties may have been more minor, and were dealt with by the Green Howards' medical officer.

For a time, Charles acted as a batman to a Norwegian officer who had escaped by boat from Norway. 'He was a smashing fellow and he told us he was looking forward to the invasion. At the last minute he was ordered to Scotland to help train soldiers and he broke down in tears. After that they sent a new officer and he was a bugger, he used to inspect my rifle and all sorts.' Charles got out of being a batman, and sees it as one of the worst jobs in the army – 'Looking after an officer and having to carry his radio about.' Charles remembers that the veteran soldiers, when they got to know about the invasion, used to wind up the younger ones with their war stories, but also to tell them how easy life might be once they got to France and got their feet under the table.

We moved to Romsey near Winchester under canvas. We didn't do much there, but we were given a 24 hour pass and three of us decided to go home to Sheffield. (One of my friends became the first wounded on the beaches and appeared in the local paper. The other got killed on the beach.) When we returned we were confined to camp and boarded the Empire Mace. We landed at Hayling Island – a mock invasion – and also at Studland. We knew these were not the real thing because some of the landing craft were not properly loaded.

Important units of the invasion force were provided by the Royal Army Medical Corps (RAMC). As an example of the RAMC units that landed with 50th Division, 203 Field Ambulance Unit were aware that they would be involved in the invasion from early in 1944, with 59th Infantry Division as a follow-up force. By the middle of January, a War Office selection board had tested men in the unit for fitness to stand up to battle conditions, and intensive training was taking place. By the end of the month, they were on an active war footing administratively. During February and March, they were involved in exercises, and a number of officers took part in exchange visits. But from 20 April, the HQ and A Company were temporarily attached to 56th Infantry Brigade because of the high casualties this brigade was expected to take. Despite some consternation over splitting the unit, it had to be, and HQ and A Company moved to Lymington, to be later attached to 56th Infantry Brigade as they moved to the New Forest. They did not take part in the 'Smash' series of exercises, but did take part in

'Fabius'. After Exercise Fabius, there was much pre-invasion training going on, as well as the pre-packing of vehicles. On D-Day, it was planned that three medical officers would land with seventy-five men in eleven vehicles. These moved to Pennerley Camp in the New Forest on 18 May, joining 56th Brigade. A further 100 men and twenty-seven vehicles would be landed in the two days following D-Day, and these moved to Felixstowe for loading as part of Force L. Two important problems had to be sorted out in quick order: on arrival, it was found that the waterproofing of vehicles had been badly done, and needed doing again; and the ten ambulance jeeps arrived minus their stretcher racks, which had to be fixed. The War Diary noted: 'The fifth year of war and this can still happen!'[21]

Ken Stone was called up in 1940 into the RAMC. After training at Aldershot and service in Northern Ireland, his unit was centred in Gainsborough. Interestingly, like the infantry, he attended landing craft training in Scotland.[22]

Captain Peter Johnson[23] trained as a doctor at the Middlesex Hospital and Mount Vernon at Northwood between October 1937 and October 1942, when he was called up and joined the RAMC. Two years after Ken Stone, he was training at the same initial camp – Crookham Camp, Aldershot – but this only lasted one month. He was first attached to 177 Field Ambulance, stationed in Hull, Plymouth and finally Pulborough in Sussex. After a two-week medical course in Liverpool, he was posted to 31 Field Dressing Station (FDS) back at Crookham Camp, then York and three different places in Scotland. During this time, it is interesting to note that he attended the Battle Training School at Haytor in Devon for a course lasting over four weeks. By the end of March 1944, 31FDS was based in the New Forest at Lymington. During the unit's movement to Lymington, Johnson was able to drop in on his family: 'Dropped into home for a few minutes. A spot of food and an attempt to reassure the family that I wasn't going over to France tomorrow. – at least that was as far as I know.'[24] Arriving at their destination after dark, the unit spent some time bumping into trees and falling down holes while getting organized! Evidently, they were in adequate, but cramped, tented living accommodation, located in what Johnson describes as a beautiful pine forest, with the camp organized by the RAF.

One of the very important tasks to be carried out by a small unit attached to 50th Division on D-Day was the capture of the small port of Port-en-Bessin by the 420 men of 47(RM) Commando. The point of capturing Port-en-Bessin was that it was intended to be the coastal junction between British forces landing on Gold Beach and US forces landing on Omaha Beach, and it was an important small harbour. Most importantly, it had been identified as the place where fuel would be pumped ashore to supply the armies before the hoped-for capture of Cherbourg, when pipelines (PLUTO) would be laid direct to Cherbourg from the Isle of Wight. Landing at Le Hamel two hours after the main assault, it was expected that 47 Commando would march via Ryes to La Rosiere – both of which, it was anticipated, would be captured by this time – and advance further west through German-held territory, avoiding the Longues battery (a D-Day target for 2 Devons). Using Point 72 (Mont Cavalier) north of the port as a firm base, an attack would be launched to capture Port-en-Bessin from the south after a 12-mile march from the point of landing on Jig Green. This tactic for capturing the town had been decided upon, rather than a frontal assault from the sea, because, in a similar way to Arromanches, but on a larger scale, Port-en-Bessin lay in a fold in the coastal cliffs, and heights rising to either side meant that the German defences totally dominated the seaward approaches, harbour and town beneath. These dominant heights, on what was termed in British plans the Eastern and Western Features, rose to over 50 metres on the Eastern Feature and over 60 metres on the Western Feature. As well as this, both features and the port installation were heavily defended. On the Western Feature was situated WN57, the port area was defended by WN56, and the Eastern Feature was defended by Stutzpunkt Port-en-Bessin. The entrance to the town was defended by WN58, standing above the approach road further back of the Western Feature. On the face of it, this scheme seemed unlikely to succeed; the two things that gave it a very good chance of success were the extreme fitness and will of the Royal Marines in 47 Commando and the very heavy artillery, naval and air support expected to be controlled from the ground.

However, considering the above task, less than a year earlier, 47(RM) Commando had not been in existence. As related in an earlier chapter, Commando Units had been formed through the enthusiasm of Churchill from 1940. However, it is not always realized that these Commandos were army units. It was later in the war that Commando units were raised from Royal Marine battalions. Numbers 40 and 41(RM) Commandos took part in the invasions of Sicily and Italy; it was the onset of the 'Second Front' that galvanized the raising of further units from the Marine Corps. Coming out of 10th Battalion Royal Marines, 47 (RM) Commando only began to be formed in 1943 at Dorchester.

Ted Battley[25] volunteered to join the Royal Marines in 1941. Training at Chatham to begin with, he moved to the Exmouth, Devon, area for further training, but quite often was involved in helping with farming work.[26] His take on morale in 10th Battalion is that it was not high, due to the type of work they were involved with. However, all this changed in August 1943, when the 10th Battalion formally became 47(RM) Commando. Its new commander was Lt Col. Philips. He was known as a strict disciplinarian. The whole unit moved to Dumfries and Galloway in Scotland to commence the tough commando training. All ranks had to pass Commando Basic Training, held at Achnacarry in the Highlands near Spean Bridge,[27] and gain the right to wear the coveted green beret, and 47(RM) Commando were slated for their trials during the month of December. There was a standard syllabus, with an accent on fitness and speed marching, and a high priority on weapons skills, using British, Allied and captured German weapons. Many of those in the unit were not to succeed in completing this training phase, in which a standard of 'Commando fitness' had to be reached, and hence 10th Battalion RM was reduced to a Commando establishment figure of 420 men.

Much of the training during the six-week course at Achnacarry was very hard, especially as 47(RM) Commando were there during the harsh Scottish winter. Some reminiscences of Ted Battley point this out, plus the guile of a typical British serviceman:

> We had to undertake various sorts of training, for example they sent us out on initiative training to get from A to B with no more than sixpence in your pocket.

Some got round that by sewing extra cash in their battledress. The weather was so bad we put up in a wood one night and it constantly rained and we were absolutely soaked. I remember breakfast was supposed to be dried scrambled egg, but by the time we had finished it was scrambled egg soup! We hitched a ride on a post van to our next destination.

Typical of the type of situation that assault troops found themselves in while practising landings is this memoir from Battley – again from Achnacarry:

It was Christmas Eve 1943. The Commando were practising a night landing on a steep, stony beach on a pitch-black, freezing night. A motley collection of craft was being used including RN lifeboats and the ubiquitous Dory – her with her nose in the air. To jump off her bow meant going into free-fall. The drill on B Troop's Dory was that the Bren team, Roy Emsley and myself, hop off first, tear up the beach to the high ground and give covering fire to the hoi polloi behind. Simple. Like blind men wearing sun-glasses we are perched on the bows. Suddenly the boat grinds on the bottom and almost stops. We both take a flying leap and sink out of our depth into eight foot of turbulent water. I force my way forward, find my footing and lope like a half-drowned hare up the beach until I realise that I'm alone. Turning back to look for Roy, I find him emerging from the sea minus the Bren gun. The boat had hit a reef and then over-ridden it and in the process had hit Roy in the back making him drop the weapon. – Despair! Never mind, it's Christmas tomorrow and we might get a beer and a fag before the Court Martial.

In the morning, half a dozen volunteers and we two 'irresponsibles' formed a swimming party to search for the missing gun with orders not to come back without it. It took half an hour floundering about in freezing conditions before the final successful dive. I was so cold; I couldn't bear walking on the pebbled beach. I literally crawled back to the transport.

After drying off and getting dressed, our spirits were given a huge boost by being invited to that Holy of Holies, the Officers' Mess where, plied with tots of whisky, our Christmas celebrations began. [28]

After Achnacarry, 47(RM) Commando went to the Ardnamurchan Peninsula for live-fire exercises. In March 1944, the Commando moved down south to Herne Bay, Kent, until nearly the end of May. It was allocated the landing ship *Princess Josephine Charlotte*, an ex-cross-Channel ferry, and the men carried out a number of exercises with it, getting used to trans-shipping into the LCAs carried on deck.

Jim Madden was also a commando, but with a very different task to perform on Gold Beach. Madden was called up on 11 November 1942. His father had been a soldier, and his two brothers were soldiers, but Jim wanted to join the Royal Navy, and asked for this at his initial interview. His journey, from Newcastle via Birmingham, Bristol and Exeter to Plymouth, was something to remember. Just a sandwich and a pack of playing cards for company in a very full train full of men the same age. Travelling round the coastal railway at Starcross and Dawlish, he marvelled at the beauty of the scenery – 'nothing to do with war!' Arrival at Plymouth showed a bombed-out city and barracks in the St Budeaux part of the city; meeting new people from all parts of the country, and the issuing of all kit – including hammocks. He remained in training in Plymouth for six months, learning all about how to dress and act as a naval rating and all about his new 'trade' of signalling. He had to learn signalling using Morse Code and by using flags. 'We didn't go into pubs that much. We made up our own concerts of singing and comedy. Things like learning to row in these huge cutters, and swimming was a disaster, but climbing ropes in the gym came easily. I made some very good friends and became class captain.'

He was drafted to HMS *Renown*, a large battlecruiser at Rosyth dockyard. On a ship of this size, the whole mess deck was for signalmen. He learnt that he was already marked out for a commission, and he was sent for quite soon and was allowed to spend a few days in each working part of the ship. He was sent to HMS *King Alfred*, a shore training establishment for officers in Hove, Sussex. After another long, tiring and interesting journey to Brighton, James felt slightly lonelier now, as he had left his friends behind. At *King Alfred*, he did many tests and had an interview with a board of officers. The result was that he had to return to Plymouth to learn some further aspects of naval life, but after a short time he was back at *King Alfred* as a potential officer with all 'quality boys', a very different class of person and different expectations of how you would behave. Each group had an old chief petty officer to advise and keep an eye on them. 'You run everywhere, and take turns to be in charge of the parade. Then you had to go to Lancing College' (still a well-known public school; then, of course, the boys had been evacuated, and the Navy used it as part of HMS *King Alfred*). Eventually, passing out in January 1944, he was sent to Hayling Island, learning more about signals, including radar, and hearing whispers of strange frightening things like Combined Operations and Pilotage Parties.

The outcome was that he was drafted as a signals officer in Combined Operations to Dundonald in Scotland, near Troon.

> Two of us as officers had a Beach Signals Section in charge of a group of signallers and coders. You had to learn how to land on a foreign shore (the Isle of Arran). Our training was different, some was very physical using trees they had cut down to throw to each other and run with. Oddly one part of the training included sailing in darkness in a landing craft around the island of Ailsa Craig. Suddenly it was May 21st and it was time to go to Southampton to HMS Squid – when I got there it was just an office! And we moved to Beaulieu area under canvas with many sorts of odd parties like ours. I knew something was going to happen, but we had no idea what. We saw no maps, the whole world was Khaki, tanks, armoured cars, lorries hidden under the trees. Out to sea all you could see were ships at anchor and thought we could walk across them to the Isle of Wight. June 1st you have got to go, everybody's going, but we are not going together. I have to take my lot. We end up on an LSI Empire Arquebus with the LCAs on the side. We opened an envelope of information there telling us what we were to do. We were given bigger maps but also an escape kit of silk maps, French money etc. By the night of 5th June you knew it was on.

Officers and men of 56th (Infantry) Brigade went through similar experiences, although only landing 'under command' of 50th Infantry Division and expected to complete the task of capturing Bayeux by the end of D-Day, at which time it was planned that at least part of the brigade would operate with 7th Armoured Division/8th Armoured Brigade. But, as will be seen, post-D-Day events meant that they more or less stayed with 50th Division until August 1944, when they were transferred to 59th Infantry Division, and later to 49th Infantry Division. Although not an experienced brigade like the other three brigades in 50th Division, nevertheless 56th (Independent) Infantry Brigade was as effective in action as the other brigades, and was made up of three 'regular' army battalions. Because of this historical link, many were already proud of the traditions carried in from their parent regiment. B Company, 2nd South Wales Borderers, in particular, was still 'Rorkes Drift Company', and the singing from this, the only Welsh battalion of infantry to land on D-Day, was well remembered – particularly the singing by the battalion from the decks of the LCI (L) in Southampton Docks the evening before sailing for D-Day.

The brigade carried out training at Inverary in late March 1944. However, none of its motorized units or support companies appears to have had any proper practice at 'wet' landings. On the subsequent practice landings at Studland Bay, and then on Hayling Island, any 56th Brigade vehicles were fed in 'dryshod', that is, formed up and inserted from the land. This author assumes that this had something to do with the extensive waterproofing of all vehicles required before a landing, and the time and cost this would have required. Also, at this point, 56th Brigade drivers had not been trained in waterproofing their vehicles. Landing at either Studland or Fabius seems not to have involved any real tactical practice. Advances took place as per orders, and both exercises seem to have been straightforward landing rehearsals, apart from the unfortunate drowning of 2nd Essex D Company HQ members during Exercise Fabius. Also, it should be noted that in March 1944, all three battalions were short of men, especially 2nd South Wales Borderers and 2nd Essex. Neither of these battalions was up to strength until days prior to embarkation, 2SWB in particular, being short of a company of infantry. Also, it appears from War Diary excerpts that psychological testing of units was carried out, and a number of men were removed as being not fit for overseas service through age or temperament, adding to the need for reinforcements. This was the inevitable consequence of using these units as reinforcement and Home Service units between 1940 and 1944. The difference here, perhaps, was the exacerbation of the situation by the very short time frame available.

Nor was a great deal of time available from the formation of the brigade for tactical training, and, again, the situation of the brigade, being formed in Essex, gave it little or no opportunity to practise its likely role once in Normandy. In the War Diaries of all the infantry divisions across 50th Division, there is evidence of liaison work that took place between, for example, infantry and armour. These were often short officer exchange visits between the infantry and armoured units, but did occasionally involve exchanging small units of men. Overall, though, it must be said that a full awareness and expertise of infantry/tank co-operation was not developed enough for the forthcoming invasion, and it was not until after the Normandy Campaign that the two arms worked in complete concert. While, of course, many men in the normal 50th Division battalions would have seen more than enough of warfare, Major General Graham does report that 50 per cent of the men in his division joined in the United

Kingdom after the return from service abroad, and, as related above, for many this would be their first time in action, begging the question about Montgomery's decision to put in an experienced infantry assault division.

The period spent at assembly areas in the New Forest was not enjoyed by many: a period of waiting, and the weather was variable. However, for all the officers and men, valuable time was spent looking at models and photographs of the landing areas. As reported by Brigadier Hargest, 1,000 men from 50th Division apparently went absent without leave (AWOL) during the time in the New Forest. Most returned voluntarily, and a number were brought back under arrest. In this respect, 56th Brigade seems to have had its fair share of deserters, though most made their way back voluntarily, and for many it was just to go and have a drink in a pub. The fears by senior officers of invasion secrets and marshalling details getting out was certainly the reason for the high security, but in the minds of the ordinary men, the need to see their families or even just get out for a drink was the simple over-riding reason explained to this author by a number of interviewees.[29]

One new member of the signals unit, who was clearly a veteran at 56th Brigade HQ, notes the organizational work needed to be done, and also gives a very good indication of what life in the camps was like leading up to embarkation in a letter home:

> As you know we had the misfortune to join a new Brigade some months ago which was scheduled for a useful part in the opening phases. We did not know this until two or three days before D-Day. Being new we had a great deal of spadework to do, a lot of 'detail' work, documentation and so on. We started from nothing. For me it was like 1939 all over again.
>
> New Forest … every day merged into the next. Time was not a factor of significance and work often went on into the night. We are lucky to have a very well-run camp, run on common sense lines and lucky also to include among those organising, some Yanks. Thanks to these latter we had our own cinema in a marquee, big enough to hold about 300 or more and a recreation tent which supplied books, magazines sports gear and generally a singsong round the piano every evening led by a Yankee sergeant. The daily paper was 'Stars and Stripes' and every week there was a mad rush on 'Yank'. We were briefed on maps, photographs, seats provided, the centrepiece a large-scale model in relief of the sea and coast of the spot to be invaded. Maps and models had fictionalised names on them. This area itself was in barbed wire guarded by sentries.[30]

Death was also present in the concentration areas. Three of the twenty-five Commonwealth War Grave Commission graves in St John (Boldre) churchyard visited by the author date from May 1944, pointing to fatal accidents that happened to men waiting to embark. One can surmise that there may have been more, but these will have been buried in their home-town cemetery, as, for example, were the men drowned on Exercise Fabius.[31]

Preparing for Gold Beach: Britain
November 1943–May 1944

The British forces that landed in Normandy on 6 June 1944 mainly comprised of men who had not fought before, and many who had not fought since 1940. Tasked with landing on Gold Beach, 50th Division was one of only four 'experienced' divisions that had been brought back from the Mediterranean to take part in the landings.[1] But all four of these divisions had to be brought up to effective strength once back in the United Kingdom, and integrate and prepare their inexperienced reinforcements for war.

Fighting across the world, the British Army by 1944 was a very large and complex organization of Regular Army, Territorial Army and conscripted soldiers. Much had changed since 1939, when a small Regular and Territorial Army had gone to France. Training had been greatly modernized. What Montgomery had brought to the army in Southern England after Dunkirk, and then the Eighth Army in the Western Desert from 1942, was a concentration on what it could do well. Later, for the North West Europe Campaign, it is less clear that time and opportunity prevailed before D-Day for Montgomery to inculcate the ideas he had developed in the desert from 1942 and in Italy by the end of 1943 into a very large army preparing for the invasion of Europe. A criticism often levelled at Montgomery was the slow and overwhelming build-up he required before committing to the attack. But he had to operate with limited manpower, and if he had to blast his way ashore and through Normandy to keep his casualties to a minimum, he probably had the most effective artillery of any army, an arm that he believed in implicitly, and his friend and mentor Brooke was also a 'gunner' with an outstanding reputation as a planner. A report by Montgomery on 4th Division, written in July 1940, commented that the Divisional HQ did not 'understand the power of artillery as a battle winning factor'.[2] It has been noted that 'the key to British success from Alam Halfa onwards was that they had discovered how to employ the weapons they possessed in such a way as to exploit opponents' weaknesses'.[3] Montgomery was the general who made this happen in practice.

A fear of casualties and lack of reinforcements was in Montgomery's mind in the lead-up to the assault, when he wrote on 19 March 1944 to the Deputy CIGS Ronald Weeks: 'The situation re reinforcements is not good, as you say. But we must take things as they are and find the best answer. I cannot *now* give you back 56 Inf. Bde; it is in my order of battle, has been given an important task, and has begun planning.'[4] Weeks had asked to use 56th Brigade as some sort of reinforcement unit rather than on D-Day itself. The letter later goes into detail, clearly appreciating that manpower in the infantry was a critical factor.

By 1944, all units were expected to undertake rigorous training, including the use of live ammunition, even though this could produce casualties. This was not always welcomed by the experienced troops newly returned to the United Kingdom. 'He gave them no respite; formations like 50 Division, with years of battle experience, put in long, hard days of training alongside divisions which had not been overseas.'[5] Of course, the very units that had remained in the United Kingdom would point out the strenuous training that they had been carrying out, sometimes over several years. What 50th Division did not take account of, and nor was it pointed out to them, was that this new enterprise would be different. The rolling sand hills and scrub of the desert, the Sicilian and Italian mountains and garigue, were to be replaced by the bocage, orchards and wheat fields of Normandy. They knew their enemy was implacable, but perhaps did not quite realize how their enemy would behave with their backs to the wall.

Obviously, men and their officers had to be militarily fit, mentally fit and physically fit, and the Montgomery way of achieving this was not new. In October 1940, Montgomery had instituted weekly cross-country runs for the personnel of his 5th Corps HQ under the age of forty. For a time, until he was persuaded otherwise, Montgomery, in his fifties, undertook this regime. Commanders of lower units had to follow suit. When he took over 21st Army Group in 1944, he made sure that more elderly battalion commanders and other officers about to take part in Overlord were transferred, a practice he had been following for some time and that can be traced back at least to when he was commander of 5th Corps in 1940 in Southern England. One company commander from 2nd Essex, a battalion in training for landing on Gold Beach, remarked on the transfer of their battalion commander – an event in February 1944 that shocked many in the battalion:

> Bill Marriott was, I suppose, old enough to be the father of some of us. This was a positive 'beneficial factor' at that time. He was excellent at administration and training and did a very necessary job in educating his young officers and in maintaining the morale of the battalion during three years of uncertainty. He delivered the battalion to John Higson in a very good state ready to undertake the additional and more arduous training necessary for war.[6]

The 1st Dorsets also lost their battalion commander, Lt Col. Ray, on 18 March, replaced by Lt Col. Norie; Lt Col. Valentine of 2nd Devons had already been replaced by Lt Col. Nevill. 'This was a result of the Commander-in-Chief's ruling that commanding officers for the coming operations had to be around thirty five years of age or under.'[7] It is of interest how closely to the actual event these important replacements happened. The reader might like to reflect on the number of important events and changes that took place close in time to D-Day, considering the size and complexity of the operation. This shows to some extent that the Allied military machine at all levels was adaptable and able to cope with change.

Two memoirs from veterans make some telling points about training, army life and Britain in 1944, the difficulties faced by units training for Normandy, and possibly the mentality within 50th Division at the time. Michael Holdsworth, a major commanding a company with 2nd Devons, was an experienced officer who had trained at Sandhurst prior to the war. He recalls the following account:

> We came back to England and went to near Braintree in Essex. No battle training or live firing areas nearby. We went to the East Coast for a few days training. But you need more than a day to learn about street fighting for example. The training had little value for us. Again no field firing opportunities were available. Very little training for war took place. Also having fought in the more open Mediterranean country we were not really briefed about the type of country – the Bocage – we would fight in. I can only assume that it was thought that as we had been in Sicily and Italy we knew all about it. The new recruits were expected to follow the example of the veterans. It has always struck me how much training was needed for battle, and yet we did very little back in England.[8]

Neville Howard had enlisted in the Royal Artillery in 1937 as a boy soldier, and joined 73rd Anti-Tank Regiment RA in 1941. He had served in the Mediterranean, and returned home from Sicily in late 1943. His unit ended up in Felixstowe. Receiving the good news that, despite some minor offences in the desert, he now had a clean sheet, he and the rest of the unit went on leave, proudly displaying the medal ribbon of the Africa Star medal. Feted at home for returning safely for Christmas (his elder brother had been killed in the desert), and bringing with him the welcome gift of a pound of almond nuts from Sicily, unavailable through the ration system, he spent a typical family Christmas. 'I returned to Felixstowe where, because we had no guns or equipment, the next few weeks were spent idling the time away as best we could.'[9]

By early 1944, an infantry division generally comprised three brigades of infantry. Each brigade had three battalions, with around 850 men in each battalion. A brigade HQ had around 250 officers and men. Each standard infantry battalion had four infantry companies, ABCD, of 120 men, plus a support company of 250 men who mainly used Bren carriers to transport and operate a platoon of extra Bren guns as fire support, a platoon of six 6 lb anti-tank guns, a platoon of six 3 inch mortars and a pioneer platoon for mine clearance and later even flame-throwing from converted Bren carriers known as 'Wasps'. In total, each battalion had battalion transport of thirty-eight carriers, fifty-five cars (usually jeeps), trucks and lorries. There was a smaller HQ company. Each company and platoon was organized through a small company or platoon HQ. All companies were commanded by officers of captain rank, although by D-Day the infantry companies were led by majors. Each infantry company had three platoons. The company commander had a signaller with a man-packed thirty-eight set, and each platoon commander had a thirty-eight set. Each platoon had a Bren gun carrier attached to it for carrying extra equipment such as greatcoats and ammunition. The platoon commander was a 2nd lieutenant or lieutenant, and had a signaller from his platoon with the thirty-eight set and a batman. The batman or another soldier acted as a runner for the platoon commander. This was a very important role, as wireless signals were often very poor and unreliable.

The platoon HQ sergeant ensured there was enough ammunition, and he also held back men with a 2 inch mortar, generally at this time only using smoke bombs, as the high explosive (HE) they fired was not considered to carry much of a punch. Each platoon was divided into three sections of ten men, with a junior NCO in charge of each section. In each section, two men also operated a Bren gun. The Bren gun was a very good light machine gun. With an effective range of over 600 yards and a maximum range of 2,000 yards, its rate of fire was 500 rounds a minute, with the bullets held in a 30-round curved box magazine. No. 2 on the Bren carried a spares 'wallet' and cleaning kit, including a spare barrel. It was a very accurate, robust and popular weapon, and accounts exist of it being used in virtually a sniping role on odd occasions in Normandy. The two men operating the Bren gun formed the 'gun group', while the rest of the riflemen formed the 'rifle group' within a platoon. The rifle group might further be split into two for rapid fire and manoeuvre. The standard rifle in British Army use was the 'Rifle No. 4 Mk 1' with a spike bayonet. This was an accurate weapon with a ten-round box magazine. Its drawback was that it had a bolt action and was not semi-automatic, giving a slower rate of fire. The spike or so-called 'pigsticker' bayonet does not really seem to have found favour with the troops, but it was a functional, if basic, weapon. In jest, soldiers would say that it was useful for piercing holes in tins! In its intended use, it was, of course, capable of inflicting mortal wounds. The US Army had adopted the Garand semi-automatic rifle from 1937, but, despite some interest in semi-automatic rifles as early as towards the end of the First World War, the British maintained the tried, tested and reliable bolt-action Lee Enfield line. Again, an effective range of over 500 yards was achieved, with a maximum range over 3,000 yards. Battalion snipers were equipped with an adapted No. 4 Mk 1 with telescopic sight chosen from rifles proven to be particularly accurate at manufacturer testing. The Bren gun and No. 4 Mk 1 rifle both fired a .303 inch bullet. NCOs and officers were issued with the Sten sub-machine gun. Handy and easy to use, it was equally cheap and could easily produce an accidental discharge. It had a straight box 32-round magazine attached to the side of the weapon. It used a 9 mm bullet with an effective range of just over 100 yards. Some officers and NCOs 'exchanged' their Sten guns for the similar, but better-built, German MP 40 once in Normandy. Officers and NCOs also carried the No. 2 Mk1** .38 revolver. With six rounds, this was a robust weapon, but only really useful at close range. It was not always carried. The fairly new PIAT was issued officially, one to each platoon. Designed in 1942, this man-portable anti-tank weapon fired a 2.5 lb bomb around 100 yards. Spring operated, it required a great deal of strength to cock. First used in Sicily, it was relatively effective and inexpensive. One great advantage was that, being smokeless, its use did not give your position away. The PIAT used hollow charge rounds for increased penetration. Trials carried out before D-Day showed that even an experienced operator missed 40 per cent of shots, and the bomb only detonated 75 per cent of the time due to faulty detonators. However, 7 per cent of the German tanks destroyed in the Normandy Campaign were attributed to PIATs.[10]

The numbers of men given above could vary a lot within the various levels of unit once in action, because casualties caused units to rapidly shrink in size.[11] A battalion attack across open ground was often organized using two companies up front, with a supporting company behind and one company kept in reserve. Similarly, within a company, an advance was made with two platoons forward and one behind. The small company HQ advanced in the centre between forward and rear companies, and the platoon HQ advanced similarly. Attacking built-up areas, or advancing along a single linear feature, such as a road, required a different tactical deployment of companies and platoons, all outlined in 'Infantry Training Part VIII. Fieldcraft, Battle Drill, Section and Platoon Tactics' issued by the War Office in March 1944. Consider the date. 'The Co-Operation of Tanks with Infantry Divisions. Military Training Pamphlet No. 63' was issued only a few weeks before the invasion in May 1944. In the packed and strenuous training period allotted before D-Day, one wonders how well the details of these booklets could be properly understood by senior and junior officers, NCOs and men, and be implemented into the training schedule.

Montgomery writes about how he would 'get round to see his troops that were to be involved in Overlord'. He had a special train called *Rapier* at his disposal to travel around the country. In his *Memoirs*, Montgomery claims to have visited every formation in the United Kingdom by the middle of May 1944. This is not so, and, although he certainly visited many units, both British and US, he was not able to visit them all. His technique was to inspect two or three parades a day of up to 10,000 men at a time, with the men drawn up on three sides of a hollow square. The men would be 'stood easy' as Montgomery walked among them so that each could 'inspect' the other. Montgomery would then stand on the bonnet of his jeep and talk to the men about what lay ahead.[12] Typically, he would tell them that he had absolute confidence in them, everything was organized, they would have terrific back-up and knock the Germans for six.

It is interesting to note that the experienced units that had already served under him were not always compliant or complementary. Two good examples follow, one anecdotal, the other written soon after the war, while Montgomery still held high military office. A third will be reported afterwards, and make reference to the more serious problem of soldiers going AWOL. What is interesting is that the dissent is delivered by relatively large bodies of men, whom little could be done about.

Michael Holdsworth, 2nd Devons, recounts the following:

> We were visited by Eisenhower and when he left he got a tremendous reception, as did the King when he visited us in Essex. But when Monty turned up he stood on his jeep and told us to close up for a talk, and when he left the RSM called for three cheers, but Montgomery was booed by enough men to make themselves heard![13]

As a more senior officer in the battalion, Holdsworth probably had enough to think about, but an extra worry was that, against his advice to his CO, his twin brother David had wangled his way into the battalion as a platoon commander. 'I had joined the Army in 1938, he the Police and I did not believe that it was good for close relatives to be in the same battalion. However, when we reached the Beaulieu camp area his wife had arrived before us and rented a property because she had already worked out where we were likely to be!'[14]

On 15 February, Montgomery inspected the whole of the Durham Light Infantry 151st Brigade on Haverhill football ground, and then gathered the men around him.

After praising the work of 50th Division and 151st Brigade, he informed them that he had decided to give 50th Division a prominent role in the projected invasion of Europe.

> To those who had recently had a glorious reunion with their families this statement was received with no great enthusiasm. Many of the men, well aware of the fact that there were in England several divisions which had never been in action, saw no reason why 50 Division should lead the assault against Hitler's Atlantic Wall.[15]

Later, in 50th Division camps established in the New Forest, despite high security, there appear to have been a large number of men absenting themselves, effectively deserting. Most had the intention of returning, but, realizing that they would soon be involved in an invasion again and stood a chance of being killed, only wished to return home, possibly put things in order, and see their families, perhaps for one last time. Many of the men did return to the New Forest, some under their own steam and some via the military police. Few saw the inside of a cell for long, and often served out any sentence while taking part in the invasion! Brigadier Hargest, a New Zealand observer with 50th Division, recounts:

> In England (before D-Day) there was a lot of resentment by 50 Div about being asked to do the assault on D-Day. 69 Bde call Monty 'fling 'em in Monty!' The numbers of men going Absent Without Leave (AWOL) in the New Forest amounted to well over 1,000.[16]

One very important 50th Division member to arrive in January 1944 was the new divisional commander, Major General Douglas Alexander Graham MC. He already had a distinguished record, being a commissioned officer with the Cameronians before 1914; he had reached the rank of captain by 1916, and was a brigade major less than a year later. By the end of the First World War, he had been wounded, twice mentioned in dispatches and awarded an MC. He graduated from Camberley Staff College in 1925, and by 1939 had commanded a battalion in Palestine. He played an important role in the Desert Campaign, and was further awarded a Distinguished Service Order, and later a Bar to his DSO. Continuing to Italy, where he was wounded, he had completed his recovery in the United Kingdom before being appointed to command 50th Division. Reported as an 'old war horse never far from the scene of battle' and with strong religious convictions, he was much appreciated by Montgomery. After Graham had damaged his knee in October 1944, Montgomery wrote: 'I am sending him UK 23rd by air for treatment after which I am anxious he should have a rest. He is a most valuable and experienced divisional commander and we need him in army when he is fit again.'[17]

Graham took over the division at Bury St Edmunds on 19 January 1944, still under the impression that it would be one of the 'follow-up' divisions.

> It was not long however before we were warned that we would be the assault division of 30 Corps. This meant a complete alteration in the training on hand and that a great deal would have to be done in organising and carrying out the specialised training necessary for an assault. We were in a most unsuitable part of the country for combined-ops training.[18]

The change of orders gave Graham new problems and decisions to make. It left very little time to reorganize and train the battalions in their new task, with only sixteen weeks left before the invasion. But Graham was a man up to the task that faced him. He was clearly quite tough, as well as organizationally capable; one of his company commanders commented: 'General Graham had his wits about him and an interest in what was going on.'[19]

Graham believed the division needed experience with some of the new and secret specialized armour that would be used by 79th Division, and that 50th Division still required more training in combined operations. This was partly because he foresaw that the assault in Normandy would require different landing techniques by the assault battalions than those practised before, and also because around 50 per cent of his assault troops were new replacement recruits to the assault battalions. He felt, as well, that his units needed to carry out further training with the Royal Navy and the RAF. Graham points out that, while all this was going on, his staff still had to continue planning in London. Added to the naval problems of Force G, outlined in chapter 'Revised Plans, Neptune, Force G and K, and Airpower', these aspects neatly outline the extra problems faced by all in having to prepare to land and exploit the landing on Gold Beach. An obvious point is that, if each of the 50th Division battalions was 50 per cent short of manpower, to be filled mainly by new recruits, Montgomery's reasoning for having an experienced division as the assault division was flawed. A further important point about the divisions brought back from Mediterranean service was the large numbers of men who suffered from recurring bouts of malaria. The problem of officers and men falling sick through this disease was to dog 50th Division and the other experienced divisions from their return to the United Kingdom and throughout the Normandy Campaign.

We will never, of course, know whether 49th Division, already starting to organize for the assault, would have been as efficient and successful as 50th Division. What we do know of 49th Division is that, once ashore, they certainly carried out their tasks in Normandy, Belgium and Holland in an exemplary fashion, sometimes having to face and win through against the fiercest of German units.

General Graham sent each brigade in turn to the Southwold training area for up to two weeks to see and train with the new mysterious AVRE from 79th Armoured Division that would be used to overcome the obstacles, bunkers and pillboxes on and just off the beaches.[20] This armoured division had been built as a highly specialized division under the command of General Percy Hobart, often known as 'Hobo', the brother-in-law of Montgomery. Seeing action in the First World War on the Western Front, and then in what was then called Persia with the Royal Engineers, Hobart had gained experience and insight into air warfare and armoured cars. An adherent and friend of Liddell-Hart, a military theorist who strongly influenced armoured warfare, Hobart realized after the First World War the potential of the tank, and in 1923, he transferred to the Tank Corps. Hobart was responsible for a number of changes in tank warfare, including the introduction of radios. By 1930, he was a brigadier in charge of the 1st Tank Brigade, and was promoting tactics similar to the later German Blitzkrieg tactics. However, as a visionary and forceful commander believing in the tank against the pre-Second World War cavalrymen, he made many enemies. Despite gaining the rank of general and building 7th Armoured Division in Egypt, by the beginning of the Second World War he was retired aged fifty-five. Back in Britain, Hobart became a corporal in the Home Guard, but Liddell-Hart, among others, campaigned for his reinstatement. It was no less an authority than Churchill who forced the issue and had him given back a command, this time raising and training to an excellent level 11th Armoured Division. Again, using age and illness as an excuse, Hobart was not allowed to serve actively with his new division, and this time, the intervention of Churchill was to no avail.

However, in the long run, this proved to be to the advantage of the British Army. In October 1942, Hobart was given command of building the new 79th Armoured Division. By March 1943, CIGS Brooke had had a brainwave about the use to which 79th Division might ultimately be put, as a specialized armoured unit in the invasion of Europe: '11th March 1943, In afternoon had a long interview with Hobart to explain to him a new job I wish him to take on connected with flotation tanks, searchlight tanks, anti-mine tanks and self-propelled guns' and '1 April 1943, Then Hobart on questions of organisation of his division to handle various specialized forms of armoured vehicles such as amphibious tanks, search light tanks, mine destroying tanks, flame throwers etc.'[21] What became known as 'Hobart's Funnies' were to precede the infantry on landing and set about destroying minefields, pillboxes and other German defensive positions. These 'funnies' were adapted from the basic Churchill and Sherman tanks.

Although slower than the Sherman, and designed under an obsolete doctrine of having 'infantry' tanks as close support for ground troops, the Churchill tank was more heavily armoured than the Sherman. As adapted, these became AVREs. The most important adaption was the removal of a main gun and replacement by a 29 cm Petard spigot mortar. This fired a 40 lb bomb, 29 lb of which was the explosive charge. It had a range of 80–100 yards, and had to be reloaded by a crew member leaving the protection of the tank via a sliding hatch. However, the bombs it fired – nicknamed 'flying dustbins' due to their shape – were capable of demolishing the concrete shelters and protective concrete walls that the Germans were busy installing on the Atlantic coast. Thus armed, these tanks were further adapted to achieve secondary goals apart from demolition. These Churchill AVREs carried a crew of six, including a trained demolition NCO. As well as their armament of Petard mortar and machine guns, they carried a number of 'General Wade charges'. These were arched linear charges that gave a cutting and pressure effect. Such charges could be passed fairly easily through the Churchill tank side hatches, and the demolitions NCO in each tank could dismount and lead on foot, or advise the placing of such charges.

AVREs were further adapted for specific tasks. The 'Bobbin' could unroll a length of track material wound round a drum and suspended from two arms. This was made of canvas and tubular steel, and was 225–350 feet long. This laid a roadway over soft sand or clay, and was deemed vital on Gold Beach, where some areas of soft clay had been identified when Royal Navy frogmen had reconnoitred the beach in December 1943. To help with this problem, another method specifically for Gold Beach was to have a steel bobbin attached in the front of an LCT, to be pushed out on landing and rolled forward. The 'SBG', or small box girder, bridge, Class 40, was 34 feet long and could support 40 tonnes. This was attached to the front of some AVREs, and could be laid onto a sea wall to provide access or bridge anti-tank ditches. On Gold Beach, there was a significant anti-tank ditch in front of the Mont Fleury battery and around part of Asnelles, as well as many other ditches across the landing area. In a throwback to the First World War, some AVREs carried a 'fascine' on the front. This consisted of a 4 tonne bundle of chestnut paling (sometimes noted as 'chespal' in orders), 8 feet in diameter and 12 feet wide, which could be dumped in anti-tank ditches or craters to fill them in. For the landing, AVREs had their exhaust extended upwards to allow a certain wading capability.

It was 79th Division that proceeded with the testing and development of the duplex drive (DD) 'floating' tanks. After experimentation using the Valentine tank, this method was deployed using the Sherman tank, provided with a canvas collapsible flotation screen raised around the tank, and a pair of propellers powered by the tank engine. Ashore, the screen was collapsed and the propeller disengaged, allowing the tank to engage the enemy as normal. Its advantage was that it approached the shore as a very small target, and would emerge from the sea ready to fight. The D-Day plan was that these would be launched from LCT while up to 2 miles from the shore. Their effective speed in the water in good conditions was 3–4 mph, with about a yard of freeboard at the top of the screen. Rough seas could severely hamper them, as in the incident during Exercise Smash in April 1944, when several Valentine tanks were lost and sank in training. On D-Day, these tanks were to arrive first on the beaches and suppress the immediate enemy gunfire, allowing engineers to get on with their tasks of removing obstacles and mines, while the infantry and further tanks carried in landing craft arrived. As important as the DD tanks and the AVREs was the flail or 'crab' tank. This was an adapted Sherman tank. Two arms projected from the tank, carrying a rotating drum with fifty chains attached, which, when engaged, flogged or flailed the ground ahead, exploding mines. When not flailing, the tank was able to use its 75 mm gun. Exploding mines destroyed some chains, which had to be replaced. The ground could be flailed by up to three tanks, overlapping their flailing to produce a safe flailed width of road of 24 feet (7+ metres) at a speed of less than 2 mph. It was the projecting arms that earned these tanks the name 'crab'.

A large addition to Graham's force happened 'fairly early on in the planning stage', when 'it was clear we had not enough soldiers to make sure of success. We therefore asked for and were given a fourth Bde – 56 Bde'.[22] This brigade started operating under 50th Division from 1 March 1944, when they officially moved to set up in the Clacton area. From 50th Division message logs, we can glean the following information: On 19 February 1944, 56th Infantry Brigade was first mentioned in 50th Division message log with reference to 56th Brigade move to Inverary. On 27 February, the message log states that '56 INF BDE (2 Essex, 2 Glosters, 2 SWB) is moving from Exercise Eagle under arrangements of NORCO to Clacton move to EASTCO' and finally on 1 March, '56 BDE come under command 50 (Northumbrian) Div'.[23]

With the training on landing craft taking place at Inverary, rumours had been rife among the rank and file. Many realized that they were carded for some job in the invasion that was obviously soon to take place. Philip Maillou in S Company 2nd Essex remembers that 'we thought we were going to be a back-up mob, putting up tents and organising camps. We had done a good job on this in Wales on Exercise Jantzen'.[24]

In the end, the new brigade found out the news: 'On a cold February 1944 day, in a Durham cinema, the gathered battalion were informed by the Divisional Commander that we had the honour of being selected to take part in the invasion of Europe.'[25]

The 56th (Independent) Infantry Brigade was formed by three 'Regular' 2nd Battalions from the South Wales Borderers (2SWB), Essex and Gloucester (Glosters) Regiments. However, after service in 1940 in France (Norway in the case of 2 SWB), they had remained in the United Kingdom, and had been used as coastal defence and reinforcement battalions. In 1940, 2nd Glosters had suffered very high casualties and had been completely rebuilt; it seems to have been in a higher operational state by the end of 1943 than the other two battalions, which were not up to establishment strength and seem to have had a higher proportion of older soldiers in their ranks. Indeed, 2SWB had spent some time in East Anglia in the autumn of 1943, engaged in helping farmers lift turnips and other crops which were vital to the war effort. These units had never worked together before, and a new Brigade HQ had to be built. This was commanded by Brigadier EC Pepper.[26]

So, although the new brigade was needed for an important task, again we see that a lot had to be done in a very short space of time. This brigade only started to be formed in the last week of February around Clacton, and not only had it to be brought up to establishment level, but it had little or no experience of combined operations, and, of all the infantry brigades in 50th Division, was in sore need of this. It completely missed the opportunity of training with the AVREs of 79th Division. It will be noted that this brigade had the word 'Independent' in its title. What this meant in practice is that 56th Brigade was only 'under command' of 50th Division for the assault. It was further tasked to train with 7th Armoured Division for exploitation immediately after the landings. The XXX Corps plan was that, after the landings, at least some units from the brigade would be added to 7th Armoured Division to form a formidable force of armour and infantry, and quickly sweep south from around Bayeux, through Tilly-sur-Seulles, and capture Villers-Bocage.

A further problem of the British Army, especially in infantry battalions, was a shortage of junior officers. On 9 October 1943, Major General HFG Letson, the Canadian adjutant general, was having lunch with Sir Ronald Adam, the British adjutant general and confidant of Brooke, when Adam mentioned that 21st Army Group was desperately short of junior officers, especially for the infantry. General Letson said that he thought Canada could lend some officers to overcome this shortage. Under a scheme known as 'Canloan' and finalized in February 1944, Canadian junior officers were loaned to the British Army. Over 670 volunteered their services and underwent rigorous selection in Canada before being sent to the United Kingdom. Five hundred had arrived in the United Kingdom before D-Day. During their period of service, Canloan officers were awarded one OBE and 42 MCs, and received twenty-six 'Mentions in Dispatches', plus ten other awards from the United States, France, Belgium and Holland.[27]

As far as can be seen, twenty-five Canadian officers joined 231st Brigade, ten joined 69th Brigade, fourteen 151st Brigade and twenty-one 56th Brigade.[28] These will not all have landed on D-Day, but it does give an idea of the problem faced and the impact of this generous Canadian offer, especially when it is remembered that 800 British junior officers who trained for the RAC had been found surplus to requirements and had already received brief retraining as infantry officers from late 1943 to early 1944.

To fulfil the tasks expected of Graham, other units were attached for D-Day. Two very important attached units were the 8th Armoured Brigade, led by Brigadier Cracroft, and elements from 79th Armoured Division. The 8th Armoured Brigade comprised the Nottinghamshire Sherwood Rangers Yeomanry (SRY), who had seen extensive service in Palestine, Libya and Tunisia, and 4th/7th Dragoon Guards (4/7DG). These two units provided the DD tanks. The artillery for 8th Armoured Brigade was provided by 147th Field Regiment RA, equipped with 'Sexton' 25 lb self-propelled field guns. The battalion of infantry with this brigade was the 12th King's Royal Rifle Corps (KRRC), while 24th Lancers were to land on the second tide. The tank regiments were equipped with the M4 'Sherman' tank, which was armed with a 75 mm gun. These included DD tanks capable of 'swimming' ashore, plus some M4 'Firefly' tanks equipped with the more powerful 17 lb gun. Each regiment normally had four tanks in its HQ troop, a reconnaissance troop of eleven light 'Honey' tanks carrying only a 37 mm gun, and three 'Sabre' squadrons of tanks. Each squadron was made up of four troops of four tanks plus an HQ troop of three tanks. The fourth tank in each troop was a so-called 'Firefly' 17 lb-gun Sherman. 'Firefly' was not an official name, but is believed to have come from the large flash made upon firing the 17 lb weapon.[29] Anti-tank units were re-equipping with the 17 lb anti-tank gun, though some troops still had 6 lb anti-tank guns. The 79th Armoured Division units – whose specialized armour was nicknamed 'Hobart's Funnies' – included HQ 6th Assault Regiment (Royal Engineers) RE, 81st Assault Squadron RE, 82nd Assault Squadron RE, 149th Assault Park Squadron RE, B and C Squadrons of Westminster Dragoons RAC, and 13th and 15th Troops, C Squadron, 141st RAC. To help in the assault and bombardment of obstacles, the 1st Royal Marine Armoured Support Regiment comprising 1st Battery (A, B, C and D Troops) and 2nd Battery (E, F, G and H Troops) were added. This unit used the obsolete Centaur tank (an early version of the Cromwell tank), modified by having a 95 mm howitzer fitted. A small but very important group of men were the Royal Navy demolition teams or Landing Craft Obstacle Clearance Units (LCOCU), who were among the first to land. They had to disable or demolish the obstacles placed in the sand before they were covered by the rising tide. They were very obviously vulnerable to rifle and machine-gun fire.

All four infantry brigades in turn went to Inverary in Scotland, where they took part in extensive landing craft and assault training during February and March, as described by some of the veterans above. Exercises Smash I–IV, 4–20 April 1944, took place at Studland beach, Dorset. This beach was an ideal practice ground in a few respects. Although different in orientation, it had similar features, and was about half the size of Gold Beach. The layout of the inland roads was similar to an extent. The town of Wareham stood in as a near-perfect proxy for Bayeux. The exercises would involve a realistic 'run-in' firing live artillery rounds and use of the rocket-firing landing craft. As Studland had been previously used for live fire events, a large impressive bunker named 'Fort Henry' had been built on the clifftop by Canadian engineer troops in 1943. This allowed fairly safe observation over the beach. Dignitaries who watched Smash III on 18 April from Fort Henry included King George VI, Churchill, Eisenhower and

Montgomery. Smash I and Smash II involved brigade landings by 69th and then 231st Brigades, while III and IV included the follow-up 151st and 56th Brigades following in after 'their' assault brigade had gone in. There were worries about intervention by the Luftwaffe or Kriegsmarine E-boats, so air and naval cover was carefully employed. One disaster that did occur on Smash I was the sinking of six DD tanks, with the loss of several men: 4/7th Dragoon Guards were using Valentine tanks adapted through raised canvas skirts and a DD system to be launched into the sea from LCT and come ashore under their own power. The skirts collapsed in the prevailing weather conditions, and the tanks sank, drowning some of their crew members. A memorial commemorating the tragedy has been erected next to Fort Henry.[30] The paucity of landing craft meant that during these exercises many men entered the exercise 'dryshod', that is, fed in from the wings along the beach and not landed. Up to 400 officers on each of the four days, not required to take part in the exercises, were able to observe the landings from a roped-off area. These officers then walked forward and rejoined their units at specific map references after the landings.

As would be expected, not all went well on the Smash exercises. Oliver Perks, now nominated to be a forward observation officer (FOO), well remembers a number of incidents. By now, his unit had converted to the self-propelled 25-pounder Sexton Ram, based on the Sherman tank chassis and manufactured for the British Army in Canada. Able to carry 105 rounds of HE or smoke shells and fire up to eight shells a minute with a range of 7 miles (12 kilometres), they gave greater manoeuvrability and protection to the crews in the artillery regiments equipped with them. As a FOO, Oliver's job was to go forward with the infantry and organize artillery bombardments by radio back to the regiment:

We went down to Bournemouth to learn our trade on the new Sextons. I was sent to Rhyll to learn how to waterproof these things. Everything had to be covered in various plastics to waterproof them, including 30 spark plugs and five coils per Sexton. We then went into Wales and drove them into a special lake to check the waterproofing worked. When I got back the Regiment were in the forest near Beaulieu. We had a number of training assaults on Studland. On one occasion we were on an LCT and grounded on a 'false beach' and the pioneers who were to precede us on foot stepped off the craft and went underwater having to be pulled back on. Another live fire practice I was an observer on the beach but got away with it somehow and another time we had landed and driven into a bog and my carrier got stuck. But the tall figure of the Battery Commander appeared and I thought we were in for a hell of a bollicking, but he beamed at me and said 'hello Oliver, I wonder if you can help me, I have got my Sexton stuck!' On one of the Smash Exercises at Studland we were to go through the full run and shoot into the beach with live ammunition. There was a Motor Launch (ML) containing all the senior officers from Divisional Officer down. They were to observe from 1,000 yards offshore. All six of our LCTs formed up about 8,000 yards out and we were to fire three rounds. We got the word to fire and 24 rounds sailed off. We immediately got the word to STOP! (Cease fire). What had happened was that the Royal Navy navigator had plotted us in the wrong square and 24 rounds had fallen all around the observing ML, luckily without hurting anyone. We knew we were in the clear so we all laughed our heads off![31]

The series of Smash exercises were debriefed in Montgomery's usual way on 25 April 1944 at a conference held in the Regal Cinema in Ringwood and attended by senior officers. No doubt the problems of organization on the beach were discussed, including the problems of congestion of armour and vehicles when the strip of landing beach narrowed as the tide rose. Certainly, the lack of landing craft was being felt. We do not appear to have the results of this conference, as Montgomery ordered all papers burnt at the conference's end. One can only wonder why this was necessary.

The final full-scale exercise was named 'Fabius'.[32] This exercise took place between 30 April and 4 May, and was a practice landing for many of the elements for D-Day. The three British practice landing areas for Fabius were around Littlehampton for the 3rd Infantry Division, whose task was to land in Normandy on the most easterly beach around Ouistreham, to be known as Sword Beach; around Bracklesham Bay for the 3rd Canadian Infantry Division, who, on D-Day, were to land in the middle of the British area at Juno Beach around Courseulles; and finally 50th Division, who were to practise landing on Hayling Island. The order of landing beaches was the mirror image of the actual landings. After the disaster to US forces on Exercise Tiger in Lyme Bay, there were many fears, and the possible intervention of German naval or air forces could not be countenanced. Even a successful German aerial reconnaissance could show the scope and readiness of the Allied forces. There also needed to be at least four weeks between the final exercise and D-Day, so that enough time had elapsed to prepare the landing craft. An elaborate defence and deception plan was put into operation.

In many respects, this exercise was purely a movement rather than a tactical exercise, to see how problems with the expected thousands of movements to ports in the south-east of England prior to D-Day could be ironed out. Yet again, though, the transport and carrier elements were not to be part of the landing exercise, but, in the case of 50th Division, were to drive around and assemble at the north end of Hayling Island. To enable the exercise to go ahead, the British minefield off Littlehampton and West Solent was cleared, and ferries in and around the Solent were stopped during the exercise. The opportunity was taken to check arrangements with civilian authorities, and give the police, both military and civilian, practice in controlling the vast amount of traffic to be generated during the real invasion phase. No correspondents were allowed to witness or report any part of Exercise Fabius.[33]

By using the south coast, it was realized that there was a strong possibility of detection by the Germans, informing them about plans for the naval part of the invasion, code-named 'Neptune', and the land part, code-named 'Overlord'. Further, there were fears that this exercise might help them uncover the complicated deception plan, called 'Fortitude', undertaken to persuade the enemy that the invasion would take place in the Pas-de-Calais. An outer naval cover of eighteen destroyers with standing air patrols of up to four squadrons of RAF fighters was deployed throughout the exercise, and German aircraft were shepherded away from the exercise area during its operation. In the end, it was decided to use the exercise as a means 'to induce the enemy to believe that Fabius was the first of a series of exercises with Overlord and Neptune to be the second'.[34]

The weather was not at all helpful, although it did at least foreshadow the weather on D-Day itself, and thus, in one sense, gave everyone a useful experience. One Admiralty document, worried about the increasingly poor weather, stated: '2300hrs. 5th May: Wind

WSW Force 6 in sheltered waters reaching gale force in exposed areas veering slowly NW late in afternoon and decreasing. Showers, moderate to good visibility. Waves 8 feet. Immediate: All craft are to haul down barrage balloons.'[35] Barrage balloons in a high wind, especially attached to smaller craft, could lead to disaster.

The increasingly poor weather did cause the death by drowning of seven men from 2nd Essex as they attempted to get back aboard their LCI (L). Both 56th (Independent) Infantry Brigade and 151st Infantry Brigade were intended to land as follow-up infantry, and the intention was to land them direct on D-Day from the fairly large LCI (L). The landing procedure was for a naval person to swim/wade to shore with a line and fix a thicker rope between the landing craft and the shore, enabling the soldiers to have a steadying handline as they disembarked down a ramp either side of the bow. In this case, the same procedure was employed for getting back on the landing craft. On Exercise Fabius, when some of the men were re-embarking on LCI (L) 295, the ship was moved away from the shore by the swell and the rope became tight, pulling a number of soldiers holding the rope up into the air until they had to let go. Seven were drowned. As it happened, this was virtually the whole of the 2nd Essex D Company Headquarters section, and this was a difficult group of men to replace with only just over four weeks left to D-Day.

Unfortunately, an attempt by Generals Bucknall and Graham to get an award for the brave actions of two members of LCI (L) 295 (Canadian 264th Flotilla), Sub-Lieutenant J. A. Gibb RCNVR and Ordinary Seaman M. K. Macdonald, who tried to rescue the soldiers, was not acted on by higher authorities.

> On 4th May 44, during a landing exercise a party of troops of the 2nd Essex Regiment were endeavouring to re-embark on LCI (L) 295. The craft surged back from the beach, however, and a number of them were dragged out of their depth by the starboard steadying line and left struggling in the water in full equipment. Although they had already spent a considerable time in the water in the course of their duties Sub-Lieutenant J. A. Gibb RCNVR and Ordinary Seaman M.K. Macdonald V/62175 immediately went to their rescue. By their efforts they were able to save one man. One officer and six other ranks were drowned.[36]

There was a court of enquiry into the incident, and, as a result, for D-Day itself the plan was revised so that infantry on the LCI (L)s of 56th Brigade and 151st Brigade were to be transferred to shore by smaller LCM, and, according to the 2nd Glosters War Diary for 15 May 1944, 'Part of Bn. transferring from LCI to LCM for beach transfer. This was found to be quite easy to do.'[37]

But, even so, some members of the battalions, especially the transport of various types, including S Company, never trained for landings before D-Day. Also, all the brigades, especially 56th Brigade, were being reinforced with new men virtually up to the last moment. In fact, 2SWB only received a draft of a complete company when they were in the 'sealed camps' in the New Forest, a few days before loading the landing craft for the invasion.

The final plan for Gold Beach was to land two assaulting brigades, 69th Brigade left, around the seaside village of La Riviere, and 231st Brigade right at Le Hamel, and to exploit southwards and outwards, 69th Brigade through Ver-sur-Mer and Crepon, and 231st Brigade through to Ryes and beyond the coastal village of Arromanches. Following them up would be 151st Brigade behind 69th Brigade, and 56th Brigade behind 231st Brigade. The two follow-up brigades would pass through the assault brigades, fill the widening gap and exploit to the south via the village of Meuvaines, 151st Brigade as far as the Caen to Bayeux lateral Route Nationale, and 56th Brigade to capture Bayeux and the high ground to the west and north of Bayeux. The left (eastern) brigades would make a junction with the Canadians landing on Juno Beach, while 56th Brigade would join with US units landing on Omaha Beach. Further, for the landings and exploitation, a unit of 4th Special Service Brigade, 47 Commando, would land after the assaulting brigades, move south, then west, and by the end of D-Day, capture the small port of Port-en-Bessin. By the evening of D-Day, 7th Armoured Division should be disembarking in force to follow up an earlier exploitation by 8th Armoured Brigade via Bayeux to the south. It was hoped that 8th Armoured Brigade, with other elements, including 2nd Glosters as an additional infantry battalion, might have reached as far south as Villers-Bocage by the end of D-Day. For organizational purposes, Gold Beach was divided into two main areas: left, code-named King, and right, code-named Jig. King and Jig were further divided into Green (right) and Red (left), and each of these into East and West.

An important element of all military operations involved the RAMC and also the men from the infantry battalions trained as stretcher bearers, probably what we today would class as paramedics. Casualty figures were expected to be high, and, in fact, during later June and July, casualties reached the same proportions as those during the First World War. A figure of 75 per cent casualties within the seven British infantry divisions and 37 per cent within the three armoured divisions during the Normandy Campaign has been calculated. On average, for each infantry division, this meant the loss of 341 officers and 5,115 infantrymen out of 7,200 men in the nine rifle battalions in each division during the Normandy Campaign. During the Third Battle of Ypres (Passchendaele), between July and November 1917, casualties numbered on average 2,324 per day, while during the Normandy Campaign, British Army losses were higher, at an average at 2,354.[38] What was evidently different about the British Army by 1944 was that fewer men died, despite the high casualty figures, due to improved medical science and treatment of casualties. Also, those casualties suffering from shell shock, or what was termed nervous exhaustion, were dealt with in a different way. The aim was to give this type of casualty rest and restoration of morale, to be returned as quickly as possible to his unit and the battlefield. For D-Day, the following RAMC units landed to give care to the wounded: 149th Field Ambulance, 186th Field Ambulance, 200th Field Ambulance and 203rd Field Ambulance units and 25th, 31st and 32nd Field Dressing Stations. A field ambulance unit comprised thirteen officers and 231 other ranks, while a field dressing station was made up of seven officers and ninety other ranks.[39]

Landings on this scale, preceded by heavy bombing and shelling, will inevitably cause damage to civilian property. However, the Allies were mindful that they were landing on the shore of an occupied nation which they were liberating. Care was to be taken not to destroy buildings without good cause. Also, assuming a successful landing, much of the French infrastructure would be useful to the Allies; furthermore, the area of Normandy was rich in historic buildings and artefacts.

In 50th Division and Brigade intelligence summaries prior to the invasion, it was clear that it was preferred not to have to bomb or shell Bayeux, as the streets were narrow, and the hoped-for quick exploitation on D-Day would have to move through or around Bayeux. Although a squadron of heavy bombers was on call to bomb Bayeux if necessary, and 56th Brigade orders mention that a whole brigade attack with artillery might be required, the hope was that large-scale destruction of this ancient town could be avoided. The 50th Division Operational Order No. 1, published on 9 May 1944, and issued to its brigades and battalions, makes clear that there were a number of important buildings and objects which should be preserved as far as possible. From Appendix M to 50 Div Operational Order No. 1, the following gives a flavour of the hoped-for preservation of buildings in Bayeux:

> PTT (Postes, télégraphes et telephones) building, Bridge 788788, Hospital, Sanatorium, Reservoir, – Destruction of civil communications installations, cable and lines to be avoided as far as possible. Particular care will be taken to avoid damage, where possible, to any medical or monastic buildings suitable for medical purposes in addition to the above hospitals. If possible power cable should not be damaged. Preservation of Antiquities: Bayeux, Cathedral de Notre Dame, *Maison de Gouvernement*, Library and Tapestries, Palais de Justice (picture galleries).

Two weeks later, in 'Amendment No. 3 to 50 Div Operational Order No.1, 23rd May 1944', it was added that Grade I buildings like the Cathedral 'should not be subjected to bombardment unless it is beyond doubt that they are in use by the enemy'. Grade II buildings such as the Maison de Gouvernement 'should have guards provided to prevent occupation for military purposes'. Grade III buildings such as the Library and Tapestry 'should have guards provided to prevent damage or loss'. To the previous list of buildings was added a general outline of facilities, adding twenty-three types of buildings or materials, including abattoirs, bakeries, garages with repair facilities, railway bridges etc., to which damage should be avoided.

However, in 56th (Independent) Brigade Operational Order No.1 Appendix H,[40] it is clear that two unwelcome possibilities might occur on D-Day and ruin the plan for a quick exploitation to the south:

> 3a The town of Bayeux which covers the approaches to area 7777 from the EAST. In the event of the town being held in str, no adv to the high ground 7777 can be undertaken without first clearing either BAYEUX or the eastern portion of BAYEUX. To do this might however, necessitate a BDE attack supported by all available arty [Artillery].
>
> 4. The time factor on D-Day may make it impossible to clear both Bayeux if held in str, and to be firmly est on the final objective. Plans must therefore be made to ensure that if BAYEUX is so strongly held as to prevent an attack on D Day on to the high ground 7777 the BDE is still in a posn to meet a counter attack on the morning of D+1.

The optimistic result for the Gold Beach landings was a link on the right flank (West) with US Forces landing on Omaha; a link on the left flank (East) with Canadian forces; capture of Port-en-Bessin by 47 Commando, an advance south to capture the Caen to Bayeux lateral main road, and capture of Bayeux and exploitation south to Villers-Bocage. Clearly, an experienced commander such as General Graham was trying to cover all possibilities as D-Day unfolded. Within the constraints of time and materiel, all three services had done as much as possible to prepare for Gold Beach.

The 50th Division and its supporting units were ready to go. In the sealed camps in the New Forest around Beaulieu, men had looked at maps and taken in the details of the terrain from superb models, all furnished with bogus names which would only be revealed to most when they were issued final maps and orders on the landing craft. Depending on the task they were assigned, the different units left the camps by order of loading, and made their way to Southampton or ports like Lymington for embarkation. The assault infantry boarded the large LSIs and anchored in the Solent. The follow-up infantry joined their LCI (L) later, and sailed round to Southampton.

Across all the beaches to be assaulted on D-Day, one worrying aspect observed through aerial reconnaissance was the steady increase in the number of obstacles being erected below the high-water mark. On 1 May, at a meeting held at Supreme Headquarters, it was decided that these must be dealt with by the LCOCU while the obstacles stood in less than 2 feet of water. Tide times and this aspect of the operation were an important factor that decided practical dates from a naval point of view for the assault as being between 5 and 7 June, with 7 June being used only in extreme necessity. Eisenhower fixed 5 June as D-Day on 23 May. The king, accompanied by Admiral Ramsay, visited the Portsmouth area on 24 May; Churchill had already visited on 13 May. At 2330 on 28 May, all holders were to open their special orders. The exact date and time of D-Day were not communicated, as this had still not been definitely fixed.[41] The Solent was packed with the ships for three landing beaches – Gold (West Solent), Juno (East Solent) and a portion of ships and landing craft for Sword Beach. There appear to have been, literally, no free berths.[42] Later, when Gold Beach shipping was loaded at other ports, for example, the LCI (L) at Lymington with 151st and 56th Brigade, these ships and men were accommodated in the liner quay at Southampton, and the men unloaded and were able to use facilities adapted in the large customs sheds. This organization of the anchorage, and the smooth departures of the many convoys, deserve recognition.

By this time, the camps in the New Forest had been 'sealed', with no movement in or out without special permission of officers commanding units. Mail was impounded, and any communication outside, such as telephone, was forbidden. Men of all ranks were extensively briefed on models of the area, seeing photographs and maps of their particular objectives. Alan Norman, a subaltern with 1st Hampshires, remembers many hours spent before the landings poring over the aerial photographs, using magnifying viewers which gave a 3-D image. 'I recall the Sanatorium was one of A Company's early objectives. One of the foreshore photos showed a horse and cart with men around it':

> We thought they were probably fixing anti-tank Teller mines to the beach obstacles to sink landing craft. The German Army extensively used horse drawn transport in infantry and non-mechanised units. I remember that at one of the briefings, held I think at Beaulieu, a senior officer gave a stage by stage description of the offensive, the overnight bombing, the naval bombardment and the rockets on the beaches,

whilst an aide gave a running total of the high explosives. We, the inexperienced Subalterns, were brain washed, we all thought everything would be flattened and the Germans surviving would be very keen to surrender. Little did we know![43]

It was, of course, the weather that led to postponement from 5 to 6 June. With the Germans believing that no invasion could be launched in such weather, Rommel returned home for his wife's birthday and a meeting with Hitler, and thus was in Germany on 6 June. The slower convoys started leaving the anchorage at 0900 on 5 June; their bad luck was to spend longer at sea in the poor weather. The faster ships left during the evening. The wind was Force 5 with a sea state of 4, conditions that, despite the forecast, were 'unexpectedly severe and imposed a high test on the landing craft crews'.[44] The vessels from all five landing beaches went through an area south-east of the Isle of Wight called area 'Z' from the afternoon of 5 June, and then left this area towards Normandy, out through what was called 'The Spout', along swept lanes. One of the early leading convoys for Gold Beach was forced out of its swept lane, first by a convoy bound for Omaha Beach and later by overtaking infantry ships and light cruisers. It is reported that it spent less than one hour in the swept channel during the passage! During the voyage, Force G lost five LCT, one Rhino ferry and three Rhino tugs, an LCP (L) and seven LCAs (HR). All were important, particularly the LCA, as their job was to approach and bombard the beach with spigot mortars (Hedgerow), blasting mine-free lanes across the beach.[45]

To keep the Germans guessing, there were three feints towards the French coast on the night of 5/6 June 1944. Six harbour defence motor launches (HDMLs), operating in the Channel, sailed towards beaches in the Pas-de-Calais area (Operation Glimmer); eight HDMLs feinted towards Bruneval and Fecamp (Operation Taxable); and four HDMLs operated in the Cape Barfleur area to draw the attention of radar in the north-east Cotentin Peninsula (Operation Big Drum). These very seaworthy craft (despite the title 'Harbour') carried balloons and other equipment to draw the attention of any German radar station by replicating a large convoy approaching the coast. These attempts were backed by air force operations.

Equally, the Allied air forces were playing their part. 'The weather had broken as forecast before noon on Sunday (4 June 1944), but operations on Sunday and Monday were carried out regardless of the conditions.'[46] On 5 June, 3,500 sorties were made throughout the day, attacking fifteen radar stations in the chain along the French coast, five chateaux listed as German HQs, six coastal batteries, railway targets and three bridges over the River Seine. Altogether, 13,000 sorties had taken place from 2 June, including raids on non-Overlord targets such as the V1 launching sites. Also standing fighter patrols were kept over the English Channel to prevent German reconnaissance planes from overflying the invasion fleet ports.[47]

Overnight, Allied light bombers ranged inland to attack any road or rail targets, and night fighters covered enemy air bases as well as the English Channel. Coastal Command aircraft were equally involved in making sure that U-boats and German surface craft were destroyed and monitored from the invasion area and further afield towards the U-boat bases in the Bay of Biscay and Norway. It was believed that 100 U-boats would be available at any one time to counter the invasion, and these were a very serious threat.[48]

On the night of 5/6 June, as an important part of Operation Taxable, the RAF flew sixteen aircraft from 617 (Dambusters) Squadron from 0030 to 0407, flying in a box four aircraft abreast, 12 miles wide and 8 miles deep, over the naval units. Dropping silver foil strips of 'Window', they flew thirty very accurate orbits, each one ending 0.82 miles nearer the coast and replicating the approach of a large convoy. Supporting Operation Glimmer, 218 Squadron, with only six aircraft and using the same technique as Taxable, created a similar impression. Operation Mandrel, by 199 Squadron, RAF and 803 Squadron, USAAF, jammed enemy radar during the airborne and air landing operations. In Operation ABC, 101 Squadron flew between the Taxable and Glimmer areas, jamming German night-fighter radio-telephone communications. Operation Titanic I, III and IV dropped window to confuse any coastal radar station still in one piece, and then dropped dummies and noise simulators to persuade the Germans that airborne operations were taking place north of Rouen, and around Maltot and Marigny. Also around Marigny, a small number of SAS troops were dropped.[49]

The sea journey from the Solent had been very rough, especially for those on the smaller ships and flat-bottomed LCTs, who had been tossed about mercilessly. The LCTs with flatter bottoms slid all over the sea. Perhaps the best off were the assault troops of 231st and 69th Brigades and 47 Commando in their larger LSIs. Even so, one member of 1st Dorsets remarked on 'being tossed about in the English Channel'.[50] On the same LSI, David Bushell remembers being woken around four in the morning, and thought it was strange that for breakfast they had corned beef hash and porridge![51] Alan Norman, as a junior officer in 1st Hampshires, had 'proper food' in the wardroom alongside Merchant and Royal Navy officers on *Empire Crossbow*. They sailed at 2100 on 5 June. They had a model of the landing beaches on board, and now the code names had been taken off and replaced by the real names of the towns and villages. Norman had decided to land cleanly dressed, and so, while many of the men were already sleeping, he had a shower and changed into clean kit. Deciding he did not want to take his dirty clothes with him, he threw them, packaged up, overboard – and was then worried a U-boat might find them and realize it was a troopship! From deck, he had 'never forgotten seeing the landing craft tank going almost sideways on, because of the rough seas and wind'.[52] But in the same battalion, Major Mott of B Company recalled that 'beer was available and a number of officers had a pleasant party'.[53]

Ahead of Convoy G1 carrying 231st Brigade, the 6th Minesweeping Flotilla, consisting of eight minesweepers and four attached Danlayers,[54] was already hard at work, closing with the coast of Normandy and sweeping a lane clear of mines as far inshore as the lowering positions for the LCAs. Engine Room Artificer F. Merrill on HMM *Postilion* wrote home on 19 June 1944 that they 'cut the mines. There was no fire from the shore batteries. One mine surfaced less than six yards away.' He stayed on deck all night, with his life vest on, fully inflated. 'Just after dawn we steamed away, the first part of the job done. We hadn't gone very far when we saw them. Hundreds and hundreds of ships as far as the eye could see. Overhead planes were roaring continuously.' They stayed on station all day, observing the continuing lines of ships approaching the shore and the stream of planes overhead, and continued to sweep channels clear.[55] The similarly sized minesweeping group of 18th Flotilla preceded Convoy G2, carrying 69th Brigade. Men who came up on deck observed the lights and flags of the Dan buoys laid to mark safe passage. From the minesweepers, a serrated 'sweep' wire sawed through the cables between mine and anchor. When the mines surfaced, they were destroyed by gunfire. The sweep wire was marked at its end by an Orpesa float, the wire's end kept down in the water by an otter board. Ahead of the precious leading minesweeper in the flotilla sailed two smaller motor launches, themselves trying to sweep clear any mines endangering the larger minesweepers. It is reported that in the (British) Eastern Task Force area alone, 550 mines were swept from 6 June to the end of the month.[56] Nearly 300 minesweepers and Danlayers of several types took part in the whole operation.

In the LCI (L) carrying 151st and 56th Infantry Brigades, the men had spent a difficult night, with up to 200 men per craft cramped together lying on bunks, often with just their belts unbuckled for some comfort and the lower decks crammed with kit and equipment – Bren guns, PIATs and 2 inch mortars, extra ammunition, extra kit. On deck, many of the LCI (L) had light airborne cycles stowed centrally on deck, for each battalion in the follow-up brigades had one 'speedy company' whose task was to press forward and keep up with the battalion Bren gun carriers during an expected quick advance from the beach. Some men in these companies, it turned out, could not ride a bike, let alone carry the heavy equipment, rifles and Bren guns they had to keep with them.

> On Landing Craft Infantry (Large) the housing system was not quite as good as battery hens! Below deck there are stanchions from floor to ceiling and racked around the wall would be six shelves folded down with the distance from one to the next above was not quite enough to raise your head when sliding into one. You are not allowed to get out because the alleyway between these rows of shelves is full of our equipment. If you stood on the floor you were standing on everyone's equipment, packs, respirators, ammunition, entrenching tools, full size picks and shovels. All the weapons including my Bren gun were all on the floor. If we were hit we were all done for.[57]

Men were not allowed on the upper decks, although some did go up to get some air or to be sick, and this 'rule' does not seem to have been rigidly enforced. Often there were not enough 'vomit bags' carried aboard the less stable craft in the pertaining weather conditions. 'As we passed the Needles it started getting a bit choppy and overcast, some of the lads were violently seasick, I decided to stay on deck until later. I wasn't sick until just before landing.'[58] Officers were luckier, and Pat Barrass OC of B Company 2nd Essex stayed up all night with the ship's officer, receiving a can of self-heating soup. All D-Day men remember tins of self-heating soup, a marvel to many, and perhaps a lifesaver after a soaking. George Jesson, also of 2nd Essex, remembers, though, that 'a tin exploded and scalded a man on the landing craft.'[59] Some men did manage to sleep. Tony Atcherley travelled on an LCT with the Brigade Signals truck:

> The weather was bad and the seas lashed by gales. When Eisenhower released us the Channel felt rough indeed and we had over a hundred miles to go poor Ken was terribly sick and spent a sleepless night, but as was the case in all my sea voyages, this my first had no effect on me. I happily consumed the special rations

we had been issued with. Everything we needed was provided including a tiny heating contraption to warm our drinks. Then I lay down and curled up in my blanket. The deck was of steel and the boat was surging up and down but despite the excitement of making history, I managed to sleep for several hours.[60]

Also travelling on an LCT, with his motor bike stashed on the South Wales Borderers signal half-track M14, was Frank Dilworth, 56th Brigade Dispatch Rider:

We were fed these tins of self-heating soup. There was no shelter and we had to sleep where we were on the checker plating of the vehicle. Facilities were limited, only a little wash place and small toilet. Some of the vehicles were shifting so they lashed them together. Then we moved off and all night long we could hear bump, bump, bump, from the waves. I wasn't seasick but had a real headache.[61]

There was also humour, even between a lowly private and an admiral. As he drove his unit landing officer's jeep onto an LCT on 2 June, Les (Titch) Holden remembered:

As I sat at the steering wheel, Admiral Ramsey touched me on the collar with his baton, then pointed to the name I had painted on the fascia of my jeep. I had previously noted that most vehicles in our convoy were named after famous lords, such as Haig, Roberts or Kitchener. I had christened my jeep Lord Elphus. Giving me a smile, the Admiral said, 'I'm sure He will, driver.'[62]

Neville Howell, with his M10 on another LCT, recalled: 'We knew we were in for an uncomfortable night, there were no sleeping quarters for us on-board.' Issued from the ship's stores, they received a blanket sewn up as a sleeping bag, and 'my crew and I took it in turns sitting in the seats of the driver and wireless operator in an attempt to doze.' Like many of those awake, and despite the sound of the ship's engines, sea and wind, they could at times hear the 'roar of aircraft engines passing above us'.[63]

Major Holdsworth of 2nd Devons makes a useful observation here as to the possible mental state of soldiers during the journey across: 'Just imagine yourself, crossing the Channel, feeling very sick, somewhat frightened of what you had to do, and knowing that there was no real cover for you on the beach to prevent you being shot up while you waited.'[64]

The infantry brigades, of course, were split over a number of ships. The assault brigades and 47 Commando were accommodated on the LSIs, and the follow-up brigades on the LCI (L). Their jeeps, M14 half-tracks and Bren carriers were to land separately off LCTs staged to arrive as required, and the majority of their lorry transport was carried by LSTs, mostly to be landed on the second tide, although items like the infantry battalions' 6 lb anti-tank guns were loaded onto DUKWs and landed from LST.

When we finally loaded a few days before D-Day we had our 6lb Anti-tank guns loaded onto a DUKW. They hauled the gun up onto the DUKW with about five of us. The Carrier and driver went off on a LCT we were loaded with our DUKW on a LST. All six guns were spread out on other craft. We were split up into sections of two guns, Nos. 1, 2 and 3 Sections.[65]

Some of the men from the support companies went with the vehicles, while others went with the infantry portion and had to join the vehicles at rendezvous after landing. The plan was for 151st Brigade to land on King Beach and move inland to concentrate around the village of Meuvaines before advancing further, while 56th Brigade was to land on Jig Beach near Le Hamel and concentrate in orchards near the farm of Buhot on the right flank before advancing further, with the hope of taking Bayeux before nightfall.

Even those landing on the second tide off the LSTs had concerns: 'We took all the top deck up with Gloster vehicles, while the tank deck was loaded with Jerry cans of petrol. We thought if this gets bombed there will be no swimming away!'[66]

D-Day: Morning

Several elements of the Gold Beach force did not survive the journey. The plan for landing 151st and 56th Brigade went awry well before the beachhead, when the two flotillas of small craft, intended for use to carry the men to shore from the LCI (L), had to turn back to England because of the sea state. It will be remembered that these craft were added after the drownings during Exercise Fabius. Now the LSI (L) of the follow-up brigades would have to beach directly in the rough weather. Also, seven of the LCA (HR) being towed to the beach sank through being swamped, while another had a tow rope part, which then fouled the propeller. Because of their poor seaworthiness, four LCT (A) also had to return to port. This had an effect on the Royal Marine support group with the Centaur tanks, who were being carried in these craft. A number of men were drowned. The (A) stood for armoured, and because of the extra armour and carrying of heavy tanks, there was very little freeboard; it was no wonder that in the conditions such craft sunk or were swamped. Those LCT (A) carrying on to the beach struggled, and appear to have arrived later than planned. The eight LCA (HR) that did survive the journey and arrived on time found that their explosive mortars did not reach the upper beach obstacles. However, by falling in among the obstacles in the water, it was observed that the explosives set off a number of the mines and shells that were attached to them, and in that way gave a helpful service. 'Under the extremely bad weather conditions it is most creditable that the remaining eight fired their pattern according to the fire plan.'[1] Many of the more open ships, such as LCT, shipped water, and being packed with men and equipment, made the journey miserable for all.

As the invasion force was arriving, the air forces were bombing their targets. At close to 0430, bombs were dropped blind using radar on the Longues battery. Although the target markers were initially seen, cloud soon obscured them. Despite opposition from ground fire being reported as very light, one bomber from 582 Squadron was lost without trace. Shortly after, the Mont Fleury battery was bombed, again by the RAF. A 76 Squadron Halifax was shot down on the approach to the target, with all seven crew killed, and another was shot down by ground fire over the target, with three survivors. Over 1,000 Lancaster, Halifax and Mosquito bombers attacked ten selected batteries across the invasion area. Lighter bombs, up to 1,000 lb, were used, as the intention was to disorientate and confuse the gun crews, drive them to shelters and destroy battery communications. Most of these raids were carried out very close to first light, after which the bombarding ships took over suppression of the batteries. The

Longues battery received 538 tonnes of bombs and the Mont Fleury battery received 540 tonnes of bombs.[2]

Crews on these raids were warned that they might see a large number of ships in the Channel, and had received orders not to directly overfly the ships, one presumes because of the fear of friendly fire. Even so, RAF crews were surprised by the actual number of ships they saw.[3] The crew of Halifax bomber LKN of 578 Squadron, returning in the first light of dawn from bombing Mont Fleury, saw the great armada of ships below them, and spontaneously cheered and wished the men below good luck.[4]

Then the US VIII Air Force took over bombing of the beaches just before the landings took place. The original idea of this bombing mission was to 'drench' the beach *Wiederstandnester* with many 100 lb and 500 lb bombs. This mission was supposed to end only five minutes before the landings. 'The first mission involved 1,361 bombers about 1,000 of which were to attack four assault beaches and the remainder to bomb military headquarters in Normandy and choke points in Caen.'[5] On D-Day, due to the weather and cloud cover, it was appreciated that ten minutes clear would be required for the safety of the troops on the shore. As bombing would take place by radar because of the increasingly cloudy weather, it could not be as close to the shoreline as planned, and extra distance should be given to ensure the safety of the troops. Despite this, three bombs fell in the sea near Le Hamel, but with no consequences to the ships massing below.[6] Although the mission went ahead, the bombs inevitably missed their targets, and on Gold Beach fell between 300 yards and 3 miles from the beach.[7] Between Courseulles on Juno Beach and the Longues battery, plus Caen, the US VIII Air Force employed 75 Squadrons of B. 17 'Flying Fortresses' in this task. Bombing of Gold Beach took place between 0655 and 0725, with the Longues battery being bombed from 0645 to 0735. The cloud level was reported as being at 10,000 feet, with patches of cloud down to 1,000 feet.[8] This allowed the lower-flying spotter aircraft helping the naval bombardment group to operate fairly adequately as long as communications could be maintained.

The naval bombardment ships had already been in action since 0530, when HMS *Ajax* opened fire on the Longues battery and HMS *Belfast* (initially firing on Gold Beach targets, but then shifting to Juno Beach) engaged the Marefontaine battery beyond Ver-sur-Mer. By 0630, a spotting aircraft reported that this battery showed no activity, and HMS *Belfast* ceased fire on it at 0716. HMS *Argonaut* was narrowly missed by the Longues battery at 0534. A small battery near Mont Fleury appeared to be firing on the headquarters ship *Bulolo* at 0617, but this battery was silenced by HMS *Cottesmore* by 0630. The Mont Fleury battery was engaged by HMS *Orion* at 0632, and was reported silenced within eleven minutes, a spotter aircraft reporting that it had observed twelve direct hits on its three guns still in open positions. A reported problem from 0630 was that smoke from the 'American Sector' obscured the beach. As several ships firing guns from 8 inch to 4.7 inch were now bombarding the beach, and the two air forces had been bombing the area since 0430, it was not surprising that the area was covered in smoke and dust, and according to one source: 'From 0545 smoke shells were used to baffle the enemy's long range guns.'[9] (Various battalion war diaries and individual memoirs mention that the burning *Marais* gave useful cover, and later aerial photographs taken around midday still clearly show smoke from these areas as they still burnt.) From then on, the bombarding group started on the 'run-in' fire plan, which meant targeting specific points while the landing craft made for shore.[10]

HMS *Bulolo*, leading Assault Group G1, arrived at the swept anchorage at 0510; by 0537 these ships were all anchored. At 0300 the men had an early reveille, maybe managing some breakfast, and from 0500 the leading companies of assaulting infantry were forming up on deck, and their LCAs were being lowered into the water by 0600. The supporting companies would have the unenviable task of descending the scrambling nets, carrying all their kit and arms, to get into the bucking LCAs as they returned to their parent LSI. The LCAs got away with the first waves fairly promptly. Alan Norman, 1st Hampshires on Empire Crossbow, remembers his experience at the lowering point:

> We had breakfast early and were called forward to get into the landing craft. Everything went right. We got into our craft and we were lowered down into the water and immediately moved out so others above us could be lowered. Then we went round and round the LSI until we had all formed up. This was about seven miles out. I remember one of the major warships firing on shore and the waters around the ship was frothing. Then one of the Landing Craft was firing their rockets with a great 'whoosh!' as we passed them and the lads in the boat were cheering all of them.[11]

Lt Kenneth Taylor, signals officer of 6th Green Howards from 69 Brigade, wrote in his diary:

> Had a very good breakfast despite the rough sea – probably the last for a long time. Got dressed up and went to action deck about 0430hrs. Everyone in high spirits and singing to the mouth organ. Whisky and rum being passed round freely. After a long time went up and embarked into LCM about 0530.[12]

On their small LCAs, a platoon to a craft, the assault infantry were away moving towards shore, along with the LCT carrying the AVREs, Crabs and DD tanks.

At 0557, the Longues battery opened fire on *Bulolo*, and by 0630, near misses forced the decision to weigh anchor and move to another position. *Bulolo*, of course, was packed with senior officers, including General Graham. As headquarters ship, it carried extra technical staff and signalling equipment, and was 'grossly overcrowded for this operation'.[13] The wind was reported Force 4, and made the anchorage and the sea towards shore very rough. A decision was made that it was too rough to launch the DD tanks from as far out as planned (7,000 yards), so their LCTs started to make towards the shore; some DD tanks were let go in shallower water, and some landed without the need to raise their protective canvas screens. It meant that the DD Shermans of B and C Squadrons Sherwood Rangers (Jig) and B and C Squadrons Royal Dragoon Guards (King) landed later than the assault infantry and breaching teams instead of just before, and were not in a position to support the infantry assaulting the beach positions or LCOCU and Royal Engineers working in the water and on the beach.

As the day grew brighter from twilight, it was possible for the men to identify some of the landmarks from their briefings, photographs and models of the landing beach.

However, soon these became obscured by the dust and smoke from the air and naval bombardment. The craft approaching the beach came under fire from about 3,000 yards out. This fire was 'desultory and inaccurate'.[14] During the final 800–900 yards, the craft were brought under fire by a wider range of artillery pieces, mortars and machine-gun and rifle fire. It was still unknown to the British that the larger weapons could only fire in enfilade, being protected on their seaward flank. Adding to the bombardment of the beaches by naval gunfire, the seventy-two 25-pounder guns from the self-propelled artillery of 86th, 90th and 147th Field Regiments were now firing on their run-in to the beach, and the four LCT (R), ranged on Jig and King Beaches, each fired its 1,000 65 lb rockets to smash beach defences and explode mines, though some salvoes fell short. Many men well remember this spectacular display, and Lt Cmdr Humphries on HMS *Glenroy* tells of seeing 'banks of fire behind us and a sound like a dozen express trains going overhead. This scared the living daylights out of us as this was something we hadn't experienced before.'[15]

The very brave LCOCU and Royal Engineer Field Companies were first ashore, with little close covering fire from tanks. The Force G Narrative noted: 'Their work is deserving of the highest praise.'[16] LCOCU were organized by the Royal Navy, and each unit consisted of one officer and ten ratings. Four LCOCUs operated on Gold Beach, Nos. 3 and 4 on King and Nos. 9 and 10 on Jig. They were equipped with rubber suits and shallow-water diving apparatus. They carried explosive charges to demolish the beach obstacles, and were supposed to be working in water between 10 feet and 4 feet 6 inches. But the bad weather seemed to pile up the water on the coast faster than anticipated, and this led to many obstacles becoming submerged earlier than expected. Because of the problems of landing the armour, this meant that the LCOCU were also initially the only targets visible, and at the mercy of German snipers and machine guns while they worked in the water. As well as this, there were many more obstacles than anticipated and planned for. The after-action report pointed out that there were not enough LCOCU on Gold Beach, and that their allocation of explosives and stores was inadequate.[17] Equally at the mercy of the Germans were the 145 men in each of 73rd Field Company RE (Jig) and 280th Field Company RE (King), who had to complete similar tasks to the LCOCU's but further in, destroying obstacles in water shallower than 4 feet 6 inches and on dry land. The LCOCU travelled in LCAs, while the men from the Field Companies travelled with the AVREs in the LCTs. One LCA followed one LCT, allowing them to disembark simultaneously. Each man carried two 3 lb demolition charges. Other equipment for the Res, such as hawsers for towing obstacles by AVREs, reserves of explosives etc., were eventually placed in folding rubber boats to be towed off by the AVREs, evidently carrying some of the REs.[18] 'There was considerable surf on the beaches and a strong wind. The tide was higher up than expected and rising by one foot every ten minutes.'[19]

These operations suffered quite a number of casualties and difficulties, as a later history by 73rd Field Company was to show. The outline tasks of the Field Companies were to clear metal and concrete obstacles on the beach below the high-water mark. The company of five officers and 140 other ranks was loaded into six LCTs carrying AVREs on 5 June in the Solent. They beached on Jig Green at 0730. LCT 2025 launched an AVRE that was 'drowned', after which LCT 2025 became the target for shore batteries, and two men were killed and several wounded. From LCT 2026, one section of the Field Company got ashore on the back of an AVRE and commenced demolition. Two sections were unable to disembark and returned to the United Kingdom. On LCT 2027, one folding boat of stores was disembarked, another was wrecked. A section and stores were transferred to an LCA. One man was killed. From LCT 2028, both folding boats got away, but were holed, and the section swam to shore. While reporting to his company commander, Captain Smith was killed by machine-gun fire. The men from LCT 2029 swam ashore, except for five in each of the folding boats. In LCT 2030, both folding boats were ripped on the ramp. Personnel and stores were transferred to another LCT, but this struck a mine and settled while still 300 yards out. The men and equipment were transferred to yet another LCT, only then finding out that it was already returning to England! They transferred yet again, and eventually reached shore at high water. Despite all these setbacks, the company had cleared 2,000 yards of beach by the end of D-Day, and suffered nine killed and twelve wounded.[20]

On King Beach, 280th Field Company suffered similar problems as 73rd Field Company. It was reported that the obstacles on this side of the beach were not as thickly laid. The folding boats were equally useless in carrying stores ashore. The nearer the heavily defended eastern side of King Beach at La Riviere, inevitably, the heavier was the fire, from small-calibre weapons, mortars and anti-tank guns. When under the sea walls, Germans lobbed hand grenades over at the troops sheltering beneath. Two 200 yard gaps in the obstacles were made by 0830, when, as on Jig Beach, the tide and the large number of landing craft now streaming ashore made further work impossible. In the first hour, the company lost eight killed and twenty-six wounded, and the LCOCU one killed and four wounded. Resuming work later, they completely cleared 1,200 yards of beach by 2030 that evening.

Harry Billinge was with one of the RE companies, and came ashore on a small landing craft. With shells screaming overhead, he set to work in a shallower area, demolishing obstacles. 'Blowing up anything impeding the boats. Things were booby-trapped and we had to make things safe for the following troops. It was an easy thing to defend the beach, very hard to attack.' He saw men killed in the water and the water turn red. He remembers a terrible noise from the bombardment 'hell on earth'.[21]

Under continuous fire from Le Hamel, La Riviere and the strongpoints in between, these men and the LCOCU worked for an hour until conditions became impossible as the tide rose. They were not only threatened by enemy sniper, machine-gun and mortar fire, but very quickly had to dodge the mass of craft that were bringing in all the assaulting units.[22]

The other important unit to help neutralize the beach defences and force a way inland was, of course, the 'funnies' from 79th Armoured Division. On each of Jig and King, it was planned to land twenty AVREs from 82nd Assault Squadron (Jig) and 81st Assault Squadron (King) and thirteen flail tanks from B (Jig) and C (King) Squadrons Westminster Dragoons, plus three bulldozers (two armoured). The aim on each of Jig and King Beaches was to clear a gap, free from obstacles, 250 yards wide to allow further LCTs to land safely, and to construct three mine-free exits or 'lanes' in each of Jig Green and Jig Red and King Green and King Red, 24 feet wide, for tracked vehicles to use within the first hour.[23] The 'funnies' were landed as a mix of AVREs and flails organized as twelve 'breaching teams'. On each LCT, each breaching team was tasked with opening a lane inland and providing support for the infantry. The AVREs would prove particularly effective against the pillboxes and fortified houses.

As pointed out, things did not go well on Jig Green Beach. The breaching teams landed between 0720 and 0730. Starting at Jig Green (West), the first AVRE off LCT 2025, which was pushing a roly-poly mat, drowned, and the LCT had been hit in the engine room and bridge and, losing power, had beached side on. The LCT and AVRE were jammed on the beach, and the rest of the AVREs and flail tanks could not be unloaded. From LCT 2026, a flail tank blew up in the minefield. On one AVRE, the gears jammed in reverse, and it had to be abandoned. The command AVRE with the officer commanding (OC) of the unit, Major Elphinstone, engaged pillboxes with machine guns, but Major Elphinstone was killed directing fire from the turret of his tank. However, this breaching team did manage to complete a beach exit. Of the armour from LCT 2027, one AVRE was hit by the 75 mm gun at Le Hamel, but carried on until mined. The AVRE carrying the fascine was hit and overturned. The two flail tanks both became bogged down and then hit from Le Hamel, one of them three times, and both were put out of operation. A troop of one Sherman and four Centaurs of the RM Support Group also landed in this sector close to Le Hamel. The 75 mm gun there hit the Sherman lead tank twice, and one of the Centaurs. Two of the other Centaurs had tracks blown off by mines. It was proving very problematic to exist on Jig Green. Further left, on Jig Red, LCT 2028 had drifted half a mile too far east, but its vehicles landed safely. Planned to land at the exit leading to Les Roquettes, one of its flails worked its way successfully off the beach, but became bogged in the marsh behind, while the second flail was bogged on the beach. One of its AVREs got to the lateral road and turned towards Le Hamel. It met with another AVRE, held up by a large crater in the road, reported to be 50 feet wide and 10 feet deep. The crater was causing a significant traffic jam. The other AVREs from LCT 2028 were called up, and using fascines, the hole was filled to the extent that vehicles could creep by. LCT 2029 again landed 500 yards too far east, and all vehicles got out. Within 15 minutes, they had cleared a path to the lateral road and went on towards Les Roquettes until they joined the queue by the large crater; when cleared, they continued towards Les Roquettes. One of the flail tanks carrying this breaching team commander was unluckily hit in the fuel tank, probably by a mortar, and burst into flames – the crew safely evacuating. LCT 2030 landed 1,000 yards east of its intended position, but managed to open a lane to the lateral road within 22 minutes, and shortly after a second lane was opened. Between 0745 and 0752, only half the lanes were opened, two on Jig Red and a third on Jig Green.

Landing on Jig Green, Lt Jack Booker RNVR reports his LCT 'hit several times by shell-fire, two of which shot away our starboard winch and wire'. They got their tanks ashore partly due to the bravery of the anchor winch controller, Stoker Mountain. He stood by his winch totally unprotected from bullets and shrapnel, slowly easing the LCT up to the beach during the half an hour or so it took to offload our tanks. For this act, he was awarded the Distinguished Service Medal (DSM). A corporal of the Royal Engineers was killed in the tank hold. Due to the broken winch wire, the craft had to back off the beach until a mile offshore, where eventually the problem was fixed.

From there, they had a grandstand view of the landings, waves of follow-up craft landing in the area cleared by the Royal Engineers. One of the sadder sights was 'that of seeing several of our AVRE tanks being hit and bursting into flames and their crews jumping out to save themselves'.[24]

The King Beach breaching teams had drifted somewhat eastwards from their planned objectives, landing between 0725 and 0730, with two lanes opened by 0750. Whereas the 82nd Squadron Jig Beach breaching teams had landed across a wide stretch of coastline of well over a mile wide between Le Hable de Heurtot and close to the eastern edge of Le Hamel, the 81st Squadron breaching teams landed within a half-mile of each other, starting at the eastern edge of La Riviere. Landing between 100 and 150 yards from shore in 5 feet of water, the armour was launched. One AVRE was run down and swamped by an LCT. The roly-polys when launched would not work in the strong current, and were allowed to float adrift from the AVREs laying them. Number One breaching team, launched from LCT 2412, sent an AVRE to help 6th Green Howards overcome the position near Le Hable de Heurtot (WN35), and, joining with the two other AVREs from breaching teams Two and Three, this group helped 6th Green Howards overcome the position.

One flail from Team One got bogged down, but the other flailed to the road and made its way to the crest of the hill, completing its task. DD tanks soon followed up. Meanwhile, on the beach, AVREs from Team One were busy dragging obstacles away, aiding 280 Field Company. The two flail tanks from Team Two flailed to the road and turned east, where one got stuck in a crater in the road and the second bogged down nearby. Both flail tanks of Number Three breaching team were hit by the 88 mm gun at La Riviere and disabled as they entered the beach minefield. On King Red near La Riviere, the first AVRE from Team Four was hit by the 88 mm gun and blew up, a second AVRE drowned and the two flail tanks become bogged before they could reach the lateral road. From Team Five, one AVRE was hit by the 88 mm gun and exploded, and both flail tanks became bogged down and supported the attack on La Riviere by

Photo 5 The present-day remains of WN35. A good idea of the coastal erosion since 1944 is obvious from this picture. To the left in the sea lies the open 50 mm emplacement. All the wooden groyne structure is modern and clearly did not work. Currently the strategy is to lay large blocks all along this coastal strip to stop erosion.

Photo 6 The present-day remains of WN36. Similarly this picture of WN36 shows even worse erosion. The open 50 mm emplacement can be seen in front of the concrete gun crew shelters. A photograph taken in 1947 and used in 1st Dorset book *Three Assault Landings* shows this emplacement still in position with its gun and the sea not yet encroaching upon it. This photograph also graphically illustrates the fields of fire available to all defensive weapons across Gold Beach. The modern oyster beds can also just be seen at the tideline.

firing HE and smoke shells, also giving cover to Number Six Team. Finally, Number Six Team had one AVRE break down on the beach. The two flail tanks successfully got to the lateral road, but one became bogged down and another lost a track when it went over a mine. However, it was one of these tanks – Captain Bell, Westminster Dragoons – that got into La Riviere and dealt with the 88 mm gun from only 100 yards, firing directly into the embrasure of the position. Later, the crew of the gun were captured hiding in the casemate. One of the exploding AVREs, carrying 'General Wade' demolition charges and extra explosives for the assault, virtually wiped out two supporting infantry platoons.

As the tide came in on King Beach, it was decided that those AVREs helping remove the obstacles on the beach were not required, so they, along with a number of the DD tanks, made their way into La Riviere and helped assist the East Yorks to mop up the area by demolishing part of a house that had been holding up the attack with spigot mortar bombs. They then moved through the Mont Fleury area and on to Ver-sur-Mer. Naval forces, too, had helped significantly by sailing as close as possible to the shoreline and subjecting the village and coastal defences to a withering fire from destroyers; particularly effective were the LCG and LCF, destroying a 50 mm gun and a number of fortified houses and mortar positions. None could touch the 88 mm gun with its flanking wall until Captain Bell had dealt with it from landward.

From the naval end of the landing, it is interesting to note their perspective. On LCT 442, carrying five Sherman tanks of the SRY, Midshipman Stan Smith remembers:

On our arrival at the launch position the sea conditions were unsuitable to launch so, in accordance with sealed orders, which we were not allowed to open until we were well out to sea, we beached over the obstacles at H-Hour at Asnelles-sur-Mer. My job was to supervise the lowering of the ramp, then to stand on the end of it, very mindful of the 'horns', and measure the depth of the water with a sounding pole. It was sufficiently shallow here to allow the first three tanks to swim a few yards before touching down on the sand. Then a mortar bomb exploded about thirty feet behind me on the tank deck. I was unhurt, but one of my sailors was wounded, and the flotation screens of the two remaining tanks were ripped. The captain therefore had to drive the landing craft in closer so that these tanks could leave dry-shod. As they did so, another mortar bomb exploded alongside the last tank. Captain Eldridge was riding on the turret directing operations, and must have been mortally wounded. He still managed to get his troop ashore, but we lost sight of them as they made their way up the beach. By then we were busy with our own problems.

Our landing craft was badly damaged by the first mortar bomb and by Teller mines, which had blown a 10-foot hole in the port side, opened up the plating of the port bow and twisted the port rudder hard-a-starboard. Also, another LCT had broached to across our stern and severed the stern anchor wire. Having driven the ship so far up the beach, the captain was having great difficulty getting her off without the stern anchor to heave on. I was busy raising the ramp, and, with the aid of the coxswain, Leading Seaman Armstrong, taking care of our casualty.

Eventually, our landing craft slid back into deeper water and floated off. As she moved astern, a stick of three mortar bombs exploded in the water immediately ahead of us – just about where I had been standing a few moments before. We made our way to a hospital ship lying off shore and transferred Able Seaman Laurence into their care. We then proceeded to a pre-arranged collecting area for damaged vessels and joined an 'old crocks' convoy for a night passage home.[25]

Telegraphist William Cooke on LCT 1087 remembers that his station was in the radio cabin below the bridge. The only way to see out of this was through three portholes. They went in later than expected, and at a more easterly part of the beach, due to the tide and sea state. As they were about to come off the beach, William was invited to have a look, and the main thing that shocked him was a line of twenty dead on the beach. After unloading a mix of tanks, lorries and Bren carriers, they reversed off by kedging, but hit either an obstacle or a mine, as the engine room became flooded. They drifted away around 20 miles, but were eventually brought back by an American tug. William had been sleeping, and he woke up to find that they were tied to another LCT, and they were both filled with German prisoners.[26]

On another LCT, Eric Krull from New Zealand found himself in the thick of it as he and his friend Tony Gregson lowered the ramp. Again, the first tanks off 'drowned':

And then we pulled off again, we kedged off with this thing and the deck officer said well there's only one way we're going to do it and that's to go full speed ahead and see what happens. So we pulled off the beach and we ploughed into all these obstructions and it was then that all the chaos started because we weren't actually under fire at this stage. So we made full speed ahead at the beach and we got onto the beach but we couldn't get quite on, there was a bit of water to go through and the sea was very rough and it was then that one of the mines exploded. There were two winch houses, one on each side and wire rope coils and that lowered the door from these winches and you put that down. And I was in one winch house and Tony was on the other.

I suppose we were only two to three metres apart and I suddenly saw him disappear with this explosion under water and it blew the bottom of the boat right through the whole thing, he just went up in the air and came down and absolutely one side of him was all shattered and he just landed on the deck and so I thought 'Oh my God!' So we had what's called the Neil Robertson stretcher which wraps around and keeps him horizontal. We had a lot of morphine aboard and I just pumped him full of morphine and thought if he dies I rather hope he does because he was terribly wounded. He just kept saying 'I'm cold'. Then I thought if we can get him back – so I signalled the destroyer to send a boat to collect a wounded officer. Miraculously the doctor on board was Tony's best mate and I believe he survived.[27]

With the tide now going out, the LCT remained beached all day. Despite being badly damaged, it was able to return to Tilbury Docks for repair. Eric Krull sustained shrapnel wounds to his hand and injured a knee in the explosion.

It must be remembered that, at the same time as these events were taking place, the infantry assault companies had landed across Gold Beach among the chaotic scenes taking place between the water's edge and sand dunes, and were adding to the targets for German weapons, making strenuous efforts to take their objectives and force a way inland. On the west of Gold Beach, 231 Brigade had planned to land with 1st Hampshires on the right to capture Le Hamel and the village of Asnelles just inland (the two virtually merge together) and then move west to capture the cliff strongpoints, Arromanches, Tracy-sur-Mer and Manvieux. At the same time, 1st Dorset, landing on the left, was to capture WN36 and move inland to Les Roquettes. Leaving a company to hold this area, the remainder was to push on and capture the westerly commanding heights – Point 54 – above St Come-de-Fresne. Following this, they were to capture the Puits de Herode strongpoint WN41 and assist the attack of 1st Hampshires on Arromanches. One company was to stand in a blocking position south of Buhot, itself the forming-up area for 56th Brigade. Forty minutes later, 2nd Devons was to land, push south to capture Ryes and hold it with a company, push on to capture La Rosiere prior to the arrival of 47 Commando, and then capture the Longues battery. Should this be successful, they were expecting to exploit beyond Port-en-Bessin and link with the US forces (16 Regimental Combat Team) from Omaha Beach.

With the unexpectedly high resistance from Le Hamel, and the fact that the 1st Hampshire LCAs landed much further east, on Jig Green (East) rather than Jig Green (West), nearly opposite WN36 and with no supporting DD tanks, the plan was foundering. A Company 1st Hampshires captured WN36, while B Company and HQ made its way inland to Les Roquettes. Each company took a number of casualties on the beach and moving inland. C Company landed near the same place twenty-five minutes later, and its commander could see about twenty soldiers from A Company fighting and mopping up what was WN36. C Company was ordered to join the remainder of A Company's' attack on Le Hamel, and attempts were made to approach the area, but, despite the help of a Crab tank from the breaching team, it was becoming impossible to move along the beach against what was described as heavy machine-gun, mortar and shell fire. As the Crab tank moved closer to Le Hamel along the beach, it was hit and caught fire.

Dennis Hawes, 1st Hampshires, was on his third assault landing and '… vaguely remember dressing many ghastly wounds as I made my way along the beach, experiencing a terrible sense of helplessness'.[28] George Davis, from the same regiment,

> felt like a one man band, carrying a wireless set on my chest, a huge pack on my back, a shovel stuffed behind it and a reel of cable under one arm as well as rifle and ammunition. When the ramp was finally flung down our Sergeant Major shouted 'follow me men' and jumped. But he wasn't there to follow; he simply disappeared under the landing craft. Once on the beach we made for a ridge at the top. Our company runner was there lying down. We called a greeting but it brought no response, he was dead.[29]

The 1st Hampshires War Diary records that that the assault and reserve companies landed as per orders on Jig Green Beach, but:

> The aerial bombardment did not seem as effective as expected. Enemy machine gun nests survived the aerial, naval and Arty bombardment and made the fullest use of their underground, well-concealed and well-built positions. The narrowness of the beach and the presence of mines added to the difficulties of the Bns. task.[30]

As he approached the beach, Lt Alan Norman of A Company, 1st Hampshires, recalls:

> The coxswain sending someone around with a tot of rum each. Normally only one or two would be seasick, but every one of us including me was sick. Not too much firing coming our way. We are chugging in, binoculars up and I said to Tony Boyd, my superior, 'I can't identify anything!' He said I will have a look. 'Oh my God. It's not our area!' I don't remember seeing the other two craft of A Company near us either. We had drifted too far east. We were supposed to land on the ramp near the 88mm gun, and the other two platoons along the sea wall of Le Hamel. As we are coming near I get my Bren Gunner – who had brought a great steel case full of 30+ Bren Gun magazines – to fire at any target on shore he fancied. He said to me that he had not fired as many rounds for a long time, and even had to change the barrel and dangled it in the water to cool it! As we came in we were told to get under cover. I was looking through two slots in the ramps. We grounded and with not a shot fired at us – remarkable! My sergeant said that ours would be the first footsteps in the sand and we were of course. Out we come, everyone is supposed to run up the beach but we were so groggy. One man was so ill we had to carry his equipment, I carried his Bangalore torpedo and they dragged him up the beach by

his epaulettes. Jogging is the best we could manage. Get up to the top, get down and almost straight in front of us is a pillbox. I immediately get one section to attack it on the run with a flanking attack while the other two sections lay down covering fire. Soon there was a great cheer and they all trooped back – it was empty!

While they congratulated themselves and formed back up, someone said: 'Look over there sir'. Nearby could be seen a slit trench, concreted in – and with helmeted figures moving about. 'Quick as a flash one of the lads squirted his Sten Gun over the top'. Norman delegated a section to go and round them up, and the Germans surrendered immediately. He sent them off with one of his men, who was suffering from malaria, as guard to these prisoners. Norman relates that many of the veteran men in his platoon were taking Mepecrine for malaria.

The assumption is that this was part of WN36, actually a target for 1st Dorsets, although between WN36 and Le Hamel further west, reconnaissance photographs taken in May appear to show a single pillbox and fortified position. Doubtless some of the soldiers were still sheltering in the trench from the bombardment, and should have been manning the pillbox.

Wondering what to do next, Norman tried to make contact by radio, and finally sent a runner, who came back with an order to move to attack the original target. By this time, they were still lucky enough not to have received any casualties. Quickly, they trotted along a track behind the sand dunes towards Le Hamel; the next thing Norman knew was that he was lying on the track in considerable pain with his arm at a funny angle. 'My platoon had disappeared, apart from two or three, who I shouted at to "get on" but I am not sure they were alive.' He had been shot and spun around, with the bullet going through his arm and into his body and taking out two ribs. He could not move. Coming up the track was an AVRE, and Norman was very worried it would run him over. He waved his arm and was shot again through the upper arm. He could see the sea and two or three wounded men there moving around by the water's edge. But as the tide came in, they drowned, and the bodies floated. Later, one of the sergeant majors from another platoon came by, took off Norman's boots and rubbed his feet, which were hurting. The sergeant gave him some morphine which Norman was carrying, marked him with an 'M', and after a short conversation, went off.[31]

After the 'run-in' of an hour and a half, B Company 1st Hampshire Regiment arrived several hundred metres further east of A Company. When near the beach, Major Mott reported that 'some shells or mortar bombs began to fall in the water, but nothing really close to us. Ahead we could see LCTs disgorging tanks and the underwater obstacles were high and dry being tackled by intrepid sappers.'[32] Jumping in too early, in water well over his head, Mott grabbed a chain and was dragged in. He was soaked to the skin, his army issue watch stopped, his binoculars were misty and he had lost his map case. As his men and others moved forward through a crookedly white taped route through the high marsh grass and reeds, they were hit by mortars, and men from Company HQ and eleven Platoon were killed and wounded. Carrying on, and realizing they were in the wrong place, they reorganized around Les Roquettes, which was ruined and deserted. A and C Companies had gone directly towards Le Hamel, being held up considerably by WN37. Now Mott organized a move on Asnelles as the Hampshires D Company arrived, followed by the first platoons of 2nd Devons, who had landed at 0810. These moves were resisted heavily to begin with by the Germans, despite the use of the tanks ashore. Also, the Hampshires had already lost the CO of A Company, Major Baines, and several other platoon commanders alongside Alan Norman and a number of senior NCOs. Their commanding officer, Lt Col. Nelson-Smith, was badly wounded on the beach, and radios had been disabled by water and enemy fire. They had lost communication and could not call on fire support from the warships. The situation was not helped when the battalion second-in-command, Major Martin, landed around 0930, and was killed instantly. And not only had the RE tanks been badly hit, but the three supporting DD tanks from the Sherwood Rangers B Squadron drowned when they landed, and another was disabled by gunfire (C Squadron supported the Dorsets' landing; the A Squadron tanks were not DD tanks, and had to be more or less landed dryshod).[33]

On the Hampshires' left flank, the other Jig Beach assault battalion was the 1st Dorsetshire Regiment. It had been tasked to deal with WN36, but, like the Hampshires, had drifted much further east. Frank Wiltshire's memoir states the following:

> I jumped from the LCA straight into about 7ft of deep water. I was the number one of the mortar team of five men. There were six mortar teams. After landing in the water, I had to jettison the base of my mortar as it weighed over 50lbs and it would have kept me under the water. After wading out of the water, I had a 100 yards dash across sand to reach the bank. Eventually we managed to assemble one mortar out of the six, the other five were lost. I got the mortar in a firing position, but the barrel was full of sand and water, where somebody had dragged it along the sand. After seeing my friends killed and injured around me, I thought it would be my turn any moment.

Wiltshire believes it was about two hours from landing to getting inland before they could get their mortar into action.[34]

The young infantryman David Bushell of 1st Dorsets remembers that:

> Going in to land, and this Marine (one of the small crew and in charge of lowering the ramp on the boat), came around with a big rum jar. I said I don't drink mate, in fact I think everyone said no – especially the ones being sick! He said 'your loss is my gain' and put the jar on his shoulder and drunk from it like some American Hillbilly! We sat on the middle bench which was the seat for the assault section. George Davey was an old regular soldier from about 1934, only 5' 8" tall and was to be first out with me following. We had landed on a ridge of sand and the Marine - who was about 6'2"- jumped in up to his chin and then George jumped in and went under the water. The Marine leant over and grabbed him by the hair to keep him above water and walked him in nose above water. When I jumped in I was prepared and jumped in with my rifle above my head landing on tip toes and the water was still up to my nose! I was still laughing at George – and he had lost his tin hat and rifle! Effectively that put me first on the beach and I was aware of the whistling of shells – we had seen a boat blown out of the water.
>
> On the way in we were told to keep our heads down. Then we hit this sandbar and had to get out. We ran forward through some obstacles on the sand and we

were being fired at by machine guns and rifles. Bullets were whistling nearby. We charged up to the top of the beach and laid down in rough grassy cover waiting for further orders. We were near the road at the back of the beach. George soon replaced his helmet and rifle from a soldier that had been killed on the beach.

We were told to move off and went up this fairly gentle grassy slope. The guns were firing at us from the buildings further to the right. Walking forward we came to a village and there were children playing! Just an hour later! Then these French women started shouting at us because of the shelling.[35]

The 1st Dorset War Diary records that '0725. A and B Coys touched down on the beach. A Coy right, B Coy left. Both Coys landed approx. 600 yards east of correct posn. A Coy pushed forward to line of road running E. from Le Hamel without difficulty.' The Diary then reports, though, that within 500 yards of landing, A Company lost Major Jones, Lt Ellis and CSM Howell, all wounded by shell and infantry fire. Captain Royle took over command of A Company. B Company, meanwhile, was suffering 'considerable casualties' from shell, mortar and machine-gun fire, but pushed on to firm base at Les Roquettes. At 0745, C and D Companies landed. Some of C Company landed opposite WN36, and finding it already suppressed by 1st Hampshires, pushed on to Les Roquettes. C Company took casualties from mines and mortar fire. Joining C Company was a FOO with two signalmen and another observation post (OP) assistant from 90th Field Regiment. They were expecting to meet with their armoured vehicle on the beach and use the RM Centaur tanks for initial shoots. They could find neither, and proceeded on foot with C Company. They reported that the beach was becoming crowded and also under shell, mortar and rifle fire, with casualties also being caused by mines. Apparently, their journey inland through a burning hayfield to Les Roquettes was aided by 'an ancient Boche who obligingly pointed out the path through the minefield'. They report observing four 88 mm guns being brought into action on the Meuvaines Ridge; they were able to do little about it. At 0750, the 1st Dorsets Tactical HQ landed alongside D Company, again about 600 yards east of the planned beach area of landing. D Company pushed on to Les Roquettes. C Company, meanwhile, advanced towards Buhot, and joining with some of 1st Hampshires, faced 'considerable opposition' during the advance. Houses on the southern side of Asnelles contained numbers of Germans willing to fight, and six were killed and ten captured.[36]

Harold Lewis came in slightly later, with part of the battalion transport. On their lorry, they were carrying rations and spare clothing for A Company, plus the battalion records and grave markers. Spare ammunition was on another lorry. Luckily, their lorry got ashore all right, only slightly wet, but deep enough for Harold to get his boots full of water. Leaving the lorry on the beach, George reported to Captain Whittington, the beachmaster. He was sent just inland to where HQ had been established near Les Roquettes. It was noisy, shells and mortars were still landing on the beach, and naval shells were flying inland. He started to collect details of the dead men and help ensure the injured were looked after.[37]

Back on the beach, and despite the bombardment, mines were proving a considerable problem both on and leaving the beach. One of the colourfully named 'Thug parties', 295 Field Company, was attached to 231 Brigade for the landings. Its men were now needed to deal with the mines. T. Curran had landed from the *Empire Spearhead* and, feeling queasy, had wrapped his D-Day breakfast in newspaper, placing it in the map pocket of his battledress. Wading ashore, he passed 'a frog man' – a member of the LCOCU. He noticed a flail tank on fire on the beach, and his unit started to sweep the beach using mine detector equipment. Finding no apparent mines, they laid white tape around the searched area, but one of the bulldozers clearing the beach turned over a number of mines. Made of wood and with few nails or other metal parts, they were undetectable. The sappers promptly got down on their knees, and, using their bayonets, probed the soil. Later, remembering his breakfast, Curran removed a sticky mess of bread and fried breakfast from his map pocket.[38]

Now on the Jig section of beach, it was the turn of the reserve battalion of 2nd Devons to land. They started for shore at 0705 from HMS *Glenroy*, and A and B Companies landed just over an hour later at 0810, after a difficult ship to shore journey. 'The sea was very rough, and there were many cases of sea-sickness on the run in.'[39] The War Diary also records that the 'landing was extremely difficult and hazardous due to the rough seas' and 'The landing was rendered more difficult by the presence of enemy beach obstacles.'

Lt Col. Nevill reports that, despite being in touch with 231 Brigade HQ by wireless, they could get little information on how the assault was going, and only realized the problems caused by resistance at Le Hamel and Asnelles after they had landed. Running in, they used the church spire of Asnelles as a marker. Also, realizing that many of the mined obstacles were still in place, and on a rising tide, speed had to be reduced to manoeuvre the LCAs safely to shore. This loss of power helped the tide to push the landing craft eastwards. Lt Col. Nevill landed around WN36, and observed dead German bodies around the strongpoint.

> We expected to see a nice clear beach with all the correct signs neatly arrayed pointing the way to our assembly area. A very different picture greeted us. The beach was covered with a swarm of troops lying flat on their faces, ostrich-like, trying to make as small a target of themselves as possible. All was not well.[40]
>
> Before the majority of the Devons were to land Lt. 'Chancer' Pearson was in charge of the Pioneer Platoon and on landing they had to lay Bangalore Torpedoes through the barbed wire and blow it up so that the wire was already blown when the troops landed. On jumping out of the LCA the depth of water was considerably deeper than thought and the fuses of the Bangalore Torpedoes refused to light.[41]

Trying to make sense of the situation – and not in contact with any of his men – Nevill with his intelligence officer, Captain Wood, walked towards Le Hamel along the beach. They noticed knocked-out tanks on and just off the beach, and they were aware of the 'considerable noise of rifle fire from Le Hamel, and an occasional anti-tank round opened up'. On this journey, they came across the wounded CO of 1st Hampshires, still directing the attack on Le Hamel. Not able to breach the coastal minefield or find any of his men, Nevill turned back and made contact with Brigadier Stanier, who had just landed. Apparently, Nevill said to Stanier: 'If I can find any of my chaps I will bypass Asnelles and go straight for Ryes – anything to get away from this unhealthy beach.' Shortly after this, he made contact with his battalion and started to get it reorganized.

Tom Hewitt was one of the B Company 2nd Devons landing here:

We got near to the shore, and one of the older chaps went off the ramp first with an officer – and the landing craft went right over them. [*This was Major Howard from B Company, who suffered crushed ribs and CSM Bembo, who was also severely injured.*] I jumped in and the water was up to my armpits. It was difficult to make progress with your rifle and two haversacks, one on your back and one on your side. We just about pulled our way onto the beach. There was not a great deal of fire on the beach, nor much in the way of obstacles, and we rushed to the edge of the beach and got down. Then we caught some fire. The man next to me put down his Bren gun and a bullet ricocheted off it. We got more and more fire as we went in. We got down in this gulley and we were always taught never to get up where you go down. We did what we were trained for, but some of the officers got up and caught a bullet in the head. Further in we came across pillboxes and trenches but we went past them. We got into column and started moving up the road.[42]

Ten minutes later, at 0810, Battalion HQ landed, followed by C and D Companies. They report that 'the beach was under fire from snipers and spasmodic gunfire and mortar fire'.[43] A and B Companies dealt with some of these problems, and remained firm based for a time in the sand dunes, while C and D Companies advanced. 'The battalion left the beaches in single file, along a narrow footpath the sides of which were supposed to be mined'.[44] By 0915, C and D Companies were approaching Le Hamel from the east, and A and B Companies followed them at 0955. With the expected concentration area of Asnelles still in enemy hands, the Devons HQ had to reorganize, and there was some difficulty in the new orders reaching the rifle companies with changes of plan. Partly, this was because C and D Companies had already become embroiled in the fighting to clear Asnelles, and with C Company fully committed, D Company was extracted to lead the advance directly to the village of Ryes, with A and B Companies following.

At some time, Lt Col. Nevill was informed that the C Company commander, Major Duke, had been shot and killed at Le Hamel. In fact, he had been talking to Lt Pearson just after the Bangalore torpedo incident, and was standing up when he was shot at the instant Pearson told him to get down.[45] During the advance, D Company received considerable mortar fire, and their company commander, Major Parlby, was wounded in the leg. Lt Col. Nevill makes the point that he lost three of his company commanders in half an hour. A company went into the lead around 1130, with the stream of La Gronde Riviere as the axis of advance. The 2nd Devons were more or less back following the original plan. One minor problem was with the name of the stream they were following; its small size belied its grand title (which apparently had been read as Grande), and initially officers had a problem identifying it!

At least now all of the riflemen of 231 Brigade were ashore, along with some supporting AVREs, the Field Artillery Regiments and other armour. The follow-up vehicles of Bren carriers, jeeps, further dryshod armour and beach battalions were all beginning to land, and the beach area was becoming very congested. But already the plan was falling well behind schedule, due to the greater number of obstacles in the sea than expected, poor sea conditions, and the unexpectedly heavy German resistance from Le Hamel and Asnelles – and the next expected line of German resistance, at

Ryes and on the hillside above Arromanches, to be tackled by the Devons and Dorsets respectively, was only just being approached. Le Hamel was to remain a serious problem on the right flank of the landing for most of the day. As well as being missed by the bombing due to the weather conditions, the German soldiers manning the positions had received another early stroke of luck. The 147th Field Regiment was planned to bombard the area on the run-in with its 25-pounder Sextons. This bombardment was to begin 10,000 yards from the beach and continue virtually until landing. But the motor launch leading the 147th Field Regiment LCTs as navigating vessel broke down, and it was decided that 147th Field Regiment would join with 90th Field Regiment and their leading Motor Launch (ML), and both regiments bombarded the target of the 90th – Les Roquettes, apparently already abandoned by the Germans.

Meanwhile, on King Beach, the assaulting companies of infantry were also coming ashore with the AVREs and DD Tanks. The 5th East Yorks landed on the left to take La Riviere, with D Company left and A Company right. C and B Companies landed as support left and right, respectively. The assault companies were to clear the beach and sea front defences, with the follow-up companies advancing to take a crossroads east of La Riviere (left) and Ver-sur-Mer inland a mile on the right flank. They lost no craft on the run-in, and landed on time at 0725. The Battalion War Diary reports that the landing was 'very wet in up to four feet of water'. A and B Companies appear to have had a reasonably straightforward landing against 'spasmodic' opposition, and advanced to take the Mont Fleury lighthouse battery (WN34) fairly quickly. They took only eight casualties themselves, and captured thirty Germans. They report that the German battery commander committed suicide.[46] At 0750, B Company landed, passed through A Company and continued to Ver-sur-Mer. It appears that the earlier bombing around the lighthouse was accurate and effective, and A Company found the 75 mm and 50 mm guns here undamaged but covered with debris from craters over 10 metres away. One underground bunker was destroyed, and another badly damaged, along with a number of buildings. This almost certainly explains why resistance here was lighter and a German platoon surrendered quite quickly.

On the left flank of the battalion landing, it was a different story. D Company met strong opposition from the enemy around the 88 mm gun in its protected casemate at WN33 and other weapons. Wading ashore through deep water, they were 'picked off by small arms fire and were unable to reach shore'.[47] The 88 mm gun knocked out supporting tanks, and it was here that an AVRE exploded, causing many casualties. Two platoon commanders were killed, and when finally the shelter of the sea wall was reached, the men were showered with grenades. The bombing and bombardment had not diminished the fire from the 88 mm or 50 mm, or from several machine-gun and mortar posts. Equally, the men of the field companies and LCOCU, still working on obstacles in the sea, were taking heavy casualties.[48] It was the arrival of C Company over twenty minutes later that began to relieve the situation, although they took heavy casualties themselves on landing. By moving further right, they reached the beach and began to make inroads into the enemy positions. At the same time, the naval forces had been contacted, and as related earlier, particularly LCG and LCF vessels moved close in and started to destroy the enemy positions. C and D Companies now began fighting through the rear yards and gardens of houses, advancing towards WN33. Until the arrival of Captain Bell and his tank, the 88 mm gun position still held out. The

Battalion War Diary reports forty-five prisoners of war taken, all from 736 Infantry Regiment. By 1000 hours, the battalion transport was starting to land, and reported the loss by drowning of a vehicle carrying all maps and documents for the battalion. C and D Companies were reorganized into one composite company, and then started moving towards the village of Crepon. A and B Companies were already on their way. The advance was inevitably contested by snipers and small groups of Germans standing to fight.[49]

Bert Cooper landed with 5th East Yorks, remembering

> the very rough journey in the LCA with 32 men and four marines, two working the engine and two at the front with guns. When we landed they dropped us near to shore and we were dashing up beach – there were a tank, shell hit that and when I heard him fire I dropped and at the side of me were Nobby Clark and he was split in two, and he were still talking till he died. There were bodies all over and everyone made for a big wall on the left. All at the front were barbed wire and they were all shouting for Bangalore torpedoes and when the wire was blown we started getting through then. I got to where the gun emplacement was facing right down the beach. I couldn't fire my Sten Gun as it was all full of sand. We dropped behind some cover and I said to a kid from Sheffield 'they have just sniped four of us!' Give me some grenades (we only carried two). I threw four grenades into this emplacement and they all surrendered. In front of us was a minefield; in it was a flail tank with the front blown off. We started using our bayonets to check for mines, but when the Germans started surrendering we knew which areas were clear. We ended with about fifty odd prisoners. Another of our corporals was killed by a stick grenade about then. Then we moved up past this great big house. I was surprised to find a naval bod with us who it turned out was with the Forward Officer Bombardment directing the fire of the warships. When we were moving forward he gave instructions to fire on an 88mm anti-tank gun we spotted. He contacted a ship and got a direct hit first time and blew the 88 out of its position![50]

Dennis Bowen also landed with 5th East Yorks, but he had only joined D Company in the battalion at the last moment before sailing around 4 June. Aged just eighteen and a half, he had been in the reserve detachment to sail to France later as part of the reinforcement holding unit for casualties, but he and several others replaced men who fell sick through malaria on board the LSI. He held the men who already wore the Africa medal ribbon in complete awe, recognizing that many had served in France in 1940 and through the desert war. He only became aware of the invasion on the LSI where he saw for the first time maps of their actual invasion area. Some of the veteran soldiers were clearly fed up that they were yet again to be in the spearhead of a major landing.

> On the LCA that I was on, we got into it while it was just on the LSI davits then lowered into the sea. It was staffed by several Royal Marines. We sailed from the ship and there were already other empty LCAs coming back from shore to our LSI. Men were getting into these by scrambling down nets to. The sea was very rough and you could see some men having to jump or fall into the LCAs. We got into

a formation led by a motor launch that sped around shouting orders through a loud hailer. We could see the land, and as we approached the noise got louder and louder and eventually was so terrific. I was not scared as it had not really got into my head that this was a real action.

We were told in the LCA to 'get your bayonets on'. When the front of the LCA went down and I saw the beach it hit me that this was double serious. I was halfway down the craft and the first few off jumped into fairly shallow water, but with the swell going up and down we jumped into deeper water just above our knees. The Marines kept the engine going to keep the bows on the beach. We were under fire as we landed. On the beach was a Sherman tank burning and every NCO was shouting 'get forward, get forward!' Everybody ran and got down under a little lip of sand at the edge of the road. Our platoon had a specific task to attack a large gun emplacement over to our left and we had to knock it out. When we got over the road we were to go left towards the lighthouse and take the emplacement from the rear. We had an AVRE with us to help knock out the emplacement. We went about three hundred yards inland and turned left, but as we approached the emplacement the AVRE was hit by the Germans and blew up with a massive explosion causing quite a few casualties. But another tank had approached from the front and hit the emplacement, so as we approached the Germans ran out and surrendered. We then moved forward towards Crepon and Creully and at some point were joined by tanks from 4/7 Dragoon Guards.[51]

The Germans resisted stoutly, and made a fighting retreat from the village house by house, driven back by a combination of tanks from 4/7 Dragoon Guards and AVREs battering through or blowing down the high garden walls and the East Yorkshire infantry following up. By the end of the action at La Riviere, C Company had lost its CO wounded and second-in-command killed, while D Company had lost two platoon officers killed and the company commander wounded. The War Diary also reports eighty-five Other ranks (ORs) as casualties between the two companies. Nor was this the end of action in this area.

Landing at 0740, the King Beach security battalion, 2nd Battalion Hertfordshire Regiment, got involved in fighting to clear the area. George Church remembers that:

We crossed the channel on the 'Empire Lance' and had been split from our battalion through lack of space on their transport. The battalion had been trained as proper infantry though tasked as a beach group. My Platoon landed with the East Yorkshires near the old Tram Station on King Sector, Gold Beach. We landed at 0740. I was a Section Corporal. We moved up the road with E. Yorks towards 'Lavatory Pan' Villa and the Mont Fleury Battery. However before we reached the villa our HQ, now landed on the beach, called us back. Our job then was to clear the beach huts from the track bottom towards Ver sur Mer of German snipers. Clearing these huts involved chucking a handful of grenades and then mopping up. The Germans had dug down into the basements and cellars of buildings and created firing slits. Having cleared this area we moved through the old town into the lighthouse area and there we copped it. We came under Spandau fire and a mortar or light shell fell amongst us killing the Bren gun team. As we withdrew I saw that our Platoon Sergeant and a corporal were out in front and badly wounded. Against the advice of the remaining members of the section I decided to have a go at getting them back. I crawled out and got hold of both of them and managed to get them back. Anyone would have done it.[52]

For his bravery, George Church was awarded the Military Medal.

Immediately to the west of La Riviere, 6th Green Howards landed at 0735. Again, their War Diary makes a comment on the sea state: 'The LCAs made their hazardous dash for the mainland in a sea that did not favour a landing so important, whilst Allied cruisers and destroyers heavily engaged enemy shore batteries.' On the left, D Company had to land and advance and take the Mont Fleury battery at the top of the rise. On the right, A Company had to take the coastal position of WN35 and then continue up the track and take WN35b, a smaller position in a quarry. The D Company landing beach was not directly defended by any emplacements, and here 233 Field Company managed to cut the enemy wire and clear the minefield to the lateral road fairly swiftly.

Charles Hill in D Company was in the first wave ashore, and in the same LCA as CSM Hollis, who was to win the only VC awarded for bravery on D-Day. On the run-in, Hollis had fired at what he thought was a small position, as related in the Introduction, and burnt his hand on the Bren gun. His VC was awarded for two outstanding acts of bravery: in clearing a German position in front of the Mont Fleury battery that had been bypassed in the initial assault, and later, in Crepon, by charging into an area under fire and retrieving some men who were pinned down. Charles can remember the padre waving as they left the ship and his platoon got into the LCA and were then lowered into the sea.[53]

> We all had to carry extra items like a case of 3inch mortar shells, a six foot scaling ladder or bangalore torpedo. I carried mortar shells. I was up to my chest in water as we landed and at least one man was drowned. [*This was Sergeant Hill, who fell into a submerged shell hole and was run over by a landing craft.*[54]] The motor launch saw us all the way in. Once ashore I could not immediately use my rifle as it was full of sand. We more or less landed in the right place. Mortar bombs were landing on the beach and we were being fired at. There was a flail tank ahead clearing mines and we were very quickly up the track towards the Mont Fleury battery. All the gunners came out and were crying and had all their family photographs spread out. The Colonel came out and seemed about seven feet tall; I kicked him up the backside!

After landing, Hollis charged up to the high-water mark, where he and some Bren gunners laid down a smokescreen using the 2 inch mortar to aid the crossing of the minefield. There was already so much smoke and dust, it hardly seemed worth it.[55]

Only one of the battery positions was complete with its gun inside. It may have fired its gun, but had taken a direct hit by a 500 lb bomb and was wrecked. The other three guns were in open positions to the rear and their casemates had not been completed. They had been effectively dealt with by HMS *Orion*, which hit the three guns with twelve rounds from its 6 inch guns.[56]

A Company landed east of WN35 and then turned to take it. A sea wall up to 3 metres high ran in front of WN35, and the men of A Company faced increasing machine-gun and mortar fire coming from the occupants of the pillboxes, trenches and shelters. Some of the company had to shelter by the sea wall, but three AVREs and a 4/7 Dragoon Guards DD tank helped in the final brave assault by A Company. Faced with the infantrymen and tanks inside their positions, the remaining Germans surrendered.

Following the assault quite closely, Signals Officer Lt Kenneth Taylor wrote:

Eventually approached beach and found things difficult. Kept grounding and hitting obstacles with shells falling in water. Made a few attempts to get close in but failed. Eventually decided to climb out but the ramp refused to go down at first. Shrapnel hitting craft so we jumped for it at 0800hrs and water only up to waist. 27 set got wet thro' and would not work. Cairns hit in leg. Stopped a few minutes at edge of beach. Woods hit in eye. Got on to coast road where things were unpleasant owing to mortars and shells flying around and minefield on both sides. Some logs on the side of the road provided welcome protection.[57]

The War Diary recounts that the assault on Mont Fleury Battery and WN35 was highly successful, with surprisingly low casualties.

B Company, following up, had loaded into the LCAs using scrambling nets. Lt John Milton remembers that he was not actually seasick, though many were:

We had to jump down from the bottom of the netting into the boats and I don't know how we didn't lose anybody over the side. We circled round and round until all the craft were gathered together and we then we set off in. It was incredible that these two young Royal Marines landed us exactly in the right place and we were lucky to miss all obstacles. We went up towards the house with the circular drive which we could clearly see. [*From the shape of the drive in aerial photographs, some wags had nicknamed this 'Lavatory Pan Villa'. It was situated to the front of the Mont Fleury battery at the top of the rise from the beach. It is still there today, surrounded by new housing.*] Flail tanks were already there at work and we followed them up to the house. We did not have any casualties at that time. The assault companies were several hundred yards ahead of us. Hollis probably saved my life by taking out the pillbox. Our CO Robin Hastings was very much the boss and very good too, although only a few years older than me.[58]

According to the 6th Green Howards War Diary, B Company cleared the quarry containing WN35b east of Lavatory Pan Villa. C Company moved forward quickly to clear and occupy the hilltop area around Pt 52 on the ridge overlooking the village of Meuvaines. This was the battalion forming-up area. By 1000, the Battalion HQ and Support Company had landed, and before 1100 the area of King Beach was under control and men and vehicles started to stream ashore, some diverted to these beaches and part of Jig Red Beach because of the heavy fighting still taking place around Le Hamel and Asnelles.

After the difficulties in coming ashore. Kenneth Taylor gives a good description of the move forward:

Glad to find myself not unduly worried and able to walk around and see how people were getting on. Most of them OK but a few rather shaken. Quite a number of prisoners coming in looking completely dazed. 'Achtung Minen' notices on roadside stick in my mind. Very glad to move up road away from the beach where things a little quieter. Grass on fire provided a useful smoke screen. Moved thro' Ver sur Mer and was 'Spandau'ed' a little. Talked to a few prisoners including Russians.[59] [*To be 'Spandau'ed' was to come under the withering fire of a German MG42.*]

Lt Sidney Beck gives a very good account of 86th Field Regiment coming ashore after its run-in shoot, and the help it was able to give to the Green Howards in particular, and one gets a very good idea from his description about how events on this part of the beach were developing:

The three craft carrying A, C & E Troops beached first. A Troop went into action immediately on the narrow strip of beach with water lapping round their tracks. With this support the Green Howards rushed and overpowered the enemy battery, the enemy gunners being demoralised by the very heavy bombing and naval bombardment during the assault. By 0845 the second half of the Regiment was due to land. It was getting difficult to find a clear spot on the beach. The strong wind and tide had made the first boats ground almost sideways to the coast instead of head on. Boats which should have pulled away after unloading had been damaged or stuck and the beach was fast becoming jammed.

The Royal Engineer detachment on board the B Troop LCT rolled out the roly-poly and the Sappers waded ashore. They were a Beach Maintenance Party. The guns had a short distance to run through water, dragging behind them flat 'porpoises' containing ammunition. Capt Hall, already landed, his part in the run-in shoot having been most effectively carried out, was waiting on the beaches to direct the vehicles and guns. We joined the single line of traffic making for the only exit from the beach. The beach was by now a narrow strip between high water mark and the tide, crammed with boats and vehicles and men in seeming confusion. Rolling clouds of smoke from burning buildings and grass formed a fitting background. The first German prisoners standing dazed and bewildered amid all the activity were a centre of interest. One prisoner lifted a wounded Tommy out of the path of the vehicles. B Troop went into action alongside the knocked out casements of the Mount Fleury Battery, only recently captured. The Command Post was established in a bomb-crater. Three Centaur tanks, manned by Royal Marines also occupied the area and for the first and last time in the campaign B Troop had 7 guns. As soon as they were in action, the other half of the Regiment were moved up from the beaches and A Troop came alongside B to form a Battery Position.[60]

Neville Howard with his M10 tank destroyer was also ashore with 73rd Anti-Tank Regiment. Their LCT had hit a mine on landing, and drifted seaward with a flooded engine room. While they were drifting, they pulled some injured soldiers out of the water, including a Royal Marine captain. Eventually, another landing craft nudged them to shore and they began unloading:

Somehow a jeep, under the control of a captain (I think he was a medical officer) squeezed onto the ramp just in front of us. The jeep, almost submerged, came to a halt at the bottom of the ramp. The captain stood, up to his chest in the water, waving to me to halt our descent down the ramp, but I ordered my driver to proceed and the jeep was pushed gently to one side. We had no trouble getting off the beach, which, because of the rising tide, had narrowed to a thin strip of sand at this point, backed by a shallow bank of dune.

Other parts of our battery, including the remaining vehicles of our troop, were already ditching what they could of the materials used during water-proofing when we joined them just off the beach, and we learned that we had been landed well to the left of where we should have been. We soon moved off in a column of vehicles, climbing a slope of land running parallel to the sea. About halfway up our column halted and I dismounted to attend to the wants of nature. I heard the boom of a heavy gun and the sound of a shell coming our way. I turned to remount just as the shell, a dud (or I wouldn't be writing this) landed a yard away. I was splattered with earth as the shell left a steaming hole where it had buried itself. My crew, and the troop sergeant, Sergeant Kitchen, who was travelling on my M10, found it rather amusing.

We came to a halt again about a mile or so inland from where we should have landed. We were stopped beside a gate surrounding part of a large garden and two elderly ladies came to talk to us, while from the direction of the sea came the sounds of a heavy battle. After a couple of minutes one of the ladies told us there was a German soldier in the large shed in the garden and would it be safe for him to come out now. I assured her he would not be harmed, and to tell him to come out. He came with arms raised, and on our side of the gate I motioned him to lower his arms. As soldiers go, he was an old man, and he had tears in his eyes as he tried to interest me in family photos he took from his pocket.

There was a narrow road leading in the direction of the sea, and I pointed down the road for him to go. After a quick farewell to the ladies he went, with a look of disbelief, that so soon after becoming a prisoner, he was set on his way alone. I've often wondered if he made it to the beach. The time would have been mid-morning, about 10am. Our column continued its advance inland.[61]

The supporting battalion of 69th Brigade was 7th Green Howards. After landing, they were to exploit south through the 5th East Yorks and 6th Green Howards. They beached from 0800 in the order B and D Companies, followed by C and A Companies and Battalion HQ. They found the beach still under slight mortar fire with grass fires burning. One of their objectives was the casemated gun battery of WN32 or Marefontaine battery, consisting of four 100 mm guns, one to each casemate. This battery had been shelled by HMS *Belfast*, which had fired 224 rounds of 6 inch shells at it, seemingly successfully, as it had remained quiet, although after capture it was found to have fired 87 rounds in total.[62] In fact, like the Mont Fleury battery, it had not been completed, with protective blast shields missing from the casemates. When B, D and A Companies came in sight of the batteries, movement was seen, but the Germans surrendered to C Company, supported by two 'Crocodile' flame-throwing tanks from 13 Troop, 141 RAC, giving forty to fifty prisoners.[63] The tanks did not engage using flame, but fired two rounds from their 75 mm guns and supported C Company with machine-gun fire. On D-Day, none of the specialized flame-throwing tanks was used in its flame-throwing role. As the battalion proceeded along two parallel routes, increasing numbers of snipers and machine-gun fire were encountered. Progress continued, and the battalion was joined by five of its carriers with 3 inch mortar and anti-tank guns. Also, it had support from 4/7 Dragoon Guards and 86th Field Regiment artillery.[64]

Alongside the infantry, armour and artillery, very important units of the RAMC were being landed just after the assault battalions went in. Peter Johnson remembers that he was to land on Jig Green East by 0900 and set up a beach dressing station (BDS) in the pillboxes on the beach, if possible, or even on Item Red, which would have taken him directly in front of Le Hamel. From the LSI, he and his men clambered down into an LCT, jumping the final few feet. The sea was very rough, and as they approached the shore, Johnson picked up various landmarks from the prior briefings.

> As we came closer, the noise increased, and the rattle of small arms went on to a background of the Fleet doing its stuff behind. We got to within a mile, and then out came a couple of LCAs to offload. We got off our two first parties, and waited for more LCAs. None came near, and so we began to edge in to land. We were shooed off by a naval control, who told us that our beach was not yet captured, and we couldn't go in until some guns had been silenced up the hill above Cabane. Borrowing the skipper's glasses, I could see the battle going on. Then we saw a tank creep round the shoulder of the hill, and two quick rounds into each of the embrasures, and all was over. The infantry swarmed over the hill, and in we went, watched more tanks skirting another hill, and dashing over the skyline.
>
> As we came closer, we saw that we should have a long wade, – indeed, it was nearly 500 yds to the top of the beach. We couldn't come far in because the ship had lost her anchor. And so couldn't winch herself off again. We saw the wrecked craft, drowned tanks, the obstacles and mines, – all so suddenly brought into focus and held there even more firmly as the door clanged down in 3 foot of water. No one was shooting at us, there was just a few shells dropping haphazard, and quite a number of mines going off. Although we heard bullets crack and whizz no one knew where they were coming from or gone to. I got my crowd off the LCT, and we waved goodbye and set off. Just like any other water – cold, and wet; and having an unpleasant tendency to get deeper in odd places. It did, and we got wet to just below the armpits – which wasn't too bad, I suppose. As we trudged up the broad beach I passed a war correspondent wading in, and said Good Morning to him – he looked at me as if I was stark mad.
>
> Not much organization on the beach that I could find, and nowhere to set up my show. Dotted everywhere were sodden bundles of the Hampshires, Devons and Dorsets that had led the infantry spearhead. Tanks still burning, LCTs blown up by mines, houses afire, craters, smells, Achtung Minen and skulls and crossbones. And crowds of French civilians rushing down to the LCTs, and getting taken back to England. And a few prisoners – and so many, many wounded and nowhere to put them. So we moved gingerly through a minefield to the first lateral road – just a track, and we set up on the grass verge, which was 3 feet wide and bounded by traffic one side, and a minefield on the other. Here we looked after our first wounded.[65]

The men of 47 Commando had a very difficult run-in to the shore. They had been split between two landing ships: one was the *Princess Josephine Charlotte*, with eight LCAs that they knew well, and crewed by the Royal Navy; the other was the SS *Victoria*, with six LCAs and most of the medical personnel aboard. From their landing ships, the men of 47 Commando watched the assault battalions of 231 Brigade in their LCAs move towards the shore. The Commandos loaded into their LCAs at 0730 and started towards shore at 0800. About a mile offshore, things began to go wrong, as spouts of water started to erupt between the craft and the shore. A number of German guns on the western slopes above Gold Beach were easily in range, let alone any of the larger guns of the Longues battery still capable of firing. According to 50th Division War Diary, they were especially fired on by units in Le Hamel. An LCA from Q Troop was hit and started to list, twenty-six out of its thirty-six occupants dead or wounded. As the remainder approached Jig West, the beach appeared deserted, with only disabled and blazing tanks apparent on its shores. Now, a run eastward of a mile and a half was required to reach a safer landing zone. The problems on Jig West, therefore, do not appear to have been communicated to 47 Commando. An LCA from Y Troop next hit a mine, and with the front blown off it started sinking: eight killed and a number wounded. Three more of 47 Commandos' LCAs were sunk through mines or swamping, and seven others damaged by mines or gunfire. The remainder landed at around 0925. Only two of the fourteen LCAs that left the LSI that morning were fit after landing for a return journey to their parent craft.

The casualties among the Marines were high, and many had lost equipment and weapons. With the survivors gradually joining together on Gold Beach, and many having to swim ashore minus their kit, an immediate march on Port-en-Bessin was clearly impossible. One Marine even came ashore on Juno Beach, and wrenching a Lewis gun off a beached LCA, made his determined way after laying up overnight to Gold Beach, where he eventually met with the 47 Commando Support Carrier Troop![66] The commandos were originally to rendezvous in Le Hamel. This was clearly impossible, and after receiving information direct from Brigadier Stanier, they gathered together on the road just east of Les Roquettes and were not able to move off until around 1130.[67]

Ted Battley was a member of B Troop in 47 Commando and recalls the following:

> Going into the beach we were still under fire. The Y Troop craft just blew up. I was in the cockpit of our LCA with my Bren Gun and had a view of the whole landing. The whole beach was covered with stranded landing craft and wrecked vehicles. Our coxswain headed for a gap, but there was an underwater obstacle there. The craft hit a spike and we got stuck there. We could not lower the ramp so we went over the side. I expected it to be waist deep, but it went over my head! By lunging forward I managed to get up to the beach and even kept hold of my Bren Gun. The Beachmaster sent me over towards our rendezvous. When I arrived there were already some of our men there. I settled down with my No. 2 (on the Bren Gun) and we stripped down the gun and cleaned it. Checked and reloaded the magazines. Colonel Philips was missing at the time and arrived only just before we set off.[68]

A number of men already on the beach from army units remark that, despite its problems during the landing, the calm and ordered way that 47 Commando went about reorganizing itself was a fine example and raised morale. After 47 Commando moved off, its first contact with the enemy was only 800 yards beyond Buhot. X Troop came under fire and a short exchange of shots ensued. B Troop, passing through, surprised and captured a German battery OP group, seizing a marked-up map of their battery only a few hundred yards further on. The Commando continued towards La Rosiere.

The landing of further tanks, artillery and units of the 104th Beach Sub-Group to organize and control the beaches and clear up any remaining opposition meant that with the incoming tide, great queues of men and vehicles began to form on the narrowing strip of sand. Despite the beach area becoming increasingly organized and its borders cleared of mines and obstructions, there were still few cleared tracks leading from the beaches.

Now, late morning, the decision was taken aboard the command ship *Bulolo* to send in the 'follow-up' 151st and 56th (Independent) Infantry Brigades. Three problems presented themselves. First, Jig Green, the proposed landing area of 56th Brigade, was still under fire; second, the ground between Le Hamel and Ryes, their planned line of advance, was not yet clear; and finally, with the available clear landing space around the borders of Jig Red and King Green, it was not advisable to send in all eighteen LSI (L) carrying both Brigades with nearly 4,000 men between them at once. The first to be sent in was 151st Brigade, landing from its United States Navy (USN) LCI (L) s between 1020, when the Brigade HQ seems to have landed, and 1130.

Captain Peter Goddin, with 151st Brigade HQ, describes a busy scene at the beachhead:

> Our LCIs ran us onto GOLD beach with a wet gap between the vessels' bows and the dry beach. We disembarked down ramps on each side of the bows, so if we were lucky we only got our trouser legs and boots soaking wet. With tapes marking a safe route, we got off the beach and through a minefield as speedily as possible to an assembly area. There we linked up with our jeeps and Brigade HQ command vehicles, half-tracked American all-purpose carriers (M14S). DUKWs were busy ferrying stores ashore, some of them soon to be patients in a drowned DUKW parking area. Brigade HQ lost two officers killed in the landing operation, but we quickly became a cohesive body and off we moved in the direction of our planned D-Day objective, the Caen-Bayeux road.[69]

John Cummer, US Navy, reports:

> I served as Gunner's Mate aboard USS LCI (L) 502, which on 13 April 1944 was detached from US LCI Flotilla Eleven, and designated as group 31, attached to RN Assault Force George. The group was composed of US LCIs 499 (flagship), 500, 501 502, 506, 508 and 511. On D-Day we landed troops of the Durham Light Infantry on Jig Green sector, Gold Beach at 1040. These details are taken from a copy of the log of the 502.[70]

The plan to trans-ship the men from the larger LCI (L) to LCA and LCM was abandoned due to the number of the small craft that had hit obstacles, foundered on landing or broached on the shore, or were simply still playing catch-up with the programme of landing other troops from the LSIs. The US landing craft carrying the Durham Brigade approached shore and grounded as far in as they could. Many men were seasick, and had spent an unpleasant crossing in these smaller craft.

Aboard US LCI (L) 501, Eric Broadhead of 9DLI remembers: 'Time passed, I felt more ill than ever before, it was beyond dawn. About 05.00 am I made a supreme effort and crawled on deck. The Yankee sailors were manning every gun aboard all dressed in sheepskin clothing and wearing a revolver as only a yank dare wear it.'[71] Now they had to leave the crowded decks, carrying their heavy loads, via gangways dropped from the decks.

> Ahead only yards ahead was the French coast, but it was too far away to keep dry. Naval personnel were shouting 'get ashore', ships were everywhere like a traffic jam, down the ramps went but this only led to the ship in front, across its decks, then came ten horrible yards between ship and shore with water in between. Over the ships side, still dizzy from seasickness, and into water 4 feet deep, each one let out a gasp as the water swirled around, and we struggled for shore.[72]

Charles Eagles, also of the 9DLI, must have been on the same LCI as Eric Broadhead.

> We were very crowded going across and thought that if anything happened few of us would get out. One man older than me was obviously very upset, telling me about his family. The stink down there with sweat, bodies and fuel. Gambling schools had opened up. They had issued us with these stupid waders that came up to our chests. They made us sweat and feel even worse. They called us up on deck, C Company then S Company. We had to walk across another LCI before landing. I went right the way down to the bottom and then popped out and I was pulled out. We landed and were all assembled and we were given these bikes from a pile that was already there. We had only gone about 200yds when some mortar or artillery fire made us dive into a ditch. When we got up no-one picked up their bikes! Pretty chaotic on the beach trying to organise all the men as well as our battalion. Also odd bodies lying around. We got straight off the beach up a track. German prisoners were trickling back. None of us thought it would develop the way it did, those who had been in action before were the most surprised. A sniper seemed to be waiting around every bend.[73]

The idea of issuing the waders mentioned above to 151st and 56th Brigades seems to have come about after Exercise Fabius. Despite the best of intentions, their waterproof nature meant, for any man landing in deep water, that the waterproof trousers filled with water, restricted movement and dragged men down. A number of men have mentioned having a desperate time wading ashore in these, and even ashore fighting to get them off, as the wet tapes holding them had tightened. A number were certainly cut off, and many must have added to the detritus on the beach and floating in the sea. Enough bicycles were carried on the LCI (L) to equip one company in each of the follow-up battalions, and were intended to enable one rifle company to keep up with the expected quick advance led by the Bren carriers from Support Company. They were never popular, and no practice beforehand seems to have been carried out. Amazingly, in 1940s Britain, some of the men could not ride a bicycle! Also, they made the men a higher target when cycling along the lanes and tracks. Many were dumped or 'lost' within the first few days, at most, of landing.

As 8DLI landed, around 1130, they encountered difficulty in approaching the shore because of obstacles from wrecked tanks and landing craft in the water. A and B Companies and Battalion HQ landed in only a few feet of water, but C and D Companies landed in deeper water, and US sailors swam ashore with ropes that the men could follow and use for support. Both companies were ordered to remove their waders by Captain English, possibly saving some lives. One D Company man is reported as saying that 'it's a good job there are no Germans about. We are so wet we could not even argue with them, let alone fight them.'[74]

Within an hour or so of landing, the three battalions moved through Ver-sur-Mer fairly quickly, and 151st Brigade started assembling in fields west of the town. By noon, although 69th Brigade had started to ably exploit the left flank of the landing, there was still stubborn resistance on the 231st Brigade front from 352nd Infantry Division troops and units under their control. Le Hamel, Asnelles and the heights above Arromanches were proving a tougher proposition than expected. Artillery and mortars still threatened any approaching craft and the men and vehicles already ashore. The follow-up troops of 56th Brigade had still not landed, and this part of the plan was now some two or three hours behind schedule; 47 Commando had only just set off, realizing that for the first part of their advance the ground ahead was not clear of enemy as planned, and any fighting would further hold up their advance. The hoped-for quick exploitation south to Bayeux and Tilly-sur-Seulles and west to Port-en-Bessin was already falling well behind schedule.

D-Day: Afternoon and Evening

The Tactical HQ of 50th Division was ashore by 1000, but unable to immediately move off the very crowded and narrowing beaches. Only an hour later, General Graham left *Bulolo* for shore, and by 1300 he had joined his Tactical HQ, now established in the village of Meuvaines. Within half an hour of Graham's arrival, Tactical HQ at Meuvaines had taken over responsibility for the majority of communications from *Bulolo*. Later in the afternoon, additional signals sets and office equipment had arrived, considerably aiding communications and organization. One worry under consideration from 1645 was that Brigadier Senior from 151st Brigade was missing, presumed killed or captured, and it was believed that he had with him the divisional code signs and other codes for the following fourteen days.[1]

The infantry companies from 56th Brigade had not yet landed, although quite a number of men with jeeps and Bren carriers from this brigade had landed earlier with the first wave of assault battalion vehicles from 231st Brigade, coming ashore between an hour and an hour and a half after the assault landings. Using a jeep as their transport, unit landing officers (ULOs), with an NCO and two ORs, had the task of marking the way to the assembly areas for their battalion. Simple chalk and self-made wood and canvas signs were the means by which this important task was to work. However, all the jeeps were flooded on landing, and the ULOs proceeded with their task on foot. Wet landings meant the end of the chalk handily packed in ammo pouches, and the signs were lost too.

The 2nd Essex jeep nosedived into the sea after the LCT ramp had been blown off by a mine, and the driver, Les 'Titch' Holden, Captain Chell, Sergeant Giggens from S Company Mortar Platoon, and a corporal from the battalion intelligence section were dumped in the sea, and ended up fighting for their lives before they landed on the French shore. Les Holden has left this vivid memoir as the ship's tannoy blared:

'Number one, prepare to drive off.' This was where I had to come into action. I pulled the starter. The engine sprang to life. Then came a sickly crunch. The ship next to us received a direct hit from the guns of Le Hamel. It went up in flames and smoke. A sailor from a deck above us crashed down, dead, behind my jeep. Then, an almighty explosion sent our ramp crashing upwards against the bows, severing the arm off a sailor. We had hit a mine. Despite the shock, I was surprised that I was still ready to drive off. The ship backed off and made a fresh run-in. This time I drove down the ramp, in spite of it being detached at one side. My orders were to clear the ramp, turn starboard and on no account to foul the exit for the following vehicles. I cleared the ramp. Water came up to my armpits. My passengers stood up in an effort to avoid the angry sea. We were making good progress, but it was short-lived.

A massive wave, funnelling its way between the ships, broke over the jeep, washing my team-mates overboard. The wave receded, carrying the jeep and me out to sea to sink ignominiously behind the landing craft. I discarded my helmet, scrambled out of my seat only to find the Intelligence Corporal hanging onto the jeep shouting for help. Somehow his lifebelt was tangled around his neck. I told him to thrash his hands and feet up and down while I untangled the belt. By a miracle I got it tied under his arms and, as swimming was about the only skill I could boast of, and with supreme effort we managed to make fifty yards to climb, aided by others, onto the turret of a drowned tank to regain our breath. It was not a safe haven, and two men were washed off and drowned in the swell. Eventually, a large wooden cylinder floated by and I jumped into the sea and grabbed hold of it. My jeep-mate followed, but two others remained there. Within wading distance of the shore the outstretched arms of Captain Chell and the signaller came to our rescue, but within seconds I was to be lost from sight, as an underwater mine blew me up into the air and dumped me into the sea again. My next memory is of heaving up sea water and the Captain pumping my chest and stomach with his hands.

We sheltered by the side of a burned out tank from the gun fire from the Le Hamel emplacement. This was our plight – all our equipment lost; the wireless on the signaller's back out of commission. It was now 9.15 and the brigade were due at 10.00. Captain Chell re-organised our tasks. We were to keep in touch with the Engineers and keep a sharp lookout for our Battalion Commanders, mending our radio or share with another signaller's. We were to report back to our base, by the tank every 20 minutes. We set off in different directions. I learnt quickly that when someone shouted, 'DOWN!' You went down, no matter what lay ahead. Dead and wounded seemed everywhere. Le Hamel gunfire raked the beach; bullets that did not find their target sent sprays of sand into the air; larger guns concentrated on the incoming ships; snipers in the reeds and marshes were picking off men from time to time.[2]

Being informed that the brigade would land much later, around 1200, Holden was left on the beach with instructions from Captain Chell on how to greet the battalion when it landed. With no signs, and useless wet chalk, Chell and Giggens nevertheless proceeded to Buhot. Once they had found the forming-up orchard near the farm, Captain Chell returned to the beach to show the way. Sergeant Giggens kept lonely watch in the concentration area at Buhot.[3]

The 2SWB jeep ended drowned in a shell hole as its crew took shelter from mortaring and shellfire behind a tank. Similarly, Captain Talmadge and Sergeant Philips proceeded on foot to mark the way for the battalion. They came under machine-gun fire on the way, and saw a section of one of the assault battalions mown down. Philips remembers:

The unfortunate part of that was we saw these young chaps with the Africa Star lying in the surf. I thought these poor buggers; they have been through North Africa. They even didn't get up on the sands you know. When we landed there was a lot of shelling and it was a bit hairy. So I said to the driver get behind that knocked out tank for protection. A shell had shattered the tracks and we drove into the hole where the shell had exploded. So the jeep went down and we had to leave them. Captain Talmadge and I grabbed hold of the battalion signs and took them towards the rendezvous area. As we were leaving the beach there was a chappie going up the bank and a shell exploded at his feet in the sand and we saw his body coming toward us in the air. We got away with this and then there was a farmhouse surrounded by a high wall with double gates and there was an elderly lady outside there and she was jumping up and down, clapping her hands.

The shelling was still pretty hairy but we got to the rendezvous area. There was only the two of us and there was quite a lot of firing going on. I would still like to know whether these fellows were taking cover or cut down. We were on the road, when these groups were going through a field. The corn in there was quite high, about a yard high. Then suddenly the Germans opened up with machine guns and whether the chaps had gone down first or been scythed down, I don't know, but they disappeared. We went on and there was a car with four German officers dead in it. In one field near the RV they must have had naval guns trained because there was loads of German bodies there, absolutely blown to bits.[4]

Other 56th Brigade men came ashore earlier in small signals units attached to each of the assault brigades. They landed pushing what they termed a 'pram', and, indeed, their radios were transported in an affair similar to a baby's carriage, with the equipment well waterproofed. After difficulty getting ashore and moving up the beach under fire, Robert Metcalf realized that his radio was useless, as it was riddled with mortar fragments. He converted immediately from signaller to infantryman, and spent the rest of the day helping one of the assault battalions – probably 2nd Devons or 1st Dorsets – winkle out snipers. At one stage, he and an NCO hunted around a field boundary for hiding Germans. He did not find his way back to 56th Brigade HQ, and then 2SWB, for forty-eight hours.[5] Similarly, the Support Company Bren carriers had come ashore before their infantry had landed, and in some cases were the first to arrive at the brigade concentration area.

Frank Dilworth was a 56th Brigade HQ motorcycle dispatch rider, and came ashore with some of the 2SWB Bren gun carriers landing from an LCT on Jig Beach:

My bike was loaded on the SWB half-track, an M14, which had a big radio in. There was a driver called Jones, a Scots lad called Fraser (later they got badly injured by an airburst) and a South Wales Borderers officer who was rather quiet. The grass was all burning. The ramp went down about 10 o'clock and I was high up looking down from the M14 and there were two rows of carriers. At first I thought that's all right, as the carriers only looked to be in two feet of water. The next thing is they had nearly disappeared! We had stopped one side of a sandbank with a big dip on the other. Our driver was a bit cautious and instead of putting his foot down we stopped in about two feet of water. I then had the job of getting out and running our winch wire to an armoured bulldozer to give us a pull out.[6]

Philip Maillou of 2nd Essex came ashore around 1130 with his 6 lb anti-tank gun carried on a DUKW, and was deposited at the Buhot rendezvous by the DUKW. He and his team set up covering the road with only the half-dozen shells carried behind the gun shield for ammunition.[7] Charles Benson and his men, landing off an LCT, had to use pick and shovel to demolish part of a sea wall to get his Bren carriers off the beach.[8] The different individuals making their way to Buhot kept a lonely watch until numbers of brigade men and vehicles started arriving much later in the day. Each battalion had a large orchard field to assemble in next to each other.

It was now midday, and finally the infantry of 56th (Independent) Infantry Brigade was preparing to land. It was carried by 264th RCN Flotilla, but three of the landing craft – those allotted to 2nd SWB – were attached from the US Navy: LCI (L) Nos. 400, 421 and 511. It appears that the army officers aboard were not made aware that they were to land around and east of Le Hable de Heurtot on Jig Red and King Green, rather than Jig Green beach as planned. The three battalions landed in the order of Glosters, then Essex, then SWB, from east to west: 2nd Glosters landed at 1158, with the War Diary commenting that 'some ranks were seasick, but this passed off before landing. Everyone was in good spirits and keen to get on with the job'. It was reported that the three LCIs touched down in the Le Hable de Heurtot area, and the men quickly cleared the beach via King Red and then moved towards the brigade concentration area at Buhot. An important point, again, was that due to the number of small landing craft casualties, the LCI (L) came ashore directly onto the beach, rather than trans-ship the men afloat to LCA and LCM. On this journey some mortar fire was encountered, causing two casualties, and it was clear that the enemy was still in force on the hills above Buhot, the Meuvaines ridge and the ground between to the south. The rough landing in the wrong place meant that, according to the War Diary, it was not until 1607 that the Glosters Battalion HQ arrived at Buhot, after the area had been cleared by 'Marine Commandos', one assumes 47 Commando.[9] Similarly, 2nd Essex landed at 1230, also suffered from mortar fire as the battalion moved towards Buhot, and were told that Ryes, only a short distance from Buhot, was still in enemy hands. Major Barrass, the officer commanding B Company, remembers the colonel holding an impromptu order group on the beach with the maps out, deciding exactly where they were.

On the beach, two members of the ULO party were waiting to greet 2nd Essex after spending several difficult hours. Holden recalls that around 1130 a great cheer went up, as the large bunker at Le Hamel had just been put out of action by a shell from a 147th Field Regiment (Essex Yeomanry) Sexton commanded by Sgt Palmer – an act for which he received the MM. This allowed work on the beach to proceed more quickly. Just before noon, the two men saw the 56th Brigade LCI (L)s coming in. As 2nd Essex landed, Holden remembers:

We watched them climb from the ships and wade ashore. In complete order they formed up two abreast and with the Colonel and Adjutant leading, they marched up the Beach. It was all so different from the previous few hours and I watched them with pride. I cannot say that I was excited to meet the Colonel, [I was] a somewhat bedraggled soldier, smothered in mud and water and bereft of helmet and equipment. Not only that, I had lost my jeep, and Commanding Officers do not take kindly to that sort of thing. Now it was my duty and honour, not by choice, but by circumstance, to welcome my Colonel and Battalion to France and to give them their marching orders. With no hat on, it is not customary to salute, so I raised my hand to a halt and stopped the Colonel in his tracks. I braced myself for a dressing down.

He looked at me as though I had just popped out of the sand, the expression on his face of total disgust. Before he could explode, I said, with as much authority as I could muster, 'Sir, Captain Chell has instructed me to welcome you and the 2nd Battalion of the Essex Regiment to France. He is arranging emergency plans for transport.' He looked at me again, 'I now recognise who you are. Walk on with me. You look as though you have had a rough time.' Briefly, I explained what had happened and told him that Black Route was open. I still expected a dressing down, but instead was given a thump on the back. 'Well done, now go back to the Beach, recover your jeep if possible and catch us up when you can.'

I stepped aside and watched as the Battalion marched past, loaded like pack horses, some with fold-up bicycles. I shouted farewell to the Signaller as he marched by with his own platoon. I was never to meet my three compatriots again, though, fifty years later, paid homage at the graveside of Captain Chell who died, age 24, on 12th August 1944. Two days later than that, at Esson, I received the injuries that were to end my wartime service.[10]

At 1200, 2SWB landed, but seemed to have the worst of the landing in terms of men stumbling into deep water and submerged shell holes. Brigade HQ landed at 1215, and also proceeded to Buhot via Meuvaines. The Brigade War Diary has the brigade complete at Buhot by 1745.

As 56th Brigade men debouched from their LCIs, the marshy area was still blazing. The beach did not appear to be under direct fire, although one of the Canadian LSIs later found bullets embedded in the 'plastic' armour around the bridge of the ship.

The 2nd Glosters advanced up the track and arrived at WN35a, where some remember finding German bodies flung into trees near the position from the bombardment. Moving from here was the point where they came under mortar and artillery fire. The experienced soldier Bill Robinson was from S Company, but landed on foot with the LCIs:

On D-day I was fortunate in one respect that I had been under fire and knew what to expect, most others hadn't. So when we got to the top of the track we were in open country. There was a road running across the top of the track and from the top of this road you could see another road going down on the right. It was more like a plain. We were on top going down and on the left in the direction of Caen a shell whistled down and there was a puff of smoke where it hit. It was a smoke marker. Some of the eight or so with me said 'what was that?' I told them that another one would be coming in a minute on the other side. While we were looking the Germans shelled the area and hit a couple of Bren Gun carriers that were down there. If we had gone on we would have been in it.[11]

On the beach, 2nd Essex men remember:

> We had the self-heating cans of cocoa and soup, which were lovely. When we landed our boat got within a few hundred feet of the shore so I only got my knees wet. Others were wet up to their waists. Our boat did very well! So we walked ashore and carried on. There were still dead laying about and tanks and Bren Carriers drowned in the water.[12]

Tony Mansi remembers that one of the first things he noticed was a member of the Army Film and Photographic Unit taking pictures of our landing. This was Sergeant Midgeley, whose Normandy work can be viewed at the IWM Photographic Department.

> From the beach up onto the road a flail tank was beating the ground exploding mines and engineers were putting iron stakes in the ground and putting white tape on them marking the way between so we had a safe pathway to get up onto the road. Once we got onto the road it wasn't quiet, there was a lot of firing going on. When we looked further down the beach we could see houses from where we were. Also there were German prisoners being taken down to the beach. There were dead bodies about.[13]

Men from the 2SWB landed in deeper water. Bill Evans from B Company believed that 'someone was looking down on us kindly at that moment, a miracle we all survived the landing'. Bill Speake from C Company, Lt Sam Weaver, the signals officer, and Lt Nicholas Somerville, the battalion intelligence officer, all report the deep water, having to fight against the water to get ashore, and many men progressing under water. The LCIs had a much deeper draught than the LCAs and LCMs and had to 'beach' further out. The US naval men helped considerably. It seems that where 2SWB landed, a series of deep underwater runnels, as well as shell holes, crossed the front of the landing craft.[14]

Log entries from the US LCI landing 2SWB detail some of the difficulties faced, as this entry for LCI (L) 400 by Lt MJ Rand USNR shows:

> 1145 Beaching stations sounded. 1157 Let go stern anchor. 25 fathoms out when ship hit sand bar 100 yards from shore. Lorenzo J sent ashore with line. Bomb craters make water overhead in spots. Army senior officer decided to send men in at 1209. Some men nearly drown as they go in. Burgman J sent to help Lorenzo J with Army men that are going under. 1215 passage of men ashore stopped. 1218 all men aboard, ramps retracted. 1227 LCA sinking; lines thrown to her and pulled alongside. All men brought aboard our ship. 1234 heaved in stern anchor. Began manoeuvring to new landing place. 1315 let go of stern anchor; endeavour to bring ship near stranded LCT. Hit sand bar. Bow about 20 feet from stem of stranded LCT. Ramps out with 1 foot of water. 1412 Troops ashore, ramps in. Tide far out, unable to get off beach.

LCI (L) 400 was only able to leave the beach at 2125 that evening, and within the hour was anchored as directed from *Bulolo*. Similarly, LCI (L) 421 remained beached until a similar time. The log of LCI (L) 511 gives the position as one and a half miles east of Le Hamel on Jig Red. Lifelines were taken out at 1215, and it was noted that the water was very deep on landing, but, as with the other two craft, a rapidly lowering tide left them stranded. However, they were able to take aboard eight British officers and thirty men from three stranded LCTs, termed 'survivors'. Later, they took aboard thirty-eight wounded British soldiers and one German. Again, they were not able to get off until 2130.[15]

Brigadier Pepper seems to have done a good job back in Britain, preparing 56th Brigade from untested battalions within a very short period of time. An interesting thing about senior officers is the number of them who drove about with only their soft hats on, or even hatless, and often seemed to drive themselves, having their drivers in the passenger seat! Pepper was no exception, as his signaller for the landing, Syd Lee, explains:

When we landed I was Brigadier Pepper's wireless operator. Obviously I was told this before D-Day. We landed off a small landing craft – an LCM probably – with just a couple of jeeps in it. We were lowered from HMS Glenroy and put in the water about half past five in the morning just circling around and I was violently seasick. The Brigadier was in the same craft as us. When we drove off the landing craft we had a dry landing in the jeep. I was sitting in the back with the 22 Set. As we drove off the beach I remember the barbed wire and we were driving up this dirt track with the infantry plodding up either side. The Brigadier was driving at the time and I remember the infantry were pushing bicycles and he ran into one of the bicycles as he was driving past![16]

One important 56th Brigade HQ vehicle was the ACV, an armoured communications truck or 'armoured command vehicle', based on the AEC Matador chassis, weighing some 17 tonnes. As signaller Tony Atcherley explains, their landing does not appear too fraught with difficulty:

We had no difficulty getting our truck through the water and on to dry land. This was about noon. Then we joined the long line of traffic crossing up the beach along a taped route through the mines and onto the high ground beyond. The very high ground was at about two o'clock from us as I recall. We were very fortunate in our landing on Gold Beach. A little way inland we halted for a short time. I was sitting on the right as the truck was American and had a left-hand drive. A Frenchwoman from a nearby farm came out and held a huge gleaming golden lump out to me. Used as I was to dealing in tiny portions, it took me some seconds to realise it was butter! There must have been a kilo of it, my first spoils of war, except it was freely and gladly given. My schoolboy French was not good enough to understand all that she was saying, but I thanked her as best I could.[17]

It seems a feature of the Gold Beach landings that quite a few French persons, often women or girls of all ages, made contact with the British from early on in the landing, waving and clapping hands or swapping foodstuffs, and even, in the case of 1st Dorsets, castigating the men for bringing danger to their door. This seems especially the case on the right flank of the landing. One can only speculate, but it may be that the bombing on this flank, landing far from its objectives and less severe, was less stressful to the civilians despite the naval bombardment. It also clearly shows that the Germans had not moved civilians away from the coastal defended crust in this area. By evening, on King Beach at least, fishermen appeared to tend their pots.[18]

With the two 'follow-up' brigades ashore, it is important to return to how the assault battalions and supporting armour were advancing along with the thrust by 47 Commando.

On King Beach, 69th Brigade was well established ashore, with 5th East Yorks suffering the worst casualties and having to regroup around Ver-sur-Mer. The two battalions of the Green Howards had started to push into the hinterland. The trick was not to be held up too long by enemy snipers or machine-gun positions. It was important to try to push forward and reach the planned objectives, and trust that all the follow-up men and materiel would do their jobs in the areas behind the emerging front line. Thus, 6th Green Howards War Diary reports at 1300: 'Strong enemy resistance reported west of Crepon, the Bn proceeded to advance along the Bn axis and the CO fwd with the Coys, informed them that any resistance encountered was to be by-passed unless absolutely unavoidable.' John Milton remembers that Lt Col. Robin Hastings was 'a very good Boss, definitely in charge in spite of his young age'.[19] When a party of Germans resisted near Crepon at 1400, they came under 'a substantial dose of Bren and Sten fire, and came out under cover of a white flag'. It was, of course, at Crepon that Stanley Hollis performed his second act of outstanding bravery that day, in retrieving some men under fire in a farmyard. By 1500, the battalion was approaching the village of Villers-le-Sec, the Battalion HQ clearing Crepon half an hour later and reporting back to the brigade the successful completion of phase two of the day's plan. Part of Crepon was cleared by 5th East Yorks by 1510.[20]

Similarly, the War Diary of Signals Officer Kenneth Taylor records the following:

> Held up at Crepon by 88s and Spandaus but by-passed them and stopped for a brew-up. On moving forward shelled and mortared and made one hasty exit from M14. Rainford killed. Dug in then moved fwd to overlook St Gabriel and dug in again. Drinking Champagne when disturbed again by Jerry. At about 2000hrs saw 4 of our tanks blazing. Put in final attack S of St Gabriel and stopped in wood at dark. Gibson wounded. We are the furthest forward troops of the whole invasion and fairly near our objective. The morale was very high and we have moved very quickly, by-passing any opposition where possible.[21]

Similar heavier resistance was faced by 5th East Yorks when they ran into Battle Group Meyer from 352nd Infantry Division. This battle group comprised two infantry and a reconnaissance battalion, and included self-propelled guns, infantry guns and anti-tank companies. However, by 0530 on 6 June, this group was travelling from its positions south and east of Bayeux in the opposite direction, towards the American parachute drop zones on the Cotentin Peninsula. Too late, the German commanders realized that the major threat came from the British landing on Gold Beach, and ordered the battle group to return and stop the British landing. Already short of an infantry battalion sent to Omaha Beach, it only came into action in the St Gabriel area late in the afternoon. Only some elements were in action by 1600, although at 1630 they did capture Brigadier Senior of 151st Brigade at Bazenville, just over 2 kilometres south-east of Ryes. He later escaped, wounded.[22]

The War Diary of 5th East Yorks reports that at 1500, Lt Col. White was wounded and Major Dixon took command. North of St Gabriel, they were involved in heavy fighting against a company of German infantry supported by two 75 mm self-propelled (SP) guns. It took them more than two hours to capture St Gabriel, and they reported that the Germans they captured were from the Fusilier Battalion of 352nd Infantry Regiment and 915 Regiment. The 6th Green Howards report the heavy German shelling of St Gabriel. As 5th East Yorks advanced further, two 88 mm guns and machine-gun posts in a wood held them up and caused further casualties. In the end, what is reported as 'Bde attack supported by 4/7 DG pushed enemy back through Brecy, which was occupied by battalion approx. 2300hrs. Quiet night'.

Probably, the senior officers in these advance battalions and Brigade HQ were worried. Information was being received that over 100 enemy tanks and much transport was on the move west of Caen, and 86th Field Regiment was reporting enemy tanks advancing north-east from Rucqueville. Eventually, at 2100, worries about this enemy concentration forced 6th Green Howards to halt, under orders from their brigadier, west of St Gabriel, and dig in, supported by fire from 86th Field Regiment and the Medium Machine Guns of B Company, 2nd Cheshires.

Dennis Bowen from 5th East Yorks recalls that when units of 50th Division advanced, they never counted the rounds, but advanced in a hail of gunfire. The style of fighting was completely different between 50th Division and 3rd Division, with which he served later. In 50th Division, they had great sympathy towards the enemy once captured or wounded, and were rarely rough with prisoners, giving them cigarettes and so on. It was the style they had learnt in the desert. The difference was that 50th Division had been doing it for real for a long time, while other divisions had spent years training for war in the United Kingdom.

> We followed up to the east of Crepon supported by Sherman tanks from 4/7 Dragoon Guards and on towards Creully. We had been told 'do not stop' if a mate gets hit leave him. People following up will attend to him. We had these firefights, perhaps up to ten or twelve little actions, all the way to Creully really – sometimes up to Company size attacks. It appeared to me that we were coming among enemy who were not well organised. We had men killed and wounded of course. Germans were either shot or surrendered and each time we took a little position we just indicated with our bayonets that the Germans should make their way back to the beach. That night we arrived near our objective and dug in.[23]
>
> We had one man killed by a tank skidding into him. We had little firefights all the way forward once we left Ver-sur-Mer.[24]

Charles Hill from 6th Green Howards remarks: 'I grew up a bit on that first day. We were rumoured to have had nearly fifty men killed and wounded on D-Day. Those of us who had not been in action before were no longer novices!'[25]

Now 7th Green Howards were also in a position advancing on the enemy, as the front broadened. They also began to encounter heavier opposition. By mid-afternoon, they had taken a further forty prisoners. Their D Company helped the situation at

Crepon and then moved towards St Gabriel in support of 5th East Yorks and 6th Green Howards. The main battalion group was moving towards and through Creully, with B Company leading as the mobile column, supported by Bren carriers and tanks of 4/7 Dragoon Guards. They now began to reach more open country, and soon crossed the valley of the River Seulles.

A Squadron 4/7 Dragoon Guards were glad to have passed through the narrow confines of Creully. They were moving across open fields towards Fresnay-le-Crotteur with a column of tanks either side of the road when they ran into trouble. Two tanks of 2nd Troop were hit and exploded 'in a sheet of flame'. The left-hand column of tanks had rushed for the cover of some trees. As one nosed carefully through the trees, it was hit, and 'a near solid column of dense black smoke spiralled vertically upwards for about 100 feet' and became an instant inferno. A fourth tank was hit and instantly caught fire, but the flash of the German gun had been spotted, and some careful shooting destroyed it. As this happened, though, the ground around the remaining tanks erupted into geysers of earth as heavy fire fell all over the area. The 7th Green Howards, who were supporting the tanks, suffered severe casualties. Also badly injured and killed were some members of 4/7 Dragoon Guards who had dismounted to see more clearly where the German gun was. The shelling quickly stopped, the soldiers realizing it had come from behind them. This incident was later proved to be HMS *Orion* following a fire order.[26]

> 1940 ORION engaging tanks as ordered 1847
> 2005 FOB reported HQ 86 Fd. Regt. RA reported naval gunfire falling amongst own troops.
> 2012 ORION ordered to cease fire on tanks
> 2012 Orion reported three tanks destroyed [27]

To add insult to injury, as the 4/7 Dragoon Guards tanks and infantry were ordered to withdraw slightly to a better position, they were attacked by US Thunderbolt aircraft. Eventually, with the use of orange smoke grenades, the pilot realized he was attacking Allied armour.[28]

So, by midnight, 69th Brigade had stopped about a mile and a half short of its hoped-for line of advance, the Route National 13 road running between Caen and Bayeux. Partly, this was because the infantry battalions were often slightly withdrawn and ordered to stop in less exposed positions than might have been the case. Men were very tired, having spent a rough night at sea and most having been in action for sixteen hours.

By now, 151st Brigade was well established and organized in its forming-up area. For example, 8DLI used the short time for D Company to collect the cycles from other companies, as they had been trained for a mobile role, and others tried to dry out some of their clothing, particularly C and D Companies, who had suffered the wettest landing. The plan was to advance along two centre lines with a battalion leading each. The right had 9DLI in the lead, supported by a platoon of 2nd Cheshire machine guns, a troop of 6 lb anti-tank guns from 288/102 Anti-Tank Battery, a FOB party and a FOO party from 90th Field Regiment RA. Ambulance support came from a section of

149 Field Ambulance. They were followed by 8DLI, with similar support, and then by Brigade HQ, 2 Cheshires providing Medium Machine Gun (MMG) and heavy mortar (4.2 inch) support. On the left line of advance was 6DLI, similarly supported and with a squadron of tanks from 4/7 Dragoon Guards.

As they were preparing to move off in the direction of Bayeux, at 1345, a shell landed in the area and seriously wounded the battalion MO and another soldier, 8 DLI's first casualties. They continued the advance through the village of Meuvaines with A Company leading. By early evening, they were dug in and patrolling the orchards around the village of Sommervieu. D Company occupied a forward position about a mile south-east of Sommervieu; 6 DLI moved off with a similar mobile column in the lead of 4/7 Dragoon Guards tanks, Support Company Bren carriers and a cycle company. After encountering some resistance in Villiers-le-Sec, they reached the Bayeux to Caen road by 2030, and dug in around Esquay-sur-Seulles. As 9 DLI moved off, they suffered an attack from the air: 'RAF fighters zoomed overhead, peeled off one by one and machine gunned the column, this was far from pleasant and we dived in all directions as bits of dirt among other things were flying everywhere.' On another occasion, they were fired on by a Sherman tank. Mounted on tanks and Bren carriers, they reached the Sommervieu area around 1830, and cleared it of enemy within an hour. The battalion dug in in south-east of the village around Cauge Ferme. In one instance, a farm cart was used to provide an extemporized barrier across a road. Some small engagements took place in the woods and orchards very early the following morning, and a second member of the battalion was killed, joining another killed in the air attack.[29]

Photo 7 View from the Meuvaines ridge. This picture is taken from near 151st Brigades assembly area on the Meuvaines ridge looking west. In the foreground is the church and village of Meuvaines, beyond can be seen the spire of Asnelles church. This photograph clearly shows the dominating nature of the ridgeline across the valley of La Gronde Riviere. The Puits d'Herode position is just out of shot on the far skyline ridge.

Charles Eagles remembers that

the lads who got the biggest shock were the veterans who were used to open warfare. They were not ready really for these country lanes with a Spandau, sniper or what have you waiting around every corner. No wonder we were slow. Germans coming back didn't look very smart, with hands up or on their heads. They did not look like first class troops. We were up and down into ditches all the time. Interestingly at around 1600 we were shot at and I went straight down in the ditch and found three French religious medallions which I kept throughout the war and still have.[30]

As indicated in the first paragraph of this chapter, Brigadier Senior, in charge of 151st Brigade, had gone missing. Simply, around 1500 the brigadier had gone forward to visit the mobile column, and his jeep had been ambushed and his driver and signaller killed. The brigadier had been wounded and taken prisoner. This incident is one of a number showing that, despite large bodies of British troops advancing, there was plenty of room available for the enemy to avoid capture, and also that such groups, big and small, remained very aggressive.

Peter Goddin with Brigade HQ recalls: 'Our CO, Brigadier Senior, was wounded, so for the remainder of D-Day the Brigade Major virtually commanded the brigade. We couldn't pull in the senior battalion commander, as he was too committed in command of his battalion of the Durham Light Infantry.'[31] It took a considerable time for the senior Lt Col. Lidwell of 8DLI to take command of the brigade. This seems to have occurred around 2230.[32]

A patrol from 8DLI sent to try and locate the brigadier that night was unsuccessful, and mainly blundered into positions held by Geordies, who had not been told the new password.

On the 231st Brigade, or right flank of the invasion, 2nd Devons had now assembled south of Asnelles, minus C Company, which was still heavily engaged around Le Hamel, and Lt Col. Nevill decided that they were through the German coastal crust and could now advance rapidly towards the village of Ryes and capture it. The village of Ryes was an important point, as it was here that 56th Brigade was expected to pass through and on to Bayeux. However as the 2nd Devon advanced, they ran into 'intense LMG and Spandau fire at close range from enemy hidden in thick hedges'.[33] Without artillery or mortar support, they became embroiled in more close fighting, slowing down the advance. The only heavy weapon they could call on was a destroyer, and the FOB brought down accurate fire onto the outskirts of Ryes. A Company tried to press on using their small 2 inch mortars to provide smoke cover, while trying to turn the enemy blocking troops around their flanks. B and D Companies made little progress in the open country of the wide valley floor. In these attempts, one platoon commander was killed and two wounded, and two captains were wounded.

Nevill was losing more and more of his officers and NCOs in this protracted German defence. Lt Foy and part of his platoon were actually taken prisoner. In the end, Nevill left A Company containing the Germans around the river and decided to push B and D Companies, with support from some armour supplied by M10s of 102nd Anti-Tank Regiment, straight up the road to Ryes. Eventually Ryes was reached, and after some less intense fighting in the village, the objective was consolidated. It was 1600. It had taken eight hours and many casualties to advance from the beach.

Thirty-two members of the battalion had been killed. Michael Holdsworth had landed with the follow-up Devons and met Nevill in a field checking his map at around 1500. Nevill outlined the casualty situation as he knew it, and told Holdsworth that he was now in charge of B Company. Holdsworth asked where they were, and Nevill told him that 'they are about half a mile over in that direction'. The first task that Holdsworth had to perform once he found the B Company was to brief his platoon officers, one of whom was his twin brother. It was his brother whom he tasked with the job of leading the forward platoon on their move towards the Longues battery. But the idea of pushing on and taking the battery had to be shelved for that day. An elderly French couple next approached Holdsworth, she needing to get water from the village tap, while the man was offered a cup of tea, which he accepted![34] C Company only rejoined the battalion from Le Hamel at 1900; they were moved straight through to open the way towards Longues, and reached La Rosiere after more fighting. It was only during this time that the majority of 2nd Devon Support Company of mortars and anti-tank guns with their carriers started to arrive with the battalion.

Tom Hewitt from B Company remembers the advance:

> One of our officers 'caught it' there, and we moved back across the other side and we were lined up and moved across a field, then we were called back! We were under sniper fire! One or two shouted at the officers for being silly beggars. We stayed down on the deck and then went back some way. We went up in single file and pinpointed where the sniper was and eliminated him. We went on until we were sniped at again. Our job in B Company was to land and make our way inland to take a hill. I was really only concerned with my section. We had to ignore any Germans left or right of us. Anyway eventually we got there and dug in, it was quite placid and the place was almost like a shallow quarry, and we consolidated there for the night.[35]

Meanwhile, 1st Dorset had moved towards their next goals of eliminating German resistance around Point 54, the Puits de Herode battery lying across the minor road between St Come-de-Fresne (WN40) and Arromanches, then WN41 on the minor road which followed the high ground between Arromanches and Ryes, and further positions along this line to consolidate on the hill above and north of Ryes, while still keeping an eye on the approaches to Le Hamel from the south-east. One of the approaches to Point 54 was via a steep wooded lane from the Ryes road near Buhot. This area was reached around 1330. Initial moves by C and D Companies were repulsed, and casualties started to be taken. It was obvious that the Germans were on Point 54 in greater force than had been thought. C Company quickly made a second assault, killing two German officers and capturing fifteen others, and taking Point 54 by 1400. At about the same time. D Company, pushing through Buhot, captured a company of German pioneers and their transport. David Bushell remembers the action as follows:

> We went into this orchard and we were fired upon suddenly and a nearby Corporal fell shot across the head. We carried on through this orchard and cleared the Germans out. One of George Davy's friends was killed by a booby trap in the orchard. When we returned fire each time, we moved forward, and the Germans sort of disappeared![36]

An attack on WN40 – le Puits de Herode – was now prepared. This appeared to be a heavily defended position. D Company attacked, with C Company giving supporting fire from the area of Point 54. Also, C Squadron of the Sherwood Rangers went forward. Initially, D Company was successful in clearing the enemy from forward of Point 54 towards the position, over-running several machine-gun posts. But, already depleted by casualties, they could not carry the final position. Finally, Lt Col. Norie launched A Company into the assault around 1700. Covered by the fire of the two other companies, the Sherwood Rangers tanks and artillery from 90th Field Artillery (whose CO, Lt Col. Hardie, was with the 1 Dorsets Tac. HQ, Puits de Herode) fell with A Company in close combat, killing a number of Germans and capturing forty others. At one stage during the attack, C Company beat off a German attack on their flank.

Advancing A and C Companies to the second position of four 150 mm guns, it was found by 1830 that the enemy had retreated and abandoned all their equipment. B Company was now ordered at 1800 to proceed to Ryes from Les Roquettes, and the rest of 1st Dorsets cleared the ridge southerly to above Ryes, consolidating the area held by 2nd Devons. Battalion HQ established itself in a comfortable series of German dugouts with double bunks on the hill just north of Ryes. Also, in the meantime, Major Bredin had landed in the afternoon, and from the beachhead had extracted parts of 1st Dorset Support Company, especially the anti-tank component, plus parts of the main Battalion HQ. These he moved up via Buhot to Ryes, and established a secure anti-tank defence covering the valley of La Gronde Riviere. This move meant that 2nd Devon were now free on the following day to advance towards the Longues battery and work towards joining 47 (RM) Commando at Port-en-Bessin. During the day, they had lost four officers and seventeen ORs killed, and ten officers and eighty-eight ORs wounded. Nine men were missing.[37] The total of 130 casualties was a typical cost to the assault battalions on Gold Beach.

On the right flank, 1st Hampshire was still battling through Le Hamel, which, despite close support from LCG, LGF and destroyers, was proving a very tough nut to crack. On its eastern side, the large gun emplacement firing in enfilade across Jig Beach had been seemingly silenced a number of times, but kept coming to life. The nearby sanatorium complex was also proving a hotbed of resistance. Also, there were a number of other concealed machine-gun positions and Tobruks built into the sea wall. The 1st Hampshires were taking more and more casualties, and clearly there were more Germans here than expected and of a very different fighting quality than some of the coastal units defending King Beach. The influence of 352nd Infantry Division was easily seen in Le Hamel, Asnelles, and the areas taken during the afternoon by 2nd Devons and 1st Dorsets. Not surprisingly, considering the intensity of the fighting and the casualties, 1st Hampshire War Diary lacks hourly reports.

A plan was made in the early afternoon for B Company to give fire support to C Company as they established themselves within Le Hamel east, and bring them within 250 yards of the sanatorium position. C Company started its advance at 1345, but it took an hour of difficult fighting to attain dominance in the area. B Company now moved up to about 50 yards from the sanatorium in order to put in a final attack, but was held up by heavy fire. Luckily, at the same time an AVRE from Assault Breaching team 2 had managed to find its way from the beach, leaving Lane No. 3, and began to be very usefully employed. When it fired a 'dustbin' bomb at the sanatorium, a huge amount of smoke and dust erupted, but German fire was only temporarily disrupted. Five further bombs caused considerable damage, and the 1st Hampshires were able to get inside and 'mop up' any remaining resistance. Major Selerie from the SRY describes this event as five of his Sherman tanks being joined on the outskirts of Le Hamel by an AVRE, whose commander (Sergeant Scaife) told him his AVRE was the sole survivor of the troop. They then proceeded into Le Hamel, where 'the main enemy fire was coming from a tall many-storeyed house. The five SRY tanks supported the AVRE with machine gun and 75mm rounds.' He describes the effect of the Petard bomb hitting above the front door and part of the building collapsing 'like a pack of cards, spilling the defenders with their weapons and an avalanche of bricks into the courtyard'. The AVRE then commenced further excellent service by moving to the rear of the large concrete position (WN37) that had caused so many problems on Jig Beach. One round into the back of the bunker finally brought to an end German resistance there. Over thirty prisoners were taken in these two actions, and Le Hamel east was finally in the hands of 1st Hampshires, but the protracted and deadly German resistance meant that it took till around 1700. Part of the problem had been that, as well as the early bombing falling 3,000 yards away from the target, and WN37 in particular being well protected from naval gunfire on its seaward flank, the casualties among 1st Hampshires officers and the close nature of the fighting meant that radio contact with naval bombardment forces could not be effectively exploited. 1st Hampshire C Company was now able to advance more easily through Le Hamel to take the 50 mm gun position (WN38) at the west end of the village. Even so, the Germans in the area fought back, and Sergeant Scaife's AVRE was put to further good use, bombarding fortified houses. A further twenty prisoners were taken.

Photo 8 Eastward view across the front of Le Hamel. WN38 is the obvious 50 mm emplacement nearest the camera. The far end of Le Hamel with WN37 is indicated by the tall white modern coast guard tower, which is situated next to the WN37 casemate. The high sea wall is obvious as is again the field of fire available along these beaches. It was across here that Captain Johnson drove in the late afternoon/evening of D-Day to set up his dressing station in buildings behind WN38.

Meanwhile, D Company of 1st Hampshire had advanced around Le Hamel and moved to attack WN39, described as a 'half troop' position in reports. This comprised a 75 mm gun and an 88 mm gun in separate concrete bunkers, wired in with minefields fronting them. Both guns were sited to enfilade the beach in front of Le Hamel, and could also engage craft to the east of the position up to 3,000 yards away. Gunboat *Flores* had engaged the battery at 0630, and it was engaged again by the destroyers HMS *Undine*, HMS *Cottesmore* and HMS *Cattistock* at various times during the morning, up to 0930, when the position was observed firing on the beaches. At a similar time, Admiral Vian, the overall naval commander of the Eastern Task Force, got in on the act when visiting the area in his flagship HMS *Scylla*, firing forty rounds of 4.5 in at Arromanches at a range of around 8,000 yards between 0924 and 0931 after being ineffectively engaged by the shore batteries. HMS *Scylla* then returned to Sword Beach area in the east. The guns at WN39 were two of the most effective on D-Day, firing between them over 150 rounds. Investigation after D-day showed that, again, the early bombing had missed, but naval bombardment showed numerous hits within 20 yards of the casemates, eighty for the 75 mm emplacement alone. However, only one direct hit was recorded on this casemate, and none on the 88 mm emplacement.[38]

It appears that D Company was able to capture both WN39 and continued to take the radar station (Stutzpunkt Arromanches) on top of the cliffs relatively easily; however, the War Diary reports: 'Enemy 88mm guns and Spandau teams put up a determined resistance.' At any rate, after Le Hamel seemed under control, B and C Companies joined D Company at the radar station, and the move into Arromanches itself was organized. Some of the battalion Support Company Bren carriers had arrived, and several AVREs seemed available. D Company had taken about forty prisoners, some

Photo 9 Looking west from WN38. A closer view of the gun position WN38, this time looking west. Arromanches can be seen in the distance in a fold in the cliffs. The immediately apparent buildings on the slope to the cliff top did not exist in 1944 and mask the very active WN39 or 'half troop position'. In the private gardens behind the emplacement are other concrete shelters and positions.

coming up from Arromanches under a white flag. A bombardment on the battery beyond Arromanches by naval vessels and 147 Field Regiment was arranged, and D Company advanced to the south and rear of the town to take this objective. Major Mott then descended into Arromanches with C Company, and he reports little opposition and that 'Arromanches was full of French people. Flowers came out and Tricolours and Union Jacks. I had been told that all coastal inhabitants had been moved inland, but these were delighted to see us.'[39] Further advance into Tracy-sur-Mer was thwarted by very active sniping, and it was felt better to leave this until the morrow. The right flank of the Gold Beach landing was now securely held. Brigadier Stanier came up and congratulated the men for 'a magnificent show'. Major Mott had been worried that 'we would be getting a rocket for being so slow, as we hadn't done Tracy and had taken 14 hours for a 6 hour task'.

It is worth considering some of the wounded left as units continued to advance. Despite promises that men following up would deal with the wounded, this was not always possible. We had left Lt Norman shot twice by a sniper and badly wounded just off the beach early in the morning. He had lost a lot of blood, but lay out all day. It was half past four in the afternoon before he was picked up by a four-stretcher jeep ambulance and taken to a dressing station. His clothes were removed and dressings applied. He remembers the line of casualties being quite long. He was given a can of self-heating tomato soup and malted milk. He remembers when he wanted to pee he was given a tin to urinate in, as they had not got any proper bottles. The following day, he was evacuated by LST, landed at night and put on a hospital train to a hospital near Slough.[40] Many wounded were able to be dealt with promptly, but many suffered the

Photo 10 View of Gold Beach from the cliffs east of Arromanches. Taken looking east from the cliff between Le Hamel and Arromanches and within Stutzpunkt Arromanches (the remains of the radar station are just behind the photographer) this gives an excellent view of Le Hamel, the area of Le Marais and the point of land which is Le Hable de Heurtot. In the distance are La Riviere and the Mont Fleury lighthouse. The dark areas are modern oyster beds.

fate of Lt Alan Norman; it was a very large and intricate beach area, and opposition had been much more ferocious than expected.

The 56th Brigade was forming up in the orchards just south of the farm at Buhot. Like all the infantry brigades, they had seemed slow to move and concentrate. But, as with many of the landings, it must be remembered that they landed in an unexpected place, later than planned. The earlier landing craft casualties had also caused problems, ending the idea of trans-shipping. Also, fairly accurate mortar, sniper and machine-gun fire had the effect of making infantry go to ground. The fear of mines meant that many diversions were made, and signs proclaiming *Achtung Minen* seemed to be everywhere. The evidence of seeing occasional bodies or men with legs and feet blown off would have reinforced this fear.

All units suffered because the landing was dislocated through resistance and poor weather, and the marrying up of infantry with their tank support often took time. Units had to wait their turn, as by midday there were many units ashore, all needing to make progress along the few narrow roads and tracks. Villages like Ver-sur-Mer and Meuvaines that were open to movement became choke points. The 2SWB turned right along the beach and became enmeshed in the vehicle jam on the narrow beaches. Once off, Lt Col. Craddock became impatient with using the 'safe' roads. Turning to his signals officer, Sam Weaver, he told him to ride a motorbike across the field ahead, as he did not believe it was mined. Doubtless with his heart in his mouth, Weaver complied, and luckily found that the signs marked a dummy minefield. Henceforth, progress by 2SWB was quicker, but not without a small number of casualties from the ever-present mortars.[41] Craddock had discovered what many officers and men were beginning to realize: that inland many of the minefields that were marked with signs were, in fact, dummies, and it was found that dummy minefields were marked with white signboards and real ones with yellow boards.

By 1730, all 56th Brigade units had arrived at the concentration area. No doubt the unit landing parties and lonesome groups of anti-tank gunners were grateful for the appearance of their battalions. Even while waiting, though, numbers of Germans emerged to surrender. One surprised Sergeant Frank Clarke, who after a busy day had retired to a quiet corner of the orchard to go to the toilet. Pulling up his trousers, he was surprised to be accosted from nearby bushes by a German anxious to surrender![42]

At 1745, Brigadier Pepper ordered the brigade to advance in the order already planned in the United Kingdom. The 2SWB were to advance via Ryes and La Rosiere to Vaux-sur-Aure, 2nd Essex to St Sulpice via Ryes, while 2nd Glosters remained as brigade reserve with Brigade HQ. By 1930, Ryes and La Rosiere were reached. The 2nd Essex and 2SWB were moving into unknown enemy territory, and for the first time the majority of their men were in the forefront of the battle. In their various ways, each battalion had its introduction to modern warfare on its first day in Normandy.

Tony Mansi, 2nd Essex, recalls:

> In the open we kept quite close to the tanks for protection. As we got into more dense countryside with hedges and trees, the tank commander asked us to go in front to scout out if there were any German 88mm guns around. Some places we stopped when we came under sniper fire. Then the platoon officer had a couple of

our own snipers sent forward to try and spot them. They were mainly up in trees. At one place there was a small village and I remember seeing this long brick wall and of course we couldn't see over this wall. Sergeant Chandler said, 'Right over you go! When you get to the other side start giving us covering fire.' When we got over the wall there was nothing but green fields and trees in the distance. He shouted for covering fire and as it was our first day in action we were just firing off our weapons into an area to see if we could attract fire back. Finally we arrived at St. Sulpice where we stayed for the night. I don't think we felt frightened it was just the unexpected, not knowing what was in front of you.[43]

By 2130, the forward patrols of 2nd Essex had secured the St Sulpice crossroad, and the rest of the battalion moved in. Civilians told them that the Germans had left hours before and that they had probably left Bayeux as well. During the night, with tanks of the Sherwood Rangers for support, patrols 'felt' towards Bayeux and the anti-tank ditch to the north-west of the town, but returned after being fired upon. With only four men wounded, the advance from beachhead to such a commanding position above Bayeux seemed miraculous. Phillip Maillou and the 6 lb anti-tank guns of S Company were strategically placed, covering junctions around St Sulpice in case the expected counter-attack developed:

We run into St. Sulpice. We went into the fields on the right. We were getting into Bocage country. We sighted the guns to cover the road and a bit of the village in case they came at us. We pulled about twenty yards off the road and had to cut down some of the hedgerow to get a field of fire. We were all chopping away. We heard a bit of firing away to our left. A German motorcycle and sidecar came down the road and the Vickers (Medium Machine Guns, 2nd Cheshires supporting 56th Brigade) opened up and got them. It shows you how close everything was to have the Vickers up with the Battalion. A little later a staff car came up and they copped it as well. I think they were German War Correspondents. We spent the night in the ditch there. Next morning one of the older members of the gun crew was sent back. Probably aged about 35, he looked an old man to those of us aged 18! His knee was all swollen and that was the last we saw of him.[44]

The nearness of Bayeux was perhaps menacing as well as an indicator of a successful advance. Major Pat Barrass, officer commanding C Company, remembers that:

As dusk was falling you could see the spires of Bayeux beguiling in its closeness. Junkers 88 were taking off from Carpiquet near Caen and turning over our position to go and bomb the shipping. If you had a long stick you could touch them they were so low. Later you could see the AA fire in the sky. There was background noise, but quiet where we were so I caught up on some sleep. The nights were short. 'Stand to' was before dawn.[45]

The 2SWB took a different axis of advance after Ryes than 2nd Essex, and moved via La Rosiere, where they were fired upon. This was dealt with by bursts of fire from the lead Bren gun carrier with seemingly hardly a pause. Moving south, more determined resistance was met, and a minor action was fought near the farm at

Photo 11 Bayeux from St Sulpice. 'The spires of Bayeux Cathedral were beguiling in their closeness.' This view of Bayeux is taken from the St. Sulpice crossroads and reflects the thoughts of Major Pat Barrass from 2nd Essex as he stood here on the late evening of 6 June 1944.

Pouligny, where for a while German troops defended a radio direction finding (RDF) station before setting fire to it and abandoning it as a company-size attack was put in by D Company. In the gathering darkness, the exploding ammunition from the RDF station lit up the sky. Early in the action, one of 2SWB's Bren carriers had hit a mine in the roadside verge and blown up. Then, Major Peter Martin, the company commander, was talking to a FOO in a tank which, as it moved off, set off another mine, badly wounding Major Martin in the stomach. He was immediately evacuated by an ambulance jeep.[46] By 2350, the forward party were able to report the capture of the bridge at Vaux-sur-Aure, and they held it until the main body arrived. During the night, 'Bn established defensive locality Vaux-sur-Aure. Active patrolling by enemy during the night twelve prisoners taken.'[47] During their day in battle, 2SWB had lost four men killed: two by mortar fire on the way to Buhot, Sergeant Reynolds and Private Price, and two from sniper fire, Privates Massey and Parr. Ivor Parr was killed in the locality of Magny, and initially a local French family buried his body. Later, as things calmed down, he was reinterred by locals at the church of Magny, where his grave remains today. The other three are buried at Bayeux. The battalion also had about twenty men wounded.[48]

Carrying a heavy load, and often under fire for the first time, the infantrymen of all the units involved must have been incredibly tired by the events of the previous forty-eight hours. Most had had little sleep and a very rough sea crossing to contend with, before a long day in the field. They were also keyed up, expecting a serious counter-attack overnight. Probably many could not believe that they had not seen a single German tank. Upon reaching Vaux-sur-Aure, Lt Dennis Davis found ten Panzerfaust anti-tank rockets abandoned around the little bridge. His next task was to lead a quick patrol into the woods to advance on the reported 105 mm gun emplacement, where they expected to find four pieces of artillery. This position had been bombed earlier in the day. They did not find any Germans, but came across the German horse lines, including wagons from the abandoned battery position. In one wagon, Dennis shot the padlock off a locker and liberated two bottles of Benedictine. After reporting the results of his patrol, Davis returned to his slit trench by the bridge. As a good soldier and officer, he began to clean his Sten gun, but promptly fell asleep sitting up.[49] Nick Somerville remembers feeling that they had been extremely lucky, and was also very concerned at the non-appearance of the US units that 2nd South Wales Borderers were supposed to link with. Lieutenant Somerville had been very lucky himself, as twice during the day, the man behind him had been killed by enemy gunfire from the ridges dominating the Ryes valley.[50] Private Bill Evans remembers that the very narrow roads had high banks. When they stopped, he simply got in a hollow covered by a low tree and improved his position by breaking the branches down to cover him.[51] At one stage during the night, two of the South Wales Borderers Companies exchanged fire, luckily without harm being done. Sergeant Phillips of the Intelligence Section provides this picture of his first night in Normandy:

> At Vaux we were in a farmyard and the little Padre, who was about five foot tall, was soaked to the skin. There was a lot of firing going on between two of our own companies, but there was also an attack. We were quite safe inside the actual farm. This firing had been going on between the two companies and then this lot (Germans) came with automatic weapons, but we were safe and sound where we were. Probably they came from the west. They came in, gave us a quick burst of fire and withdrew.[52]

At 1940 back at Buhot, Brigadier Pepper decided to move forward to Magny with Brigade HQ and 2nd Glosters. On the way, 2nd Glosters ran into German opposition, took thirty-one prisoners and had four men wounded. They arrived at Magny near midnight, and dug in around the church. Their War Diary reports being dug in by 0026. Brigade HQ was established in the farm to the rear of the church. Patrolling was carried out, and a troop of 105 mm guns was captured, possibly the four expected to be found at Vaux. Brigadier Pepper had held a conference with the 2nd Glosters CO, and they had concluded that as it was so late, he did not wish to get his battalions tangled up in street fighting in Bayeux, and decided to send them in the morning. What the brigadier could not know was that most German military personnel had left Bayeux much earlier in the day, and German reaction to the 2nd Essex reconnaissance was only caused by a light covering force, but his decision was very sound. Getting battalions of infantry with tank support fighting in the dark through a town full of substantial fifteenthth to seventeenth-century buildings with very narrow streets would not be a good introduction to this type of warfare for troops unused to working together.

In any event, by midnight, the four brigades of infantry from 50th Division may have been short of some of their hoped-for D-Day targets, but with tank squadrons supporting them and artillery well ashore and organized, the strongly held beachhead area seemed secure, and contact had been made with Canadian forces on the left flank of Gold Beach. The main concern was the open right flank and the expected German counter-attack.

The one unit with an important individual task not yet dealt with since they landed on Gold Beach, and moving towards Ryes, was 47 Commando. They had reorganized on the beach and moved off after the very difficult landing, causing high casualties. The planned forming-up point was Le Hamel church, clearly now impossible to reach. Heading off at 1200 via Les Roquettes and Buhot, the Commando made a slow advance, avoiding minefields and Germans. They had turned west inland before reaching Ryes using farm tracks and lanes. Their job was to push on to Port-en-Bessin as unobtrusively as possible. Initially, Colonel Philips was missing, but luckily he turned up just as they left the beach. Odd things really were observed; a farmer ploughing a field with his two horses as if the battle around him were not taking place. Ted Battley, in the leading troop, remembers it as a progress of carefully dodging Germans where possible. He describes it as more of a walk than the 'march' it is sometimes described as. Lying low when a couple of German convoys of trucks passed them, heading, he believes, towards Omaha Beach, they carefully followed hedges to provide cover.

> At another point we came across a slit trench with three not very attentive Germans in it. They were a bit surprised! They were interrogated by a couple of Commandos from 10 (IA) Commando who were attached for the purpose. While this went on a German charged down towards us shouting and screaming. Captain Isherwood said 'shoot him'. Well I had this pistol as a personal weapon and it just went 'click!' I had cleaned my Bren Gun, but forgotten the pistol. But there were plenty of others around to shoot him down. We came across an open road we were forced to cross. A shot rang out from a small copse and we could see movement within it. It was decided to attack it after a second shot. When we got into the copse there was a listening device for detecting aircraft. The only other thing around was a magnificent shire horse – which we took prisoner and passed down the line! I believe Colonel Philips told the men to get rid of it.[53]

Behind Batley's leading troop, other events took place. A well-remembered person was the MO, 'Doc' Forfar, who has provided us with an excellent account of 47 Commando in north-west Europe.[54] This is a very useful piece of primary evidence, often quoting commandos and French people involved in the events, and helps fill the gap left by the missing War Diary for this period. A German officer riding a horse was shot and killed; a small German vehicle stopped ahead and fired an MG. Hit by a rifle grenade, the German died soon afterwards. At La Rosiere, the commandos had a short sharp battle to subdue the enemy here. Obviously, Germans remained in the area, because later in the afternoon/evening, both 2nd Devon and 2SWB reached this area and had clashes with a German force. A number of commandos who had been wounded in this action, including one who was paralysed by a bullet in the spine, were left at La Rosiere and were later picked up by 2nd Devon. Of course, according to the planned timetable, La Rosiere would have already been reached *before* 47 Commando had to pass through it. Again, all these actions on the right flank of Gold Beach point to the effect of the more highly trained German 352nd Infantry Division.

Forfar makes the point that French civilians looked after marines injured on the march, while walking wounded had to make their own way back to the beachhead. By the end of the action at La Rosiere, it was apparently about 1530, and Colonel

Philips held an 'order group' with his officers. One marine had been killed and eleven wounded so far on the march from their already depleted forces, and by this time, the Commando numbered about 360 men. Over 100 men had caught up with the Commando at La Rosiere. They handed over twenty prisoners to 2nd Devon, who were now on the scene. Waiting until 1945 to leave the area of La Rosiere, 47 Commando formed a new plan, to reach Point 72, which dominated both the valley to Port-en-Bessin and the main road leading to Bayeux.[55] The comment is made that 'many of the men were now armed with German rifles and machine guns and there was no shortage of ammunition'.[56]

> Eventually we got to Hill 72 above Port-en-Bessin. Often on our journey we didn't see anything or anyone. As often as we could we were cutting across country. We settled down here and put the hill into a defensive position.[57]

Forfar mentions that at the base of Hill 72 was a large concrete bunker that was a German medical centre. Again, Germans smoking outside the door were surprised to find themselves faced with marines arriving from the landward side. One of the 10(IA) commandos was able to interrogate the German doctor, and they got on well, first, because the German doctor was not happy to be involved in the war and second, because they both came from Vienna![58] The men had little sleep that night and were digging in until 0300. Several patrols towards Port-en-Bessin exchanged shots with the enemy.

Of course, throughout the day, a large variety of units continued to come ashore. A number of these were Royal Navy Commando units: sailors specially trained to act in a combined operations mode. On Gold Beach, RN Commando units were J, Q and T Commando. Each comprised ten officers and sixty-five ratings. As specialized 'beach parties', their job was to see to the control of men and vehicles across the beaches and aid the men manning the landing craft on the beach. As trained land fighters, they also played a part in subduing beach defences, but that was a secondary role. T Commando landed at La Riviere at 0730. Q and J Commando landed further west, but, as with most other units, early in the landing they were not in the correct beach area. Some members of Q Commando dealt with a pillbox using grenades.[59] They remained in the area, helping with beach duties and on Mulberry B, for at least a further six weeks after D-Day.

One small but important unit of Naval Commandos was led by the young naval officer James Madden and was to help with the work of Royal Naval Beach Signal Section B7.

> When we went in about 9 o'clock we could see that some of the obstacles had been cleared, but that we were landing on the wrong beach, not the one planned because of the trouble at Le Hamel. The first thing that I was given on landing was a can of self-heating soup. Immediately we set up the radio, and RT, a decoder, Aldis signalling lamp and so on.

Principal Beach Master Lt Cmdr Whinney told Madden to wait and organize his group there on the beach. At around 5 o'clock they were sent to Le Hamel and the sanatorium, and reorganized in some rooms in the sanatorium. The building was quite a wreck.

They did not touch anything for fear of booby traps which they had been warned about, including toilets and the water supply.

> Lots of other people were coming in, especially the first aid people. I remember some Germans being interrogated there and there was a complex of tunnels that the Germans had built. We took watches but had no sleep that night. The area was in a real mess from the fighting. Another group were looking after the dead. All the incoming people and cargo had to be dealt with. Everything was very well organised and as coasters came in people knew what each carried.

Their signalling task was ship to shore and keeping in touch with all the vessels coming in. They linked with the Royal Engineers, who were unloading the ships as they arrived. As the organization ashore expanded after D-Day, they had contact with other port areas on Sword and Juno beaches as well as Arromanches as the Mulberry harbour grew. For example, they had men living on the Gooseberries off Juno and Sword. Much of the ship-to-shore signalling was done by Aldis Lamp. This small unit was, therefore, a very important part of the continuing delivery of materiel over the beachhead, and eventually through Mulberry B as well.[60]

Clearing the Germans from the area of Le Hamel and Asnelles also meant that after a long day spent organizing a dressing station just inland on the coast road very near to the east end of Le Hamel, Captain Johnson RAMC could now move to set up a covered dressing station in the village. 'So I went along and found a likely lot of buildings, getting them cleared of booby traps, and while I was away, after I had been over them, a dozen Huns who were found hiding in the roof – what the eye doesn't see!'

> Back a mile along the beach again, a race against the tide, passing the now so familiar corpses, and dead tanks, to collect the lads and move them in. Time had ceased to matter now, and it was getting dark by the time we had settled in our new quarters. They were very comfortable, and I think, well chosen, being a couple of houses and 3 or 4 garages, with a summer house for the Border SBs [Border Regiment Stretcher Bearers] who always liked to be on their own. We soon made ourselves at home, and managed tables and chairs, and white dishes and whatnots. We were sent a couple of dozen prisoners, so we put them in a garage – we couldn't evacuate them that night.[61]

Johnson took over a building and several garages literally just behind WN38 and its 50 mm gun. In going backwards and forwards, he drove along the beach fronting Le Hamel, avoiding the chaos within the village. As shown in his memoir above, by no means all the Germans had surrendered, and movement across the beach remained a risk for some time.

A small number of men from a specialist unit that was tasked with gathering maps, plans and other intelligence were from 30th Assault Unit (previously 30 Commando). Some of their members inspected and photographed the radar station above Arromanches, and even found secret documents in an abandoned vehicle near the radar station.[62]

The RAF also had a ground force presence on the D-Day beaches. On Gold Beach, No. 4 RAF Beach Squadron, 107 and 108 Beach Flights were landed, as were 980 RAF

Beach Balloon Squadron, 54 and 55 Flights and an 83 Group Code and Cypher section. The duties of the Beach Squadron were to work with the army beach organization to supervise the discharge of RAF personnel, stores and equipment across the beaches and their onward journey to the new landing grounds to be built for fighter, fighter-bomber and reconnaissance aircraft. Unlike the naval men, who wore khaki uniforms, the RAF men wore blue battledress with red brassard armbands. The Beach Balloon Squadron's task was to help defend the beachhead from low-level attack using barrage balloons. They were administered by the Beach Squadron, but operationally were under the control of the army anti-aircraft defence set-up. The beach flight squadron leader landed around 0850 on King Red, as did two NCOs with a jeep. A further three members of the flight had travelled with 151st Brigade and arrived with them before midday. The bulk of the flight arrived on D+1. Their main bivouac area was in the dunes at the back of the beach. They lost one man, killed here on 15 June. While he was digging a new dugout, his pickaxe struck an undetected mine. Elements of 108 Beach Flight landed in the safer part of the Jig area around 1030. One of their jeeps was drowned when their LST sank, but this was later recovered. Further men arrived with transport, and eventually they set up in Le Hamel around 1800. Again, the bulk of their men arrived early on D+1. The Beach Squadron returned to the United Kingdom in late August 1944.[63]

The work of the RAF was very important. As well as providing barrage balloon cover over the beaches, the building of the airstrips meant that fuel and time were saved getting fighters and fighter-bombers into the air, and the important 'spotter' planes working with the artillery and warships were quickly airborne and refuelled. Also, the larger strips allowed wounded men to be evacuated quickly by air using Dakota transport aircraft. In the Gold Beach area, the first emergency landing ground was open near Asnelles (B-1) from D+1, while an advanced landing ground (B-2) with a runway a mile long, and housing up to 1,000 personnel in tents, was started between Crepon and Bazenville on the night of D-Day and completed by 11 June 1944, and another advanced landing ground (B-3) was opened on 10 June at St Croix-sur-Mer. This had a runway 1,200 metres long, and a small memorial marks its position today. RAF and engineer personnel working on building these strips were often under sniper and mortar fire before the beachhead was extended.

By the late evening, barrage balloons were being established, anti-aircraft units were organizing themselves, and the many units belonging to the beach organization, who were now vital for the next stages in the campaign, were digging in and marking out their territory.

Overnight, and for many nights, enemy aircraft would intrude and attack targets, and the area became a cacophony of anti-aircraft fire between those established on land and the many boats going in and out of the beachhead. It must be remembered that bringing in men and materials was now a 24-hour job, only curtailed in the worst of storms. Coasters, LSTs and LCTs arrived regularly, some beaching ashore at high tide to be floated off after unloading on the following high tide, or were unloaded by the constantly busy ferrying DUWKs.

Something often forgotten was the work done by the Rhino ferries. On Gold Beach, Captain Ted Hunt RE was in charge of fifteen Rhino ferries of 935 Inland Water

Transport Company. The ferries were 180 feet long by 42 feet wide by 5 feet deep. They had 6,000 square feet of deck space, and when fully loaded they had little freeboard, but were designed to be very buoyant, and could carry loads, for example, of twelve Churchill tanks. Hunt says that he carried up to sixty Bren carriers on one journey! Each ferry was designed to take half the load of an LST. Its main drawback was the possible failure of the engines which propelled it. The Rhino ferries were towed across the Channel behind LSTs for D-Day, and a number were lost through parted tows in the rough sea.[64]

So, by sometime after midnight, all the advancing infantry battalions with supporting armour and artillery and other support had taken position for the night. Because of the weather conditions and tougher German resistance, very few of the elements of 7th Armoured Division had been landed, and the casualties to 8th Armoured Brigade tanks meant that the projected drive south to Villers-Bocage was not yet possible. The infantry battalions had all made very good progress, but had not quite attained the distance of advance that had been hoped for. The 69th Brigade were anchored by 6th Green Howards on Brecy, with 5th East Yorks and then 7th Green Howards east of them, around a kilometre apart and just over a mile short of the Bayeux to Caen main road. To the west, 151st Brigade had 6DLI at Esquay and 8th and 9th DLI at either end of Sommervieu. West again, at St Sulpice (2nd Essex), Magny (2nd Glosters) and Vaux-sur-Aure (2SWB), stood 56th Brigade above Bayeux. The 231st Brigade was covering some of the area behind, with 2nd Devons companies between Ryes and La Rosiere, and 1st Dorsets covering Ryes and the high ground to the north, while 1st Hampshires had the coastal strip and high ground from Le Hamel to Arromanches. In the beachhead area were very many units with infantry protection provided by 6th Border Regiment and 2nd Herts. But there were an unknown number of German soldiers variously active within this area. Perhaps the most dangerous were the remaining elements of *Kampfgruppe Meyer*, mainly 1/915. But there were also other small units across the whole area, some prepared to be quite aggressive and certainly ready to take up sniping activities as soon as it was light; and, of course, in June the nights are short. On Point 72, 47 Commando were ensconced, but Port-en-Bessin was still strongly held, in fact more strongly held than these men knew. To their rear were important German HQs at the chateaus of Fosse Soucy and Sully. The Longues battery, approximately halfway between Port-en-Bessin and Arromanches, had still not been approached.

We often see in books about D-Day maps showing large areas of land blocked in colour, as if all these areas were under complete Allied control by the end of the day. This was certainly not the case. Claims had been pegged out by the relatively small numbers of men in the infantry battalions, but between these battalion positions, the enemy could be anywhere.

Exploitation of the Landing, 7–15 June 1944

Few men could have slept well. Long daylight hours meant that the night was very short, and the expectation of a German counter-attack and the knowledge that German units were still at large in the area caused great concern. Patrols bumped into some German units, and in the tension, British patrols sometimes fired on each other. The noise of sustained anti-aircraft fire from the beachhead as the Luftwaffe made attempts to bomb the beach area equally kept men alert. There were a number of important objectives to achieve as soon as possible. The first priority was to make sure that all German units had been eliminated from the area gained by the advance of the previous day, and to set about making the area inland from Gold Beach into one vast safe supply dump. The second was to stabilize the front line. For this purpose, 2nd Devons needed to make sure that the Longues battery was secured; 47(RM) Commando had to take Port-en-Bessin; 56th Brigade needed to secure Bayeux and the area immediately to its south. Because of the tougher German resistance, loss of many landing craft and the continuing poor weather, follow-up supplies and units could not be landed to the expected timetable. In particular, 7th Armoured Division was only able to land a small part of its force on D-Day. Above all, perhaps, the western right flank of the landing needed to be secured and contact made with US forces from Omaha Beach. Thought could then be given to attempting significant advances southwards from the positions of 56th, 151st and 69th Brigades. However, inland from Gold Beach, not all German units were prepared to surrender or retreat easily.

The beach itself was being cleared up as quickly as possible to help all the follow-up landings, but was still something of a complete mess. Elements of 2nd Cheshires landing around 1400 on D+1 report that:

> as the tide receded it revealed numbers of vehicles which had been overturned, damaged or drowned, tanks, lorries, DUKWS and many other vehicles. The beach itself was a shambles, LCTs; LCIs had run up onto beach obstacles and were either overturned on their sides or balanced precariously on top of the obstacles when the tide went out. There was evidence of bitter fighting having taken place on the beaches; bodies were still lying strewn on the beach. The Beach Group was working overtime to clear the beaches with bulldozers, cranes etc. and to rescue those vehicles which weren't too badly damaged.[1]

The 1st Hampshires had suffered a high number of casualties the previous day, including its commanding officer. Lt Col. Howie took command, and the battalion cleared Tracy-sur-Mer and carried on to clear the village of Manvieux, encountering little opposition. The battalion then spent the day securing the area. A patrol of four jeeps was sent to Buhot to capture some snipers reported in the orchards there, and carrier patrols were sent towards Bazenville, one of these patrols capturing three prisoners and not returning until 2330. The following day, the battalion was moved north-east of Bayeux to the village of Ruberay.[2]

The 1st Dorset was situated mainly in and above Ryes, with a rearguard party back near Les Roquettes. Just off the beach, in the firm base he had arrived at with a lorry of equipment on D-Day, was Harold Lewis of 1st Dorset. He had been up since 0530 to help make breakfast to be taken up to the forward companies. Suddenly, one of the drivers exclaimed that 'there seemed to be a load of blokes coming across the field towards us'. These were quickly identified by the senior sergeant as Germans, with the obvious intention of attacking them. Quickly preparing some Bren guns, the post opened fire and accounted for seventeen Germans.[3] Further forward, above the village of Ryes, David Bushell was still in wet clothes that were barely starting to dry out, as were most of the men who had landed. The night had been spent patrolling the line of La Gronde Riviere to their east and across to 2nd Devon on their right, or west. By 0530, Ryes had been completely taken over by 1st Dorset from 2nd Devon. Around 1030, D Company, including the battalion chaplain, partly acting as a burial party looking for casualties, encountered a group of Germans, and in a short action took thirty of them prisoner in an area north-west of Ryes, not far from Point 54: ground that several units, including 1st Dorset and 47 Commando, had crossed the previous afternoon. An important task undertaken by 1st Dorset, starting at 1215, was to clear the enemy remnants out of Bazenville and La Croix, and a fighting group consisting of B Company supported by two sections of Bren carriers, including 3 in mortars, and a troop of tanks from the SRY was sent on this task. This area is approximately just south and east of where the modern Bazenville CWGC Cemetery is today. SRY intelligence had been led to believe, after interrogating a POW around 1400, that there was at least a company of Germans at La Croix, only 2 kilometres from Ryes. The infantry moved down the right-hand side of the road in the attack, while the tanks and carriers gave direct fire support and acted in a cut-off role if the enemy retreated.

By 1600, after a two-hour battle, forty Germans had been killed and seventy others became POW's from 915th and 916th Regiments from 352 Division. This successful action had a sting in the tail, as the Germans brought the group under artillery bombardment at 1730, immediately killing an officer and OR and wounding several others. B Company returned to Ryes by 1900, where it was learnt that during the confusion of the battle, Brigadier Senior from 151st Brigade had made good his escape. However, he was wounded and had to be returned to the UK to recover. Among other posts, he later commanded 56th Brigade in north-west Europe.[4]

At 0530, 2nd Devon B Company had relinquished Ryes to 1st Dorset, and now the complete battalion moved off to take the area known as Masse de Cradalle, high ground just beyond La Rosiere which C Company had not been able to take the previous evening. This feature was occupied by 0700, and the way was open to continue the advance on the Longues battery. Two companies were left to consolidate this area, while C Company, supported by B Company, moved off towards Longues. Longues battery was a complicated position to take. The village of Longues, south of the battery itself, had to be checked and cleared of any Germans first. Further north, near the cliffs, the battery was wired in, and obviously many mines had been laid protecting the position. The main position consisted of four large concrete casemates containing four 152 mm naval guns with a range of 20 kilometres (12 miles). There was also a 122 mm gun in an open position (similar to those at Mont Fleury) used especially in this position for firing illumination shells in night actions, but also capable of firing normal artillery shells. A large two-storey concrete fire control centre stood closer to the cliffs. The site was protected by several Tobruks containing Machine Gun (MG) and mortars, and underground concrete passageways joined its defensive trench system. It also had several 20 mm anti-aircraft guns. However, the infantry unit protecting the gunners had been called away the previous day to put in an attack towards Bayeux, and had not returned. As C Company 2nd Devons approached, they did not know that two of its main guns had been put out of action by HMS *Ajax* the previous day, with a further bombardment from the naval bombardment force protecting Omaha Beach in the afternoon of D-Day finally shutting it down. The D-Day aerial bombardment had not caused significant damage to its artillery, but had ripped up the position's signalling cables, and on D-Day visual signals had had to be used to set the guns to shoot the 115 rounds the battery fired.[5] The C Company attack was to be preceded by another bombardment from HMS *Ajax* until 0845, then a five-minute air attack by fighter-bombers. A platoon from 2nd Cheshires provided MMG support as the attack went in at 0900.[6] Photographs taken after the action show the casemate front openings partially buried by the debris of the bombardments it had suffered.

Michael Holdsworth had not been expecting to lead the attack, but the previous day's casualties to officers meant that he now became a company commander once again. He also had an unwanted burden in that, against his wishes, one of the platoon commanders was his twin brother! On the day they had boarded HMS *Glenroy*, Holdsworth had received some photographs of the Longues battery. He went to talk to the company commander, Palby, to discuss these, and in discussion with Palby, Holdsworth came to certain conclusions regarding how he thought the operation to take the battery should be run. This turned out to be a good thing, as Palby had been wounded on D-Day and it was Holdsworth who took his place as company commander.

I gave the Platoon Commanders including my twin brother my orders. We sat around on the ground with a cup of tea and I explained how we were going to do the attack. It was my brother's turn to be the leading platoon. I could see signs up to the right saying Achtung Minen everywhere which spread out to the right. Up to the left was some very difficult area covered by trenches. Spreading out one platoon behind the other we advanced very slowly using bayonets to check for mines, one platoon behind the other. We started off and it went extremely well. The guns seemed to be pointing down into the earth. I knew about the cliffs, an impossible way of attacking the position. My brother got some grenades and threw them through the embrasures. I was about 50 yards away and out came the

Germans. It was all over and done with in about a quarter of an hour. Unfortunately we had one casualty during the mopping up operation around the cliff. Captain Clarke the mortar officer told Lt Pearson that he had seen 7 Germans about 100 yards away who he thought were coming towards them to give themselves up. As Clarke went to meet them they opened fire and killed him.[7]

Over 100 prisoners were captured (sources vary between 90 and 120), and before 1100, 2nd Devon had completed this task and set about making sure the area was secure, with B Company at Masse de Cradalle, C Company at Longues, A Company protecting the battalion rear, and D Company moving on to secure the hamlet of Fontenailles. Lt Col. Nevill was aware that 47(RM) Commando were having a tough time at Port-en-Bessin, so the Carrier Platoon was sent to help and 'got seriously embroiled on the outskirts of the port'. As Lt Col. Nevill later remarked, they had completed their D-Day tasks just twelve hours late.[8]

At their forward and exposed position on Point 72, 47 Commando had little rest. Nearby two chateaus housed German units; the one at Fosse Soucy was a sniper school. Halfway towards Port-en-Bessin, the road was covered by German weapons pits. There had been no real contact overnight with other British forces, even trying the wireless link. Some French people had proffered advice and information. The early morning had been enlivened when a small group of German soldiers, led by an NCO, marched up to the first aid bunker. It was the morning sick parade, and clearly the Germans were not at all aware of the presence of British soldiers in the area. The Germans surrendered fairly meekly, and joined the rest of the prisoners in the rear room of the bunker.

It was not until 1100 that Lt Col. Philips made contact with 231st Brigade, using the single wireless of a FOO from 147th Field Regiment, who had managed to make the difficult and hazardous journey from Gold Beach in a Bren carrier. It was decided that the move on Port-en-Bessin should be made at 1600, giving time for arrangements to be made for air support and bombardment ships. A plan was made, with an order group forming at 1350. The tasks were to deal with the weapons pits using X Troop, and then take the town and the dominating German positions on the cliffs above and east and west of the port, known as the Eastern Feature and the Western Feature. A Troop were to take the Western Feature and B Troop the Eastern Feature. Only a small group of fifteen men (Y Troop) could be left as rearguard at Point 72, with others from Q Troop guarding the village of Escures.

An unplanned bombardment of the port took place at 1400, but then, on time at 1500, HMS *Emerald* started the planned shoot on the town until 1600, followed by a Typhoon fighter-bomber strafing of the Eastern and Western Features, then a ten-minute shoot by 147th Field Regiment 25 lb guns from the Gold Beach area firing smoke shells. MMGs had been brought up and fired on the Eastern Feature for several minutes, but had to stop because of the smoke. The Commando advanced, including 'Doc' Forfar, who moved forward to establish a first aid post within the town. In fact, as he was passing the weapon pits' slit trenches via the road, he noticed that there were still Germans there. However, at that time the X Troop attack took place, which appeared to be a straightforward old-fashioned bayonet charge from close range (only 200 yards). The cover provided by commando mortar fire was pretty haphazard, as they had lost the sights to the mortar on the landing. Luckily, little opposition was encountered, and an officer and nineteen ranks surrendered. The commandos were surprised to find a wealth of food, drink, ammunition and clothing there. At about 1745, this troop had the first encounter with US troops when an American officer turned up driving a jeep.

Meanwhile, A and B Troops, with the help of local gendarme Henri George Gouget, made their stealthy way into Port-en-Bessin. Ted Battley remembers that:

> We advanced towards the town, the usual things advancing and being fired at – goodness knows what. When we got to the town it was a bit difficult. We didn't know which streets to go down or anything. So we headed for the church where more plans were laid for the next stage. Our problem was the splitting of the Commando to attack each side of the town and they were chucking mortar bombs all over us. Later on we found in the Eastern Feature a really good German map with ranges marked on it. They could drop the mortar bombs on a sixpence. We had a couple of goes at the Western Feature but couldn't get anywhere. We even had chaps coming across from the Western Feature asking if anyone had any helmets to protect them, but hardly anyone had helmets after the problems of the landing. We carried our helmets with us on the landing craft and wore our berets.

Things were difficult for A Troop. First, they had had to blow some obstructive wire in the narrow street leading to the Western Feature; then, not only did they come under sustained fire from there, but as they climbed the hill, it was realized that there were two German flak ships in the harbour, unleashing rapid machine-gun and cannon fire on them from behind. Previous reconnaissance pictures had shown the harbour empty. Several marines were killed or badly wounded in this attack. A British ship outside the harbour warned them via loudhailer that German troops were approaching from the west along the clifftop, and there was little option but to fall back. Also, in the streets of Port-en-Bessin the marines had to deal with German patrols and snipers. At great risk, the French people of the town took in wounded marines and treated them. At least one civilian was shot out of hand by a German for this. Also, several townspeople were wounded or killed in the British bombardment. B Troop, advancing on the Eastern Feature, overcame the first defences straightforwardly; Sergeant Fuller (actually Kagerer-Stein) from 10th (IA) Commando advanced, and in a loud voice ordered the men in the pillbox to surrender, which they meekly did. However, this whole group then came under sustained MG fire, forcing them to get into cover in nearby houses, with one marine dead and eleven seriously wounded. Other marines were wounded by the mortar bombs from the Eastern Feature. Again, French people started looking after the wounded.

Marine Battley was hit by mortar fragments and wounded quite severely. A mortar bomb landed near where a number of them were standing. Several were wounded, including Battley. Doc Forfar looked at him and said 'you are for home!' He was put on a stretcher jeep eventually, taken to a hospital ship and back to Britain. He remembers the ship as being well staffed. He was back with 47(RM) Commando within several weeks.

By 1930 that evening, then, 47(RM) Commando was caught in the town, and there was worse news from outside: Point 72 was under fire, and German units were closing in, bringing the road between Point 72 and Port-en-Bessin under fire even though the 47(RM) Commando and some 2nd Devon carriers had arrived at Point 72. In itself, this had been an interesting adventure. Having not been able to pass La Rosiere the previous evening, Lt Bennett, with the carriers, had set out early, deciding to go via Bayeux, which he had been told was in British hands. As 56th Brigade had still not arrived, this group of carriers was probably the first to briefly enter the town. Realizing it was still occupied, they quickly got out and got to Point 72 via La Rosiere and the Longues Battery, observing the 2nd Devon attack on the way. Having had some carriers damaged, they joined with the 2nd Devons carriers that Nevill had sent to Port-en-Bessin. In the end, a platoon of Germans captured Point 72 temporarily at 2200 hours, and a battle had developed at Escures. Back at Port-en-Bessin, Forfar had now established a first aid post in a stable-like building in the town, and several of Lt Bennett's carriers had made it into the town. Effectively, 47(RM) Commando was now trying to continue an offensive action against an enemy well dug in on the two dominating features above the port with much depleted numbers, and it seemed that the enemy were now slowly closing in from the rear.

There was some better news from the harbour. As the tide had come in, the two flak ships had risen to be visible above the harbour wall, and a protracted exchange of fire took place between them and two destroyers, HMS *Ursa* and the Polish destroyer ORP *Krakowiak*, lying outside the harbour. Both ships moved to within 300 yards of the breakwater, and then at 2230 sent boarding parties in cutters into the harbour, and found that one of the flak ships had been partially sunk and the other abandoned. Apparently, the Commandos ashore were heartened by the volume of English swearing taking place within the harbour as the action took place!

It was now decided to concentrate on capturing the Eastern Feature, using the Bren guns from the carriers to cover an attack and smoke laid by the Heavy Weapons Troop. An attack was put in again at 2200. This caused more casualties to the Marines, including Captain Cousins, who it was felt deserved a VC, but did not receive one. The attack was pressed home with much aggression and determination, and only thirty men managed to kill or capture well over 100 Germans. The Western Feature still had to be dealt with. However, the morale of the Germans weakened, and the following morning, 8 June, twenty-three 'surrendered' to Corporal Amos, a marine they had captured the day before and who, at some points of his capture, felt that he was near to execution. He descended to the town with the Germans; any others fled across the top of the plateau. On examination, this clifftop proved to have been as well prepared as the Eastern Feature, with pillboxes, underground shelters, concrete trenches, fixed flame-thrower positions, barbed wire and mines. Radio contact was made with Omaha Beach, and 'Doc' Forfar received some much-needed medical supplies by parachute from a small spotter plane.

Escures and Point 72 had also been secured by the Marines and 2nd Devon with armour support. Now, carriers and jeeps could bring supplies through to Port-en-Bessin. Contact was established with US forces that evening by a small officer patrol, and the wounded were evacuated via Omaha Beach back to the United Kingdom on 9 June. From this small unit of 420 men on the LSI on the morning of 6 June, only 276 could be mustered at Port-en-Bessin on 9 June. Forty-six had been drowned or killed in action on land, sixty-five wounded – a number very seriously – and six captured. Twenty-eight were missing, the majority of whom had been picked out of the sea and returned to the

United Kingdom; they rejoined in Normandy before the end of June. However, they had taken over 300 prisoners and killed a large number of Germans. Within forty-eight hours, the fit members of 47(RM) Commando had switched flanks and were back in action supporting the parachutists who had landed inland to secure Sword Beach! Before this, they were congratulated on their achievement by Generals Montgomery and Dempsey. Dempsey was to later pick out this operation for special mention, and the later XXX Corps commander, General Horrocks, wrote: 'It is doubtful whether, in their long and distinguished history, the Marines have ever achieved anything finer.'[9]

A very important result of the taking of Port-en-Bessin was that the plan to use the small port for bringing fuel ashore could begin, and the town became the first Allied 'petrol port'. As early as 9 June a Port Operating Company arrived, and began construction and organization. From 9 June, fuel was brought ashore in jerry cans,[10] while storage facilities were constructed near the port. Then an offshore facility was constructed, allowing larger tankers to discharge fuel from a kilometre away directly through a pipeline to the storage facility at a rate of 600 tonnes an hour, while smaller tankers could discharge fuel within the harbour walls. The fuel was then pumped inland for two miles in pipelines laid along the country lanes to the village of Etreham, from where it was distributed by lorry. When the early capture of Cherbourg failed to materialize after D-Day, and the projected opening of PLUTO (Pipe Line Under the Ocean) between the Isle of Wight and Cherbourg had to wait, Port-en-Bessin remained an important place for the offloading of fuel. The offshore facility first operated on D+19. In the meantime, hundreds of thousands of gallons of fuel had been landed in the harbour contained in jerry cans.[11]

As related, Point 72 was back in British hands, but occasional fire was directed on it from the nearby chateau of Fosse Soucy, situated on higher ground across the valley to the south. The chateau was an important area command post. On 8 June, 2nd Devon had started to clear positions towards Port-en-Bessin along the coastal belt. By 1320, they had captured thirty-eight Germans north of Le Mesnil, and then pushed on towards Point 72 with C, D and A Company and tank support, while B Company patrolled the Masse de Cradalle. Arriving in the area of Point 72 and deciding to attack the chateau, Lt Col. Nevill had to first persuade 50th Division HQ that the chateau was occupied by Germans and not American troops, as it lay in the US sector of operations. The approach to the chateau was difficult. Two rivers had to be crossed, and temporarily checked the advance of A and D Companies, supported by a squadron of SRY tanks and 2nd Cheshire MMGs. Some support was given by 147th Artillery Regiment, but at 1800 they had another shoot to perform. The infantry were now faced with an assault across the open ground of the park in front of the chateau. The assault had to be pressed home, as both 2nd Cheshires and the tanks were expending ammunition at an alarming rate, having fired on the chateau for forty-five minutes. One of the officers leading the attack was Michael Holdsworth:

> About 5.30pm I was sent for by the CO and he told me we had to attack and take the place. 'You will be in command of D Company. You have got to get moving because you will lose the gunners at 6pm, they have another job to do.' I told Frank Saddler of A Company that he would go to the right of the mansion and I would

go to the rear. I did not know that there were the two rivers in the way, in ditches about 100 yards apart from each other and about 6-7 feet deep and 10 feet wide. This was all on a completely open piece of ground about 400 yards wide plus as I discovered later there was a moat around it fed by a lake. The distance we had to go was about 700 yards.

An A Company runner arrived as we reached the first ditch to tell me they have found a bridge. We used that and then found a second one at the next ditch. So far we had no casualties and I told my soldiers to get a bloody move on!

The lake/pond was thigh deep and I found my sten gun was not working properly and we then came under fire. My spare magazine didn't work and I knocked it on my knee and replaced it and fired on the windows up and downstairs in the chateau. We came out of the pond and I was walking around the moat and I told my men to go in the front door which they did.

My sergeant major was with me and suddenly from only around 20 yards away a Spandau opened up on the two of us but missed. The sergeant major said to me, 'Excuse me sir I have a little job to do.' He fixed his bayonet and charged into the German trench and killed them both! At the same time my men came out of the chateau with some prisoners. That was really the end of the action; A Company had been equally successful and both companies had successfully cleared the chateau.

On the radio I was asked by the Colonel if I thought I could hold the chateau with my company alone, as a large German force was heading our way. I told him I didn't think so as we had about 85 prisoners and had used a lot of ammo. He told us that was all right and to come back to the hill (Point 72).

Immediately after this I noticed two of my men talking to two German prisoners and one of my men pulled out a packet of fags from his pocket and offered a cigarette to the L/H German prisoner. This prisoner I noticed put his hand in his pocket and I knew instantly he had a pistol. He had, and he used the bloody thing and killed him. The German threw the pistol into the moat and both of them ran into the middle of the German prisoners. There was nothing I could do about it as we had to move off in a hurry. I lost one man only in that attack and to have this one man killed through lack of forethought. As a postscript less than a week later I was called at night by a sentry to see the Sergeant Major. He had a heart attack and had to be returned to the UK. He had been a bloody fine sergeant major since Sicily. This is what happens and you can lose your best man.

In his memoir, Lt Col. Nevill mentions: 'It was a very anxious moment, but owing to the inspiring leadership of both Major Mike Holdsworth and Major Frank Saddler, and to the intrepid gallantry of all ranks under their command, all difficulties were overcome.' The final assault took place to the 'accompaniment of ringing cheers' from those on Point 72. One of the captured Germans, a medical officer, said that he had never believed that men could advance across such difficult ground in such perfect order under fire. The action took only an hour and a half from the time the CO issued his orders. The three companies arranged themselves back on Point 72, but the counterattack never came. By 2130, full contact had been made with US troops at Escures. The only man killed during the day's actions was the one Holdsworth witnessed at Fosse

Soucy, killed by the captured enemy he was handing a cigarette to. Eight others were wounded.[12]

Now to return to 7 June, and how 56th Brigade was progressing, literally just over the hill, to the south of the above actions. By just after midnight, the Brigade, with support from SRY, had secured the three villages of St Sulpice, Magny and Vaux-sur-Aure. At Brigade HQ, situated just behind 2nd Glosters at Magny, signaller Tony Atcherley awoke to the whine of a sniper's bullet hitting the ACV. It was his nineteenth birthday. The Brigade War Diary states that at 1000 there was no news of US progress. More optimistically was written: '3(Br) Div in CAEN', something unfortunately not to be achieved for several weeks. At 1100, 2nd Essex was ordered to advance, skirting Bayeux to the east and via the railway station to take up position on the high ground known as the Monumirel feature, south of Bayeux, while 2nd Glosters was to clear the centre of Bayeux. Starting from St Sulpice, 2nd Essex reported a quiet night. Moving off to Bayeux, the leading companies passed round Bayeux and through part of St Vigor-le-Grand, and reported that apart from a short action around the railway station, their progress was through quiet and shuttered streets. But by the time the main body was moving through, around 1300, 'The local inhabitants showered flowers on our troops and many bottles of wine were brought out. The Tricolour was soon to be seen flying from many houses.'[13] The only casualties seem to have been Captain Hearne, the signals officer, and his driver Downes, badly wounded when the Bren carrier they were travelling in hit a mine on the way into the town. Arthur Dyer was the signals sergeant travelling in the Signals section half-track M14:

> Moved off about 0830hrs to follow Carrier in our M14 (Armoured half-track radio vehicle). Carrier went ahead out of view; we went along and pulled up to negotiate trip wire across road. This done we again moved forward speeding and ran into a lot of bumps in the road. George (the driver) steered his way through the maze just in case they were mines. By a miracle we missed every one. A Battalion Carrier behind us hit one and it turns out they were mines. The Signals officer was seriously wounded. We had gone ahead looking for the leading Carrier and stopped short of a corner and sent the DR *[Dispatch Rider or Don-R]* to investigate, he returned immediately saying there were Jerries around the corner. We had taken the wrong road and arrived in Bayeux before our troops. We stayed here quite a while before proceeding back to Bayeux. Here our forward troops had just got in and were being showered with roses red and white. The French really are happy and old men salute us, women wave and cheer, amongst each other they kiss and weep – their happiness has no measure. Prisoners are coming in steadily all the time – some are very old, others look about 16.[14]

By 1900, 2nd Essex had secured the Monumirel feature and deployed its infantry companies forward of Bayeux.

At Magny, 2nd Glosters did not have a 'quiet' night, having 'dug in' at the village by 0026. Under cover of darkness, a number of Germans in the area, who had been lying low, tried to get away. A few ran past the Bn. HQ, where Sgt Davis of the Pioneer Corps shot one with his Sten gun, thus winning the £5 for the first person to 'bag' an enemy. Later, Lieutenant Tucker was walking along the road near the slit trenches and started to engage a figure in conversation in the gloom, thinking it was one of his own men. Realizing suddenly that they were a group of Germans, he fired on them at the same time as they fired at him. Both missed, and the Germans ran for the hedge across the road and up some steps cut in a bank. Everyone in the area fired at the Germans, but missed.

On arrival at Magny, 2nd Glosters had captured a troop of 105 mm guns, including some horses. At least two of these horses became an A Company possession, pulling a wagon full of kit in the charge of an ex-Gloucestershire farmhand:

> In an apple orchard we found the deserted transport of a local gun battery with the horses standing in their traces, and from then on for the next three weeks our 'platoon truck' consisted of two splendid Norman horses pulling a German cart driven by Private Deeley. He was a countryman and fully conversant with the needs and behaviour of horses.[15]

As morning broke, the sniper who had probably hit the ACV Tony Atcherley was in fired occasional rounds, and his 'nest' was identified as being in Magny church tower – interesting in itself, as some Glosters had spent the night inside the church, from where the Germans running off several hours earlier had apparently erupted! Frank Rosier from D Company fired a Bren gun at the outside tower; marks remain that can be seen to this day. The German surrendered only after a Sherman tank levelled its gun towards the tower. Gordon Duffin of A Company was coming back from the advanced position he had occupied that night when four Germans jumped out of the hedge with their hands up to surrender.

Then, 2nd Glosters moved off towards Bayeux, and entered through the centre of the town around 1220. 'Civilian population very pleased to see us.' Some German soldiers were captured in Bayeux, and by now a party was in full swing, but some Frenchmen were looking for retribution. Sergeant Frank Clarke had captured some prisoners from the cellar of a large house and lined them up outside the garden wall. An increasing number of French appeared, and began to get very ugly with the prisoners. Only by threatening to use their weapons on the French did Clarke's men get the prisoners away safely towards the beach. That evening, 2nd Glosters took up positions in the area of what is today the CWGC Cemetery. The Germans had blown one of the main railway bridges, and the railway embankment was one of the Glosters' patrol lines and main defensive lines while occupying this position.[16]

A covering force of 2SWB was left at the bridge at Vaux-sur-Aure, with the main body moving off at 0515. Their War Diary gives a final position in the north-western suburbs of Bayeux, where they were treated by the French to the normal celebrations. However, how many of the battalion made it here is debatable, as the following day they were operating mainly from around a farm called Le Parquet between Bayeux and Chateau Sully. Also, one platoon commander admits to nothing more than a recce of Bayeux with two ORs. Major Gillespie was wounded by a sniper on 7 June and had to be evacuated, and all sources, written and oral, agree as to the trouble snipers caused the battalion while moving forward on this day. Another task on 7 June sent A Company to make contact with US forces via Chateau Sully and Vaucelles. At both places they met resistance, and at Sully this was very determined and unexpected, from what turned out to be a German Regimental HQ.

Sully was also a natural fall-back position for those German troops retreating from 47 Commando and 2nd Devons' coastal push, and also for units escaping Omaha Beach. US troops were now beginning to consolidate and advance south from their hard-won beachhead. We know that tanks and self-propelled guns moved back via Sully. The movement of A Company over the small bridge attempting to enter the village was heavily contested, and A Company had to withdraw, realizing that they had been asked to bite off more than they could chew. Also, of course, there were clearly no Americans in the area!

The following day, 8 June, it was decided at divisional level that the situation at Sully had to be 'cleared up' even if Sully was in the US area of operations, and so a larger assault was planned. A and B Companies, two troops of tanks, a 4.2 inch heavy mortar platoon from 2nd Cheshires and a field regiment of artillery were given the task. The guns of a cruiser could not be used due to fire-control difficulties in the bocage and wooded areas surrounding the chateau. As the infantry went in, one carrier exploded on a mine, and the field artillery had to cease fire, as many of the shells were exploding in the trees and too close to the infantry. The tanks themselves had great difficulty fighting in the narrow confines of the bocage, their first experience. Also, the enemy had deployed two 88 mm guns. The action became very hotly contested. One platoon officer missed a turning on a track in the close country. The small village held snipers and machine-gun teams, and it was not known that as well as the chateau buildings, there were concrete underground bunkers and trenches built into this HQ of 726 Grenadier Regiment, as well as barbed wire obstacles. In fact, the SWB was faced by larger numbers of enemy fighting from well-defended positions. Things did not improve when it was seen that at least one, and possibly more, German self-propelled guns or tanks with infantry were moving into the chateau grounds via a bridge previously unseen across the River Drome. These counter-attacked 2SWB. With Brigadier Pepper on the scene, a decision was taken to withdraw under cover of smoke from artillery. Casualties were severe enough. Captain Noble, the Royal Horse Artillery FOO, lost his life when his tank went through the parapet of Sully Bridge. His is the only CWGC grave in Sully churchyard. During the two days of action, 2SWB suffered thirteen deaths and over fifty wounded. Lt Col. Craddock, commanding 2SWB, was wounded and had to be evacuated, and his second-in-command, Major Barlow, took command. It is again notable that fairly senior officers were often in the thick of the action. Craddock was almost notorious in the battalion for wearing his soft hat and carrying only a sidearm and swordstick.

Also as a matter of interest, the gendarme Henri Gouget, who had helped 47(RM) Commando move forward into Port-en-Bessin, had been captured by the Germans later on 7 June when returning to retrieve his cycle from near Point 72. On being searched, he was discovered to be carrying a grenade and a map. He was being interrogated in the basement at Chateau Sully with the intention afterwards of shooting him. This all changed when the chateau was subjected to bombardment on 8 June, and in the confusion Gouget was able to escape. The self-propelled guns and infantry may well have been the same force that threatened Chateau Fosse Soucy after the attack by 2nd Devons. Also, some 47(RM) Commandos in the area away from Port-en-Bessin report seeing a force of 200–300 Germans and a self-propelled gun, probably all the same unit.

On 9 June, patrols into Chateau Sully discovered the chateau abandoned and burning. Later that day, 2SWB also made contact with US forces, and so on 9 June a continuous bridgehead was established across the whole invasion front, and 50th Division's right flank was secure from the front line to the sea. The chateau no longer exists, and was badly damaged in 1944, being one of three in the immediate area of Sully. At the time, its proper name was Chateau de Petit Sailly. Traces of its existence can be seen on the ground and from the air. Anthony Gross, the war artist who landed with 50th Division on D-Day, made an excellent sketch showing the tree-lined drive to the chateau littered with equipment.[17]

On D-Day, 151st (DLI) Brigade had been able to move forward successfully, and broadly speaking, been able to occupy the line Sommervieu to Esquay. Along with 56th Brigade, it had dominated the high ground north of Bayeux and formed a blocking force for any German drive on the beachhead, but with the German units in the Bazenville area to its rear. At 0700, 8DLI moved off from Sommervieu, and in just over an hour A Company had captured no fewer than one officer and eighty-five ORs. It seemed that the Germans in this area had little stomach for a fight. The hamlet of La Bergerie was now under control, which was just south of the Bayeux to Caen RN13 main road, effectively cutting off Bayeux from Caen. The battalion dug in and patrolled the area, capturing further enemy. By 1645, they reported linking with 6th Green Howards. They reported tanks moving towards them at 1720, but little developed, and by night they were patrolling forward of La Bergerie.

At 0500, 6DLI had already moved off, crossed the Bayeux to Caen railway line, and dominated the high ground and railway north of Conde-sur-Seulles by 0730. It had lost two carriers in a mistaken attack by two US Thunderbolt aircraft, but had shot up a German truck convoy. It patrolled into Conde, with the intention of forming a joint post with 69th Brigade. This post was attacked by about a company of German troops in the afternoon, and the post unit of a platoon of 6DLI, an anti-tank gun and section of carriers was reinforced with a further section of carriers around 1700. The enemy were dislodged from their position in woods overlooking the 6DLI position, but later, after armoured cars were heard, it was decided to hold the village. Further platoons were sent into Conde from D Company, and Conde was made defensible against attack, with the main body of 6DLI established between Conde and Neuville towards 8DLI at La Bergerie.

At first light, 9DLI moved forward and occupied the area between 6DLI and Bayeux, forming a junction with 2nd Essex of 56th Brigade at Gueron by the end of the day. They dominated the high ground above the River Aure, which ran north into Bayeux. Patrols on foot and carrier were sent forward on reconnaissance, and enemy concentrations to the south were reported and engaged by 90th Field Regiment RA. As the Brigade HQ moved forward, it captured five officers and twenty-eight ORs. This purposeful advance by 151st Brigade meant that by the evening of 7 June, Bayeux was completely isolated, virtually surrounded as it was by 56th Brigade and 151st Brigade and their supporting units. Control of both the main road and railway line connecting Bayeux and Caen was achieved, and 151st Brigade was on the high ground dominating the river valleys of the River Aure and River Seulles south and south-east of Bayeux. Importantly, it appeared that the road to Tilly-sur-Seulles, only 8 miles away, and therefore Villers-Bocage, a further 7 miles beyond Tilly, lay open. If Tilly could be attained, a further German east–west connection would be cut, and similarly, if Villers-Bocage was taken, not only would the Allies dominate major east–west road lines, but the way into the heart of Normandy, well south of Caen, would be open. However, the projected armoured/infantry thrust to the south had still not taken place, and did not seem imminent. The point is made that the small German units defending the small villages and hamlets in the area seemed out of touch with their HQ, had little in the way of supporting arms outside MGs and armoured cars, and were surprised at the speed of the British advance.[18]

To the east of 151st Brigade, 69th Brigade also began to advance. After holding a company commanders' conference at 0815, 6th Green Howards started advancing south. By 1000, it had passed through Ruqueville and then crossed the RN13 between Bayeux and Caen. By 1100 hours, it was in view of the Bayeux to Caen railway line, having passed through Ducy-St-Marguerite. However, there was significant opposition, which began to make itself felt through mortar fire and snipers. C Company ran into some German tanks (probably SP guns), and it was decided after the brigadier arrived to move back 1,000 yards north of Ducy, in line with the rest of the brigade and away from their exposed forward position. Numerous Germans were seen, and sixty Germans were reported as making southwards for their own lines from near the RN13 behind 6th Green Howards' forward positions. At 1930, it was reported (wrongly) that German paratroops had been dropped in the Canadian sector and that they should look out for them. By 2000, armoured cars were reported in Ducy, and at least one fired on the 6th Green Howards' B Company without causing any casualties. That night, patrols were sent forward, but reported finding nothing. The following day, positions were maintained, enemy moving around 6th Green Howards' front was engaged by 86th Field Regiment, and a C Company platoon went to La Riviere, a hamlet near Carcagny, establishing a joint post with 8DLI at a bridge over the River Seulles. For the following two days, 9 and 10 June, positions were maintained and men allowed to get as much rest as possible. The main excitement was eight Focke-Wulf 190 fighter planes going south on 9 June at 2200 over the battalion area, to the accompaniment of heavy anti-aircraft fire.

At 0530, 7th Green Howards moved off, and advanced through Coulombs in two parallel columns. Short of the RN13, they were stopped by resistance from MGs and 20 mm cannon at a farm called Le Parc. The buildings were surrounded by a minefield of wooden box mines and Bakelite mines. This was, in fact, a Luftwaffe radar station. Plans were made to attack it. C Company gained the farm entrance, and A Company gained the farm from the west. Tanks of the 4/7 Dragoon Guards fired in support. Sixty Germans were captured, and much valuable intelligence information and wireless equipment was discovered. A staff car knocked out at a crossroads contained a long-range movie camera. The battalion formed an eastward-facing block across the RN13, and by 1500 a joint post had been made with the Canadians in Brouay. Contact was also made with 6th Green Howards.

On 6 June, 5th East Yorks had suffered heavily, and after ending the day at Brecy, it was decided that they would be brigade reserve. On 7 June, after reconnaissance, they moved south to occupy the village of St Leger and established a further block across the RN13. For the following four days, the battalion rested and refitted here.

By 1150 on 7 June, 69th Brigade HQ was established in an orchard just to the rear of 5th East Yorks. Because of losses of equipment during the landing, Brigade HQ was to suffer from rear link communications with 50th Division for some time. C Squadron of 4/7 Dragoon Guards had helped in the reconnaissance of St Leger and then continued forwards to the railway line, but lost two tanks to 88 mm guns as they attempted to cross the railway embankment. Further north on 7 June, a position containing a concrete pillbox and four 75 mm guns was cleared early in the morning by a composite force of twelve men from 86th Field Regiment acting as infantry, No. 1 Troop Westminster Dragoons and two 'Crocodile' flame-throwing tanks of 141 RAC. Over sixty of the enemy were captured. Later in the day, some RM Centaur tanks were used to round up snipers in an area 86th Field Regiment wished to move to. It needs to be remembered that artillery in this type of warfare were involved in a fluid battlefield situation, and it was not necessarily unusual for them to take part in 'infantry'-type actions.[19]

By 9/10 June, the Allies had a secure front line from Omaha in the west to several miles across the River Orne north-east of Caen. Sword, Juno and Gold were secure, with only a unit of Germans holding out at the radar station at Douvres-la-Deliverande. The first Gooseberry harbours of sunken ships were being put in place, and the concrete and metal constituent parts of Mulberry A off Omaha, and Mulberry B off Gold, were on their way. The weather was still unsettled, and unloading across the beachheads was working well, but behind schedule. The particular problem for the Allies was that Caen had not been taken, and the city formed a particularly difficult defensive wedge to the front of the Canadians and British forces from Juno and Sword Beach. Although 7th Armoured Division units such as 5th Royal Tank Regiment had already been in action with 2SWB at Sully, the division was not yet complete, and its supporting infantry brigade, drawn from the Queen's Regiment, was only just landing. At Sully, 5RTR from 7th Armoured Division had already lost a 'Firefly' Sherman tank and a Cromwell, and had begun to realize what fighting in this close country meant for armour and infantry, while 49th Infantry Division was only just about to start landing.

Meanwhile, of course, the Germans had not remained idle. Caught out by a landing they thought improbable in the weather conditions, and with Hitler and his generals believing that the main assault on the coast was still to come, the realization had sunk in before the first twenty-four hours was up that something had to be done to gain back the lost ground. The expected strategy of throwing the Allies back into the sea had obviously failed on 6 June. The only Panzer division very close to the scene was 21st Panzer Division under General Major Feuchtinger. This division on D-Day had 117 Panzer IVs and 16,200 men.[20] Some 6th Airborne troops landed on top of some 21st Division units, and by the morning of D-Day, the division was taking active action on its own responsibility against the paratroops. Later in the day, it received orders to attack the British landings, and reached Lion-sur-Mer between Juno and Sword, where in the late afternoon confidence was lost with the arrival of the 6th Airborne air train of gliders bringing reinforcements and equipment to those already landed, and obviously landing to the rear of the 21st Panzer Division.

On its way to oppose 50th Division was the powerful Panzer Lehr Division of over 14,500 men, 237 tanks and assault guns, including eighty-nine Panzer V (Panther) and eight Panzer VI (Tiger) tanks, and over 650 armoured half-track personnel carriers. Their journey was not easy, and although reported numbers vary, they had lost over a hundred vehicles and a number of men. Their commander, General Major Bayerlein, had orders on 9 June to take Bayeux. This division had a march distance of between 75 and 120 miles, depending on where units were situated, starting from D-Day. Slightly closer to the battle was 12th SS Panzer Hitlerjugend, with ninety-six Panzer IV and sixty-six Panzer V and over 20,000 mainly young men aged eighteen to nineteen, who would confront both Canadians and units such as 49th (WR) Infantry Division inland on the left flank of Gold Beach. This division had a march distance of between 45 to 110 miles, starting on D-Day.

The 716th Infantry Division had virtually ceased to exist as a unit. As far as Gold Beach is concerned, General Richter reported in a post-war interrogation that early in the morning, Ost Battalion 441 'retreated in flight', while the remainder of the troops held the woods and Crepon. Later, between Ver and Courseulles, British forces had broken through by 1030, sending another company of Ost Battalion 441 into flight. British tanks and infantry attacks were successful, as the German troops had few anti-tank weapons. By 7 June, Richter had met representatives from both Panzer Lehr and 12th SS Panzer. Both reported the difficulties of movement during the day because of the threat by Allied aircraft. Panzer Lehr had to be refuelled from another division because it had lost so many of its fuel trucks in the march to the battlefield. The field hospitals were full of casualties from the advancing Panzer divisions. Richter, remarking on the small number of casualties in hospital from the coastal divisions, says that 'this was not surprising since hardly anybody came back from the most advanced line'.[21]

As we have seen, 352nd Division held firm on the west flank of Gold Beach until late into the afternoon of D-Day, while the only mobile reserve, Kampfgruppe Meyer from 352nd Division, had had its forces split, one battalion going to Omaha Beach while the rest could not stem the tide when they arrived after midday on D-Day, and any remnant was dealt with in the Bazenville area by the end of D+1, or had retired south on Brecy. The picture painted for the Gold Beach area by 352nd Infantry Division by the end of 7 June was that between 716th and 352nd Divisions a gap had been opened, so large that it could not be closed with the available forces. Between Bayeux and Tilly, only a 'thin screen' was in existence, formed by the remnants of 915th Regiment and other survivors, including Fortress Pioneers. It was noted that British 50th Division was able to 'reinforce his troops without difficulty'.[22]

Despite all this, 50th Division had not been able to push forward fast enough to prevent the arrival of the Panzer divisions disrupting future plans. This was not surprising, considering the resistance put up on the 231st Brigade area of operations on D-Day and the significant casualties taken by the assaulting battalions. In the follow-up battalions of infantry, small actions such as that at Sully showed the cost in dead and wounded that would be extracted for any advance in Normandy. The armoured element had taken significant casualties, and armoured units used to fighting in different terrain learnt quickly that the old tactics would not work in this close countryside. Time was not on the side of 50th Division or the Allies as a whole. Despite the dominance of the Allies in the air, German units did make it to the front and react more quickly than hoped. By 8 June, elements of Panzer Lehr were infiltrating towards Bayeux. This same day, carrier patrols from a number of the British infantry battalions explored a long way forward before hitting significant opposition. Charles Benford from 2nd Essex remembers:

> Captain Harrison – our officer – took us out on reconnaissance and he took us out miles. We drove into one village, which was full of Germans. We had to spin round and get out of it. If they had had an anti-tank gun covering the road we would have had it! Later I was detailed off to lead the Battalion down towards the Tilly – Hottot lateral crossroads in my carrier. Once I got there the officer in charge was to detail where we were to take up defensive positions. However as we got near to a village called Ellon the road bent round in an arc and as I came round the bend I suddenly spotted the offside of a tank further along the bend. I stopped my driver immediately and shouted to him to Back up! Back up! We got down (out of the carrier) and crossed the road. I took my PIAT Gunner with me.

As it happened, this was a British tank, but it was engaged in a duel with German tanks. Panzer Lehr had arrived, and Ellon is 4 miles short of Tilly-sur-Seulles, and a potential opportunity had been lost. Now, 50th Division had a problem, because not only were any reconnaissance patrols seriously opposed, but the enemy suddenly became much more aggressive in shelling and mortaring British positions and in counter-attacks. Perhaps the first indication of this was a move towards Tessel and then Bretteville and the main road to Villers-Bocage, effectively bypassing Tilly-sur-Seulles, by a column from 8th Armoured Brigade with 8DLI attached. On 9 June, this column comprised 8DLI, 24th Lancers, 147th Field Regiment, armoured cars and a troop of anti-tank guns from the Northumberland Hussars. They moved first towards Audrieu, but having established that this was heavily held, bypassed the village and advanced towards St Pierre, which is situated just across the east side of the River Seulles from Tilly. C and D Companies moved into the village at 1745 on 10 June, and after some savage fighting costing several casualties, they took the village and held it overnight. Vicious German counter-attacks took back part of the village next day, but 8DLI still held their ground for the next thirty-six hours. German tanks, though, were dealing effectively with the British armour support from 24th Lancers, knocking out three of them, and later the Sherwood Rangers Yeomanry, having relieved 24th Lancers, lost their CO, adjutant, intelligence and signals officers to a single shell burst while they were attending an Order (O) group. In the confined streets of St Pierre, it became impossible to make progress; nor could the crossing of the River Seulles be forced to give a back entrance to Tilly, and 8DLI and 8th Armoured Brigade were withdrawn from this dangerous salient, with the loss of thirty-six killed and 130 wounded by 8DLI. It was found that they had been facing a combination of soldiers from 12th SS Hitlerjugend Panzer Division and Panzer Lehr. The more powerful German tanks had sometimes been able to shoot up the area virtually at will. From a British point of view, all concerned had acted very courageously, and quite a number of gallantry medals were later awarded for this action.[23] The village was only taken some time later after a stiff fight by 10DLI from 49th (West Riding) Infantry Division.

While the thrust towards St Pierre was taking place, XXX Corps decided that 7th Armoured Division and 56th (Independent) Infantry Brigade would form a striking force south of Bayeux to force the issue to Tilly-sur-Seulles and take the next two east–west road lines to the south. First, the Balleroy to Tilly-sur-Seulles road would be secured, then the Caumont to Caen D9 between Hottot and Juvigny. This would allow 7th Armoured Division and other attached units to launch the always projected move on Villers-Bocage. Also, this move formed part of the larger Operation Perch (the code name for the line of the road from Juvigny to Hottot),[24] and if successful, would help isolate Caen and ultimately put 7th Armoured Division and 8th Armoured Brigade even further south of Villers-Bocage and on the high ground of Mount Pincon. On 9 June, orders were issued that from 0800 on 10 June, 56th Infantry Brigade came under the command of 7th Armoured Division.[25] The plan was to advance to the south on two axes. From the west, the River Aure would provide the westward boundary of the advance, and to the east, the D6 road would be the main axis of advance from Bayeux to Tilly-sur-Seulles and then Juvigny. This was to be an advance of 9 miles in, it was hoped, one fast move. The start line was the level crossing just south of Bayeux, beginning at 0830 on 10 June. The 56th Brigade was to provide protection for the armour, consolidate on the final objective and provide flank protection on the River Aure. The 2nd South Wales Borderers were to provide a guard of one anti-tank gun at each bridge over the River Aure as they were reached in the west. The 2nd Essex would move south along the line Ellon, Juaye-Mondaye to Lingevres area, with 22nd Armoured Brigade; while 2nd Glosters moved south down the main Tilly road with '86th Field Regiment, 505 Field Company RE, 198 Battery Anti-Tank M10s, AVRES etc. and 203 Field Ambulance'.[26]

Although the move down the Bayeux to Tilly road began promptly at 0830 on 10 June, 56th Brigade HQ reported by 1100 that both columns were held up only 1 mile from Bayeux.[27] In the bocage, the situation quickly became confused. There never seemed enough infantry to support the tanks. Strongly built farm houses, hamlets and small chateaus, and the monastery at Juaye-Mondaye, each, in turn, became a difficult fortress centre of resistance to overcome. All this took a great deal of time. However careful commanders were at the different levels of command – section, platoon, company and battalion – the result of each attack was often success, but at a cost at each obstruction of a few casualties dead or wounded. While the British were able to call down heavy concentrations of artillery fire or even naval gunfire to assist attacks, when infantry and tanks approached near to objectives bombardments had to cease and it was only then that the German positions revealed themselves in close defence.

Now began a slow protracted advance. It was decided that each major unit HQ, 22nd Armoured Brigade and 56th Infantry Brigade would take responsibility for an axis each of the advance, right and left, respectively. This put 2nd Essex from 56th Brigade under 22nd Armoured Brigade. By 11 June, the whole advance became bogged down. In the morning, 5RTR on the right flank lost three tanks and a number of men from its supporting Rifle Brigade platoon in orchards and woodland north-west of Lingevres in the area of Verrieres farm. The 2nd Essex were tasked to attack this woodland immediately. Lt Col. Higson seems to have been unhappy to proceed without a proper reconnaissance, but this proved fruitless, as the ground would not allow a proper inspection. The 2nd Essex attack went in with heavy artillery support, but as Lt Col. Higson had surmised, the woodland was heavily held by tanks and infantry. The 2nd

Essex took the forward edge of the wood, and despite heavy German resistance, made progress throughout the night. At one stage, Higson brought down an artillery barrage on his own position to disperse an enemy attack, and later two flame-throwing half-tracks were disposed of by the Battalion HQ 2 inch mortar. However, 2nd Essex had been badly mauled, losing sixteen men killed and over 150 wounded. When the second-in-command, Major Elliott, went to find HQ 22nd Armoured Brigade for tank support, he found that they had moved without telling 2nd Essex. Commandeering a jeep, he traversed the battlefield until he found 56th Brigade HQ, where Brigadier Pepper sorted out some support by M10s to cover the withdrawal of the battalion.[28] What had happened was that a gap in the German line had been detected even further west of these events, and it was decided to send 7th Armoured Division off through this gap to exploit past Villers-Bocage from a new direction. However, quite obviously, 2nd Essex should never have had to attack without continuing armoured support. Perhaps Brigadier Hinde forgot he had a battalion under command, or with the glittering prize in view, someone decided that 2nd Essex could look after themselves. In any event, when faced with a problem Brigadier Pepper seemed up to finding a solution: 2nd Essex was withdrawn to rejoin with 56th Brigade, although Lt Col. Higson seems to have been moved as some sort of scapegoat, with Elliott taking over command of the battalion. In his memoir of leading the battalion, Elliott states that no blame could be attached to Lt Col. Higson for what happened over 11/12 June.

On the left flank, 2nd Glosters were in the lead, with 4th City of London Yeomanry providing armour support. The CLY and Glosters also continually ran into difficulties, and although 2nd Glosters got into Tilly itself, as far as the crossroads (8DLI were less than a mile away across the river), they were ejected by strong German counter-attacks and artillery and mortar bombardments. Forward battalions of 56th Brigade were now withdrawn to the village of Buceels and La Pont de la Guillette. There now began a very protracted period of desperate fighting, in weather varying between good and poor in this area. All three battalions suffered in what became warfare of attrition reminiscent of the First World War. Some battalions from 131st Queens Brigade were also involved, but could make little difference. It was not until the morning of 19 June that 2nd Essex finally entered the empty town of Tilly-sur-Seulles. Panzer Lehr had withdrawn, but left the shattered town full of mines and booby traps. So dangerous was it that despite being badly wounded, and according to the 2nd Essex War Diary 'half dead', Lt Jack Cooper was awarded the MC for refusing all first aid until he had shepherded every man from his platoon safely through.[29] It had taken eleven days to force the issue, starting just south of Bayeux. From the night of 12 June, 56th Brigade had reverted to being under command of 50th Division, and their actions and those of 22nd Armoured Brigade, including 2nd Essex, had been against Panzer Lehr.

Also on 12 June, 6th Green Howards were moving forward with a view to occupying the village of Cristot and the dominating hill Point 102, and thus protecting the flank of 8DLI and 8th Armoured Brigade in St Pierre. During an earlier reconnaissance, the only opposition seemed to be from a few snipers. By 1600, 6th Green Howards were approaching the area, but came under heavy fire from surrounding orchards and a white farmhouse. The advance came to a halt. It was almost inevitably D Company that was fed into the fray, and once again it was the bravery of Stanley Hollis in rushing a German MG position and killing the crew that initially opened the way. There remained two problems for Lt Col. Hastings to puzzle over. First was the density of the trees and undergrowth, and second was the realization that the area was alive with the enemy, and that this enemy were made of much sterner stuff than they had so far encountered since D-Day. Then he heard the sound of an attack to his rear. A German counter-attack was in danger of cutting his force off. With little support from the armour, which could not adequately work in the restricted undergrowth, he was given permission to withdraw.

Kenneth Taylor was involved in this action, and his personal diary records:

> Lovely day. Decided at midday to put in attack on Cristot. Rather hurriedly arranged. Moved forward about 2 miles without opposition. Leading Coys then pinned down by Spandau. Reserve Coys likewise unable to advance. Went forward to try and get communications working. Very unpleasant. Heavy mortaring, shelling, and Spandau fire. Went in a Jeep to look for some casualties. Found none but got lost and was pinned by Spandau behind low bank. Spent about 20 minutes looking in hedges and buildings and expected to stumble on to a nest of Jerries at any moment. These Germans do not seem to take much notice of Red Cross and they Spandau'ed my Jeep the whole way back, but fortunately we moved too quickly to be hit. All the Companies badly hit and many said it was the bloodiest battle they ever remembered. I soon got used to Spandau bullets flying overhead. Withdrew in good order to the accompaniment of renewed enemy machine gunning. 4 officers killed, 2 wounded, and about 60 men lost. Reorganised at last light but could not get any food up. Counter-attack expected. Tried to sleep in a ditch but too cold. I don't think any action will upset me after this one.[30]

The day's action had cost 250 casualties for no gain. The enemy had been 12th SS Hitlerjugend Panzer Division.[31] Cristot was finally taken on 17 June by 49th (WR) Infantry Division.

Between Cristot and St Pierre, 1st Dorsets had been fed into the line, and took the intervening village of Audrieu after stiff fighting to the north to cross the railway line. Fighting through the night and the following day, they eventually got control of the Audrieu area, and were pushed on to provide protection for the armour and artillery around Point 103 above St Pierre. In doing so, they came across a number of the 156 Canadian soldiers murdered by 12th SS Panzer Division. 'It was men of this Division who had been foully murdered after being taken prisoner by 12th SS Panzer Division – we saw them with our own eyes, laid out in rows behind the Chateau Pavie.'[32] The 6th Green Howards were also aware of what was going on:

> Saw 3 French girls who gave information of 25 Canadian prisoners being shot at Audrieu. They are SS troops in front of us and are quite fanatical and very young. The prisoners are very haughty, although some of them had been told that we would shoot them when they were taken prisoner.[33]

On 10 June, 1st Dorset withstood a number of attacks by 12th SS Panzer Division, often from the direction of Cristot. Point 103 became known to the Dorsets as 'Tiger Hill' through the mistaken identity of Panzer V (Panthers) for Panzer VI (Tigers). On

12 June, 1st Dorsets were relieved by 5th East Yorks of 69th Brigade. They now moved west to rejoin their own brigade on the west flank of the British Amy.

On the right flank, the pressure was kept up on Panzer Lehr by 151st Infantry Brigade. The 8DLI were not to be involved, as they were being rested and reinforced after the battle at St Pierre, and the addition of eleven officers and 190 ORs was required to bring them back up to strength. For this operation, 2nd Glosters came under command of 151st Brigade and operated on the 151st Brigade left flank. The advance was not far from the area attacked on 11 June by 2nd Essex, and was to have naval artillery and air support as well as armour and RA support. On 13 June, 6DLI advanced with two companies 'up' and two in reserve from Conde, hoping to reach the Juvigny to Hottot lateral road. Just north of Verrieres, they were heavily engaged by MG fire from at least twelve weapons at only 150 yards' range from the edge of the woods. The advance inevitably halted. Artillery pounded the edge of the wood, German fire continued and the two reserve companies were committed. It took five hours to clear the wood; German positions were well dug in and prepared. A large quantity of equipment, including two half-tracks and 75 mm guns, was captured. B and D Companies continued to advance and clear Verrieres farm and hamlet, and got within 200 yards of the road before being halted by further heavy resistance. They had suffered over 100 casualties. The shame of this is that if the ground 2nd Essex had gained on 11/12 June had been reinforced on 12 June, this attack would have been easier, if not unnecessary, as 2nd Essex's final positions were very near the main lateral road.

On the right flank of the attack, 9DLI moved to directly attack Lingevres from the north with support from 4/7 Dragoon Guards, and met with very strong resistance from the beginning. The wood to their front was strafed by Hawker Typhoon aircraft using bombs and rockets, and received a 25 lb artillery bombardment. The advance of 9DLI started through fields of high-standing corn. But virtually as soon as the attack proper started, the usual fire was received from German positions. Hand-to-hand fighting sometimes took place within the wood, and the enemy were clearly in no mood to let it be taken easily. However, despite very high casualties and strong resistance by the Panzer Lehr defenders, Lingevres was eventually taken, and several Panzer Vs were put out of action by 4/7 Dragoon Guards. When a strong counter-attack was launched in the evening, the Typhoons helped to break it up. Eventually, contact was made with 6DLI near Verrieres and 2nd Glosters on the left around the crucifix east of Lingevres on the main road. Later in the night they relieved 9DLI, who went back and relieved 6DLI. Thirty-three of 9DLI had been killed, including 28-year-old Lt Col. Humphrey Woods, and over 190 wounded. One almost remarkable aspect of the battle was that mainly through the efforts of 4/7 Dragoon Guards, six Mark V tanks were destroyed for the loss of one Sherman in and around Lingevres. Overall, though, 4/7 Dragoon Guards had lost five tanks in the two battles, with five killed, eight wounded and four missing. The fields of corn preceding the woodlands and orchards had been mown flat by German MG 42 fire, some of which, at least, was fired by men able to keep down in their firing pits because of a cunning arrangement attached to the MG trigger. These pits were only vulnerable to direct or very close hits from artillery or tanks.[34]

Charles Eagles, now already promoted to Sergeant Eagles since D-Day, was in the advance of 9DLI with Corporal Woods, and they were both acting as bodyguards and runners to Lt Col. Wood: 'As we moved forward across this large triangular shaped field we had advanced about three-quarters of the way across it when the Germans opened up and the fire was so intense it cut the wheat.' One soldier passing an order to Eagles fell down wounded. Eagles picked him up and got him back to a first aid post. He returned into a situation he describes as 'chaotic'.

> When we got to the side of the wood about thirty of us burst through some wire that had been cut. Colonel Woods had just said to me 'get that tank with a sticky bomb'. Then there was an explosion and Colonel Wood was killed. *Eagles crawled across to his Colonel, whose last words to Eagles were* 'surely they haven't hit me?' A small number of us gathered and I said we must move on. We saw some of our lads lying in the grass but they were all dead. Then I saw a pair of large boots and above me a German officer cleared his throat and told us in excellent English 'not to do anything stupid'. We were surrounded and then marched half a mile down the road into an area where there were a number of German slit trenches. Three guards were left watching us and the Germans enjoyed sharing our cigarettes and they did give us food and in our ways we tried to communicate with each other.

About two hours later, the German officer came back and told Eagles that they would have to stay there as it was not safe or easy to get them back to the main German lines. The next morning, the officer informed Eagles that they were cut off, and later in the day, that it would be a good idea if Eagles helped him surrender his men to the British. Obviously this would be a tricky thing to achieve without either side getting the wrong idea. In the back of Eagles' mind was that they might be shot in the back by the Germans. They walked out, and the officer passed Eagles his pistol. Eventually they made contact with another unit, the situation was resolved and the Germans surrendered to British soldiers led back by Eagles. The Germans had dumped their weapons and were lined up waiting. 'We had something to eat with the British unit.' When they returned to their battalion it had to be reformed.[35]

Sergeant Frank Clarke, B Company 2nd Glosters, who had seen equally rapid promotion since D-Day, was with 2nd Glosters supporting the left flank of the DLI attacks, forming blocking positions south-west and south-east of the village. B Company, led by Major Basil Stephens, were approaching on their bicycles along a road with two Sherman tanks for support. The company laid down their bicycles before a slight rise in the ground. Moving across country now, the two Sherman tanks going through a hedgerow were hit by an anti-tank gun. Frank Clarke had the signallers' radio and asked for more support. More tanks appeared to help, together with an artillery barrage. In addition, three Typhoons flew in and rocketed two German tanks, to the delight of the Glosters. B Company HQ now came up, and dug in and firm-based in this area. Suddenly, Frank Clarke thought he noticed movement in a gateway in the hedge. Observed closely, a second German dived across the gap. Alerting Major Stephens, Frank's platoon was ordered to investigate. As they carefully approached the hedge, two German soldiers with two Durham Light Infantrymen appeared and offered surrender. Altogether, over forty other Germans appeared from the hedge to give themselves up. Major Stephens' surprised remark was: 'Where did you get them from!' The 2nd Glosters War Diary reports that one platoon of 352 [this probably should have read 902] Panzer Grenadier Regiment from Panzer Lehr Division surrendered to B Company from their half-tracked vehicles.[36] Quite obviously, this is the same event as Eagles refers to above.

Over 17 to 18 June, 6DLI resumed an attack towards Tilly from the area of Verrieres, and after two days' hard fighting, dominated the ground west of the town and doubtless aided 2nd Essex in its efforts to finally take this totally devastated village. For British soldiers who fought in the battles to capture Tilly-sur-Seulles, those nine days of horror remain etched in their memory. Between 10 and 19 June 1944, 151st DLI Brigade had suffered over 190 men killed.

It will be realized that, with the withdrawal from the Verrieres area of 2nd Essex, the employment of 56th Brigade towards Tilly-sur-Seulles and the movement of 22nd Armoured Brigade with 7th Armoured Division towards Villers-Bocage, the area to the west could not be left open, and into this gap was inserted 231st Brigade. While 151st Brigade had been involved around Lingevres, 1st Dorsets, 2nd Devons and 1st Hampshires, along with artillery support and 141st RAC (Crocodile flame tanks), had reached the road lateral to and beyond the village of La Senaudiere. A Mark V (Panther) and a SP gun were destroyed in the village. A second Mark V was found later, disabled by damage caused in the same action. On 15 June, Panzer Lehr withdrew from this area, and now 231st Brigade were able to take up more comfortable positions south of the road, where 69th Brigade would soon be pushed through them in the advance. The lateral of the D13 road was now held by 50th Division from Tilly-sur-Seulles west to past the River Aure and La Belle Epine.[37]

For the German Army, too, this was a terribly costly battle, and one which broke the back of its most powerful Panzer division committed so far to Normandy. Fritz Bayerlein, its commander, wrote:

> The British counter-attacked next day (10th June). They massed an unbelievable concentration of heavy artillery and I was glad when we finally were out of it. We pulled out of Tilly on 15th June and the British filled the gap. My chance to drive to the sea was lost. We pulled back south of Aunay to regroup. We had lost about 100 tanks to the British. Half my striking force was gone.[38]

To close this chapter, we return to the role taken by 7th Armoured Division from 12 June in the well known and ultimately unfortunate exploit, towards Villers-Bocage. By 11 June, it was clear that no quick advance could be made towards Villers-Bocage and beyond using the Bayeux to Tilly-sur-Seulles axis. The actions around St Pierre and Cristot showed that a short left flanking move avoiding Tilly would not work; nor would a slightly longer left flanking hook towards Fontenay-le-Pesnil. Also, German resistance stopped the attempt to outflank Tilly to the west in the countryside between Tilly and the River Aure. Further afield towards Caen, Canadian and British troops were making little progress in taking the city.

Around 10 June, intelligence came up with a possible solution further west, as US forces had forced the collapse of 352nd Infantry Division, and their withdrawal towards St Lo created a 7-mile gap between 352nd Division and Panzer Lehr. Bucknall and

Erskine (commanders of XXX Corps and 7th Armoured Division, respectively) were ordered by Dempsey to break off the 7th Armoured Division attacks towards Tilly, and from midday on 12 June, 22nd Armoured Brigade, commanded by Brigadier 'Looney' Hinde, advanced from Trungy, west of the River Aure, towards Villers-Bocage. A 12 mile near-unopposed advance was made before German resistance north of Livry called for a night-time halt. On the following day, 4CLY with a company of 1st Rifle Brigade moved towards Villers-Bocage, with the rest of the brigade group following up and forming blocking units either side of the advance and occupying Villers-Bocage, while 1 RTR and two battalions of infantry, 5th and 6th Queens, held the firm base at Livry. Some experienced officers, including Lt Col. Lord Cranley, and men were aware that they were being pushed on too fast, yet a quick occupation of the high ground east of Villers-Bocage seemed essential.

By 0830 on 13 June, Villers-Bocage had been reached, and a force from 4CLY headed through the town for Point 213 to establish observation and a defensive perimeter. At this point, there were a few cautionary notes. German forces had been engaged on either flank of the advance north of Livry by 8th Hussars, and the arrival of the brigade in the town had been noted by the Germans, as an armoured car, which had clearly observed the British, opened fire on the road and then escaped. Intelligence of the closeness of German armour was interpreted as involving SP guns and not likely to pose an immediate threat. British forces in the town and along the route to Point 213 had restricted vision on either side of the road. However, in passing through Villers-Bocage, the British had control of the road junction leading north to Juvigny and Tilly-sur-Seulles, and outflanked Panzer Lehr, leaving Panzer Lehr HQ, 902nd Panzer Grenadier Regiment, Panzer Lehr Recce Battalion and Engineer Battalion, plus a battalion from 6th Panzer Regiment, several miles to their north.

The British were unaware that a group of three heavy Mark VI (Tiger) tanks was nearby, and had spent the night only 200 metres south of point 213. Their commander, Wittman, assumed he had been spotted, and set off on an attack into Villers-Bocage that had become famous. The heavily armoured Mark VI was not easily stopped, and it outgunned anything the British had except perhaps a Sherman Firefly or M10; even then, the German tank was much better armoured. Causing massive destruction, Wittman drove into and back out of Villers-Bocage, becoming disabled by a British anti-tank gun probably around the Tilly-sur-Seulles junction. In 15 minutes, Wittman had destroyed seven tanks, including one 'Firefly', three light tanks (Stuarts), a Sherman OP tank (no main gun), nine half-tracks (troops like the Rifle Brigade kept up with the tanks in half-tracks), four carriers and two anti-tank guns. The other German tanks had destroyed at least three further tanks around Point 213, and crews that had previously dismounted could not regain their tanks. Wittman and his crew escaped on foot. Clearly, some German soldiers had got into, or were already in, Villers-Bocage, as sniping in the town began as Wittman advanced.

Next to arrive at Point 213 were Panzer Grenadiers, and they set about rounding up and capturing any tank men from fields and ditches. By 1030, it was obvious that Point 213 could not be held, and Brigadier Hinde ordered Villers-Bocage to be held at all costs. Panzer Lehr, fully alerted now and afraid of an attack into their rear, sealed off Villers-Bocage from the north using around fifteen Panzer IVs under the command of

Helmut Ritgen, moving down the road from Juvigny and spreading out to cover the road junctions. Bayerlein was with the lead elements, issuing instructions.

A battle developed between the British in the town and German units attacking it from the north and east. As the situation became increasingly untenable in the town, 22nd Armoured Brigade was withdrawn to a position, called the 'Island Position' by the Brigade War Diary, east of Amaye-sur-Seulles. Here they were continually hard pressed, and British and US artillery and Typhoons from the RAF greatly helped the position avoid being over-run. It also became clear that another German force from 2nd Panzer Division was being manoeuvred towards them. The position was carefully evacuated over the night of 14/15 June, facilitated by the RAF dropping over 1,700 tonnes of bombs in the Evrecy and Villers-Bocage area. Both 22nd Armoured Brigade and German forces had received a severe mauling. But perhaps the main point is that the British were back where they started, although the German units had also suffered high casualties they could ill afford. The Germans made a propaganda news film covering the events. Morale was not helped in the armoured regiments, and the whole episode underlined the overall weakness of the British armour when pitched against that of the Germans.[39]

Conclusion

The early chapters in this book have investigated the wider picture concerning events from 1940 onwards. These show that despite defeat in France, the British and Canadians made increasingly bold raids on the French coast to cause problems for the German occupation, give hope to the French people and eventually carry out more specific and important raids, such as capturing radar devices and putting important dry docks out of action, and culminating in an attempted landing in force to try out new techniques and weapons. In the event, this last went terribly wrong. The smaller raids carried out on the coast of France after Dieppe often had the specific purpose of reconnaissance to find out about the beach defences of the Atlantic Wall. Alongside these raids, planning towards putting an Allied army back into Europe continued, and was strengthened when the United States entered the war, allowing Allied planning and actions initially to focus on the Mediterranean.

This explanation is important in showing how ideas coalesced towards choosing Normandy as the centre of invasion plans. At the same time, some idea of what was faced by German forces preparing for inevitable invasion, and in particular how this was organized on Gold Beach, revolves around the ability of Allied airpower not only to strike at many different targets, destroying bridges, roads and railways and gradually cutting the area off, but also to strike at battery positions, radar posts and the Luftwaffe. From early in 1944, at the insistence of Eisenhower and Montgomery, the invasion plans were enlarged and two 'new' beachheads and divisions were added, the British one becoming Gold Beach. But these decisions were only taken in February 1944, and the detailed planning and preparations became rushed, with training and accumulation of men and materiel having to play catch-up in regard to the other divisions already training with clearer objectives. Apart from lack of time, the other important decision, as far as Gold Beach is concerned, was the use of 50th Division for the assault, and the good points and problems associated with choosing this division.

The 'story' of D-Day and the first few weeks of the Normandy Campaign from a British perspective are more often focused on events on the left flank of the landings from air and sea in the Sword Beach area. Many people will know stories about the airborne landings, and especially the taking of Pegasus Bridge by a small glider-borne *coup de main force* under Major Howard, and the attack on the Merville battery by only 150 men of 9th Parachute Battalion. Well-known stories from the later seaborne landings on Sword Beach include that of Piper Millin playing the SS Brigade[1] under Lord Lovat ashore with his bagpipes, and the SS Brigade advance to relieve the Ox and Bucks at Pegasus Bridge. Other well-known stories might include the Commando Kieffer attack on the Ouistreham Casino or the taking of *Le Bunker* in Ouistreham by a brave engineer officer 'blowing the door down'.[2] Major Bob Orrell, with only two men to help him, blew off the bunker door and captured fifty-five Germans. For the two previous days, *Le Bunker* had been directing fire on Sword Beach via a buried telephone cable.

As already mentioned in the Introduction, the US air and sea landings on the western part of the invasion area also seem to dominate 'the story' of D-Day, and perhaps this is not surprising, considering the number of casualties taken by the 82nd and 101st Airborne Divisions and the casualties on Omaha Beach. Much of this is still informed in memory by the 1960s book and film *The Longest Day*.[3] But in the telling of these events, it is important to remember that British and Canadian forces landed in larger numbers on D-Day than US forces, and it was some time before this balance was reversed in Normandy. Somehow, books and film such as *The Longest Day* have forgotten or glossed over the achievement of 50th Division and its attached units. Readers of this book on Gold Beach will probably not come away with the idea that 'British troops assaulting Gold Beach in the centre of the invasion front had little difficulty piercing defences and fighting their way inland.'[4] Nor will they recognize that 'many of the Germans were in the resort houses that dotted the coast .... Unlike the concrete emplacements, the houses could be set on fire by naval shells and air dropped bombs.'[5] This is a good example of why fieldwork is a very important part of a historian's work, because in 1944 there were hardly any buildings between La Riviere and Le Hamel other than concrete emplacements, anti-tank walls and other wired-in positions, and the whole area was backed by Le Marais. La Riviere and Le Hamel have only grown in size along the coast since the end of the war. Many of the buildings in these villages had been improved for defence by addition of concrete and sandbags. As we know, the widely reported pre-assault bombing on Gold Beach had missed the targets in the main by some way.

In the paragraph above, there is no intention of diminishing the achievements and sacrifice of any unit mentioned. However, it was some years ago, while investigating 56th (Independent) Infantry Brigade, that it became at least a curiosity that the efforts of 50th Infantry Division and its attached forces, and the naval and air forces involved on D-Day and in Normandy, had not been properly appreciated in the histories written since the end of the Second World War. The official history *Victory in the West, Volume 1* notes that 'apart from the hold-up at Le Hamel, the leading brigades of 50th Division were making good progress.'[6] As readers will appreciate, these notes do not seem to be informed by what actually happened, although the chapters in *Victory in the West* give a fair overall reporting of events. The US version *Cross Channel Attack* notes 50th Division as 'advancing against very slight opposition.'[7]

Yet, the chapters in this book dealing with the landing and the first ten days of exploitation of the beachhead point out very clearly the high cost in casualties of men, armour and materiel taken by all the front-line units that landed on Gold Beach. In fact, 50th Division and its supporting units suffered over 400 men killed and up to a further thousand wounded or injured on D-Day, and in the days that followed, casualties mounted rapidly. Gold Beach has particular significance to the D-Day landings, especially after the ground forces from Sword and Juno failed to take the important city and route centre of Caen in the first few days of the invasion, on the one hand, and the high US casualties and slow penetration from Omaha Beach and the high casualties suffered by US airborne troops and the difficulty of moving against Cherbourg from Utah Beach, on the other. But from Gold Beach a powerful force was at least in position by the end of 7 June, joining hands with Canadian forces on the left, and by 8 June with US forces from Omaha Beach on the right.

However, this advance fairly quickly stalled, and it is relevant to examine why. Two major things slowed the landings and caused problems. The first was the weather. Apart from the effects of a rough crossing on all concerned, the sea state meant that some units had to turn back or were sunk. The correct decision was taken, and the initial armour support from the DD tanks was landed 'dry', but this meant that the armour arrived after and not slightly before the assault waves of infantry, meaning there was no immediate fire support on the beaches for the vulnerable infantry, LCOCU or engineers. At both flanks of the landing, La Riviere and Le Hamel, stronger opposition than expected was encountered. Admittedly, the opposition at La Riviere was reduced much more quickly than that at Le Hamel, but still with high cost in men, especially to the 5th East Yorks. Both topography and the calibre of the defending troops have much to do with this. As early as Day Two, of the assaulting battalions, 5th East Yorks on the left and 1st Hampshires on the right began to take heavy casualties. The stiffer opposition meant that all armoured units became bogged down supporting the infantry fighting along the coastal defences, and could not be formed as a unit to thrust inland. The weather and opposition also meant that a large number of the craft involved were either badly damaged or broached to in the surf. Obstacle clearance was also more difficult: there were many more obstacles than expected, and the tide came in much more quickly with the following wind, so that the LCOCU and engineers were forced to stop their work early and wait for the tide to recede. This all meant that 151st Brigade and 56th Infantry Brigade had to be landed later than planned, pushing back the timetable of advance, and in the case of 56th Brigade, the majority of its men had to be landed on the wrong beach, further away from their assembly point. Before midday, the beach area had also become quite narrow and heavily congested with men and vehicles.

The naval report summary on the Gold Beach landing concludes that obstacles were considerably thicker and heavier than expected. The LCOCU and engineers had practised on mock obstacles back in the United Kingdom constructed on information from some of the *Hardtack* raids. But they found some obstacles to be more ruggedly built than expected and difficult to clear. Considerable damage to landing craft was caused by mines. The difference in the much higher numbers of beach obstacles, as shown by air reconnaissance, between April and the end of May is marked. Second, the tide was higher than expected, and there was a reluctance to use the stern kedge anchors by landing craft commanders to pull off of the beaches after unloading, 'and this in the surf caused many craft to broach, fill with water and so encumber the beaches'.[8] The Admiralty report also states that 'damage to LCT and smaller craft, aggravated by the weather conditions, was considerably higher'[9] than expected. On Gold Beach, the casualties to landing craft, lost or disabled, were reckoned as 34 LCT, 52 LCA and 3 LCP (L). Fifty per cent were reckoned to be caused by mines. This is obviously a considerable number of craft, and affected the rest of the day's operation.[10]

Le Hamel 'proved a very tough nut to crack and held out until 16.00hrs at least'. The report enumerates the difficulties faced on the right flank of the landing: it cost the 1st Battalion Hampshire Regiment over 200 casualties. The 75 tonnes of bombs planned to be dropped on the town were dropped 3,000 yards to the south on fields due to the low cloud cover. The self-propelled artillery of 147th Field Regiment that was to fire on Le Hamel during the run-in could not do so. Their navigational ML and control LCT fell astern due to the weather. They concentrated their fire with that of the regiment on their left, and Le Hamel was not fired upon. Much later, three destroyers engaged Le Hamel, but the low trajectory of their guns had little effect on the concrete bunkers and slit trenches. No calls for RN support came from the Hampshires ashore, due to the CO and second-in-command becoming early casualties. In the end, a concentrated bombardment of the position took place by LCG, LCF and destroyers, as well as the use of Petard-firing AVREs from land to demolish German positions.[11]

It should not be surprising that 56th Brigade, having to traverse a battlefield and assemble near Buhot, should be held up; especially when it is remembered that their Bren gun carrier support companies and mortar, anti-tank, pioneer and signals section vehicles were landed on different beaches from their infantry and only joined up at Buhot. These vehicles were crucial to their advance on Bayeux. Also, they had to link with their tank support from the SRY, who themselves were heavily engaged and had lost tanks in the landing. It is not surprising, then, that the taking of Bayeux was put off until the following day, Brigadier Pepper having no clear idea of any German forces in Bayeux and not being willing to commit to an all-arms battle at night in the congested streets of Bayeux with a brigade that had not yet proved itself in battle. In any case, it was after midnight before all his battalions were established in firm bases – the villages dominating the entrance and exit routes on the north side of Bayeux: Vaux-sur-Aure, Magny and St Sulpice. Similarly, on the left flank, although the advance by most of 69th Brigade and 151st Brigade had gone well, 151st Brigade had lost their brigadier, and 69th Brigade had clearly bumped into resolute opposition, with 4/7 Dragoon Guards losing four tanks and the brigade halting for the night about a mile and a half short of their objective.

We should also be mindful and sceptical of lines drawn on maps in history books. By the close of D-Day, south of Gold Beach, twelve battalions of infantry only held a loose line of outposts, usually centred on a small village. Two of those battalions had taken very high casualties, as had the armour. Only the follow-up brigades were relatively unscathed as yet. Once in their overnight positions, they had German units in unknown number around and behind them, and had been told to expect an armoured counter-attack. As they moved forward the following day to complete their D-Day tasks, the armchair historian should not be surprised after the events of the previous twenty-four hours if that advance was slow and careful. It is what did and did not happen in the following twenty-four hours which set the seal on 50th Division operations and events on the right flank of the British landings for the rest of the campaign in Normandy.

After landing, and considering Allied air dominance, two of the most potent and powerful Panzer divisions available in Normandy, Panzer Lehr and 12th SS Hitlerjugend Panzer Division, were sent quickly enough to the area to defend against the incursion by 50th Division and drive it back to the sea. One of these Divisions – 12th SS Hitlerjugend Panzer Division – was also to be drawn into fighting the Canadians from Juno Beach. This German division proved itself to be particularly imbued with Nazi ideology and capable of committing what appears to be premeditated acts of murder, outside the 'rules' of war as applied at the time. As these two Panzer divisions arrived, the advance of 50th Division became much harder, and casualties within its ranks mounted alarmingly.

There is no doubt that front-line units suffered very high casualty numbers during the Normandy Campaign. French[12] gives a figure of 75 per cent casualties within the seven British infantry divisions and 37 per cent within the three armoured divisions between 6 June and the end of August 1944, which is generally accepted as the end of the battle for Normandy. On average, during this period of time, each infantry division suffered 341 officers and 5,115 infantrymen killed, wounded and missing out of 7,200 men in the nine rifle battalions in each division. French also compares this with the losses of men in the British Army during the Third Battle of Ypres (Passchendaele) July–November 1917 as averaging 2,324 per day, while between 6 June and 28 August in Normandy 1944, the British Army lost more men per day, at an average at 2,354. This surely gives the lie to the slur about the fighting efficiency, especially in attack, of the British Army one reads in a number of books on Normandy. Montgomery had already expressed manpower worries several months prior to the invasion. In a letter dated 19 March 1944 to Lt General Sir Ronald Weeks, the Deputy CIGS, Montgomery states that he is worried about the situation regarding reinforcements, and then goes into detail, appreciating that manpower in the infantry is a critical factor, and worries about very high casualty figures.[13] After 8 June, the weekly casualty returns for the infantry battalions of 50th Division show very high requirements for replacements, usually up to 100 men (a whole company of infantry) and sometimes as high as 200.

These are thought-provoking statistics. It will be realized that if an infantry battalion suffers 100–200 casualties in a major action, that is a substantial number of men from within its four fighting companies and its support company of perhaps a total of 600 men. Second, often those numbers could not be made good for some time, and units remained in combat for several days, or even longer periods, producing a steady drip of casualties. Similarly, if a tank regiment lost several tanks and men in a day, that was also a significant casualty toll.

Very soon after D-Day, infantry units had to operate companies sometimes with as few as sixty to eighty men in them rather than the establishment of 120. Other tactics by the CO of an infantry battalion included reducing the number of companies to three rather than four. In a casualty situation reminiscent of the First World War, the same expedients were being applied to keep units up and running as became necessary in that earlier war. Further, infantry units and some armoured units had an esprit de corps, often based on the county locality they were recruited from. Reinforcement holding units initially were made up of men from particular areas, trained and inducted into one infantry regiment from a particular county. But even before the Normandy Campaign, casualties were so high that it became impractical to match men to their regiments as reinforcements. Further, men who were more lightly wounded or had time away from the front line through combat stress and recovered in the rear areas of Normandy often found themselves back in action with a different battalion.

This in turn led to many men becoming adamant that they would only rejoin 'their' unit, going AWOL from hospitalization and scrounging lifts back to their particular battalion, something not approved of by the general staff, but an eminently sensible move by men wishing to serve with their mates. This author has heard several accounts of this happening, and even wounded men somehow working the system all the way from hospitalization in the United Kingdom back to their unit at the front in Normandy. In their own amazing way, these stories underline the ingenuity of the British soldier.

Across British and US units, the casualty toll was very high for the nearly three months of combat: 21st Army Group suffered 16,138 killed, 58,594 wounded and 9,093 missing. This totalled 83,825 casualties. American units suffered more: 20,838 killed, 94,881 wounded and 10,128 missing, for a total of 125,847 casualties,[14] a reflection of the greater commitment of men to the ground battle by the United States. These figures do not, of course, reflect the losses of the Allied air forces or navies, including the Merchant Navy. Although the majority of U-boats were kept away from the English Channel, the Kriegsmarine and Luftwaffe were successful in laying mines, and there were a number of successful E-boat and midget submarine attacks.

South of Gold Beach, the cost in casualties is witnessed by the beautifully tended series of Commonwealth War Grave Commission cemeteries at Bazenville/Ryes (652 burials), Bayeux (3,843 burials and 1,808 names on the Memorial to the Missing), Jerusalem (47 burials), Tilly-sur-Seulles (990 burials) and Hottot-les-Bagues (1,005 burials). The journey to visit them all covers barely fifteen miles, and one is reminded forcibly of the similarity to the First World War cemeteries in Northern France and Belgium. Further afield, nearly fifteen miles south of Villers-Bocage, St Charles de Percy CWGC holds 809 burials and is the southernmost of the Normandy cemeteries. The point is that even St Charles de Percy CWGC holds a number of men from 50th Division and 56th Infantry Brigade from battles in July 1944, and these men were killed fighting north, not south, of Villers-Bocage. Up to the end of July, 50th Division with 56th Brigade still attached were fighting together, and the pre-planning for a swift breakout after D-Day had foundered by 8 June on the way to Tilly-sur-Seulles, nowhere near the projected objectives. Once breaking through the coastal crust and losing momentum, the enemy that 50th Division pulled onto itself was no longer the weak coastal 716th Division, but several of Germany's best trained and armed: Panzer Lehr, 12th SS Hitlerjugend Panzer Division and later, 2nd Panzer Division.

Perhaps the smallest of these cemeteries, which was started on 10 June 1944, stands as a good representative example of the range of casualties suffered by the British Army as it fought south of Gold Beach. Jerusalem is a small hamlet between Bayeux and Tilly-sur-Seulles. Within its CWG Cemetery are forty-eight burials, including a baronet, two army chaplains side by side, a sixteen-year-old boy with his Durham Light Infantry comrades, an unknown British soldier and a Czechoslovakian soldier dying in October 1944, presumably accidentally. Most ranks from major down are represented, as are infantrymen, Royal Armoured Corps, Royal Engineers, Military Police, Royal Army Chaplains Department, Royal Artillery, Royal Army Service Corps,

Royal Electrical and Mechanical Engineers, and Royal Corps of Signals. The oldest was aged thirty-nine and the youngest just sixteen, both serving with the Durham Light Infantry. Virtually all were killed in this area in June and July 1944.[15] When burials took place at the time of death, the convention was to provide a marker with name, rank and number inscribed with indelible pencil/ink. One of the identity tags was taken, the other left on the body. A description and map reference was recorded, and if possible a photograph of the site, although this last was unlikely, bearing in mind that cameras were not allowed. For set-piece battles, brigades might actually be allocated a burial area in the prior planning. After the war had ended, 48 War Graves Registration Unit, based in Bayeux, would find and mark out concentration cemeteries, and then gather in the dead from their original resting place to the new cemetery. When all was complete, the cemetery was handed over to the then Imperial (1960 Commonwealth) War Graves Commission.[16]

Although the Allies had domination of the air and sea, men still had to push forward and win the ground, and this predominately meant the infantry. The German Army had already shown in the First World War that it was excellent in defence, and the same was true now. As 50th Division and 7th Armoured Division pushed further south from Gold Beach, they ran increasingly into denser Bocage country. Each hedge line was better than a First World War trench for its defenders, with narrow lanes overhung with trees and no view of the ground for planning. Before 2nd Essex went into battle on 11 June, its CO insisted on driving around the area to get a good view of the intended area of attack. The lie of the land thwarted this ambition, as 'the tops of all woods and orchards look alike in this country at a distance of 2,000 yards and in this particular case the line of orchards to our south were on a slight reverse slope'.[17]

From the perspective of an ordinary infantryman in one of the experienced DLI battalions:

> When the DLI was attacked in the Desert they could see the dust rising, in Normandy you didn't see that. Fighting down country lanes was not the same. It was frightening. Every hundred yards was a kink in the road. Snipers, mines and booby traps were three things that I hated.[18]

The Germans fell back into this countryside, which they could mine at will and knew to an inch or centimetre the range of buildings, crossroads, hedge junctions and other salient points. In between, the rugged Norman buildings stood as strongpoints, only battered down by naval bombardment, Typhoon rockets and bombs, or incessant artillery bombardment. Before larger attacks, bulldozers were brought up to cut holes through hedges to allow tanks and infantry through them. German snipers, or at least well-trained riflemen, seemed everywhere, and the rasp of machine-gun fire – the dreaded 'Spandau' – added to the doubts and worries. In the memory of the men of Normandy, leaves continually shower off trees as MGs firing 1,000 rounds a minute let rip, or orchards were smashed in minutes to matchwood by mortar fire. Casualties from German mortar fire in Normandy were reckoned to be as high as 70 per cent, according to No. 2 Operational Research Section, 21st Army Group.[19] For the armour, pushing blindly down narrow lanes with high hedges on either side, they might be faced with enemy swarming all over their tank or a blast from a hidden anti-tank gun,

Photo 12 The bocage. Despite the passing of seventy years and many changes made to the landscape typical Bocage scenery can still easily be found south of Bayeux. Imagine the trepidation felt in June 1944 moving one's Sherman tank down this narrow leafy lane or advancing on foot expecting the sniper, MG42 or Schu mine at any moment.

mine or Panzerfaust (an efficient hand-held German anti-tank weapon). If you were in a Sherman, it would instantly roar with flames, terribly burning its crew. The Germans, with uncharacteristic black humour, christened the Sherman tanks 'Tommy cookers'. For the infantry, the battle was usually joined within small areas, where inevitably companies would have to split down and operate as platoons and even sections, with one small unit of men, officers and NCOs not knowing what was happening in the field next to them.

In this dreadful scenario, the men of 1944 had at least more hope of survival when wounded than their fathers who had fought in the First World War. Modern medicines and improved surgical methods meant that men better survived the trauma of wounding. The wounded were now rapidly transported from the battlefield by 'ambulance cars', the US 'Jeeps'. This meant that evacuation to the Regimental Aid Post and onwards to surgical field hospital could be quickly achieved. At battalion or regimental level, the medical orderlies received very high praise, often putting their own lives in extreme danger. Two memoirs by Ted Castle from A Company 2nd Glosters serve to illustrate this well, one at the time of the first attack into Tilly-sur-Seulles and the second just after 2nd Glosters had supported the attack on Lingevres by the DLI:

A Company just got to the outside, but I got into Tilly to see to casualties. I remember picking a lad up and got him on the jeep on the stretcher racks and got back up the road to the aid post, but when we unloaded him we found he had been hit again on the jeep and killed. I found stretcher bearing one of the most hazardous things you could do in battle.

Later about four of us went into the area known today as Essex Wood and helped clear it of the Essex dead. It was there that I first came across the 'Moaning

Minnie'. I had gone back to RHQ to get some more shell dressings and then came back with a mate of mine and heard a terrible bloody noise, like an express train. We threw ourselves down in the ditch. When I got up my mess tins fell out the bottom of my pack. Shrapnel had torn it open along the bottom and everything fell out. That night after we had finished I helped bury some of the Durham dead.[20]

The final thing that greatly helped in the reduction of deaths after wounding was the efficient transport arrangements away from the battlefront. Major Ted Hunt recalls how from Gold Beach the wounded were loaded onto DUKWs, which went straight out to the LSTs to unload. Some of the LSTs had been fitted out as hospital ships with an operating room. In this way, men reached hospitals in the United Kingdom within twenty-four hours of being wounded. Major Hunt reminds us about the effect this could also have on morale: 'If I am wounded I am going home this afternoon.'[21] Many of the wounded were evacuated even more quickly from the larger airstrips by transport aircraft. Len Cox, shot near Lingevres on 4 July, was flown back:

> They sent me to the Field General Hospital in big marquees in Bayeux. They took the bullet out there and they also gave us peaches and Carnation Milk. I was lucky really as I could have been paralysed. 'Mac' Macarthur was in the same ward as me and got two bullets in the side of the stomach. A Dakota flew us home. We landed at Swindon where we had a meal and they also washed a lot of blood off my face. We also wrote a card home to tell the families that we had been injured. Then we were put on a train and I ended up in Leicester Royal Infirmary.[22]

Another recurring theme from the War Diaries and interviews is that, during combat, both infantrymen, artillerymen and tank men often mistakenly identified the type of tank they were fighting against. The word 'Tigers' litters the War Diaries of British units in Normandy, but relatively few tanks of this type fought there, and the first unit to encounter any Panzer VIs while advancing forward of Gold Beach was 7th Armoured Division at Villers-Bocage. The tanks employed by the Germans in Normandy include only 138 Panzer VI (Tigers) as against 655 Panzer V (Panther) and 897 Panzer IV. Armoured assault guns and anti-tank hunters of various types amounted to another 567 fully tracked armoured vehicles.[23] There were also a number of Marder self-propelled guns, and a relatively small number and variety of other tanks employed; perhaps a total of just over 2,000 of what could be described as tanks rather than armoured cars or half-tracks. The majority of German tanks and self-propelled guns in Normandy mounted a 75 mm gun, and the majority of German anti-tank guns were of similar calibre. Only the Panzer VI tanks mounted the 88 mm gun. It can be appreciated that the 'Tiger' tank had made a great impression in Tunisia and Italy, and became the over-riding bogeyman to Allied soldiers of the Normandy Campaign. That fear was amplified after the apparent devastating impact of just a few of these tanks backed by Panzer Grenadiers at Villers-Bocage. The Panzer IV had somewhat of a similar silhouette, and with extra armour and side skirts applied, probably accounted for many identification errors.

A further effective and easily manoeuvred German weapon was the Nebelwerfer or 'Moaning Minnie', after the terrible screeching noise its bombs made in flight. There were twenty-one Nebelwerfer battalions, plus a few extra batteries in Normandy organized as three Werfer-Brigaden and one Werfer-Regiment, producing instant firepower at low cost and technology. A 15 cm Nebelwerfer battalion had eighteen launchers, each of six barrels, and within seconds could fire 108 15 cm rockets. This was a psychologically terrifying weapon as well as physically devastating, especially to the men of the infantry.

We have seen that south of Bayeux and along the Bayeux to Caen main road, the battalions of 50th Division report around the 7 and 8 June that reconnaissance was carried out far forward – usually by carrier patrol – and in front of the division there seemed little resistance. At the same time, the Germans in front seemed disorganized and not sure where 50th Division forward posts were. There are a number of reports in unit War Diaries of motorcyclists or vehicles driving into the British forward positions and being shot down or captured. Those captured seemed surprised at how far forward British units were. This was the time to strike, but Bucknall, in charge of XXX Corps, seemed at this time not to have been pushing the commanders under him. Everyone seems to have been waiting for 7th Armoured Division to arrive and provide the magic formula for the next stage of advance. They were arriving, but the beach hold-ups caused by the weather meant they landed more slowly. If they had been able to land more quickly, this powerful armoured division, including a fresh and experienced motorized brigade of infantry, might have been able to charge down the road to Tilly-sur-Seulles and beyond, brushing aside any resistance. But later on 8 June, it was already too late; Panzer Lehr were arriving and took immediate steps to plug any gaps.

Not until 12 June was a long right flanking move to Villers-Bocage attempted by 7th Armoured Division, after clear orders from Dempsey. But this was to be totally rebuffed by an energetic enemy, who, with the same will as shown on the Eastern Front, could extemporize and seemingly successfully adapt to any threatening situation thrown at them. Later, Montgomery would sack those he deemed not up to the job in Normandy – Bullen-Smith from 51st (Highland) Division in July, Bucknall from XXX Corps and Erskine from 7th Armoured Division on 2 August, and Hinde from 22nd Armoured Brigade on 3 August. Meanwhile, 50th Division, including 56th Brigade, were drawn into an outright slogging match, reflected in the casualty figures given above, slowly moving south. By the end of the Normandy Campaign, 50th Division had performed its task very well, but had exhausted itself. In early August, 56th Brigade moved to 59th (Staffordshire) Infantry Division, then made a final move to 49th (West Riding) Infantry Division at the end of August, when Montgomery was forced by the reinforcement situation to break up 59th Division. In each case, it replaced a shattered infantry brigade from within those divisions. Seemingly, it was preferred to keep this brigade together, as it was made up from regular Army battalions rather than territorial. Although 56th Brigade had proved itself serving with 50th Division, it missed the support from 50th Division's professional organization and divisional artillery when it left.

With the Germans finally beaten in Normandy in August 1944, XXX Corps, including 50th Division, raced north swiftly, capturing Brussels and Antwerp, where lack of fuel led to a pause in the advance. Many thought that this was the total collapse of the German Army. They were wrong. In late September, 50th Division was again in action in Operation Market Garden to seize the bridges over the Rhine. Famously

Table 1 Convictions for AWOL, desertion, insubordination and drunkenness – infantry.[24]

131st Bde	June 1	July 11	August 24	September 5
69th Bde	June 3	July 26	August 82	September 24
151st Bde	June 0	July 11	August 36	September 12
231st Bde	June 0	July 51	August 59	September 1
22nd Armd Bde	June 4	July 4	August 24	September 5
8th	June 1	July 1	August 1	September 0

stalled at Arnhem, the 'Bridge too Far', 50th Division had expended itself, taking another 1,000 casualties. Towards the end of the year, it was stood down and returned to the United Kingdom as a training division. However, many of its men were transferred to other active fighting units in north-west Europe as reinforcements. By this time, it had suffered nearly 7,500 casualties since D-Day.

It is pertinent to ask the question: 'How effective was 50th Division?' In the New Forest camps in May 1944, Brigadier Hargest reported the 1,000 men going AWOL from the division. But the majority came back. We know, as well, that 50 per cent of the infantrymen of the division were new, and reinforced the famous units after they had returned to the United Kingdom. In Normandy, the veteran divisions were much more liable to acts of desertion, drunkenness or going AWOL than the untried infantry divisions and armour, as shown by the figures in Table 1 taken from the Judge Advocate General's reports.

There are three things to consider about these figures. First, it is not surprising that the numbers peak during the periods of most intense fighting. Second, after the middle of June, when it was obvious that near-stalemate was occurring, men inevitably became more frustrated and anxious. Montgomery and his generals were alarmed by the increasing problems, especially that of so-called 'battle exhaustion', and medical officers were instructed to tighten up and not allow as many men away from the front line. There was a tightening of discipline. Finally, the type of countryside 50th Division was fighting in was some of the most difficult to make progress in, and actions took place at very short distances. British infantry in Normandy were often outgunned by their German opponents, who realized that large numbers of automatic weapons used in the close confines of the Normandy battlefield would cause high casualties and effectively disrupt any attacks. Once out of the beachhead area and south of Bayeux, many experienced officers and men used to much more open ground were surprised at the intensity and short ranges at which actions took place. British infantry battalions had little to counter this, and the armour had great difficulty negotiating the terrain; hence, it is not surprising that the very good artillery became the main tool.

The German Army in Normandy also had the advantage of retreating and knowing all they needed about an area they had just left. Mines were usually lifted by the hundred in areas just taken by British units, and German mortar, Nebelwerfer and artillery men knew ranges perfectly. The German infantryman was an expert at camouflage in the Bocage – he had to be. Also, the German Army was very good at an all-arms approach. As has been pointed out, a new British doctrine of co-operation of infantry with tanks was only published as 50th Division went into the sealed camps. It would be some weeks before British leadership caught up with an all-arms approach, as the lessons of fighting in Normandy were learned.

But overall, considering the difficulties found in fighting the Normandy Campaign, the division had operated very well. Brought back from long service abroad and requiring a large number of mainly 'green' replacements, it was placed in an area inappropriate for preparing and training for Normandy, and for some time there was little urgency displayed towards training. The problems of desertion experienced in the camps just prior to D-Day and reported by Brigadier Hargest do not seem to have persisted as soon as action was joined, despite the convictions quoted above. It had no more cases of battle fatigue than any other division in Normandy, and fewer than some. On 21 June, Hargest reports that 'the morale of 50 Div is still high after 15 days of fighting'.[25]

By the end of June 1944, 50th Infantry Division, including 56th (Independent) Infantry Brigade, had suffered over 4,000 casualties, one of the highest casualty returns in Normandy. That is testament to the very brave men who landed on Gold Beach on 6 June 1944.

In Tilly-sur-Seulles CWG Cemetery lies Nathan Lerner from Hackney in London, 1st Dorsets, killed on 28 June 1944. On his headstone is engraved this poignant message, summing up the reason why these men were there:

Fell fighting Fascism from Cable Street to Normandy.

Appendix A: Outline of 50 Div and 7 Armd Div Units

50th (TT) Infantry Division: **Maj. General DAH Graham.**

69th Infantry Brigade: **Brigadier FYC Knox.**
5th East Yorkshire Regiment: Lt Col. GW White.
6th Green Howards: Lt Col. RHW Hastings.
7th Green Howards: Lt Col. PH Richardson.

231st Infantry Brigade: **Brigadier Sir ABG Stanier.**
1st Hampshires: Lt Col. HD Nelson-Smith.
1st Dorsets: Lt Col. EAM Norrie.
2nd Devons: Lt Col. CAR Nevill.

151st Infantry Brigade: **Brigadier RH Senior.**
6th Durham Light Infantry: Lt Col. AE Green.
8th Durham Light Infantry: Lt Col. RP Lidwell.
9th Durham Light Infantry: Lt Col. HR Woods.

56th Infantry Brigade (attached):   **Brigadier EC Pepper.**
2nd Essex: Lt Col. JF Higson.
2nd Glosters: Lt Col. DW Biddle.
2nd South Wales Borderers: Lt Col. RW Craddock.

Reconnaissance:
61st Recce Regt RAC: **Lt Col. Sir WM Mount.**

MMG and Heavy Mortar Support:
2nd Cheshires: **Lt Col. SV Keeling.**

Royal Artillery: **Brigadier CH Norton.**
90th Field Regt: Lt Col. IGS Hardie.
102nd Anti-Tank Regt: Lt Col. AK Matthews.
25th LAA Regt: Lt Col. GGO Lyons.

Royal Engineers: **Lt Col. RL Willott.**
233rd Field Company: Maj. JR Cave-Browne.
295th Field Company: Maj. CW Wood.
505th Field Company: Maj. CAOB Compton.
235th Field Park Company: Maj. IL Smith.

Royal Corps of Signals: Lt Col. CB Stevenson.

Royal Electrical and Mechanical Engineers: Lt Col. EH Rundle.
69th Brigade Workshops Company
231st Brigade Workshops Company
151st Brigade Workshops Company
56th Brigade Workshops Company

Royal Army Service Corps: Lt Col. GW Fenton.
346th Company
508th Company
522nd Company
524th Company

Royal Army Ordnance Corps: Maj. DCH Merrill.
69th Brigade Workshops Section
231st Brigade Workshops Section
151st Brigade Workshops Section
56th Brigade Workshops Section

Royal Army Medical Corps:
149th Field Ambulance
186th Field Ambulance
200th Field Ambulance

Military Police: Capt. WR Hunter.
50th Division Provost Company

Other Units Attached for the Assault Phase:
Royal Marines:
47 RM Commando: **Lt Col. CF Philips.**
1st RM Armoured Support Regt: **Lt Col. LV Peskett.**

8th Armoured Brigade: **Brigadier HJB Cracroft.**
Notts Yeomanry (Sherwood Rangers):   Lt Col. J Anderson.
4th/7th Royal Dragoon Guards: Lt Col. RGG Byron.
24th Lancers: Lt Col. WAC Anderson.
147th Field Regiment RA: Lt Col. RA Phayre.

79th Armoured Division:
HQ 6th Assault Regt. RE
81st Assault Squadron RE: Maj. RE Thompstone.
82nd Assault Squadron RE: Maj. HGA Elphinstone.

149th Assault Park Squadron RE
B&C Squadrons Westminster Dragoons: Lt Col. WYK Blair Oliphant.
13th and 15th Troops, C Squadron 141st RAC

Royal Artillery:
7th Medium Regt: Lt Col. EJ Stansfield.
86th Field Regt: Lt Col. GD Fanshawe.
198th and 234th Btys 73rd Anti-tank Regt: Lt Col. Perry.
120th LAA Regt: Lt Col. JB Allan.
113th HAA Regt
A Flight 662 Air Observation Post Squadron: Maj. GA Hill.

US Artillery.
987th Field Artillery Battalion.[1]

Beach Group 104th Beach Sub Area.
2nd Hertfordshires: Lt Col. JR Harper.
6th Border Regt: Lt Col. HS Cooper.
73rd Field Company RE: Maj. LE Wyatt.
89th Field Company RE: Maj. AA Gray.
280th Field Company RE: Major LS Clayton.
75th, 173rd, 209th, 231st and 243rd Pioneer Companies
305th, 536th and 705th Companies RASC
24th and 25th Beach Recovery Sections
240th and 243rd Beach Provost Companies
203rd Field Ambulance
25th, 31st and 32nd Field Dressing Stations

7th Armoured Division: **Maj. General GWEJ Erskine.**

22nd Armoured Brigade: **Brig. WRN Hinde.**
1st Royal Tank Regiment
5th Royal Tank Regiment
4th County of London Yeomanry
1st Battalion, Rifle Brigade

131st (Queens) Brigade: **Brig. MS Ekins.**
1/5th Battalion, Queens Royal Regiment
1/6th Battalion, Queens Royal Regiment
1/7th Battalion, Queens Royal Regiment
No. 3 Support Company, Royal Northumberland Fusiliers (Machine Gun)

Divisional Troops:
8th Hussars
Royal Artillery
3rd Regiment, Royal Horse Artillery
5th Regiment, Royal Horse Artillery
15th (Isle of Man) Light AA Regiment Royal Artillery
65th (Norfolk Yeomanry) Anti-Tank Regiment Royal Artillery

Map 1: Gold Beach

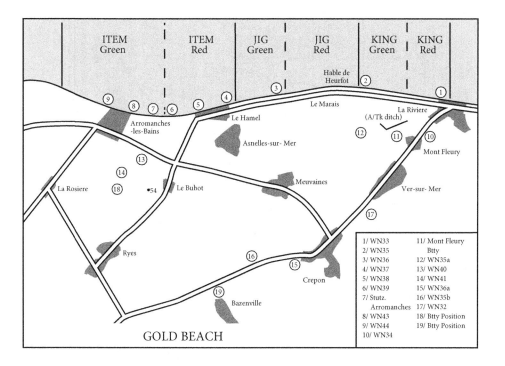

Map 2: Gold Beach to Tilly-sur-Seulles

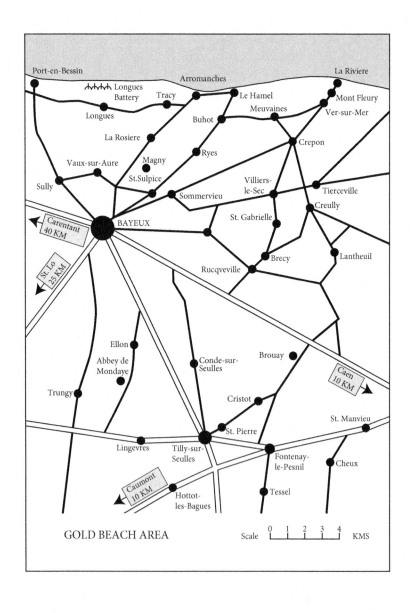

GOLD BEACH AREA

Scale 0 1 2 3 4 KMS

List of Veterans

Personal accounts and diaries used in this book have been provided by the following veterans of D-Day:

Tony Atcherley	RCS
Major Pat Barrass	2 Essex
Father, Sir Barrett-Lennard Bart	2 Essex
Ted Battley	47 (RM) Commando
Lt Sidney Beck	86 Field Regiment RA
Charles Benson	2 Essex
Harry Billinge	RE
Dennis Bowen	5 East Yorks
Eric Broadhead	9 DLI
David Bushell	1 Dorsets
Ted Castle	2 Glosters
George Church MM	2 Hertfordshire
Captain Frank Clarke	2 Glosters
William Cooke	RN
Bert Cooper	5 East Yorks
Len Cox	2 Glosters
John Cummer	USN
T. Curran	295 Field Company RE
Albert Daines	2 Essex
Lt Dennis Davis	2 SWB
George Davis	1 Hampshires
Frank Dilworth MM, BEM	RCS
Gordon Duffin	2 Glosters
Sgt Arthur Dyer MBE	RCS
Sgt Charles Eagles	9 DLI
Bill Evans	2 SWB
Peter Giggens	2 Essex,
Captain Peter Goddin	DLI HQ
Sid Hampton	2 Glosters
Dennis Hawes	1 Hampshires
Tom Hewitt	2 Devons
Charles Hill	6 Green Howards
Les Holden	2 Essex
Major Michael Holdsworth MC	2 Devons

Gordon Hornsby	RAMC
Neville Howell	73 Anti-Tank Regiment and 102 (Northumberland Hussars)
Major Edward Hunt MVO	RE
George Jesson	2 Essex
Dr Peter Johnson	RAMC
Eric Krull	RN
Syd Lee	RCS
Harold Lewis	1 Dorsets
Lt James Madden	RNVR
Philip Maillou	2 Essex
Tony Mansi	2 Essex
Robert Metcalfe MBE	RCS
Lt John Milton	6 Green Howards
Major A. Mott	1 Hampshires
Lt Col. Alan Norman OBE	Hampshire Regiment
Major Bob Orrell	RE
Oliver Perks	90th Field Regiment RA
Lt Dick Philips	2SWB
Bill Robinson	2 Glosters
Stan Smith	RNVR
Brigadier Sir Nicholas Somerville CBE	2SWB
Bill Speake	2SWB
Major Basil Stephens MC	2 Glosters
Ken Stone	RAMC
Kenneth Taylor	6 Green Howards
Sam Weaver	2 SWB
Charles Willis	RASC/2 Essex
Frank Wiltshire	1 Dorset

Notes

Introduction

1. A. Holborn, *The 56th (Independent) Infantry Brigade and D-Day: An Independent Infantry Brigade and the Campaign in North-West Europe 1944-1945* (London: Continuum, 2010).
2. C. Dunphie and G. Johnson, *Gold Beach: Inland from King – June 1944* (Barnsley: Leo Cooper, 1999); and T. Saunders, *Gold Beach-Jig: Jig Sector and West – June 1944* (Barnsley: Leo Cooper, 2002).
3. S. Trew, *Battle Zone Normandy: Gold Beach* (Stroud: Sutton Publishing, 2004).
4. B. L. Montgomery, *Normandy to the Baltic* (London: Hutchinson, 1946), p. 36.
5. This event has continued to promote lively debate occasionally in the House of Commons, the last time the author can easily find being in March 2000: http://www.publications.parliament.uk/pa/cm199900/cmhansrd/vo000322/halltext/00322h04.htm.
6. Reported in N. Hamilton, *Monty: Master of the Battlefield 1942-1944* (Sevenoaks: Coronet, 1985), p. 543.
7. Lt (later Brigadier) Sir Nicholas Somerville CBE, IO and later adjutant of 2 SWB. Interview with author.
8. B. L. Montgomery, *Memoirs* (London: Companion Book Club, 1960). Letter 14 April 1944, pp. 218–19.
9. O. Wieviorka, 'The British and the Liberation of France', in *Britain and France in Two World Wars. Truth, Myth and Memory* (London: Bloomsbury, 2013), pp. 137, 138 and 150.
10. See, for example, the letter to First Lord of the Admiralty, Secretary of State for Air, CIGs and COS Committee and Ministry of Labour. W. S. Churchill, *The Second World War: Volume VI* (London: Penguin, 1985), p. 615.
11. Montgomery, *Memoirs,* p. 219.
12. See, for example, A. R. Millett, 'Blood upon the Risers', in *The D-Day Companion*, ed. J. Penrose (New Orleans: National D-Day Museum, 2004), for an interesting account of the US airborne landings and how these were second only in near disaster to the landing on Omaha Beach.
13. L. F. Ellis, *Victory in the West Volume 1: The Battle for Normandy* (HMSO, 1962), p. 213.
14. Ibid., p. 210.
15. The other 'British' beach was Sword Beach, with the ferry port of Ouistreham as focal point; the village/resort of Courseulles for the Canadian Juno Beach; while the US beaches have no focal village, perhaps St Laurent for Omaha Beach. For the airborne landings, St Mere L'Eglise serves the US 82nd and 101st Airborne landings and Ranville the British 6th Airborne landings, although Pegasus Bridge is perhaps better known.

16. Father, Sir Barrett-Lennard Bart. Then Lt and IO of 2nd Essex. Interview with author.
17. Lt Sam Weaver. Signals officer and sometimes IO of 2SWB. Interview with author.
18. See http://vierville.free.fr/6533-Gare.html, http://www.normannia.info/cgi-bin/ aurweb.exe/normannia/rechpdoc?idn=hautsfourneaux1913.html.
19. M. Morgan, *D-Day Hero: CSM Stanley Hollis VC* (Stroud: Sutton Publishing, 2004), pp. 55–6.

Chapter 1

1. Prime minister to General Ismay, 6 June 1940: 'Enterprises must be prepared, with specially trained troops of the hunter class, who can develop a reign of terror down these coasts, first of all on the "Butcher and Bolt policy"'. W. Churchill, *The Second World War: Volume II* (London: Penguin, 1985), p. 217. Churchill had come across such a British policy before while serving in Afghanistan as a young army officer and reporter.
2. *Planning Operation Overlord.* Canadian Historical Section, Report No. 42, Ottawa 6 June 1951, p. 7. MLRS Books reprint.
3. Ibid., p. 10.
4. Ibid., p. 68.
5. N. Hamilton, *Monty: The Making of a General 1887–1942* (London: Hodder & Stoughton, 1984), pp. 269–70.
6. *Planning Operation Overlord.* Canadian Historical Section, Report No. 42, pp. 8–9.
7. M. Gilbert, *Churchill: A Life* (London: Pimlico, 2000), p. 419.
8. Ibid., pp. 748–9.
9. Churchill, *Volume II,* chapter XXIV, pp. 419–37.
10. See http://www.combinedops.com/index.htm. This website gives an excellent picture of CTC.
11. J. Terraine, *The Life and Times of Lord Mountbatten.* London: Arrow Books, 1971, p. 114.
12. Churchill, *Volume III*, p. 480.
13. Terraine, p. 115.
14. G. Millar, *The Bruneval Raid: Stealing Hitler's Radar* (London: Cassell. 2002). This is a classic account of the raid and provides a very useful account of radar development.
15. Terraine, p. 118.
16. C. E. Lucas Phillips, *The Greatest Raid of All* (London: Pan, 2000), pp. 282–3.
17. Ibid., pp. 278–81.
18. Ibid., pp. 260–2.
19. Churchill, *Volume IV*, p. 178. Letter to Roosevelt, 1 April 1942.
20. Ibid., p. 178.
21. *Planning Operation Overlord.* Canadian Historical Section, Report No. 42, p. 28.
22. T. Saunders, *Dieppe: Operation Jubilee* (Barnsley: Pen & Sword, 2005).
23. *Planning Operation Overlord.* Canadian Historical Section, Report No. 42, pp. 78–81.
24. B. L. Montgomery, *The Memoirs of Field Marshal Montgomery* (Watford: Odhams, 1958).
25. Saunders, p. 52.

26. Terraine, p. 128.
27. Churchill, *Volume IV*, p. 458.
28. Ibid., p. 459.
29. C. P. Stacey, *The Canadian Army 1939–45.* Official Historical Summary. Ottawa. 1948. Chapter V provides a good starting point for looking at the Dieppe raid from a Canadian perspective by a well-respected author.
30. Saunders, p. 198.
31. *Combined Report on the Dieppe Raid 1942. Part V.* Reported in *Planning Operation Overlord.* Canadian Historical Section, Report No. 42, p. 90.
32. Churchill, *Volume II*, p. 22.
33. Ibid., p. 503.
34. G. A. Harrison, *Cross Channel Attack* (Old Saybrook, US: Konecky & Konecky, 1950), p. 9. Harrison served as a historical officer in the Second World War, serving in five campaigns. It is the classic official US account of the European theatre of operations.
35. Ibid., p. 18.
36. A. J. P. Taylor, *English History 1914-1945* (Oxford: Oxford University Press, 1965), p. 623.
37. Ibid., pp. 685–7.
38. Churchill, *Volume IV*, p. 463.
39. Ibid., p. 541.
40. Harrison, p. 29.
41. A. Alanbrooke, *War Diaries 1939-1945: Field Marshal Lord Alanbrooke* (London: Orion Publishing, 2001), p. 282.
42. Ibid., pp. 284–5.
43. D. D. Eisenhower, *Report of the Commander in Chief Allied Forces to the Combined Chiefs of Staff on Operations in Northwest Africa.* http://www.ibiblio.org/hyperwar/USA/rep/TORCH/DDE-Torch.html#concluding, p. 48.
44. Alanbrooke, p. 351.
45. Churchill, *Volume IV*, p. 602.
46. Harrison, p. 35.
47. Hamilton, *Monty*, p. 225.
48. Gilbert, p. 749.
49. Hamilton, p. 387.
50. F. Morgan, *Overture to Overlord* (London: Hodder & Stoughton, 1950), p. 15.
51. Ibid., p. 36.
52. Ibid., p. 101.
53. R. Scott, *The Real Dad's Army: The War Diaries of Colonel Rodney Foster* (London: Penguin, 2012), p. 236.
54. Ibid. Diary entries August–September 1943, pp. 236–40.
55. Major Basil Stephens MC. 2nd Glosters. Interview with author.
56. Morgan, p. 108.
57. J. Levine, *Operation Fortitude: The Greatest Hoax of the Second World War* (London: Collins, 2011), pp. 190–3.
58. *Planning Operation Overlord.* Canadian Historical Section, Report No. 42, p. 186.
59. Quoted in Levine, p. 199.
60. Morgan, p. 114.
61. Churchill, *Volume IV*, pp. 847–8.
62. Morgan, p. 149.
63. Ibid., p. 147.

Chapter 2

1. R. Neillands and R. Normann, *D-Day 1944: Voices from Normandy* (London: Cassell, 1993), p. 25.
2. R. Jackson, *Dunkirk: The British Evacuation, 1940* (London: Cassell, 2002), p. 60.
3. Ibid., pp. 173–4.
4. The inscription on her CWGC headstone reads: *Mrs Brigadier Mary Janet Climpson. Salvation Army. 20 May 1940. Age 56. Death Takes But God Receives 'Jesus Saith Unto Her Mary' St John XX.16.* Dieppe Canadian War Cemetery, Hautot-sur-Mer, Seine-Maritime, France. (Grave reference: C.76.)
5. L. Ellis, *The War in France and Flanders.* HMSO, 1953. Reprint (Uckfield: Naval and Military Press, 2004), p. 283.
6. Bill Robinson. 2nd Glosters. Interview with author 2 May 2007.
7. A. Alanbrooke, *War Diaries 1939–1945: Field Marshal Lord Alanbrooke* (London: Orion Publishing, 2001), p. 74.
8. There is still an HMT Lancastria Association; their website is well worth a visit: http://www.lancastria-association.org.uk/index.php?page=history.
9. Charles Willis, RASC/2nd Essex. Interview with author 21 August 2008.
10. Ellis, *The War in France and Flanders*, pp. 325–7.
11. G. Maddaloni, *Liberation and Franco-American Relations in Post-War Cherbourg.* US General Staff College, 2008. http://www.dtic.mil/cgi-bin/GetTRDoc?AD=ADA483032.
12. Fuhrer Directive 18, 12 November 1940; Fuhrer Directive 19, 10 December 1940.
13. Churchill, *Volume II: Their Finest Hour*, p. 214.
14. Ibid., p. 217.
15. Ibid., p. 566.
16. J. Durnford-Slater, *Commando: Memoirs of a Fighting Commando in World War Two* (London: Greenhill Books, 2002), pp. 22–33.
17. J. O'Sullivan, *When Wales Went to War 1939–1945* (Stroud: The History Press, 2007), pp. 96–7.
18. Nr. 003830/42 Gkdos./OKW/WFSt. 18 October 1942. Fuehrer HQ. USA 1948.
19. Ibid.
20. F. Ruge, *Rommel in Normandy: Reminiscences by Friedrich Ruge* (London: Macdonald and James, 1979).
21. N. Bijl and R. Chapman, *No. 10 (Inter-Allied) Commando 1942–1945* (Botley: Osprey Publishing, 2006), pp. 22–5.
22. Fuhrer Directive 32, 11 June 1941. USA 1948.
23. B. Collier, *The Defence of the United Kingdom.* HMSO, 1957. Reprint (Uckfield: Naval and Military Press, 2004), p. 528.
24. Fuhrer Directive 40, 23 March 1942. USA 1948.
25. Commander in Chief, Navy Berlin, 27 March 1942. Skl.au.A. II 771/42 Gkdos. USA 1948.
26. Circular Telegram: Fuehrer Headquarters, 5 December 1942. USA 1948.
27. Naval High Command Berlin, 11 April 1942. B. 111. l.Skl. I Op. 8329/42 Gkdos. USA 1948.
28. W. Gorlitz (ed.), *In the Service of the Reich: The Memoirs of Field Marshal Keitel* (Focal Point Publications, 2003), p. 291.
29. G. Forty, *Fortress Europe: Hitler's Atlantic Wall* (Hersham: Ian Allan, 2002), pp. 31–3. See also K. Mallory and A. Ottar, *Architecture of Aggression: A History of Military Architecture in NW Europe 1900–1945* (D.P. & G. Doncaster, 2007), chapter 8.

30. C. Bishop, *Order of Battle: German Panzers in WWII* (Stroud: Spellmount, 2008), p. 153.
31. Some interesting detail is given in J. Levine, *Operation Fortitude: The Greatest Hoax of the Second World War* (London: Collins, 2012).
32. OKW/WFSt/Op. 662656/3 g. L. Chefs 3 November 1943, USA 1948.
33. Ibid., p. 4.
34. *German Defence Preparations in the West 1940-1944*. Canadian General Staff, c. 1955. Reprint MLRS Books.
35. D. C. Isby, *The German Army at D-Day: Fighting the Invasion* (London: Greenhill Books, 2004), p. 19.
36. R. Lewin, *Rommel as Military Commander* (Barnsley: Pen & Sword, 2004), frontispiece and pp. 245–6.
37. F. Ruge, *Rommel in Normandy: Reminiscences by Friedrich Ruge* (London: McDonald and Janes, 1979).
38. B. H. Liddle-Hart (ed.), *The Rommel Papers* (London: Collins, 1953), p. 457.
39. Ibid., p. 467.
40. Ruge, p. 99.
41. Liddell-Hart, p. 453n.
42. Ibid., p. 454.
43. Ibid., pp. 457–9.
44. See http://users.telenet.be/WMF-home/WMF_2008_3.PDF.
45. Liddell-Hart, p. 461.
46. J. A. Wood (ed.), *Army of the West: Weekly Reports of German Army Group B from Normandy to the West Wall* (Mechanicsburg, Pennsylvania: Stackpole Books, 2007), pp. 10–45.
47. Isby, pp. 22–7.
48. Ibid., p. 78.
49. N. Zetterling, *Normandy 1944: German Military Organization, Combat Power and Organizational Effectiveness* (Manitoba, Canada: Fedorowicz, 2000), p. 17.
50. Ibid., p. 29.
51. Generalleutnant Wilhelm Richter, *The Battle of the 716th Infantry Division in Normandy. 6th Jun – 23rd June 1944*. NARA FMS B621.
52. Zetterling, p. 297.
53. Ibid.
54. Ibid.
55. Ibid., p. 29.
56. Ziegelmann in Isby, pp. 122–8.
57. Zetterling, p. 17.
58. Information on defences for Gold Beach comes from a number of sources, some of them slightly contradictory: Trew, *Battle Zone Normandy: Gold Beach*; Zaloga, *D-Day Fortifications in Normandy*; Dunphie and Johnson, *Gold Beach. Inland from King – June 1944*; Saunders, *Gold Beach-Jig: Jig Sector and West – June 1944*; TNA: PRO CAB 106/967 Casualties and Effects of Fire Support on British Beaches. Army Operational Research Group Report No. 261; TNA: PRO CAB 106/975 Opposition encountered on the British Beaches in Normandy on D-Day. Army Operational Research Group Report No. 264. Also the author has extensive fieldwork experience of Gold Beach and 50th Division area June/July 1944.
59. TNA: PRO CAB 106/975 Opposition encountered on the British Beaches in Normandy on D-Day. Army Operational Research Group Report No. 264.

Chapter 3

1. Churchill, *Volume V*, p. 370.
2. Ibid.
3. G. A. Harrison, *Cross Channel Attack*. US Historical Division, 1950, p. 116.
4. A. Danchev and D. Todman, *War Diaries of Field Marshal Lord Alanbrooke 1939–1945* (London: Weidenfield & Nicholson, 2001), p. 491.
5. Churchill, *Volume V*, p. 376.
6. B. L. Montgomery, *The Memoirs of Field Marshal the Viscount Montgomery of Alamein, KG* (London: Collins, 1958), p. 206.
7. Ibid., p. 190.
8. Hamilton, p. 457.
9. Danchev and Todman, p. 499.
10. Hamilton, p. 475.
11. F. Morgan, *Overture to Overlord* (London: Hodder & Stoughton, 1950), p. 10.
12. Churchill, *Volume V*, p. 393.
13. Montgomery, p. 196.
14. It is also interesting to note that in *Memoirs* (p. 195) Montgomery states that Eisenhower told him in Algiers that 'the plan did not look good'. Also, Eisenhower was already present in Marrakesh but left early the following morning, evidently before Montgomery had talked to Churchill.
15. Churchill, *Volume V*, p. 517.
16. Hamilton, p. 484.
17. Montgomery, p. 202.
18. Ibid.
19. Both reported in Diary entries 17 and 24 January 1944. Danchev and Todman, pp. 515–16.
20. Leigh-Mallory was the brother of the famous mountaineer who was lost on Everest in 1924. D-Day was also the twentieth anniversary of Mallory and Irvine leaving Base Camp for their Everest attempt. There is still speculation that they may have reached the summit before disaster overtook them.
21. L. F. Ellis, *Victory in the West. Volume 1: The Battle for Normandy*, HMSO, 1962, pp. 33–4. Reprint (Uckfield: Naval and Military Press, 2004).
22. S. W. Roskill, *The War at Sea. Volume III: The Offensive Part II. 1st June 1944–14th August 1945*, HMSO, 1961. Reprint (Uckfield: Naval and Military Press, 2004), p. 10.
23. B. Collier, *The Defence of the United Kingdom*. HMSO, 1957. Appendix XLII, p. 520. Reprint (Uckfield: Naval and Military Press, 2004).
24. Ibid., p. 329.
25. Battle Summary No. 39, Volume 1, Operation Neptune. Landings in Normandy June, 1944. Naval Historical Staff, June 1947.
26. Ibid., p. 61.
27. Ibid., p. 63.
28. Ibid., pp. 11–12.
29. T. Robertson, *Walker RN* (London: Evans Brothers, 1956), p. 13.
30. C. Bekker, *Hitler's Naval War* (Macdonald & Jane's, 1974), Appendix II, p. 387.
31. Battle Summary No. 39, p. 44.
32. Ibid., p. 24.
33. Roskill, p. 10.
34. Battle Summary No. 39, p. 38.
35. Ibid. Figures provided by this source, p. 37.

36. Ibid., p. 64.
37. C. Douglas-Pennant, Report by the Naval Commander Force G, 15 July 1944, p. 3.
38. Ibid., p. 43.
39. Ibid., p. 4.
40. Ibid., p. 5.
41. Ibid., p. 6.
42. Ibid.
43. Secretary of Naval Board (Canada). Memorandum 21st December 1943 to Canadian Joint Staff Washington and Senior Canadian Naval Officer, London.
44. *The RCN's Part in the Invasion of France* (London: RCN Historical Section, 1945), p. 27.
45. Douglas-Pennant, p. 3.
46. J. Winser, *The D-Day Ships: Neptune the Greatest Amphibious Operation in History* (Kendall: World Ship Society, 1994), p. 90. This excellent little book gives a great deal of information and detail for anyone interested in the naval side of D-Day.
47. Eric Krull. Interview extracts by permission of the Oral History Centre at the Alexander Turnbull Library, Wellington, New Zealand.
48. William Cooke, Telegraphist LCT 1078, 53rd Flotilla. Diary and telephone conversations with author.
49. Battle Summary No. 39, p. 31.
50. L. F. Ellis, *Victory in the West. Volume 1: The Battle of Normandy.* HMSO, 1962. Reprint (Uckfield: Naval and Military Press, 2004), p. 89.
51. Battle Summary No. 39, p. 41.
52. Ibid.
53. *The Administrative History of the Operations of 21st Army Group on the Continent of Europe. 6th June 1944 – 8th May 1945.* 21st Army Group Publication. Germany. November 1945, Part III.
54. Ibid.
55. C. Messenger, *Bomber Harris and the Strategic Bombing Offensive 1939–1945* (London: Arms & Armour Press, 1984), reported p. 106.
56. Ibid., p. 160.
57. Ibid., p. 162.
58. S. Zuckerman and E. S. D. Drury, *The Effects of the Overlord Plan to Disrupt Enemy Rail Communications.* Bombing Analysis Unit SHAEF. November 1944, p. 33. MLRS Reprint.
59. Ibid., p. 3.
60. Ibid., fig. 3.
61. Ellis, p. 101.
62. Ibid., p. 111.
63. Statistics taken from: C. F. Brower (ed.), *World War Two in Europe: The Final Year* (London: Macmillan, 1998), pp. 115–25.

Chapter 4

1. Hamilton, *Monty: Master of the Battlefield*, pp. 417–18.
2. B. S. Barnes, *The Sign of the Double T: The 50th Northumbrian Division – July 1943 to December 1944* (York: Sentinel Press, 2008), pp. 53–4.
3. F. K. Hughes, *A Short History of 49th West Riding & Midland Infantry Division* (Barnet: Stellar Press, 1957), p. 22.
4. TNA: PRO CAB 44/56/57 Joslen, HF. Orders of Battle of the British Army, p. 392.

5. Information from a number of sources, but dates from TNA: PRO CAB 44/56/57 Orders of Battle of the British Army.
6. Bredin, *Three Assault Landings*, p. 44.
7. Harold Lewis, Dorset Regiment. Interview with author.
8. Lewis and English, p. 234.
9. P. R. Nightingale, *A History of the East Yorkshire Regiment (Duke of York's Own) in the War 1939–1945* (Howden: Mr Pye Books, 1998 (1952)), p. 150.
10. Oliver Perks, 90th Field Artillery RA. Interview with author. The family of the late Oliver Perks have also published http://www.oliverperks.com/. Oliver Perks' wartime blog is a marvellous resource and a fitting tribute to the man and his regiment.
11. Tom Hewitt, 2nd Devons. Interview with author.
12. David Bushell, 1st Dorsets. Interview with author and personal memoir.
13. Lt Col. Alan Norman, Hampshire Regiment. Interview with author and follow-up e-mails.
14. Captain Peter Goddin, Memoir by kind permission of the D-Day and Normandy Fellowship.
15. Charles Eagles, 9 DLI. Interview with author.
16. Dennis Bowen, 5th East Yorks. Interview with author.
17. John Milton, 6th Green Howards. Interview with author and memoir.
18. Charles Hill, 6th Green Howards. Interview with author.
19. Now known as The Derbyshire Miners' Convalescent home, it was established on the seafront at Skegness in 1927, and is one of only two such purpose-built buildings.
20. See http://www.railwaysarchive.co.uk/eventlisting.php?cause=6&showSearch=true&page=12.
21. Interview, telephone conversations and material provided by Gordon Hornsby, 203 Field Ambulance Unit and 203 Field Ambulance Unit War Diary.
22. Ken Stone, RAMC. Interview with author.
23. All references, diaries etc. from Dr Peter Johnson are by the kind permission of the Johnson family.
24. Dr Peter Johnson RAMC, Diary entry, 23 March 1944.
25. Ted Battley, 47(RM) Commando. Interview with author.
26. Lympstone, Devon, is Commando Training Centre Royal Marines – the base for Royal Marine training today. In the Second World War it was Royal Marine Exton – all the same area.
27. Nearby is the spectacular Commando Memorial in bronze with a background looking south to Ben Nevis. Next to the monument is now a small, well-visited memorial garden.
28. 47 Royal Marine Commando Association, Dispatch 10 December 2004, p. 6.
29. Synopsis of 56th (Independent) Infantry Brigade taken from A. Holborn, *The 56th (Independent) Infantry Brigade and D-Day: An Independent Infantry Brigade and the Campaign in North West Europe 1944–1945* (London: Continuum, 2010).
30. L/Cpl RS Gardiner RCS .IWM 07/13/1. Letter from Normandy 18 June 1944.
31. See http://www.cwgc.org/find-a-cemetery/cemetery/2067523/BOLDRE%20%28ST.%20JOHN%29%20CHURCHYARD. Boldre Church is also the centre for the yearly gathering of those still commemorating the loss of the battlecruiser HMS *Hood* in May 1941: http://www.hmshood.com/.

Chapter 5

1. D. Fraser, *And We Shall Shock Them: The British Army in the Second World War* (London: Cassell, 2002), p. 321. The other divisions were 1st Airborne, 7th Armoured Division and 51st (Highland) Division.
2. Hamilton, *Monty*, p. 399.
3. D. French, *Raising Churchill's Army: The British Army and the War against Germany 1919–1945* (Oxford: Oxford University Press, 2001), p. 273.
4. TNA: PRO WO 285/2 General Miles Christopher Dempsey, Letters and Directives from General Montgomery C in C 21st Army Group. 1944–5.
5. Lewis and English, p. 236.
6. Major Pat Barrass, Essex Regiment. Interview with author.
7. A. E. C. Bredin, *Three Assault Landings. The 1st Bn: The Dorsetshire Regiment in Sicily, Italy and Normandy* (Aldershot: Gale & Polden, 1946), p. 46.
8. Major Michael Holdsworth MC, Devonshire Regiment. Interview with author.
9. Neville Howell. 73 Anti-Tank Regiment and 102 (Northumberland Hussars) Anti-Tank Regiment, Personal memoir and kind permission of the D-Day and Normandy Fellowship.
10. French, p. 89.
11. Lt Col. Alan Norman, Hampshire Regiment. Interview with author and G. Forty, *The British Army Handbook 1939–1945* (Stroud: Sutton Publishing, 2002), p. 165.
12. Montgomery, pp. 208–9.
13. Major Michael Holdsworth MC. Devonshire Regiment. Interview with author.
14. Ibid.
15. Lewis and English, p. 235.
16. TNA: PRO CAB 106/1060, Brigadier Hargest Reports, 6 June – 10 July 1944.
17. TNA: PRO CAB 106/1068, M Telegrams, 16 October 1944.
18. TNA: PRO WO 223/7 Notes by Maj.-Gen. D. A. H. Graham, Operations of 50 (N) Div Normandy.
19. Major Michael Holdsworth MC, Devonshire Regiment. Interview with author.
20. TNA: PRO WO 223/7 Notes by Maj.-Gen. D. A. H. Graham, Operations of 50 (N) Div Normandy.
21. A. Danchev and D. Todman, *War Diaries of Field Marshal Lord Alanbrooke 1939–1945* (London: Weidenfield & Nicholson, 2001), pp. 388, 391.
22. Ibid.
23. TNA: PRO WO 171/152, 50th Division 'G' Message Log.
24. Philip Maillou, 2 Essex. Interview with author.
25. Les Holden Memoir. Grateful thanks to Avril Norten, nee Holden.
26. A. Holborn, *56th Infantry Brigade and D-Day: An Independent Infantry Brigade and the Campaign in North West Europe 1944–1945* (London: Continuum, 2012).
27. Report No. 145 Historical Section, Canadian Military Headquarters. Hist Sec (G.S.), A.H.Q. 5 July 1947. The Canloan Scheme, 1943 to July 1945, pp. 10–12.
28. See http://www.war-experience.org/canloan/regiments.htm.
29. J. Buckley, *British Armour in the Normandy Campaign 1944* (London: Frank Cass, 2004), pp. 16–17.
30. The monument reads: *4th/7th ROYAL DRAGOON GUARDS. Remembering those who lost their lives during Exercise Smash 1 in Duplex Drive amphibious Valentine tanks. STUDLAND BAY 4TH APRIL 1944. C.R. Gould, V. Hartley, A. V. Kirby, A. J.*

Park, E. G. Petty, V. N. Townson and all those brave men and women who ensured the success of D Day and the liberation of Europe For Peace and Freedom.

31. Oliver Perks, 90th Field Artillery RA. Interview with author.
32. Quintus Fabius Maximus Verucosus (280–203 BC) was five times Roman consul and twice dictator. He is known as 'the delayer' due to some of his tactics in war, and is often called the father of guerrilla warfare. One sometimes wonders whether all code words were picked in order from a book, as was apparently the case, or applied by a well-read officer!
33. TNA: PRO WO 199/2326. Exercise Fabius, 21 Army Group Combined Exercise, May 1944.
34. TNA: PRO WO 219/2216. Exercise Fabius, Plans and appreciation G3 Division, Operations B Plan Fortitude, May 1944.
35. TNA: PRO ADM 179/439. Admiralty: Portsmouth Station, Naval implications of Exercise Fabius, May 1944.
36. TNA: PRO ADM 1/29985. Recommendations for awards to two officers and men of HM LCI (L) 295 for attempting to rescue troops of 2nd Bn Essex Regiment from the sea in a loading accident.
37. TNA: PRO WO 171/1298. 2nd Battalion Gloucestershire Regiment, War Diary 1944.
38. D. French, *Raising Churchill's Army: The British Army and the War against Germany 1919–1945* (Oxford: Oxford University Press, 2000), p. 147.
39. TNA: PRO CAB 44/243 30 Corps, 50th (Northumbrian) Division and 7th Armoured Division, D-Day Planning Appreciations and Operations, 1950.
40. TNA: PRO WO 171/650 HQ 56 Infantry Brigade, War Diary 1944, Folder includes Operational Order No. 1.
41. Battle Summary No. 39, Volume 1, Landings in Normandy, Naval Historical Branch, June 1947, p. 70.
42. Ibid., p. 72.
43. A. Norman, 1st Hampshire Regiment, E-mail to author 1 December 2012.
44. Battle Summary No. 39, p. 81.
45. Ibid., pp, 84–5.
46. RAF Narrative, First Draft (Revised) The Liberation of North West Europe, Volume III. The Landings in Normandy. Spring 1949, pp. 60–1.
47. Ibid., p. 64.
48. Ibid., p. 237.
49. Ibid., pp. 122–3.
50. Frank Wiltshire, 1st Dorset. Written memoir by kind permission of the Wiltshire family.
51. David Bushell, 1st Dorset Regiment. Interview with author.
52. Lt Col. Alan Norman OBE, 1st Hampshire Regiment. Interview with author and various phone conversations and e-mails.
53. Major A. Mott, 1st Hampshire Regiment, DD1999/38, D-Day Archive, Portsmouth Library.
54. J. Winser, *The D-Day Ships* (Kendal: World Ship Society, 1994), p. 117.
55. ERA F. Merrill, HMM *Postilion*. Letter to parents 19 June 1944, DD 1998/22/571, D-Day Archive, Portsmouth Library.
56. Winser, p. 116.
57. Gordon Duffin, 2nd Glosters. Interview with author.
58. Ted Castle, 2nd Glosters. Interview with author.
59. Major Pat Barrass, George Jesson, 2nd Essex. Interview with author.
60. Tony Atcherley, Royal Corps of Signals. Interview with author.

61. Frank Dilworth, Royal Corps of Signals. Interview with author.
62. Les Holden Memoir.
63. Neville Howell, 73 Anti-Tank Regiment and 102 (Northumberland Hussars) Anti-Tank Regiment. Personal memoir and kind permission of the D-Day and Normandy Fellowship.
64. Major Michael Holdsworth, 2nd Devons. Interview with author.
65. Philip Maillou, 2nd Essex. Interview with author.
66. Sid Hampton, 2nd Glosters. Interview with author.

Chapter 6

1. C. Douglas-Pennant, Report by the Naval Commander Force G, 15 July 1944. Annex 3 to Appendix C, p. 371.
2. Ibid., p. 121.
3. S. Darlow, *D-Day Bombers: The Veterans' Story. RAF Bomber Command and the US Eighth Air Force Support to the Normandy Invasion 1944* (London: Bounty Books, 2007), pp. 151–5.
4. Eric Jarvis, DD 2000/36/665, D-Day Archive, Portsmouth Library.
5. *The Liberation of North West Europe. Volume III: The Landings in Normandy.* The Air Ministry, Air Historical Branch, Spring 1949, pp. 206–7.
6. Ibid., p. 213.
7. Ibid.
8. TNA: PRO CAB 44/243, 30 Corps, 50th (Northumbrian) Division and 7th Armoured Division, D-Day Planning, Appreciations and Operations, 1950, p. 96.
9. *The Story of 79th Armoured Division,* July 1945, Germany.
10. Douglas-Pennant, Report by the Naval Commander Force G, 15 July 1944, Annex 1 to Appendix C, Narrative of Bombardment Events, pp. 353–5.
11. Lt Col. Alan Norman OBE. Interview with author.
12. Kenneth Taylor Personal War Diary, www.patricktaylor.com/war-diary-1. Kind permission of Patrick Taylor.
13. Douglas-Pennant, Appendix F, p. 388.
14. TNA: PRO CAB 44/243, p. 96.
15. Lt Cmdr Humphries, Warren Tute Papers, DD 2001/1417, D-Day Archive, Portsmouth Library.
16. Douglas-Pennant, Narrative, p. 335.
17. Ibid., Appendix B, p. 345.
18. TNA: PRO CAB 44/243, pp. 92–3.
19. TNA: PRO CAB 44/243, p. 97.
20. 73 Field Company RE, A Short History of the Company in the NW Europe Campaign, DD 2000/36/115, D-Day Archive, Portsmouth Library.
21. Harry Billinge, Royal Engineers. Interview with author.
22. TNA: PRO CAB 44/243, p. 97.
23. TNA: PRO CAB 44/243, p. 79.
24. Lt Jack Booker RNVR, by kind permission of http://www.combinedops.com.
25. Midshipman Stan Smith RNVR. Personal memoir by kind permission of the D-Day and Normandy Fellowship.
26. Telegraphist William Cooke. Diary and telephone conversation with author.

27. Eric Krull. Interview by Alison Parr, permission by Eric Krull and the Oral History Centre at the Alexander Turnbull Library, Wellington, New Zealand.
28. Dennis Hawes, 1st Hampshires, D-Day Archive, Portsmouth Library.
29. George Davis, 1st Hampshires, DD2000/36/138, D-Day Archive, Portsmouth Library.
30. War Diary 1st Hampshire Regiment 6 June 1944.
31. Lt Col. Alan Norman OBE, 1st Hampshire Regiment. Interview with author and various phone conversations and e-mails.
32. Major A. Mott, 1st Hampshire Regiment, DD1999/38, D-Day Archive, Portsmouth Library.
33. S. Hills, *By Tank into Normandy* (London: Cassell, 2004), pp. 68, 79.
34. Frank Wiltshire, 1st Dorset. Written memoir by kind permission of the Wiltshire family.
35. David Bushell, 1st Dorset. Interview with author.
36. War Diary, 1st Dorsetshire Regiment, 6 June 1944.
37. Harold Lewis, 1st Dorset. Interview with author.
38. Mr T. Curran, memoir, 295 Field Company, D-Day Archive, Portsmouth Library.
39. War Diary, 2nd Devonshire Regiment, 6 June 1944.
40. *We Landed on D-Day,* memoir by Lt Col. CAR Nevill OBE. By kind permission of the Devon and Dorset Regiment Museum.
41. Major Michael Holdsworth MC, 2nd Devonshire Regiment. Interview with author.
42. Tom Hewitt, 2nd Devonshire Regiment. Interview with author.
43. War Diary 2nd Devonshire Regiment, 6 June 1944.
44. *We Landed on D-Day,* Nevill.
45. Major Michael Holdsworth MC. Interview with author.
46. War Diary 5th East Yorkshire Regiment. 6 June 1944.
47. Ibid.
48. TNA: PRO CAB 44/243, p. 113.
49. P. R. Nightingale, *A History of the East Yorkshire Regiment (Duke of York's Own) in the War 1939–45* (Howden: Mr Pye Books, 1998 (1952)), pp. 179–81 also cover the landing of 5th East Yorks.
50. Bert Cooper, 5th East Yorkshire Regiment. Interview with author.
51. Dennis Bowen, 5th East Yorkshire Regiment. Interview with author.
52. George Church, 2nd Battalion Hertfordshire Regiment. Telephone conversation with author.
53. Charles Hill, 6th Battalion Green Howards. Interview with author.
54. Lt Col. Robin Hastings, 6th Green Howards in G. Johnson and C. Dunphie, *Brightly Shone the Dawn* (London: Frederick Warne, 1980), p. 62.
55. Ibid., p. 62.
56. TNA: PRO CAB 44/243, p. 113.
57. Kenneth Taylor personal diary.
58. John Milton, 6th Battalion Green Howards. Interview with author.
59. Kenneth Taylor personal diary.
60. War diary of Lt Sidney Beck, B Troop, 86th Field Regiment Royal Artillery, by kind permission of his family. http://benbeck.co.uk/fh/transcripts/sjb_war_diaries/batterydiary.htm.
61. Neville Howell, 73 Anti-Tank Regiment and 102 (Northumberland Hussars) Anti-Tank Regiment. Personal memoir by kind permission of the D-Day and Normandy Fellowship.

62. TNA: PRO CAB 44/243, p. 115.
63. Ibid.
64. War Diary 7th Green Howards, 6 June 1944.
65. Major Peter Johnson RAMC. From notes and personal diary by kind permission of the Johnson family.
66. J. Forfar, *From Omaha to the Scheldt: The Story of 47 Royal Marine Commando during World War II,* 47 Royal Marine Commando Association, 2013.
67. War Diary 50th Division, The NA has told the author that 47 Commando War Diary for June 1944 does not appear to exist.
68. Ted Battley, 47 Commando. Interview with author.
69. Captain Peter Goddin. Memoir by kind permission of the D-Day and Normandy Fellowship.
70. John Cummer, Gunner's mate LCI (L) USN 502. E-mail to author.
71. Eric Broadhead, 9th Battalion DLI, Warren Tute Papers, DD 2001/1356, D-Day Archive Portsmouth Library.
72. Eric Broadhead.
73. Charles Eagles, 9DLI. Interview with author.
74. Lewis and English, pp. 243–4.

Chapter 7

1. War Diary 50th Division, 6 June 1944.
2. Les Holden, 2nd Essex. Memoir by kind permission of Avril Norton (nee Holden).
3. Peter Giggens, 2nd Essex. Interview with author.
4. Dick Philips, 2SWB. Interview with author. Sgt (later Lt) Philips was awarded a Mention in Dispatches for his work on D-Day.
5. Robert Metcalfe MBE, RCS, attached 2SWB. Interview with author.
6. Frank Dilworth MM BEM, RCS. Interview with author.
7. Philip Maillou, 2nd Essex. Interview with author.
8. Charles Benson, 2nd Essex. Interview with author.
9. War Diary 2nd Glosters, 6 June 1944.
10. Les Holden, 2nd Essex.
11. Bill Robinson, 2nd Glosters. Interview with author.
12. Albert Daines, 2nd Essex. Interview with author.
13. Tony Mansi, 2nd Essex.
14. From 2SWB. Interviews with the author: Sir Nicholas Somerville CBE (later Brigadier), Lt Sam Weaver, Bill Speake and Bill Evans.
15. National Archives and Records Administration, Maryland, USA. Deck Logs for LCI (L) 400, 421 and 511 attached 264th RCN LCI Flotilla.
16. Syd Dyer, RCS. Interview with author.
17. Tony Atcherley, RCS. Interview with author.
18. George Church MM. Telephone conversation with author.
19. Lt John Milton, 6th Green Howards. Interview with author.
20. War Diary 6th Green Howards.
21. Kenneth Taylor personal war diary, www.patricktaylor.com/war-diary-1. Kind permission of Patrick Taylor.
22. S. Trew, *Gold Beach* (Stroud: Sutton, 2004), pp. 70–1, 75, 80.

23. Dennis Bowen, 5th East Yorkshire Regiment. Interview with author.
24. Bert Cooper, 5th East Yorkshire Regiment. Interview with author.
25. Charles Hill, 6th Green Howards. Interview with author.
26. G. Johnson, and C. Dunphie, *Brightly Shone the Dawn* (London: Frederick Warne, 1980), pp. 72–9.
27. C. Douglas-Pennant, Report by the Naval Commander Force G, 15 July 1944. Annexure I to Appendix C, p. 358.
28. Johnson and Dunphie, p. 79.
29. 6th, 8th and 9th DLI War Diaries; Eric Broadhead – Warren Tute Papers 2001/1356. D-Day Archive. Portsmouth Library; M. C. Lewis and I. R. Major, *Into Battle with the Durhams: 8DLI in World War Two* (London Stamp Exchange, 1990 (1949)), p. 244.
30. Charles Eagles, 9 DLI. Interview with author.
31. Captain Peter Goddin. Memoir by kind permission of the D-Day and Normandy Fellowship.
32. TNA/PRO CAB 44/243 D-Day 30 Corps and Gold Beach.
33. *We Landed on D-Day.* Memoir by Lt Col. CAR Nevill OBE. By kind permission of the Devon and Dorset Regiment Museum.
34. Major Michael Holdsworth MC, 2nd Devons. Interview with author.
35. T. Hewitt, 2nd Devons. Interview with author.
36. David Bushell, 1st Dorset. Interview with author.
37. Information from 1st Dorset War Diary and *Three Assault Landings. The 1st Bn. Dorsetshire Regt. In Sicily, Italy and Normandy*, pp. 52–5.
38. 1st Hampshire War Diary, TNA: PRO CAB 44/243, 30 Corps, 50th (Northumbrian) Division and 7th Armoured Division. D-Day Planning. Appreciations and Operations, 1950, pp. 121–3; Battle Summary No. 39. Landings in Normandy, Volume 1, HMSO 1947, p. 98; *The Story of 79th Armoured Division*, 1945, N&M Press Reprint, p. 34; P. Warner, *The D-Day Landings* (Barnsley: Pen and Sword, 2004), pp. 151–2.
39. Major Mott 1999/727, D-Day Archive, Portsmouth Library.
40. Lt Col. Alan Norman OBE, 1st Hampshire Regiment. Interview with author and various phone conversations and e-mails.
41. Sam Weaver, 2SWB. Interview with author.
42. Captain Frank Clarke, 2nd Glosters. Interview with author.
43. Tony Mansi, 2nd Essex. Interview with author.
44. Phillip Maillou, 2nd Essex. Interview with author.
45. Pat Barrass, 2nd Essex. Interview with author.
46. Brigadier Sir Nicholas Somerville CBE, 2SWB. Interview with author.
47. TNA: PRO WO 171/1380, 2nd Battalion South Wales Borderers, War Diary 1944.
48. An interesting story concerning Ivor Parr is that during a CWGC attempt to move his remains from Magny to Bayeux CWGC Cemetery in the 1980s, the citizens of Magny protested, and the only result was the change of headstone to bring this into line with all other CWGC headstones. Today, the village cemetery carries a green CWGC sign, and Ivor Parr's grave has flowers and often a Union flag decorating it for the period of 6 June.
49. Dennis Davis, 2SWB. Interview with author.
50. Brigadier Sir Nicholas Somerville CBE, 2SWB. Interview with author.
51. Bill Evans, 2SWB. Interview with author.
52. Dick Philips, 2SWB. Interview with author.
53. Ted Battley, 47 Commando. Interview with author.

54. J. Forfar, *From Omaha to the Scheldt: The Story of 47 Royal Marine Commando during World War II.* 47 Royal Marine Commando Association, UK, 2013. Unfortunately, 'Doc' John Forfar passed away shortly after the publication of his revised book.
55. Forfar, pp. 47–54; Ted Battley.
56. TNA/PRO WO/223/153–161 series – Staff College 1947 Course Notes on Normandy. This is a very useful document, and much of the information it contains comes from the unit War Diaries, but quite a lot also seems to come from information given to the course staff from participants in the events on Gold Beach.
57. Ted Battley, 47 Commando. Interview with author.
58, Forfar, p. 54.
59. D. Lee, *Beachhead Assault: The Story of the Royal Naval Commandos in WWII* (London: Greenhill Books, 2006), pp. 148–52.
60. Lt James Madden RNVR. Interview with author.
61. Captain Peter Johnson RAMC. Diary and notes by kind permission of the Johnson family.
62. Craig Cabell, *The History of 30 Assault Unit: Ian Flemings Red Indians* (Barnsley: Pen & Sword, 2009), p. 111.
63. Grateful thanks to Mike Fenton, who has allowed the author the use of information at http://www.rafbeachunits.info/index.html. John Hughes Fenton served with No. 4 RAF Beach Squadron.
64. Major 'Ted' Hunt MVO RE. E-mails to author and article in *The Polar Bear News*, newsletter of the 49th (WR) Infantry Association. Issue no. 37.

Chapter 8

1. War Diary 2nd Cheshires, 7 June 1944.
2. This is a farm/hamlet just south of Sommervieu main crossroads. Other detail from War Diary 1st Hampshires.
3. Harold Lewis, 1st Dorsets. Interview with author.
4. War Diary 1st Dorsets.
5. Several site visits by the author; S. Zaloga, *D-Day Fortifications in Normandy* (Oxford: Osprey, 2005), p. 38; K. H. Schmeelke and M. Schmeelke, *German Defensive Batteries and Gun Emplacements on the Normandy Beaches* (Schiffer, 1995), pp. 24–9.
6. Nevill CAR OBE memoir, *We Landed on D-Day*. Kind permission of the Devon and Dorset Museum.
7. Major Michael Holdsworth MC, 2nd Devons. Interview with author.
8. Nevill and 2nd. Devons War Diary.
9. J. Forfar, *From Omaha to the Scheldt: The Story of 47 Royal Marine Commando during World War II.* 47 Royal Marine Commando Association, UK, 2013, p. 21 Also this synopsis taken from chapter 4 in Forfar, TNA: PRO CAB 44/247 D-Day Operations 7–16 June 1944 and TNA/PRO WO/223/153–161 series – Staff College 1947 Course Notes on Normandy.
10. In the desert war, German fuel containers were found to be much more robust than the British fuel cans, already known as 'flimsies'. The German cans were adopted by the Allies, hence 'Jerry cans'.

11. K. Ford, *Operation Neptune 1944: D-Day's Seaborne Armada* (Oxford: Osprey Publishing, 2014), p. 88; Forfar, p. 92.
12. Neville, 2nd Devons War Diary; interview with Major Holdsworth MC.
13. 56th Brigade War Diary; 2nd Essex War Diary; Major Patrick Barrass, 2nd Essex, interview with author.
14. Sergeant Arthur Dyer RCS MBE. Personal diary.
15. Major Ian Wakefield memoir provided by Gordon Duffin, A Company 2nd Glosters.
16. Interviews with Ted Castle, Captain Frank Clarke and Gordon Duffin; Lt Wakefield Memoir; 2nd Glosters War Diary.
17. See http://m.iwm.org.uk/collections/item/object/11650.
18. TNA: PRO CAB 44/247 D-Day Operations 7–16 June 1944, pp. 58–63; D. Rissick, *The Durham Light Infantry at War: The History of the Durham Light Infantry 1939–1945* (Brancepeth Castle: The Depot, 1952), pp. 241–2; Unit War Diaries.
19. TNA: PRO CAB 44/247 D-Day Operations 7–16 June 1944, pp. 63–9; Unit War Diaries; P. R. Nightingale, *A History of the East Yorkshire Regiment (Duke of York's Own) in the War of 1939–1945* (Howden: Mr Pye Books, 1998 (1952)).
20. N. Zetterling, *Normandy 1944: German Military Organization, Combat Power and Organizational Effectiveness* (Manitoba: Fedorowicz, 2000), p. 29; C. Bishop, *Order of Battle: German Panzers in WWII* (Stroud: Spellmount, 2008), p. 153.
21. W. Richter, *The Battle of the 716th Infantry Division in Normandy, 6th June to 23rd June 1944.*
22. Ziegelmann report *352nd Infantry Division on 7th June 1944* in D. Isby (ed.), *Fighting in Normandy: The German Army from D-Day to Villers Bocage* (London: Greenhill, 2001), p. 29.
23. Lewis and Major, pp. 246–54.
24. 56th Brigade War Diary, 9 June 1944.
25. TNA: PRO WO 171/650 HQ 56 Infantry Brigade, War Diary 1944, 9 June 1944.
26. 56th Brigade War Diary, 9 June 1944.
27. 56th Brigade War Diary, 10 June 1944.
28. Normandy Memoirs of Lieutenant Colonel Elliott CO and Captain H Barrett-Lennard IO, 2 Battalion Essex Regiment, The Pompadours. Essex Regiment Museum, Chelmsford. p. 6.
29. 2nd Essex War Diary.
30. Kenneth Taylor, 6th Green Howards. Personal diary by kind permission of the Taylor family.
31. G. Johnson and C. Dunphie, *Brightly Shone the Dawn* (London: Frederick Warne, 1980), pp. 80–9.
32. A. E. C. Bredin, *Three Assault Landings: The Story of the 1st Bn. The Dorsetshire Regiment in Sicily, Italy and NW Europe* (Gale and Polden Ltd, 1946), p. 59.
33. Kenneth Taylor. Personal diary by kind permission of his family.
34. War Diaries' Rissick, pp. 245–9; TNA: PRO CAB 44/247, pp. 155–60.
35. Sergeant Charles Eagles, 9DLI. Interview with author.
36. Capt. Frank Clarke, 2nd Glosters. Interview with author; 2nd Glosters War Diary, 14 June 1944.
37. TNA: PRO CAB 44/247, pp. 155–8.
38. M. Shulman, *Defeat in the West* (Chailey: Masquerade, 1995), pp. 124–5.
39. H. Ritgen, *The Western Front 1944: Memoirs of a Panzer Lehr Officer* (Winnipeg: Fedorowicz, 1995), pp. 41–5; G. Forty, *Villers Bocage* (Stroud: Sutton Publishing,

2004), chapter 3; D. Isby, *Fighting in Normandy: The German Army from D-Day to Villers Bocage* (London: Greenhill, 2001), pp. 135, 151, 155, 186, 189, 196–7, were the main sources used in this synopsis of the Villers-Bocage battle, plus War Diaries.

Conclusion

1. SS stood for 'Special Service' and in December 1944, and according to some men not before time, the designation SS was removed and replaced by 'Commando' because of the similarity of initials to the Nazi SS.
2. Major Bob Orrell. RE. Events related to the author by Bob Orrell at Le Bunker, Ouistreham, 2004. Sadly, Major Orrell died only a month after this meeting.
3. C. Ryan, *The Longest Day*, New York: Crest, 1959. Film 1962 produced by Darryl Zanuck.
4. R. Miller, *Nothing Less than Victory: The Oral History of D-Day* (London: Pimlico, 2000), p. 335. But this is a good oral history of D-Day and very much worth reading.
5. S. Ambrose, *D-Day: June 6, The Battle for Normandy Beaches* (London: Simon and Schuster, 2002). Ambrose has courted controversy with some of his evidence, but like all Ambrose books, this is a very worthwhile read.
6. Ellis, p. 178.
7. Harrison, p. 332.
8. *Battle Summary No. 39, Volume 1, Landings in Normandy.* Admiralty Historical Unit. HMSO, 1947, p. 98.
9. Ibid., p. 57.
10. Ibid., footnote 2, p. 107.
11. Ibid., p. 98.
12. D. French, *Raising Churchill's Army* (Oxford: Oxford University Press, 2000), p. 147.
13. TNA: PRO WO 285/2, General Miles Christopher Dempsey, Letters and Directives from General Montgomery C in C 21st Army Group. 1944–5.
14. Ellis, p. 493.
15. See http://www.cwgc.org/find-a-cemetery/cemetery/2032902/JERUSALEM%20 WAR%20CEMETERY,%20CHOUAIN (accessed 10 January 2015).
16. CWGC pdf available at: http://www.google.co.uk/url?sa=t&rct=j&q=&esrc=s &source=web&cd=10&ved=0CGEQFjAJ&url=http%3A%2F%2Fwww.le70e-normandie.fr%2Fwp-content%2Fuploads%2F2013%2F08%2FDepliant-anglais-sur-la-Commonwealth-War-Graves-Commission.pdf&ei=uEM-VOa1K-vW7Qbl6 YAo&usg=AFQjCNHtcBpMRHwpW2bYUbVGgIsqSsJsDQ&bvm=bv.77412846,d. ZGU.
17. Normandy Memoirs of Lieutenant-Colonel Elliott CO and Captain H. Barratt-Lennard IO, 2nd Battalion Essex Regiment, The Pompadours, Essex Regiment Museum, Chelmsford, p. 6.
18. Charles Eagles, 9DLI. Interview with author.
19. Ellis, Appendix IV, p. 550.
20. Ted Castle, 2nd Glosters. Interview with author.
21. Major Ted Hunt MVO, Royal Engineers. Letter to author and article in 49th (WR) Infantry Division Association magazine.

22. Len Cox, 2nd Glosters. Interview with author.
23. N. Zetterling, *German Military Organization, Combat Power and Organizational Effectiveness* (Manitoba, Canada: Fedorowicz, 2000), pp. 58–71.
24. J. Buckley, *British Armour in the Normandy Campaign* (Oxon: Frank Cass, 2004), p. 200.
25. TNA: PRO CAB 106/1060, Brigadier Hargest Reports, 6 June–10 July 1944.

Outline of 50 Div and 7 Armd Div Units

1. This US Artillery Battalion equipped with M12 155mm self-propelled guns joined 50 Div. in the Clacton area in April 1944 and loaded at Felixstowe on 1 June, sailing on 5 June. It arrived off La Riviere at 2000 and landed 7 June late morning. It first opened fire south of Ryes that afternoon. It reverted to US Army V Corps on 30 June. See http://www.veteransofthebattleofthebulge.org/2014/07/11/987th-fab-in-wwii-harlan-harner/.

Bibliography

Primary sources

The National Archive (Public Record Office), TNA: PRO, Kew, London

ADM 1/29985, Recommendations for awards to two officers and men of HM LCI (L) 295 for attempting to rescue troops of 2nd Bn Essex Regiment from the sea in a loading accident.

ADM 179/439, Admiralty: Portsmouth Station. Naval implications of Exercise Fabius, May 1944.

ADM 210/8, Lists of Landing Ships, Crafts and Barges. Naval Staff, June 1944 (Green List). Combined Operations Division.

CAB 44 56/57, Orders of Battle of the British Army, Colonel Joslen.

CAB 44/243, 30 Corps, 50th (Northumbrian) Division and 7th Armoured Division. D-Day Planning Appreciations and Operations, 1950.

CAB 44/246/7, D-Day Operations: Operations 7–16 June 1944.

CAB 44/248, Liberation Campaign in North West Europe: Operations 16 June–29 August 1944.

CAB 106/975, Opposition encountered on the British Beaches in Normandy on D-Day. Army Operational Research Group Report No. 264.

CAB 106/967, Casualties and effects of fire support on the British Beaches in Normandy: Report No. 261 by the Army Operational Research Group, 1945.

CAB 106/975, Opposition encountered on the British Beaches in Normandy on D-Day. Report No. 264, Army Operational Research Group, 1945.

CAB 106/1060, Brigadier Hargest Reports, 6 June–10 July 1944.

CAB 106/1066, Copies of telegrams between Headquarters 21st Army Group and War Office 1944, June–August 1944.

CAB 106/1067, Copies of telegrams between Headquarters 21st Army Group and War Office 1944, August–September 1944.

CAB 106/1088, Strength returns and casualty figures for the assault landings in Normandy, 6/7 June 1944.

WO 171/513, G Files 50 Division, May–July 1944.

WO 171/619, 22nd Armoured Brigade War Diary.

WO 171/650, 6th Independent Infantry Brigade War Diary.

WO 171/803, 203 Field Ambulance Unit, War Diary 1944.

WO 171/867, 5th Royal Tank Regiment, War Diary 1944.

WO 171/1268, 6th Border Regiment, War Diary.

WO 171/1276, 2nd Cheshires War Diary.

WO 171/1278, 2nd Devons War Diary.

WO 171/1285, 1st Dorsets War Diary.

WO 171/1295, 2nd Essex War Diary.

WO 171/1298, 2nd Gloucestershire War Diary.

WO 171/1302, 6th Green Howards War Diary.

WO 171/1305, 1st Hampshires War Diary.

WO 171/1308, 2nd Hertfordshires War Diary.

WO 171/1358, 1st Rifle Brigade, War Diary.

WO 171/1380, 2nd South Wales Borderers War Diary.

WO 177/402, Medical ADMS 50th Division War Diary.

WO 199/2320, Exercise Smash, 50th Division combined training exercise, April 1944.

WO 199/2321, Exercise Smash, 50th Division combined training exercise, April 1944.

WO 199/2326, Exercise Fabius, 21 Army Group Combined Exercise, May 1944.

WO 219/2216, Exercise Fabius, Plans and appreciation G3 Division, Operations B Plan Fortitude, May 1944.

WO 219/3077, Operation Neptune: Landing Tables for 56th, 69th, 151st, 231st Infantry Brigades, 4th Special Service Brigade and 51st Highland Division Landing Tables, April 1944.

WO 223/5, 50th Division Operational Order No.1.

WO 223/7, Notes by Maj.-Gen. DAH Graham, Operations of 50 (N) Div Normandy.

WO 223/123, Map Ryes. 1:25,000, April 1944, Includes Sully.

WO 223/136, Map Port-en-Bessin to Ver-sur-Mer. 1:25,000, May 1944, German defences marked.

WO/223/153-161 series, Staff College 1947 Course Notes on Normandy.

WO 285/2, General Miles Christopher Dempsey. Letters and Directives from General Montgomery C in C 21st Army Group, 1944–5.

Note: The prefix WO 171/denotes NW Europe Campaign 1944–5 unit war diaries. The prefix WO 223/denotes 1947 Staff College Camberley Course.

German sources

Circular Telegram: Fuehrer Headquarters, 5 December 1942, USA 1948.

Fuhrer Directive 18, 12 November 1940, USA 1948.

Fuhrer Directive 19, 10 December 1940, USA 1948.

Fuhrer Directive 32, 11 June 1941, USA 1948.

Fuhrer Directive 40, 23 March 1942, USA 1948.

Naval High Command Berlin, 11 April 1942, B. 111. l.Skl. I Op. 8329/42 Gkdos, USA 1948.

Commander in Chief, Navy Berlin, 27 March 1942, Skl.au.A. II 771/42 Gkdos, USA 1948.

OKW/WFSt/Op. 662656/3 g. L. Chefs 3 November 1943, USA 1948

Generalleutnant Wilhelm Richter, *The Battle of the 716th Infantry Division in Normandy. 6th Jun – 23rd June 1944.* NARA FMS B621.

War Office Publications, 1940s (Reprints from MLRS Books in collaboration with the National Archive/Public Record Office)

German Defence Preparations in the West 1940-1944, Canadian General Staff, c. 1955.

Infantry Training, Part 8: *Fieldcraft, Battle Drill, Section and Platoon Tactics,* March 1944.

Infantry Training: The Carrier Platoon, November 1943.

Infantry Training: The Anti-Tank Platoon, September 1943.

Montgomery, B. L., *Some Notes on the Conduct of War and the Infantry Division in Battle,* Belgium, November 1944.

The Co-Operation of Tanks with Infantry Divisions. Military Training Pamphlet No. 63, May 1944.

Tactics of the German Army, Vol. 1: *Defence and Withdrawal,* April 1944.

Tactics of the German Army, Vol. 2: *Attack and Pursuit,* July 1944.

Unit Accounts

The Administrative History of the Operations of 21st Army Group on the Continent of Europe. 6th June 1944 – 8th May 1945. 21st Army Group Publication, Germany, November 1945.

Eisenhower, D. D., *Report of the Commander in Chief Allied Forces to the Combined Chiefs of Staff on Operations in Northwest Africa.*

http://www.ibiblio.org/hyperwar/USA/rep/TORCH/DDE-Torch.html#concluding.

Gillespie, H. P., *2nd Battalion South Wales Borderers, 24th Regiment. D-Day to VE Day,* Germany, 1945.

The Liberation of North West Europe. Volume III: The Landings in Normandy, The Air Ministry, Air Historical Branch, Spring 1949.

National Archives and Records Administration, Maryland USA. Deck Logs for LCI (L) 400, 421 and 511 attached 264th RCN LCI Flotilla.

Normandy Memoirs of Capt. H. Barrett-Lennard, 17 August 1945, Essex Regiment Museum, Chelmsford.

Normandy Memoirs of Lieutenant Colonel Elliott CO and Captain H Barrett-Lennard IO, 2 Battalion Essex Regiment, The Pompadours, Essex Regiment Museum, Chelmsford.

Planning Operation Overlord. Canadian Historical Section, Report No. 42, Ottawa, 6 June 1951.

RAF Narrative, First Draft (Revised) The Liberation of North West Europe. Volume III. The Landings in Normandy, Spring 1949.

RCN Historical Section, *The RCN's Part in The Invasion of France,* London. 1945.

Report No. 145 Historical Section, Canadian Military Headquarters. Hist Sec (G.S.), A.H.Q. 5 July 1947, The Canloan Scheme, 1943 to July 1945.

73 Field Company RE, A Short History of the Company in the NW Europe Campaign, DD 2000/36/115, D-Day Archive, Portsmouth Library.

The 61st in the Western Europe Campaign, 1944. Back Badge Magazine, Various issues 1947–89.

The Story of 79th Armoured Division, July 1945, Germany.

United States Strategic Bombing Survey, Summary Report (European War).

Vince, A. A., *2nd Battalion The Essex Regiment, The Pompadours. D-Day to VE Day in North West Europe.* c. late 1940s.

We Landed on D-Day, Memoir by Lt Col. CAR Nevill OBE, Devon and Dorset Regiment Museum.

Zuckerman, S. and Drury, E. S. D., *The Effects of the Overlord Plan to Disrupt Enemy Rail Communications,* Bombing Analysis Unit SHAEF, November 1944.

CD-ROMs and DVDs

Après 60 Ans de Liberté, Tilly-sur-Seulles se souvient. DVD, Mairie de Tilly-sur-Seulles. 2004.

Army Roll of Honour 1939–1945, CD-ROM. Published in conjunction with the National Archive. Uckfield, Naval and Military Press. (From original lists, 1947.)

D-Day 6 June 1944 & the Battle for Normandy. Archive British Radio Recordings.
The Nazi War Machine. Presenter Prof C. Bullock. German Army squad tactics, infantry weapons, artillery and coastal defences. DVD, DD Home Entertainment. 2006.
The True Glory: From D-Day to the Fall of Berlin. From original Ministry of Information DVD, Film 1945/46. IWM. 2004.

Secondary sources

Books

Ambrose, S., *Citizen Soldiers*. London: Pocket Books, 2002.
Ambrose, S., *D-Day*. London: Pocket Books, 2002.
Badsey, T. and Bean, T., *Omaha (Battle Zone Normandy)*. Stroud: Sutton Publishing, 2004.
Baker, A. D., *Allied Landing Craft of World War 2*. Originally published by the US Navy Division of Naval Intelligence, April 1944. Reprint with introduction. London: Arms and Armour Press, 1985.
Barnes, B. S., *The Sign of the Double 'T'. (The 50th Northumbrian Division-July 1943 to December 1944)*. York: Sentinel Press, 1999.
Benamou, J., *Normandy 1944: An Illustrated Field Guide*. Bayeux: Heimdal, 1982.
Bijl, N. and Chapman, R., *No. 10 (Inter-Allied) Commando 1942-1945*. Botley: Osprey Publishing, 2006.
Bishop, C., *Order of Battle: German Panzers in WWII*. Stroud: Spellmount, 2008.
Blackburn, G. G., *The Guns of War: Comprising the Guns of Normandy and the Guns of Victory*. London: Constable & Robinson, 2000.
Boon, J. T., *History of the South Wales Borderers and The Monmouthshire Regiment*. Part 2: *The 2nd Battalion: The South Wales Borderers. D-Day 1944 to 1945*. Pontypool: The Griffin Press, 1955.
Bredin, A. E. C., *Three Assault Landings. The 1st Bn. The Dorsetshire Regiment in Sicily, Italy and Normandy*. Aldershot: Gale & Polden, 1946.
Brower, C. F. (ed.), *World War Two in Europe: The Final Year*. London: Macmillan, 1998.
Buckingham, F., *D-Day: The First 72 Hours*. Stroud: Tempus, 2004.
Buckley, J., *British Armour in the Normandy Campaign 1944*. London: Frank Cass, 2004.
Cantwell, J. D., *The Second World War: A Guide to Documents in the Public Record Office*. Kew: Public Records Office, 1998.
Chant, C., *Small Arms of WWII*. Rochester: Grange Books, 2001.
Churchill, W. S., *The Second World War*, vols. 2 and 3. London: Penguin, 1985.
Clay, E. W., *The Path of the 50th: The Story of the 50th (Northumbrian) Division in the Second World War 1939-1945*. Aldershot: Gale & Polden, 1950.
Collier, B., *The Defence of the United Kingdom*. Uckfield: Naval and Military Press, 2004.
Danchev, A. and Todman, D., *War Diaries of Field Marshal Lord Alanbrooke 1939-1945*. London: Weidenfield & Nicholson, 2001.
Darlow, S., *D-Day Bombers: The Veterans' Story. RAF Bomber Command and the US Eighth Air Force Support to the Normandy Invasion 1944*. London: Bounty Books, 2007.
Delaforce, P., *Monty's Northern Legions*. Stroud: Sutton Publishing, 1996.
Delaforce, P., *Churchill's Desert Rats: From Normandy to Berlin*. London: Chancellor Press, 1999.
Delaforce, P., *The Polar Bears: Monty's Left Flank*. London: Chancellor Press, 1999.

Delaforce, P., *Marching to the Sound of Gunfire: North West Europe 1944-45*. Stroud: Sutton Publishing, 2004.

D'Este, C., *Decision in Normandy*. London: Pan Books, 1984.

Dunphie, C. and Johnson, G., *Gold Beach: Inland from King, June 1944*. Barnsley: Pen & Sword, 2002.

Durnford-Slater, J., *Commando: Memoirs of a Fighting Commando in World War Two*. London: Greenhill Books, 2002.

Ellis, L. F., *The War in France and Flanders*. HMSO, 1953.

Ellis, L. F., *Victory in the West. Vol. 1: The Battle of Normandy*. Uckfield: Naval and Military Press, 2004.

Ellis, L. F., *Victory in the West. Vol. 2: The Defeat of Germany*. Uckfield: Naval and Military Press, 2004.

Essame, H., *Normandy Bridgehead*. London: MacDonald, 1970.

Fleming, P., *Operation Sealion*. London: Pan, 1975.

Ford, K. *Operation Neptune 1944: D-Day's Seaborne Armada*. Oxford: Osprey Publishing.

Forfar, J., *From Omaha to the Scheldt: The Story of 47 Royal Marine Commando during World War II*. 47 Royal Marine Commando Association, 2013.

Forty, G., *US Army Handbook*. Stroud: Sutton Publishing, 2001.

Forty, G., *British Army Handbook*. Stroud: Sutton Publishing, 2002.

Forty, G., *Fortress Europe*. Hersham: Ian Allen, 2002.

Forty, G., *Villers Bocage (Battle Zone Normandy)*. Stroud: Sutton Publishing, 2004.

Fraser, D., *And We Will Shock Them: The British Army in the Second World War*. London: Hodder and Stoughton, 1983.

French, D., *Raising Churchill's Army*. Oxford: Oxford University Press, 2000.

Gilbert, M., *Churchill: A Life*. London: Pimlico, 2000.

Graham, D., *Against Odds: Reflections on the Experiences of the British Army, 1914–45*. London: Macmillan, 1999.

Hamilton, N., *Monty: Master of the Battlefield 1942–1944*. London: Coronet, 1985.

Hargreaves, R., *The Germans in Normandy*. Barnsley: Pen & Sword, 2006.

Harrison, G. A., *Cross Channel Attack*. Old Saybrook, US: Konecky & Konecky, 1950.

Hart, S. A., *Montgomery and 'Colossal Cracks': The 21st Army Group in Northwest Europe 1944–45*. London: Praeger, 2000.

Hastings, M., *Overlord: D-Day and the Battle for Normandy*. London: Joseph, 1984.

Hills, S., *By Tank into Normandy*. London: Cassell, 2002.

Holborn, A., *56th Infantry Brigade and D-Day: An Independent Infantry Brigade and the Campaign in North West Europe 1944-1945*. London: Continuum, 2012.

Holt, T. and Holt, V., *Battlefield Guide to the Normandy Landing Beaches*. Barnsley: Pen & Sword, 2002.

Hughes, F. K., *A Short History of 49th West Riding and Midland Infantry Division, Territorial Army*. Barnet: Stellar Press, 1957.

Isby, D. (ed.), *Fighting in Normandy: The German Army from D-Day to Villers Bocage*. London: Greenhill, 2001.

Isby, D. (ed.), *The German Army at D-Day: Fighting the Invasion*. London: Greenhill Books, 2004.

Jackson, R., *Dunkirk: The British Evacuation, 1940*. London: Cassell, 2002.

Jewell, B., *Overlord: The War Room Guide*. Harrogate: The War Room, 1994.

Johnson, G. and Dunphie, C., *Brightly Shone the Dawn*. London: Frederick Warne, 1980, pp. 72–9.

Keegan, J., *Six Armies in Normandy*. London: Pimlico, 1994.

Keegan, J., *Churchill's Generals*. London: Warner Books, 1995.

Kershaw, R., *D-Day: Piercing the Atlantic Wall*. London: Ian Allan, 1993.

Lee, D., *Beachhead Assault: The Story of the Royal Naval Commandos in WWII*. London: Greenhill Books, 2006.

Lefevre, E., *Panzers in Normandy*. London: Battle of Britain, 2002.

Levine, J., *Operation Fortitude: The Greatest Hoax of the Second World War*. London: Collins, 2011.

Lewin, R., *Rommel as Military Commander*. Barnsley: Pen & Sword, 2004.

Lewis, P. J. and English, I. R., *Into Battle with the Durham's. 8th DLI in World War II*. London: London Stamp Exchange, 1990 reprint (1949).

Liddell-Hart, B. H. (ed.), *The Rommel Papers*. London: Collins, 1953.

Longden, S., *To the Victor the Spoils: Soldiers' Lives from D-Day to VE Day*. London: Robinson, 2007.

Lucas, J., *German Army Handbook*. Stroud: Sutton Publishing, 2001.

Lucas Phillips, C. E., *The Greatest Raid of All*. London: Pan, 2000.

Mallory, K. and Ottar, A., *Architecture of Aggression: A History of Military Architecture in NW Europe 1900-1945*. D.P. & G. Doncaster, 2007.

Martin, T. A., *The Essex Regiment 1929–1950*. Hazell, Watson & Viney, 1952, p. 158.

McKee, A., *Caen: Anvil of Victory*. London: Souvenir Press, 1984.

Messenger, C., *The D-Day Atlas*. London: Thames and Hudson, 2004.

Meyer, H., *The 12th SS*. Vol. 1: *The History of the Hitler Youth Panzer Division*. Mechanicsburg, PA: Stackpole Publishing, 1994.

Millar, G., *The Bruneval Raid: Stealing Hitler's Radar*. London: Cassell, 2002.

Miller, R., *Nothing Less than Victory: The Oral History of D-Day*. London: Pimlico, 2000.

Montgomery, B. L., *The Memoirs of Field Marshal the Viscount Montgomery of Alamein*. London: The Companion Book Club, 1960.

Moorehead, A., *Eclipse*. London: Granta Books, 2002.

Morgan, F., *Overture to Overlord*. London: Hodder & Stoughton, 1950.

Neillands, R., *The Battle of Normandy 1944*. London: Cassell, 2003.

Neillands, R. and De Normann, R., *D-Day 1944: Voices from Normandy*. London: Cassell, 2002.

Nightingale, P. R., *A History of the East Yorkshire Regiment (Duke of York's Own) in the War 1939-1945*. Howden: Mr Pye Books, 1998 (1952).

O'Sullivan, J., *When Wales Went to War 1939-1945*. Stroud: The History Press, 2007.

Parry, D., *D-Day 6.6.44*. London: BBC Books, 2004.

Penrose, J., *The D-Day Companion*. Botley: Osprey, 2004.

Pitcairn-Jones, L. J., *Neptune: Landings in Normandy June 1944. Battle Summary No. 39*. London: HMSO, 1994.

Place, T. H., *Military Training in the British Army 1940–1944: From Dunkirk to D-Day*. London: Frank Cass, 2000.

Rissick, D., *The Durham Light Infantry at War: The History of the Durham Light Infantry 1939-1945*. Brancepeth Castle: The Depot, 1952.

Ritgen, H., *The Western Front 1944: Memoirs of a Panzer Lehr Officer*. Winnipeg, Canada: Fedorowicz, 1995.

Robertson, T., *Walker RN*. London: Evans Brothers, 1956.

Roskill, S. W., *The War at Sea 1939-1945. Vol. 3: The Offensive. Part II, 1st June 1944–14th August 1945*. Uckfield: Naval and Military Press, 2004.

Ryan, C., *The Longest Day*. Sevenoaks: New English Library, 1982.

Ruge, F., *Rommel in Normandy: Reminiscences by Friedrich Ruge*. London: Macdonald and James, 1979.

Saunders, T., *Gold Beach-Jig: Jig Sector and West – June 1944*. Barnsley: Pen & Sword, 2002.

Saunders, T., *Dieppe: Operation Jubilee*. Barnsley: Pen & Sword, 2005.

Scott, R., *The Real Dad's Army: The War Diaries of Colonel Rodney Foster*. London: Penguin, 2012.

Shulman, M., *Defeat in the West*. Chailey: Masquerade, 1995.

Smheelke, K. H. and Smheelke, M., *German Defensive Batteries and Gun Emplacements on the Normandy Beaches. Invasion: D-Day June 6, 1944*. Aiglen, PA: Schiffer, 1995.

Stacey, C. P., *The Canadian Army 1939-45*. Official Historical Summary. Ottawa, 1948.

Terraine, J., *The Life and Times of Lord Mountbatten*. London: Arrow Books, 1971.

Trew, S., *Gold Beach (Battle Zone Normandy)*. Stroud: Sutton Publishing, 2004.

United States Army Center of Military History. *US Army Guide to Military History*. Washington, DC, 2006.

Walter, J., *Guns of the Third Reich*. London: Greenhill Books, 2004.

Warner, P., *The D-Day Landings*. Barnsley: Pen & Sword, 2004.

Watkins, G. J. B., *The War History of the Fourth Battalion the Dorset Regiment. June 1944 – May 1945: From Normandy to the Weser*. Eastbourne: Rowe, 1950.

Wilmot, C., *The Struggle for Europe*. London: Collins, 1952.

Winser, J., *The D-Day Ships: Neptune the Greatest Amphibious Operation in History*. Kendall: World Ship Society, 1994.

Wood, J. A. (ed.), *Army of the West: Weekly Reports of German Army Group B from Normandy to the West Wall*. Mechanicsburg, Pennsylvania: Stackpole Books, 2007.

Zee, Henri A van der., *The Hunger Winter: Occupied Holland 1944–5*. London: Norman & Hobhouse Ltd, 1982.

Zetterling, N., *Normandy 1944: German Military Organization, Combat Power and Organizational Effectiveness*. Winnipeg, Canada: Fedorowicz, 2000.

Journal articles

French, D., '"Tommy is no soldier": The morale of the Second British Army in Normandy, June-August 1944'. *Journal of Strategic Studies*, 19.4 (1996): 154–78.

French, D., 'Discipline and the death penalty in the British Army in the war against Germany during the Second World War'. *Journal of Contemporary History*, 33.4 (1998): 531–45.

Hart, S., 'Montgomery, morale, casualty conservation and "colossal cracks": 21st Army Group's operational technique in north-west Europe, 1944–45'. *Journal of Strategic Studies*, 19.4 (1996): 132–53.

Index